# Interactions:

# Dublin Theatre Festival 1957-2007

# Interactions:
# Dublin Theatre Festival 1957-2007

edited by

## Nicholas Grene and Patrick Lonergan
## with Lilian Chambers

**Carysfort Press**

A Carysfort Press Book

*Interactions: Dublin Theatre Festival 1957–2007*

Edited by Nicholas Grene and Patrick Lonergan
with Lilian Chambers

First published as a paperback in Ireland in 2008
by Carysfort Press Ltd
58 Woodfield, Scholarstown Road, Dublin 16, Ireland

ISBN 978-1-904505-36-5

Printed and bound by eprint limited
Unit 35, Coolmine Industrial Estate, Dublin 15, Ireland

Cover design by Alan Bennis

Typeset by Carysfort Press Ltd

This book is published with the financial assistance of
The Arts Council (An Chomhairle Ealaíon), Dublin, Ireland
and Dublin City Council

To the memory of Brendan Smith, the founder of the Festival

# Table of Contents

# Acknowledgements

This book had its origins in a conference organized by the Irish Theatrical Diaspora in association with the Dublin Theatre Festival and the Irish Theatre Institute in October 2007. On behalf of the ITD, we would like gratefully to acknowledge our partner institutions in organizing that event. In particular, we need to thank Loughlin Deegan for his encouragement throughout and for the Festival's substantial support in publicizing the conference and making the Project Arts Centre available to us. We must also thank Madeline Boughton, Ross Keane, and Shauna Lyons. For additional support in funding the conference, we are pleased to acknowledge the Arts and Social Sciences Benefaction Fund in Trinity College, Dublin, and the NUI Galway Millennium Fund. We are also grateful to Karen Fricker, who was an active and immensely know-ledgeable member of the steering committee for the conference. In the running of the conference itself, we were extremely well assisted by Lisa Coen and Shelley Troupe, our fellow researchers in a larger related project funded by the Irish Research Council for Humanities and the Social Sciences; to them many thanks. In preparing the list of DTF productions, Aoife Spillane-Hinks, the other member of the research team in the IRCHSS-supported project, carried out valuable research, while Shelley Troupe provided editorial support. We also gratefully acknowledge the assistance of Riana O'Dwyer of NUI Galway. At Carysfort Press, we wish to thank the team of Dan Farrelly, Eamonn Jordan, and particularly Lilian Chambers, who originally commissioned the memoirs from past directors of the Festival.

N.G.

P.L.

# Preface

Being custodians of such a significant cultural organization as the Ulster Bank Dublin Theatre Festival in its fiftieth anniversary year was a bracing responsibility. The challenge was to recognize Brendan Smith's great vision and acknowledge the Festival's illustrious theatrical history whilst remaining resolutely forward looking. We set ourselves high ambitions which we achieved, for the most part I believe, in fruitful partnership with many cultural and academic institutions.

One of the first meetings I had following my appointment in November 2006 was with Nicholas Grene and Patrick Lonergan of the Irish Theatrical Diaspora Project. They were interested in working with the Festival to organize an academic conference designed to investigate the impact of the Festival on the cultural life of the nation and its artists. We were delighted to work together to make such an important event happen, the results of which are contained in this very impressive published record.

The conference was personally stimulating in many ways: having researched the Festival's history thoroughly in advance, I was thrilled to have my own reading of its influence challenged by Fintan O'Toole's brilliant analysis. I, like many others, had continuously emphasized the enormous impact that visiting companies and artists must have had on a doggedly inward looking country still under the control of a conservative ruling party and an all-powerful church. Fintan, on the other hand, rightly concluded that it was the Irish work presented by the Festival that had the greater impact, challenging directly, as it did, the State who had supported the event from the outset and the Church who (initially) endorsed it. It was not, therefore, the corrupting influence of the foreign that was of concern, but the way we were representing ourselves to those foreigners through the powerful prism of our new International Theatre Festival.

As we all know, Ireland has changed radically in the past fifty years and the Festival's survival is partly a result of its ability to move with the times. Likewise, it was always our intention to use the anniversary to set down markers for how the Festival might grow and develop in the future. The Ulster Bank Dublin Theatre Festival can only maintain (and enhance) its position as one of the world's leading theatre festivals by insisting on excellence and innovation. We must present the leading artists of our time and the major works, unconstrained by venues or facilities. We must present an original programme that introduces work to international audiences and is not a carbon copy of the multitude of festivals and events that now exist around the world. We must present a diverse, interesting, and balanced programme that satisfies the Festival's diverse audiences and continues to impact on the city in real and meaningful ways.

In keeping with Fintan's analysis, this focus on innovation and excellence must also extend to the Irish work. One of my ongoing ambitions is to improve the way the Festival develops and showcases Irish work (to as many foreigners as possible!). To do this, I believe, we must begin to see and appreciate Irish work in an international context. We are all aware that the world is becoming increasingly globalized and that international barriers are being eroded in numerous ways – from Ryanair to Facebook and everything in between. Using theatre as a tool to delineate a clear sense of national identity, therefore, is becoming less urgent and it is simply a fact that the international theatre scene has developed and mutated accordingly. Irish theatre artists are also reflecting this shifting reality in the work that they create and the institutional structures must now change to accommodate this work.

What is most significant about this publication is that it addresses all of these issues. It not only maps the Festival's influence over the past fifty years, but it also provides signposts for how the Festival could and should develop over its second half century.

*Loughlin Deegan*
*Artistic Director & CEO, Ulster Bank Dublin Theatre Festival*

# Introduction: the Festival at Fifty

'Both feast and celebration: a feast of international shows and a celebration of the creative talents of Irish artists.' This was the summary of the organizers of the 1983 Dublin Theatre Festival, quoted below by John Harrington in his essay on the Beckett Festival. A quarter of a century later, how might the history of the Festival at Fifty be best charted, evaluated, or evoked? It is possible to trace its evolution from the nationwide tourist event An Tóstal, as Christopher Fitz-Simon does in his lively personal reminiscence, and to provide a social and political reading of that evolution as Fintan O'Toole does in his searching retrospect. A complete listing of all the productions mounted by the DTF can be compiled, as this volume does for the first time. Individual landmark events can be picked out: important Irish premieres at the Festival such as Hugh Leonard's Joyce adaptation *Stephen D.* (1962), Brian Friel's *Philadelphia Here I Come!* in 1964 or Máiréad Ní Ghráda's *An Triail* from the same year, Tom Murphy's *The Sanctuary Lamp* (1975), Stewart Parker's *Northern Star* (1985), Thomas Kilroy's *The Secret Fall of Constance Wilde* (1997) or Marina Carr's *By the Bog of Cats* (1998); notable foreign visits like Jean Vilar's Théâtre Nationale Populaire in the Festival's inaugural year, the Polish Wroclaw Contemporary Theatre in 1981 and 1982, the Moscow Art Theatre with Chekhov's *The Seagull* in 1989, and Footsbarn's circus *Midsummer Night's Dream* in 1990. What this book aims to do is to bring together information and analysis, interpretation and memory, to create a sense of what constitutes the history of the DTF and its meanings.

The complete listing of productions represents a crucially important scholarly resource, but is not readable except as raw data. Particular essays necessarily focus on specific parts of the Festival's repertoire, drawing out the significance of work in particular media, or individual playwrights, directors, and companies. So Sara Keating shows the importance of Irish language drama, especially in the early stages of the Festival, with the emergence of adventurous and experimental playwrights influenced by European dramaturgy such as Seán Ó Tuama, Máiréad Ní Ghráda, and Séamus Ó Néill, while in more recent years it has devolved first into the Fringe Festival and then into its own separate festival An Borradh Buan. Emilie Pine highlights the importance of Hugh Leonard, the most produced Irish playwright at the Festival, and questions why his popular gifts as acute satirist of contemporary Ireland have been increasingly devalued and not received their due academic attention. Ros Dixon, in focussing on the recurrent Russian presence in the Festival, is able to situate within the history of Russian theatre itself the visits of the Moscow Art Theatre director, Maria Knebel, to direct an Abbey Theatre production of *The Cherry Orchard* in 1968, the 1989 MAT *Seagull*, or the more radical post-Soviet productions seen in the 1990s and since. Cathy Leeney concentrates on the work of a single director, Patrick Mason, and his exceptional creative gifts in the shaping of theatrical spaces in collaboration with scenic designers and playwrights as different as Kilroy, Mac Intyre, and Carr. Tanya Dean looks at the emergence of Rough Magic as one of the key contributors to the Festival from the mid-1980s, and reflects on the relationship between their policies as a resolutely independent company and their involvement in the mainstream DTF.

The key event of the first Festival in 1957, as Lionel Pilkington reminds us, happened offstage: the arrest of Alan Simpson, director of the Pike Theatre, for his allegedly immoral production of *The Rose Tattoo*. In his essay, Pilkington provides a carefully argued interpretation of the significance of this event, with the radical subversiveness of both play and production challenging the longstanding function of Irish theatre as an acceptable instrument of modernization within the state. He concludes his account of the prosecution of Simpson over *The Rose Tattoo*: 'for the development of a modernist and radical Irish theatre, the results were catastrophic'. Fintan O'Toole's interpretation is rather different. He argues that the attack on *The Rose Tattoo* was the first sign that the Festival was not going to fulfil its designated official objective of drawing in tourists to admire Irish culture, 'a cultural version of the economic modernization project'. Instead, increasingly in the 1960s and beyond, Irish playwrights in the DTF put upon the stage not the 'deeper thoughts and emotions of Ireland' promised by the original Irish Literary Theatre in 1897, but its physical, social, and sexual deprivations. This was the more striking, O'Toole maintains, in the early 1980s, when the issue of the body was so foregrounded in Irish politics by the H-Block hunger strikes and debates over abortion and contraception, and when at the same time productions in the Festival from at home and abroad manifested a new physical language of the theatre. Shaun Richards, in his examination of Thomas Kilroy's *The Death and Resurrection of Mr Roche* (1968) and Brian Friel's *The Gentle Island* (1971) also focuses on sexuality, showing how the construction of straight masculinity as part of Irish national identity seems to have inhibited critics and audiences from attending to the plays' concern with gay men. On the other hand, *The Sanctuary Lamp*, which elicited such controversy for its anti-clericalism when first produced in 1975, as Alexandra Poulain shows, had a new and different relevance for audiences when revived in the 2001 Festival as part of the Abbey's Murphy season.

'Festivalization' has come to be recognized as a phenomenon in itself; a festival as an exceptional event, drawing larger audiences, can make possible shows that could not be produced in normal theatrical circumstances. John Harrington, with his consideration of the Beckett Festival, originally a festival within the Dublin Theatre Festival of 1991, then transplanted to New York in 1996 and London in 1999, interrogates and theorizes the form of festival itself, the ways in which it combines apparently contrary impulses towards the national and the international. The progress of the Australian epic *Cloudstreet*, an adaptation of Tim Winton's novel, is traced by Peter Kuch

from its premiere at the Sydney Festival in 1998 through its
many different stagings to the DTF in 1999. Kuch examines the
implications of its variant forms and seeks to explain its
capacity to reach different festival audiences across the world.
Robert Lepage's *Elsinore* was another regular festival traveller.
Carmen Szabó reads its appearance at the DTF in 1997, together
with Conall Morrison's experimental, technologized *Hamlet* of
2005 as symptomatic of a postmodern exploration of 'dark
play', in which any stable conception of character or identity is
called in question. In the representation of Ireland, too, the last
decade has brought innovative theatrical forms to the Festival.
The Fabulous Beast dance-drama, *Giselle*, was co-produced by
the DTF itself in 2003; as part of director Michael Keegan-
Dolan's 'Midlands trilogy' it is read by Lisa Fitzpatrick with
Marina Carr's work as a violently grotesque parody of past
theatrical traditions, subverting at once the heroic genre of
tragedy and the Irish idealization of the West as source of
authenticity.

Scholars recover the record, analyse, scrutinize, and
interpret the events of the past. Being there, however, being
involved, and then remembering how it was, add another
dimension to the sense of history. David Grant, in his
recollection of his period as Programme Director of the Festival
(1989-91), draws usefully on Stanislavsky's concept of 'affective
memory' and experiments with a memoir based on 'embodied
knowledge'. Thomas Kilroy, in the opening essay of this volume,
testifies to his experience of what the Festival meant to him as a
creative artist coming to maturity in the Ireland of the 1950s
and 1960s. He brings to uniquely vivid life the repressive
atmosphere of 1957, and how the encouragement of men such
as Alan Simpson, Tomás Mac Anna, Jim Fitzgerald, as well as
the Festival's founder Brendan Smith, enabled him to become
the playwright of *The Death and Resurrection of Mr Roche*.
Christopher Fitz-Simon, as Trinity student and actor in R.B.D.
French's impishly irreverent Players' revues at the time,
conjures up a rather different view of 1957 and the first Festival.
Necessarily for later Festival directors such as Lewis Clohessy
(1984-1989), Tony Ó Dálaigh (1990-1999), and Fergus Linehan
(2000-2004), funding and the problems of administration loom

large. Their memoirs give us perspectives from behind the scenes, the hand-to-mouth existence of the Festival, always threatened by Arts Council cutbacks and the vagaries of sponsorship, backstage 'crises, skulduggery and intrigues', the challenges of recruiting and supporting large-scale visiting shows. The juxtaposition of these informal first person recollections with the factual listing of the productions in each decade of the Festival's fifty-year-old history is designed to highlight the very different ways this story can be told.

Theatre is by its nature an ephemeral art; for the theatre-goer who did not make it to a particular production it did not happen – it will never come again. The ephemerality of the theatre festival in that context is something rather special. Because of its concentration of so much work into one short space of time it can produce an effect of unusual intensity, and by its showcasing of daringly different or innovative productions can make them appear more memorable. And yet the very overindulgence in theatre over the one limited period of a couple of weeks can lead to a blurring of effect as the experience of one play merges with another in the mind. Over the years, equally, for the hardened and recidivist festival frequenter, one whole festival tends to become confused with all the others. This book is planned to restore to distinct and distinctly understood life the theatrical phenomenon of the Festival over its fifty years. Its title of *Interactions* is intended, most centrally, to bring into focus the interrelationship within the Festival of its national and international elements, its 'feast of international shows and celebration of the creative talents of Irish artists'. It is also suggestive of the ways in which the Festival has interacted with the society and culture of its time, challenging or reflecting its assumptions in complex ways. As editors, however, we hope to have allowed the essays, memoirs, and production lists to interact with one another. Most of the essays had their origins in papers given at the 2007 conference organized by the Irish Theatrical Diaspora in association with the Dublin Theatre Festival and the Irish Theatre Institute. While many of the essayists have revised their papers for publication, we encouraged Thomas Kilroy and Fintan O'Toole, the plenary conference speakers, to retain the oral form of their talks. We have assembled the essays according to a roughly chronological order, based on the date of the first work considered in each essay, but the different trajectories of argument of the contributors have meant that they range widely over time. There are, inevitably, elements of overlap between one essay and another, between the essays and the memoirs, as certain key events and productions are re-visited from different points of view. Our belief is that these function as interactions not repetitions, confirming the multiple nature of the Festival over its half-century and the multiple refractions with which it can be viewed.

*Nicholas Grene*
*Patrick Lonergan*

**PART ONE: ESSAYS**

# 1 | A Playwright's Festival

Thomas Kilroy

The Dublin Theatre Festival was a product of that curious decade, the 1950s, with its collision of an older Ireland and an Ireland about to be reborn. What was happening in Ireland was also happening elsewhere in post-war Europe, a typical post-war process of change. The difference was the degree of resistance to change in Ireland, perhaps due to isolationism, although I remember being quite shocked by the deprivation and isolation in rural Spain when I first visited that country in the mid-1950s. At any rate, the confrontation of value systems, the opposition of aspirations in the Irish people, the choice between retaining past values or striking out into the future, is actually reflected in the events, off-stage and on, of the first couple of years of the Festival itself.

The standard reading of the 1950s is of a time of stagnation and repression, of sapping emigration with social and economic misery at home. It is true that over 400,000 people emigrated in the period and particularly notable was the number of young women who left. Areas of rural Ireland were devastated. There were other social problems. This is also the decade which we most associate with the horrors of industrial schools and Magdalene laundries, of abused and lost children, and an official indifference at the highest levels.

Like all such generalizations, however, this doesn't quite catch the complexity of the time. Brian Fallon, for one, has tried to redress this view in his book *An Age of Innocence* with his account of the active cultural life in Ireland of the period. In my own experience Dublin theatre in the '50s was very alive and it was possible to see more professional productions of European and American plays than, perhaps, is true of today – plays by Ugo Betti, Pirandello, Genet, Anouilh, Sartre, William Inge, Lillian Hellman, and so on. This was largely due to the vision of directors like Jim Fitzgerald, Alan Simpson, Hilton Edwards, Barry Cassin and his theatrical partner, Nora Lever.

My own case is a fairly typical example of growing up in those days. I came up from County Kilkenny to UCD in 1953 from a strict Catholic upbringing and schooling, a naïve, insecure nineteen-year-old, torn between Catholic guilt and a desire for a liberty which I couldn't as yet understand, much less articulate. That fear and lack of maturity was to betray me in the theatre itself, something I will be coming to in a moment.

We should also remember that the Theatre Festival began as an offshoot of An Tóstal so that its first year was part of the fifth year of An Tóstal. An Tóstal was a spring festival throughout the country, engineered by the people in Bord Fáilte to try to push back the tourist season from the summer into the spring. The Irish weather consistently played hell with this exercise in invented bacchanalia.

The point is, however, that the Theatre Festival began under this particular umbrella of official Ireland with its political, social and clerical establishment. In its first year, for example, the Festival had a garden party in the Royal Marine Hotel out in Dun Laoghaire, a Festival gala dinner in the Shelbourne Hotel, while all the suits and frocks turned out again in the dress circle of the old, long-gone Theatre Royal for Margot Fonteyn and the Royal Ballet.

It was a bit like the Irish establishment of the new Irish Free State so brilliantly mocked by Denis Johnston in *The Old Lady Says No!* I saw this play for the first time in its revival at the Gate in that first year of the Festival in 1957. And although Mac Liammóir was clearly too old for the part of Emmet, which he had first played nearly thirty years earlier, the play itself was a revelation of energetic theatricality. Its targets, too, of blood sacrifice and romantic evasion of reality, seemed entirely apt for the times, as the IRA campaign gathered momentum in the

North and the realities of Irish life of the day made romanticism of any kind irrelevant, even immoral.

The actual idea of a Theatre Festival came from one man, Brendan Smith. Although born in England he was a quintessential Dubliner, a theatre producer who ran a professional acting academy in the city. Some people looked upon him as a fuddy-duddy, conservative type, but I was to learn in the 1960s that he was a man of great courage, a risk-taker, when he produced *The Death and Resurrection of Mr Roche* at the Olympia.

When he announced the first Festival programme in 1957, he expressed regret that the one thing that was missing was the premiere of a new play. While he was involved, Brendan Smith struggled to make that goal central to the Festival and this is one of the reasons why the Festival became an important promoter of new plays down the years. The other plank of Smith's policy was to internationalize the Festival. He brought Jean Vilar's TNP company from Paris that first year performing Molière (which I did not see).

The two shows which I did see that had a considerable influence upon me in that first year were Jim Fitzgerald's productions of the Yeats plays for the Globe Theatre in Dun Laoghaire and Alan Simpson's production of Tennessee Williams's *The Rose Tattoo* at the small Pike Theatre. I already knew Fitzgerald's extraordinary work with the Globe Theatre. I didn't see all seven Yeats plays but I saw enough to learn something about how Yeats's idea of theatre could still speak to the later twentieth century. I also saw how a director with an acute sense of contemporary theatre in all its facets could do something new with Yeats's plays. The whole experience of the Globe Theatre was given a certain piquancy by the fact that they performed in the Gas Company building. To get to your seat you had to wend your way past refrigerators, washing machines, and other items of gas-powered technology.

My encounter with *The Rose Tattoo*, on the other hand, is one of the more shameful memories of my whole life. I was trying to describe this to a group of young American theatre students last year and I think they didn't know what I was talking about. I'll try again now to convey the mood of the time and how I personally failed to measure up to the challenge of it.

Three years earlier, in 1955, I was auditor of the student English Literature Society in UCD. As part of the Inaugural meeting I had to read a paper in public, which I did, on the fiction of the American South. Many of the books I spoke about were still banned in Ireland at the time.

We tried, through the American embassy, to get a real, live American author as one of the speakers to the paper, perhaps someone already on tour, which would cut down on our costs. To our horror the Ambassador, one William Howard Taft III, decided to accept the invitation himself. When he heard this, the President of the university, Michael Tierney, a notoriously conservative man and an old Blueshirt, decided he would chair the meeting to honour the Ambassador. When I also say that my professor, Jeremiah J. Hogan, was a member of the Censorship Appeals Board you can see that this mix was potentially explosive.

I was duly chastised in public at the meeting for daring to speak about what Michael Tierney called 'dirty books'. As a classicist he advised me to read the 'decent', 'clean' classics. I had studied enough of Ovid to find this advice puzzling. Moreover, a totally innocent Denis Donoghue, one of the speakers, was also reprimanded by Tierney as a junior lecturer who was leading young students astray with indecent reading. My source for the banned Faulkner and Thomas Wolfe novels was not Denis but that's another story.

I tell this story to try to convey the atmosphere of the place in 1957. I was trying to write and I was mad about theatre. I went to Alan Simpson and asked for any kind of job he could give me in the Pike. He put me in the box-office selling tickets. When the police moved in on the theatre towards the end of May I came under considerable outside pressure to leave. Among other things it was suggested to me that I might not graduate – utterly ridiculous, I know, but that was the way it was. I should say that this pressure did not come from within the university itself.

When I went to talk to Alan he told me to go home which (to my lasting embarrassment) I did, along with a couple of others of the company. It didn't make it any better that, when he took charge of the Abbey in the 1960s, Alan was responsible for the production of my play *The O'Neill* at the Peacock in 1969, twelve years after that episode in the Pike. He became a good friend until his death.

I now think that I was unable to shed the incubus of the Ireland I was born into until I finished writing my play *The Death and Resurrection of Mr Roche*. The writing was my way of growing up and facing the fear and guilt inculcated into me in my childhood. The difficulty, too, in the writing of that play was a reflection of the forces I had to contend with in my personal life.

I think I had already started to write a play about a group of people in a Dublin flat sometime in the late '50s. It was based upon a story I had heard about a group of drunken men bringing back a woman prostitute to a flat and assaulting her. I went through multiple drafts but I couldn't get it right. I thought I'd never finish it, and the problem was the presence of the woman.

Frank McGuinness has said that this is a play about heterosexuality not homosexuality and I think he's right. One day I just changed the role of the woman prostitute to a gay man and the play wrote itself in a few weeks. It was one of those miraculous gifts that the imagination sometimes offers to us, coming from a well deep beyond our reach but still somewhere within us. Using a gay figure concentrated the play on maleness, on the dynamic within which the dysfunctional world of the play had its roots and grounding. But I'm also convinced that the choice of the gay man was an important liberation of myself from the kind of forces that had led to my failure of nerve at the Pike Theatre in 1957. I remember saying something like this to Alan years afterwards. He just laughed and said at least it helped to produce a play.

In 1958 I was teaching English in Switzerland so I missed the brouhaha when the Festival was cancelled. I remember a friend sending me the statement of Archbishop John Charles McQuaid with its papal cadences, announcing that since Joyce's *Ulysses* and a play by O'Casey were featured in the Festival he would not allow the annual Mass to be said at the start of An Tóstal. Like my own wilting at the Pike, the Council of An Tóstal caved in, even though they had asked a reluctant O'Casey for the play in the first place. Brendan Smith tried hard to salvage the Festival and there was an effort to move it to the autumn, away from the dates of An Tóstal and its official morality. But that didn't work and the Festival for 1958 was cancelled.

I truly believe that this incident strengthened rather than weakened the Festival. The absurdity of it was one further step towards the dismantlement of Irish censorship. The anger which it generated in the theatre itself was no bad thing, although it took some time before Brendan Smith was able to develop the international side of his programming again. I suppose people outside Ireland didn't want to know. For a few years the Festival was very much a Dublin Festival.

His first policy, however, that of the production of new plays, was very much to the fore. Over the next decade, until my own involvement in 1968, he was responsible for new plays by Hugh Leonard, John B. Keane, Brian Friel, Eugene McCabe, James McKenna, Máiréad Ní Ghráda, M.J. Molloy, G.P. Gallivan, James Douglas, Bryan MacMahon, Conor Farrington, and many others. In effect, the Festival became known among playwrights as an attractive target for their work. People wrote specifically for the Festival itself. Plays which might be difficult to produce outside the Festival found their places within it. This, indeed, was to be my own experience.

In 1959 I had to get a job and much to my astonishment I was appointed Headmaster of Stratford College, the Jewish school here in Dublin. Over the next few years I somehow combined this with the start of an academic career, lecturing in the States and trying to write plays. I have no doubt that Stratford College suffered as a consequence. In 1965 I was appointed a Junior Lecturer in English at UCD.

Over these six years, 1959-1965, I was struggling with *The Death and Resurrection of Mr Roche*. I turned aside from it more than once and sometime in 1963 or 1964 I wrote my play *The O'Neill*. It would be true to say that the form of this play came out of my interest in Brecht. It would also be true to say that I was learning how to use stage space from a remarkable group of stage directors working at the height of their powers in

Dublin like Jim Fitzgerald, Hilton Edwards, Alan Simpson, Tomás Mac Anna, and Barry Cassin.

Hilton Edwards had been greatly taken by the Berliner Ensemble when it came to London in 1956. He would, I think, have had little interest in Brechtian ideology. What must have impressed him was the way Brecht embedded realism inside highly stylized staging, the frontal immediacy of the productions, the direct, startling way in which they engaged audiences. I didn't see these productions myself. My sense of such techniques came to me second-hand through directors like George Devine and Joan Littlewood in London and, in Dublin, Hilton and Tomás Mac Anna. I saw Mac Anna's fine production of *The Life of Galileo* at the Abbey in 1956 and Edwards's Festival production in 1961 of Brecht's *Saint Joan of the Stockyards* with Siobhán McKenna. This was a companion piece to his famous production of *Saint Joan*, again with Siobhán. But you could also see this new influence on Edwards's work in his *Julius Caesar*, in Fascist costume, in 1957. So, too, I remember the movement and stage energy of Simpson's Festival production James McKenna's *The Scatterin'*, in 1960, that rarity in Irish theatre, a local pop musical. My writing of *The O'Neill* came very much out of this stable of influences.

Dublin was going through something of a revolution in the art of staging at this time, to some extent influenced by what was going on in British theatre. The Festival was crucial to all this. I've suggested elsewhere (in the Spring/Summer 1992 issue of *Irish University Review*) that Fitzgerald's Festival production of Leonard's *Stephen D.* (1962) and Edwards's Festival production of Friel's *Philadelphia Here I Come!* (1964) marked the emergence of a new Irish theatre, a significant demarcation from what had gone before. Much of this had to do with a new sophistication in both writing and staging. These plays portrayed a traditional Ireland but they did so with a contemporary freedom in the use of the stage that was invigorating to those of us who were there on the opening nights.

I sent *The O'Neill* to Hilton Edwards and received his response in a three page letter in June 1964. He said:

> I liked the play in so far as it holds the attention, is fresh in its
> approach with, as far as I can judge, a contemporary parallel,
> and it is in the main actable and would be interesting to
> produce. I like its freedom of form.

He then went on to talk about the economic difficulties in
Irish theatre of the day.

> This latter point is of particular importance because the cast
> of your play, while by no means too big for your
> requirements, is larger than we can cope with in the Dublin
> theatre under present economic conditions – It is because I
> can no longer put on Shakespeare or anything but piddling
> little plays that I am keeping out of the scene.

It was around this time too that Hilton suggested that I get
an agent and with his help I was taken on by Peggy Ramsay, an
agent who had an enormous influence on late twentieth century
British drama. (Something of her bizarre character emerges in
the Joe Orton film *Prick up your Ears* where she is played by
Vanessa Redgrave). She was a turbulent, hugely creative
presence in my own writing career until her death in 1991. I
wish someone would publish her collected letters, although they
may have to wait until some important people in British theatre
have passed away, to avoid the impact of her savage asides.

*The O'Neill* then went to the Abbey and I got an equally
enthusiastic response from Ernest Blythe, with precisely the
same point about the economics of staging the play at that time.
The date of Blythe's letter is May 1966. He did reveal that the
Abbey readers were divided on the play but that 'some of those
who heard from others a view directly contrary to their own first
impression, expressed a wish to re-read the script before
coming to a final judgement'.

He himself, however, admired it, something which I need to
record, given his reputation as an obstacle to the production of
new work. Moreover, his enthusiasm for the play was there
despite his sense that it might cause trouble when produced.

> However, while O'NEILL is not a play which might be
> expected to be wildly popular or a money-spinner and might
> indeed even provoke some public anger, we think it is far

better than any previous play about O'Neill which has come to us and merits the most serious consideration.

It took five more years before the play appeared on the new Peacock stage, a period of great frustration because by then I also had *The Death and Resurrection of Mr Roche* ready for production. It, too, started the rounds and the two plays, so very different, became enmeshed like two unhappy partners. Certainly having both of them on offer at the same time made it more difficult to get either one staged.

Hilton hated the world portrayed in *Mr Roche* and, while he praised the writing, he demolished this world with typical aplomb. You can almost hear that booming voice in his words when he wrote to me on the subject:

> Maybe it's my generation, but, much as I appreciate its almost photographic *verité*, it reveals a side of life that I prefer to dismiss as I would the contemplation of my natural functions.

A friend, the actor T.P. McKenna, as I remember, brought the play to the Abbey and it was, of course, turned down by Mr Blythe as Managing Director. This was a year after his enthusiastic letter about *The O'Neill*. By this time Tomás Mac Anna had come into the Abbey, although working, it has to be said, under severe limitations imposed by Blythe and his board. My memory is that his title, like that of Alan Simpson after him, was Artistic Adviser, not Director, and that speaks for itself. The Abbey has always displayed a skill in its use of titles and appointments. Tomás became a great supporter of my work in that theatre over the years. One of the first letters he wrote to me, however, was on the rejection of *Mr Roche*.

> I am returning *Mr Roche* as the managing director feels that it is not our line of territory. I would add to that the one word – yet. However it does seem to me that if Jim Fitzgerald is interested, then its success at the Gate or Olympia is assured. In fact, it is the sort of play which would be excellent fare for the Festival. If I can help to have it get a first class production, you have only to call on me.

It should be pointed out in all of this that Ireland had no official stage censorship while England had. Even as I was struggling to get this play produced in Dublin, Peggy Ramsay was writing to me from London to say that she expected trouble with the Lord Chamberlain's office on the play's content if it were taken on by a London management. And, of course, by the time this happened, with Richard Eyre's 1969 production at Hampstead, stage censorship in England had passed into the history books.

I had given the play to Jim Fitzgerald when he was working as a television director at RTÉ. Niall Toibin agreed to play the lead and, suddenly, everything started to move quickly. Fitz brought the play to Brendan Smith who accepted it for the Festival of 1968.

Fitz was alcoholic and often flew by the seat of his pants. He was also a director of genius, particularly of actors in close, intimate, physical situations and at the same time a terrific reader of the text. He was a highly intelligent, well-read man who was deeply subversive of all conventional thought and practice. As with Peggy Ramsay's letters, someone should publish an account of the contribution of his company, the Globe Theatre, to Irish theatre. Its contribution, and that of Fitzgerald, to the early days of the Dublin Festival were immense. It was truly extraordinary what he achieved, in spite of the drink.

I remember coming into the Olympia Theatre after lunch for a rehearsal a week or so before the opening of *Mr Roche*. To my surprise, one of the doormen, normally so polite and helpful, did his damnedest to keep me out. I managed to get past him to find the actors in a huddle on the stage. Fitz was stretched out, plastered, on the floor in the wings, after a liquid lunch that had gone on too long. The question of the moment among the actors was: how to stop Brendan Smith from entering the theatre? I can't remember how it all ended. But I do know that all of this was soon forgotten because Fitzgerald's production of the play was superb and Brendan Smith was delighted. I owe my real start in theatre to Jim Fitzgerald.

The Festival of 1968 also featured several other new Irish plays, including Hugh Leonard's *The Au Pair Man* and Tom

Murphy's *The Orphans* at the Gate. I suppose the production which created most anticipation that year, though, was the production of *The Cherry Orchard* at the Abbey by Madame Knebel of the Moscow Arts, with Siobhán McKenna and Cyril Cusack. It was my first experience of that slow, stately, pictorial, Russian treatment of Chekhov, the whole action framed within edges of quietness and repose. Not everyone's cup of tea, though. I remember saying how interesting it was to Mary Manning, one of the more acerbic creatures of Dublin theatre at the time. 'Rubbish!' she said, 'It's like a staging of the Lord's Prayer!'

I have talked about how these very different plays, *The O'Neill* and *The Death and Resurrection of Mr Roche* became entangled together, both in the writing and in doing the rounds of managements. The Theatre Festival had an important bearing upon the life of both plays. My point is that, firstly, I don't think that *Mr Roche* would have appeared, because of its portrayal of a homosexual, outside the security of the Festival. One of the things which gave the Festival this daring and security was the presence of critics and journalists from outside Ireland. You never knew what they might write about us if we didn't behave ourselves. Secondly, I think it would have been virtually impossible to get a professional production of *The O'Neill* at the time without the success of *Mr Roche*. That, in a nutshell, represents the importance of the Festival in my own writing career.

## 2 | Theatre, Sexuality, and the State: Tennessee Williams's *The Rose Tattoo* at the Dublin Theatre Festival, 1957

Lionel Pilkington

The dramatic event for which the opening year of the Dublin Theatre Festival is most famous took place offstage, in a struggle between theatre personnel and police officers in the box office of the Pike Theatre and then on the street outside. This event was the arrest and detention of Alan Simpson on 23 May 1957 for his production of Tennessee Williams's play *The Rose Tattoo*. In an action that remains unprecedented in Irish theatre history, Simpson was arrested on a summary warrant by Irish secret police, the Garda 'Special Branch', for producing 'for gain an indecent and profane performance'.[1] To be apprehended in Ireland for a theatrical performance is highly unusual. Despite the existence of repressive, perennially renewed 'emergency' security legislation directed primarily against anti-state republicans and radical socialists[2] as well as the country's much better-known censorship laws for literature and film,[3] the institutional theatre in Ireland remains outside the strictures of direct censorship and state control. As the first section of this essay will argue, this is, at least in part, a postcolonial legacy. Historically, the theatre's role in Ireland as an institutional vehicle for modernization, its discursive function in naturalizing and reinforcing the idea of agency as delegation, and its role in demonstrating a somatic modernity possess a cumulative effect that supersedes the need for direct state control. Precisely *because* Simpson's arrest is so anomalous it offers a fascinating revelation of a set of ideological effects which, I want to suggest, are crucial to the way in which we think about theatre and modernity in Ireland.

Theatre *in* Ireland is a cultural relationship that is complicated and overdetermined. This is partly because Ireland itself is regarded as innately performative: a location for the 'drama' of rebellion and anti-colonial insurgency and possessing an ontological core that is inherently theatrical. There is our propensity for charm and flattering exaggeration known as 'blarney', our older and less charming reputation for deviousness and verbal chicanery, and the many oxymoron-type adjectives listed for the word 'Irish' ('Irish confetti', an 'Irish bridge') in the *Oxford English Dictionary*. Indeed, Matthew Arnold's famous diagnosis of the Celtic temperament in terms of 'its straining human nature further than it will stand' might well be mistaken for a description of theatre.[4] Ireland's longstanding association with the histrionic — an ability, like theatrical performance, to delve in the subjunctive and stretch the bounds of the possible either through political rebelliousness or linguistic gymnastics — means that the theatre in and for Ireland tends to be viewed as an institution that is particularly well suited for the expression and disciplining of the innate and wayward performativity of its people. As the 1897 letter to the guarantors of the Irish Literary Theatre put it, an Irish theatre would possess a special vitality because, unlike the English commercial theatre, it would draw on 'an audience trained to listen by its passion for oratory'.[5]

Theatre as a means of disciplining the drama of Irish character is a formulation with a long history. As is very well known the theatre as an institution begins in Ireland with the establishment of Dublin's Werburgh Street Theatre, probably in 1636, on the orders of the English Lord Lieutenant, Thomas Wentworth, Earl of Strafford.[6] With a company of London actors and with the English dramatist James Shirley as its resident dramatist, this was a theatre that existed, quite openly, as a vehicle for English vice-regal government and for the promotion of the values and prestige of a settler colonial elite.

Rapidly indigenized as a forum for the performance of plays dealing with Irish subjects and, briefly at the end of the 18th century as a national institution, the development of theatre in Ireland consists of the maintenance and accentuation of this early modernizing cultural function. Established as a building and urban-based site for the performance of scripted plays, the theatre (assisted by theatre historiography) attempts to set itself apart from a competing range of performative and theatrical practices associated with Ireland's rural, peasant majority: practices such as mumming, wake games, story-telling, ballad singing and elements of faction fighting.[7]

Inseparable from the modernization role of the institutional theatre in Ireland is its ideological function in seeking to naturalize and support dominant norms of representation and political agency. Thus, as I have tried to argue elsewhere, [8] the idea of the modern citizen as someone who delegates power to his or her political representative tends to be endorsed by the idea that spectatorship in the theatre is an activity that is also primarily concerned with imaginative delegation and/or sublimation. Finally, one vital but largely neglected aspect of the modernizing function of the institutional theatre in Ireland is the way in which theatrical acting seems to demonstrate a satisfyingly modern degree of somatic intelligibility. Thought of along the lines of Richard Schechner's definition of performance as 'restored behaviour',[9] the kind of performance that takes place in the institutional theatre is one that shows Irish bodies moving in recognisably modern ways. In contrast, for example, to the weird gesticulations of an ululating funeral keener, the straw-masked performances of a mummer, or the grotesque and often crudely sexual and violent indecorousness of a wake game, acting in the institutional theatre renders behaviour somatically legible. At the fundamental level of body movements and gestures, one of the enduring features of the Irish theatre — from the Abbey Theatre tours of the United States in the early twentieth century to *Riverdance* today — is to demonstrate to audiences both in Ireland and internationally the extent to which the Irish body conforms to recognisable norms of Western modernity.

That the institutional theatre in colonial, nationalist, and postcolonial Ireland is so closely bound up with an historical project of cultural modernization, that its vocabulary is frequently evoked in order to underline the naturalness and inevitability of a system of political representation based on delegation, and that it renders Irish behaviour as modern amounts to a formidable cultural power. Crucially, however, this is a power that depends on the idea that the theatre is a mode of representation that operates autonomously and outside the direct control of the state. It is in this context that the arrest of Alan Simpson in May 1957 appears such a bizarre and dramatic event.

Founded by Alan Simpson and Carolyn Swift in 1953, the Pike Theatre was a club rather than a public theatre. It modelled itself not on the dominant political aesthetic of representative nationalism that was still championed by an apparently indefatigable Ernest Blythe at the Abbey Theatre, but on the more adversarial stance of a European, modernizing elite. To this extent, the Pike belonged to the 'new wave' of theatrical experimentation that was then also taking place in London and Paris. Like the English Stage Company at the Royal Court Theatre, the Pike was self-consciously avant-garde and championed theatrical regeneration by means of reinvigorated naturalism and virile (hetero)sexuality.[10] With its small fifty-seat auditorium, its regular expressionistic designs, and a repertoire that mixed high modernist plays and facetious revue, the social and cultural atmosphere at the Pike was a mix of exclusivity and boisterous hedonism. Described by Alan Simpson as 'a revolutionary force of small means [designed to] ... stir up the theatrical lethargy of post-war Ireland',[11] the Pike's late-night revues, annual 'follies', and productions of Ionesco and Beckett, displayed an exciting and often provocative disregard for Ireland's prevailing moral and aesthetic conventions. There was irreverent *double entendre*, jibes at the G.A.A., acerbic political and cultural commentary, and actresses dancing on stage in mink bikinis. This was a cultural phenomenon that celebrated the arrival of a new, urban, liberal elite and a social space in which audience members could perform with brio this new identity. These were educated cosmopolitans for whom the shibboleths of nationality and religion were no longer as valid and for whom (hetero)sexuality operated as a more crucial site for identity formation.

The Pike Theatre was a daring and innovative cultural venture. But while its aesthetic philosophy may be described as avant-garde, modernist, and consistently subversive of what it saw as the outmoded pieties of Irish nationalism and the socio-political authority of the Irish Roman Catholic church, this same political aesthetic was also the reason why the Pike was fêted by Ireland's political establishment. What the Pike demonstrated was what the Dublin Theatre Festival also aspired to convey: an internationally accessible Irish modernity that was willing to cast off the shackles of an inhibiting past. Quite apart from the plays that were performed at the Pike, what the Pike's actors and actresses (and to some extent their audiences) performed was modernity in motion. More important than the satirical lyrics of *The Follies* ('You can't undress to kill / At the beach at Salthill / But you can, in Cannes') was their performance by actors and actresses themselves looking like fashionable theatre spectators: actresses in stylishly low-cut ball gowns and actors in well-tailored dinner jackets. Emphasized by this means was a contrast between the presence and authenticity of the libidinal body on and off stage and the stilted factitiousness of traditional Irish pieties outside and beyond the range of the theatre building. Demonstrated by the Pike at the most fundamental level of the body was Ireland's energetic adaptability to modern modes of dress, physical deportment and styles of behaviour. This trend was by no means unique to Ireland and the Pike. As Stephen Lacy has shown in reference to the English Stage Company, the idea of the body and the personal assuming a new importance conjugated well with a broad shift in European socialism from radical class struggle to liberation as personal freedom.[12] By May 1957, the Pike had become the toast of a large section of the Dublin establishment. Gerard Whelan's book *Spiked* recounts Carolyn Swift's memory of an evening dancing with the newly-elected Fianna Fáil T. D., Charles Haughey and Alan Simpson writes about a heady round of Embassy functions and parties.[13] Moreover, by 1957 the Pike enjoyed the financial support and very considerable prestige of the Dublin Theatre Festival and was considering plans to move to a larger city-centre venue.[14]

Why then did the state act with such draconian force against Simpson on 23 May? As I argued in 2001, Simpson's arrest does reflect — at least to some degree — an ideological conflict between an expansionist state agenda championed by Seán Lemass in the Department of Industry and Transport and officials within the Department of Finance and defensive reactions within the Catholic hierarchy and their allies within the government.[15] In addition, Whelan is surely correct in his assertion that the action taken against Simpson was motivated partly by an on-going controversy concerning membership of the Censorship Board.[16] As an examination of files from the Office of the Attorney General (released in 2000) clearly demonstrates, the decision to arrest Alan Simpson took place *before* the production of *The Rose Tattoo* and was instigated by an approach to the Minister for Justice Oscar Traynor by the Fianna Fáil T.D., Seán Brady. Brady alerted the Minister that if action was not taken against the production of Williams's play, then there was a strong possibility that Archbishop McQuaid would make a public statement criticizing the Minister for not pursuing a robust policy of censoring indecent material. Such a statement would have damaged Traynor's attempts to weaken the power of the Censorship Board and would have exposed him to political attack. *The Rose Tattoo*, Brady averred, was 'unquestionably indecent' and its performance had already been prohibited in several American cities.[17]

Plausible though it is, the limitation of this line of interpretation — both Whelan's and my own – is that it underestimates the subversive potential of the Pike and of Williams's play. Specifically what is overlooked is the extent to which the narrative action of *The Rose Tattoo*, and the ideological effect of its performance, makes overt that which the satirical action of the popular 'follies' had only hinted at: that a somatic Irish modernity, so necessary and so reassuring to Ireland's new climate of modernization, could spill over into the erotic. At stake in the state's attempted suppression of *The Rose Tattoo*, in other words, was not merely tensions within the Irish state regarding the pace and social consequences of economic modernization. Also at issue was a collision between the institutional and somatic features of theatrical modernity in Ireland: a clash between an avant-garde theatricality as a sign of Ireland's modernity, and the libidinousness of the Irish female body through which this modernity was expressed and reproduced. It was against this powerful force that the fury of the state's action was primarily directed.

The most objectionable feature of Simpson's production of the European premiere of *The Rose Tattoo* was the play itself: the extraordinary neo-Freudianism of the play's narrative and, not least, the analogy between this narrative and Ireland's project of modernization. Chosen by Swift and Simpson because 'the play has a theme of religion versus primitive superstition and should appeal particularly to an Irish audience',[18] Williams's play shows the indispensability of an unrepressed and commodified female sexuality to the kind of socio-political adaptations required of Sicilian immigrants in the southern United States by a modern, U.S. dominated global economy. The play begins with a scene in which the play's protagonist Serafina della Rosa eulogizes her husband's prowess at love-making and ends with a scene in which Serafina encourages her fifteen year-old daughter, Rosa, to have sex with her boyfriend. Outside of a major metropolitan venue, it is just as hard to imagine an uncontroversial and unexpurgated performance of *The Rose Tattoo* in 2008 as, presumably, it was in the 1950s.

With the developmental logic of the three-act structure, Williams's narrative celebrates a Rabelaisian eroticism. Initially rendered desolate by her husband's sudden death in a Mafia-style shootout, Serafina mourns her bereavement by isolating herself and her daughter from the rest of the Sicilian immigrant community and, more detrimentally, from mainstream American society. While Serafina's lugubriousness is portrayed as excessive, the real damage that it causes is most evident in relation to her daughter's attempts at assimilation. Serafina almost prevents Rosa from taking part in a crucial American rite of passage — her high school graduation ceremony — and, in what the play presents as the most damaging of acts, compels Rosa's boyfriend, U.S. navy sailor Jack Hunter, to swear that he will respect Rosa's virginity. It is only when Serafina discovers

that her husband was unfaithful and had himself abandoned his
Sicilian Catholic vows of marital fidelity, that she dramatically
changes her attitude. This is the moment in the play when
Serafina describes the statue of the Virgin Mary as 'a poor little
girl with the paint peeling off' and then blows out its vigil light.[19]
Following this, Serafina reconciles herself to her clumsy, new-
found lover Alvaro whose air of buffoonery — in one scene,
omitted from Simpson's production, Alvaro accidentally drops a
condom during a romantic speech – is compensated for by his
uncanny physical similarity to her former husband. Serafina
rethinks her earlier rejection of Alvaro, decides to have sex with
him (Act 3, scene 1 begins with the off-stage but unmistakable
and noisily passionate sounds of Serafina's orgasms), and then
encourages Rosa to do the same with her boyfriend.

The effects of Simpson's arrest on the fortunes of the Pike
Theatre, and on Simpson's subsequent career, were devastating.
Although the court hearing determined that a case for
prosecution could not be brought, Simpson's legal costs and the
effect of the controversy and its association of state opprobrium
drained the Pike of membership and finances.[20] Equally
crippling was the curtailing effect of the court hearing on the
Pike's programming which precipitated a move away from the
theatre's earlier and more adventurous attempts at subversion.
Plans to produce the English language premiere of Ugo Betti's
*Crime on Goat Island* — a play that explores the psychological
dimensions of female sexual need – were abandoned,
unsurprisingly, in August 1957. The repercussions of Simpson's
arrest also weakened the prospects of the Dublin Theatre
Festival championing a critical or avant-garde modernism in
the 1950s and 1960s and, more temporarily, emboldened the
Roman Catholic Church in terms of its influence over Ireland's
cultural and political life. Whatever about Archbishop
McQuaid's direct involvement in the state's initial action against
Simpson (as Whelan's book points out, the weight of evidence
suggests that McQuaid was not directly involved), there is no
doubt that Simpson's arrest and trial contributed to the
church's further involvement in the Festival. The situation went
from bad to worse when, in February 1958, under pressure from
McQuaid, the Festival committee withdrew its planned

productions of Sean O'Casey's *The Drums of Father Ned* and
Alan McClelland's dramatization of James Joyce's *Ulysses* from
that year's programme. Samuel Beckett responded by refusing
permission for his plays to form a part of the Festival and its
organizing committee then cancelled (literally 'postponed') the
1958 Festival in its entirety.

Given the devastating effect of the state's actions against
Simpson's production of *The Rose Tattoo*, it is understandable
that critical discussion of this episode tends to focus on trying to
explain the state's motivation. This discussion has concentrated
on the main political issue that was at stake: the fear within
some elements of Fianna Fáil that if Minister for Justice Oscar
Traynor did not take action against the Pike then Archbishop
McQuaid would be forced to make a public statement. It is also
understandable that those who seek to defend Simpson's
reputation as a director of courage and extraordinary merit
have tended to stress the extent to which the play was *not*
especially objectionable.[21] Ironically, the consequence of this
joint emphasis is that the transformative power of the Pike for
1950s Dublin is underestimated. This transformative power lay
in two connected features: the use of theatrical performance as
a satirical instrument to expose social conditioning by stressing
the gulf between official ideology and the libidinous body of the
actor or actresses on stage, and (in a manner similar to John
Osborne's *Look Back in Anger*) the suggestion of a new kind of
role playing and behaviour which would not be restricted to the
theatre.

Despite the modernist character of plays performed at the
Pike – Eugène Ionesco's *The Bald Prima Donna*, Samuel
Beckett's *Waiting for Godot* and Jean-Paul Sartre's *The
Respectable Prostitute* were all produced in 1956 – the Pike's
style of acting and production tended to be naturalistic. Not at
all Brechtian, what was stressed was the physical identification
between actor and role and the encouragement of a similar
identification between spectator and actor. In many ways what
was at stake at the Pike was a variation on what Herbert
Marcuse had outlined two years earlier in his 1955 book *Eros
and Civilisation*. Marcuse argued that 'the reality principle' of
western civilization was a form of alienated labour that involved

the diversion of the libido for socially useful performances and what he described as a 'mechanics of conformity'.[22] There is a striking similarity between Marcuse's use of Freudian analysis and the extent to which the Pike's theatrical agenda centred on releasing the libido from a 'mechanics of social conformity'. In many ways the intended theatrical effect was similar to the power that Freud attributes to transference especially if in re-reading Freud we substitute the words 'actor' or 'spectator' for Freud's 'patient':

> The part of the patient's [actor's / spectator's] emotional life which he can no longer recall to memory is re-experienced by him in relation to the physician [or fictional character]; and it is only this re-experiencing in the 'transference' that convinces him of the existence of the power of these unconscious sexual impulses. [23]

Williams's *The Rose Tattoo* also deals with the realization of unconscious sexual impulses with an opening tableau that contrasts the irrepressibly physical sexuality of the 'voluptuous' Serafina and her 'pretty and vivacious' fifteen year old daughter Rosa with the seven dressmaker's mannequins whose frozen bodily movements are described in the stage directions as 'like the declamatory actresses of the old school'.[24] In Williams's play, sexuality is presented as an irresistible, and impossible to repress, quasi-animalistic urge, and as profoundly mimetic. The rose tattoo of the play's title refers to Serafina's belief that her husband's tattoo transferred itself to her breast in that moment in her lovemaking when she had conceived a child.

Performance, as Schechner puts it, can be thought of as 'restored behaviour' and the corollary of this is that performing a role on stage means physically demonstrating and transmitting the plausibility of a particular mode of behaviour.

> [T]he use of restored behavior is the main characteristic of performance. The practitioners of all these arts, rites and healings assume that some kinds of behavior — organized sequences of events, scripted actions, known texts, scored movements — exist separately from the performers who 'do' these behaviors. Because the behavior is separate from those

who are behaving, the behavior can be stored, transmitted, manipulated, transformed.[25]

Thought of from the point of view of Schechner's study, the fictional roles of *The Rose Tattoo* gain an additional dimension when performed by Irish actresses and actors on the Pike Theatre stage. Quite apart from the thematic emphasis of Williams's play — the irrepressibility of sexual desire — a performance of *The Rose Tattoo* conveyed the somatic plausibility of certain kinds of action, behaviour, and physical response. If, for example, a respectable middle class young woman like Kate Binchy (the nineteen-year-old daughter of a Dublin Circuit Court judge) could take the part of Rosa delle Rose, a highly sexualized fifteen-year-old Sicilian-American, then something similar was being suggested for Irish women in general. An overt expression of sexuality, repressed in Irish public life, was asserted in the performance of Williams's play by means of a form of double transference. That is, the repressed sexuality of the actor or actress was experienced in his or her performance of the fictional characters of Williams's narrative and, by the same token, the repressed sexuality of the spectator was experienced imaginatively in terms of the physical performances taking place on stage. On one level what the production of *The Rose Tattoo* demonstrated was Ireland's modernity: the ability of Irish actors to adapt easily and fluently to new and predominantly American forms of physical behaviour and expression. It was, at least in part, this implied somatic flexibility that led to the Pike's popularity and to the apparent compatibility of this production in relation to the modernizing elements of the Irish government: the *Bulletin of the Department of Foreign Affairs* displayed an advertisement for *The Rose Tattoo* at more or less the same time that the Department of Justice was investigating how to prosecute for indecency. And yet, as Susan Cannon Harris's recent book on gender in modern Irish drama argues so forcefully, a predominant discursive feature of the adjustments necessitated by economic modernization in post-Independence Ireland was the requirement that the Irish woman compensate for these adjustments with a 'natural' purity.[26] With Simpson's nuancing

of Ireland's modernization drive in terms of newly awakened
female libidinousness, the Irish state responded with an
unprecedented show of direct and repressive action. For Alan
Simpson, who was the principal victim of this action, and for
the development of a modernist and radical Irish theatre, the
results were catastrophic.

---

[1] *Irish Press* 24 May 1957, p. 1.

[2] Michael Farrell, The *Apparatus of Repression*, Field Day Pamphlet,
11 (Derry: Field Day Theatre Company, 1986).

[3] Michael Adams, *Censorship: The Irish Experience* (Dublin: Sceptre,
1968).

[4] Matthew Arnold, 'On the Study of Celtic Literature', extract in *Poetry
and Ireland Since 1800: A Source Book*, ed. Mark Storey (London
and New York: Routledge, 1988), p. 65.

[55] Augusta Gregory, *Our Irish Theatre: A Chapter of Autobiography*
(Gerrards Cross, Bucks: Colin Smythe, 1972), p. 20.

[6] Christopher Morash, A *History of Irish Theatre, 1601-2000*
(Cambridge: Cambridge University Press, 2002), p. 4.

[7] Mark Phelan, 'Modernity, Geography and Historiography: (Re)-
Mapping Irish Theatre History in the Nineteenth Century', *The
Performing Century: Nineteenth-Century Theatre's History*, eds
Tracy C. Davis and Peter Holland (London: Palgrave Macmillan,
2007), pp. 135-58.

[8] Lionel Pilkington, 'Irish Theater Historiography and Political
Resistance', *Staging Resistance: Essays on Political Theater*, eds
Jeanne Colleran and Jenny S. Spencer (Ann Arbor: University of
Michigan Press, 1988), pp. 13-30.

[9] Richard Schechner, 'Restoration of Behavior', *Studies in Visual
Communication* 7 (1981), p. 2.

[10] See Dan Rebellato, *1956 and All That: The Making of Modern
British Drama* (London: Routledge, 2002).

[11] Alan Simpson, *Beckett and Behan and a Theatre in Dublin* (London:
Routledge and Kegan Paul, 1962), p. 1.

[12] Stephen Lacy, *British Realist Theatre: The New Wave in its Context
1956-1965* (London and New York: Routledge, 1995).

[13] Gerard Whelan, (with Carolyn Swift), *Spiked: Church-State Intrigue
and the Rose Tattoo* (Dublin: New Island, 2002), p. 61.

[14] Whelan, p. 47.

[15] Lionel Pilkington, *Theatre and the State in 20th Century Ireland: Cultivating the People* (London and New York: Routledge, 2001), p. 157.

[16] See Whelan, pp. 193-298.

[17] National Archives: AG 2000/10/535.

[18] See *Pike Theatre Newsletter*, p. 15; Simpson papers, Trinity College Dublin — MS 10813/383/14.

[19] Tennessee Williams, *The Rose Tattoo and Other Plays* (London: Penguin, 1978), p. 101.

[20] Carolyn Swift, *Stage by Stage* (Dublin: Poolbeg, 1985), p. 281.

[21] See Whelan, p. 49.

[22] See Herbert Marcuse, *Eros and Civilisation* (London: Allen Lane, 1970), pp. 111-18.

[23] Sigmund Freud, *Two Short Accounts of Psycho-Analysis* (London: Pelican, 1972), p. 82.

[24] See Williams, p. 18.

[25] Richard Schechner, 'Restoration of Behavior', *Studies in Visual Communication* 7 (1981), p. 2.

[26] Susan Cannon Harris, *Gender and Modern Irish Drama* (Bloomington and Indianapolis: Indiana University Press, 2002), pp. 267-72.

## 3 | Irish Language Theatre at the Dublin Theatre Festival

Sara Keating

Irish language theatre had a prominent role in the development of the Dublin Theatre Festival, especially during its first ten years. The Festival had developed as an offshoot of An Tóstal festival, which was founded to encourage tourism and 'depict the varied aspects of Irish life and culture' – including the Irish language – throughout the country'.[1] When Brendan Smith approached Bord Fáilte in 1956 with the idea for a festival devoted entirely to theatre to run in parallel with An Tóstal, '[t]he original idea', as he later commented, 'was to have a festival that would be, roughly speaking, given over to two-thirds Irish contributions – in terms of writing, acting and directing – and one third foreign contributions'.[2] Although funding difficulties in the early years led to a variety of changing ratios between the international aspect of the Festival and its home-grown productions – reflected in the inclusion or exclusion of the defining term 'International' in the Festival's branding logo – the production of Irish language theatre was an important part of the Festival's emerging remit.

Within the wider theatre culture of Ireland at the time, Irish language theatre certainly had a high profile, although its reputation was hardly regarded as progressive. The position of Irish language theatre at the Abbey Theatre, for example, is often used to illustrate the conservatism of Irish theatre during the 1940s and 1950s, although recent scholarship has shown that focussing on the Abbey's approach to Irish language drama can obscure the extent to which there was plenty of genuine dramatic experimentation during this period.[3] Nevertheless, it is worth briefly outlining the conflict between cultural policy and quality theatre that predominated at the Abbey in the 1950s, because doing so provides a backdrop against which we can measure the achievements of many of the Irish language writers whose work premiered at the Dublin Theatre Festival in the 1960s and 1970s.

Earnán de Blaghd – or Ernest Blythe, to give him the name by which he's better known – was a board member at the Abbey for almost thirty years and its Managing Director between 1951 and 1967. He had implemented a stringent Irish language policy at the theatre in the early 1950s. Under his Directorship, the actors at the Abbey were required to be bilingual; one-act Irish language plays were commissioned to provide interval and post-show entertainment every time a play in English was produced; Irish language pantomimes were a significant, and notorious, element of the annual programme; and Irish language translations of work by Yeats, Gregory, and Synge – specifically their plays that engaged with Irish mythology – were given especial prominence at the theatre.

However, it was less the status given to Irish language theatre during this period than the standard of the plays being produced that was at issue. As Alan Titley has characterized it, it was 'theatre of "the cow in the well" and "the fairy fort"' (118). Plays with titles such as *Prátaí Mhicil Thaidhg* ('Mike Ted's Potatoes'), *Caismirt na gCearc* ('The Battle of the Hens'), or *Cupán Tae Airt* ('Art's Cup of Tea') suggest the stagnant theatrical conception and mundane domestic preoccupations of much of the Irish language drama of the time.

That does not mean, however, that all Irish language theatre during this period was of a similarly routine, realist conception. The history of An Club Drámaíochta, which operated out of Damer Hall in the basement of the Unitarian Church on St. Stephen's Green, throws a different perspective on the status of *drámaíocht na Gaeilge* in the 1950s and 1960s. Founded in 1955, An Damer was sponsored by the Irish language preservation group, Gael Linn. According to Alan Titley, it 'produced the best and most revolutionary of Irish theatre', both in the English and Irish language, during the 1950s. As Titley observes, translations of European modernist classics were popular at An Damer, but new writing by Seán Ó Tuama, Eoghan Ó Tuairisc, Críostóir Ó Floinn, Brendan Behan, and Máiréad Ní Ghráda 'provided the most sustained period of original and creative theatre ever' in the history of Irish language drama (118).

In fact, as Christopher Morash has commented, Irish language writers at the time 'registered the same willingness to tackle hitherto taboo subjects' evident in the work of the Anglophone Irish writers who were also beginning to flourish in the late 1950s – dramatists such as Eugene McCabe, Tom Murphy, Thomas Kilroy, and Brian Friel.[4] The Dublin Theatre Festival, as other essays in this book illustrate, provided a platform for showcasing much of this (often radical) new work in English. What is less frequently acknowledged, however, is that it also did so for Irish language writing.

The first years of the Dublin Theatre Festival programme did not signal an especially auspicious beginning to its Irish language remit. In 1957, for example, the Festival's Irish language output was limited to two productions. The first was Douglas Hyde's classic one-act play *An Pósadh* ('The Marriage'), which was run as a post-show accompaniment to the Abbey's repertory productions of *The Playboy of the Western World* and *Juno and The Paycock*. The second was a bilingual late-night revue at the Pocket Theatre, based on a new translation of Merriman's *Cúirt an Mheán Oíche* ('The Midnight Court'). Meanwhile, the cancellation of the 1958 Festival meant that the premiere production of Brendan Behan's *An Giall* (which soon would infamously be 'translated' for Joan Littlewood's Theatre Workshop as *The Hostage*) was postponed.[5]

Behan's anarchic comedy became one of the most significant plays of the period, both in its Irish-language and English-language version. The play's proposed premiere within the Festival was intended to signal the beginning of a productive relationship between An Damer and the Dublin Theatre Festival, the small basement theatre becoming the chief

producing house for Irish language theatre at the Festival for
the next decade. In fact, from 1960 onwards, An Damer would
put forward at least one, if not two, productions to the Festival
repertoire (and *An Giall* was eventually produced at the Theatre
Festival in 1967, although at the Peacock Theatre).

The variety of works presented by An Damer was notable. Its
contribution to the Festival in 1960 was the world premiere of
*Spailpín, a Ruin*. The high profile of the cast and production
team is notable. The play was written by Seán MacRéamoinn,
directed by Pronsias Mac Diarmada (Frank Dermody), boasted
original music composed by Seán Ó Riada, and featured a young
Niall Toibín (who developed his craft at An Damer) in the
leading role. Meanwhile, the 1961 Festival production of *Scéal
ar Phádraig* was written by Seán Ó Tuama, who was to be
responsible for some of the most interesting and challenging
plays that An Damer presented at the Dublin Theatre Festival,
including *Gunna Cam agus Slabhra Óir*, written in 1964.

*Gunna Cam agus Slabhra Óir* marked a significant
breakthrough in the scale of Irish language work, and had a
huge influence on the imagination of Irish language playwrights
at the time. A three-act quasi-historical drama set in a castle, Ó
Tuama's play drew on a mixture of verse and prose, historical
text, and original writing, to create an intricately crafted play
that was heavily influenced by Brechtian dramaturgy, and
which used monologue, soliloquies, and asides as much as
dialogue. According to Titley, the play 'showed how far drama in
Irish had come' since the 1940s and 1950s.[6] Indeed, Ó Tuama's
work still holds a significant place in the Irish language drama
repertoire, and was used to represent Irish language drama in a
radio production on RTE Radio One's *Seachtain na Gaeilge*
celebrations in 2006.

When Ó Tuama's landmark play was presented by An Damer
at the Dublin Theatre Festival in 1967, a new play by Séamus
O'Neill, simultaneously playing at the Peacock as part of the
Festival, showed how Ó Tuama's play was already very
influential. O'Neill's play *Faill ar an bhFeart* was a three-act
play for fourteen actors, set during the 1798 rebellion and, apart
from its scale, it challenged traditional historical views by
presenting the rebellion from the perspective of a Protestant

minister rather than the revolutionary nationalists. The minister is represented sympathetically, campaigning for justice on behalf of the peasants, and in the dramatic climax, he is brought to trial for treason, and condemned to death by hanging. In both its scale and its alternative historical perspective, *Faill ar an bhFeart* mirrored the developments represented by Ó Tuama's earlier epic play.

Perhaps the most significant play in An Damer's repertoire at this time, however, involved another trial. Máiréad Ní Ghráda's poignant drama *An Triail*, which premiered at An Damer in 1964 in a production directed by Tomás Mac Anna, also illustrates how far Irish language theatre had evolved, both in its commitment to developing an exciting theatrical aesthetic, and in its willingness to critique prevailing Irish social structures.

Ní Ghráda's expressionistic play stages a psychological trial of sorts, as a young unmarried mother, Máire, attempts to cope when she is ostracized by her community and her lover. The play was an experiment in form, but was also 'experimental' in its exposure of the harrowing results of Irish social and cultural conservativism. Using such Brechtian techniques as surtitles and music, the first production of *An Triail* effectively placed the audience in the position of jury, alienating them from the story unfolding on stage, and making them the moral arbiters of the young girl's future. The critical representation of the protagonist's lover (a teacher in a position of social authority), Máire's unyielding mother, and the religious institution that she finds herself forced into – all show the radicalism of the script, both in its representation of sexuality and its critique of Irish society. The play continues to be taught on the Leaving Certificate curriculum, and is produced and toured nationally on an annual basis. In 2008, for example, the innovative Irish language theatre company Fíbín brought an extra level of experimentalism to *An Triail* with an exciting version of the play told through puppetry. However, the use of the Irish language is an especially significant aspect of *An Triail's* interpolation in the wider context of 1960s Irish society; as James J. Blake has suggested, the Irish language allowed Ní

Ghráda to stage a subversive social critique that would never have been possible in English.[7]

An Damer was also involved in producing a number of translations from the European and American repertoire at the Dublin Theatre Festival during this period, showcasing a desire to refute the criticisms of conservativism and insularity that had dogged Blythe's Irish language repertoire at the Abbey. Pádraig Ó Gaora's translation of Arnold Wesker's seminal socialist play *Roots* was An Damer's Festival production in 1963, for example; while *An Chúis in Aghaidh Íosa,* Liam Ó Bríain's translation of Diego Fabbri's 1955 play *Processo a Jesú,* was the Festival production in 1971. Fabbri's play, advertised in the Festival brochure as a play by 'duine de mhór scríbhneoirí Chaitleacha na hIodáile' ('Italy's premiere Catholic writer') was in fact more radical than the promotional material suggested, and controversially put Jesus on trial to defend his miracles.[8] In a dramaturgical device similar to that used in *An Triail,* the audience were invited to decide on the fate of the Catholic faith.

This production of *An Chúis in Aghaidh Íosa* in 1971 was in fact the last time that An Damer was represented at the Dublin Theatre Festival, although Damer Hall was used again briefly in the 1980s as an English language venue, hosting the premiere of Frank McGuinness's short play *Ladybag* at the Festival in 1985. Meanwhile, under the directorship of Tomás Mac Anna, the Peacock Theatre took over the primary responsibility for Irish language theatre productions, having already supplemented An Damer's repertoire with a second Irish language production at the Festival since 1967. When the Abbey had moved into its newly built premises on Abbey Street in 1967, Blythe had handed artistic control to Mac Anna with the proviso that the Peacock should be used primarily as a stage for Irish language productions. Under Mac Anna's directorship, the Peacock was to replace An Damer as the only significant producing house for Irish language theatre represented at the Festival throughout the 1970s and early 1980s.

The most remarkable Irish language play to emerge during this period was Críostóir Ó Floinn's monumental historical drama *Mise Raifteirí an File,* which premiered at the Peacock in 1973, and featured twenty-two principal roles, with extra parts for crowd scenes. The play's bold and experimental dramaturgy managed to blend historical material with contemporary cultural debate, resulting in a three-act drama of epic scope that, according to Alan Titley, 'never let the culture clog up the story or history slow down the action'.[9]

The late 1970s and early 1980s were dominated by the production of new stage adaptations of classic Irish literary texts and established dramatizations of Gaelic legends. These included the 1978 production of Micheál Mac Liammóir's seminal Irish language play *Diarmuid agus Gráinne,* which had premiered in the opening season of An Taibhdhearc, the national Irish language theatre located in Galway city, in 1928. This new production of the Irish language classic was followed by adaptations of Padraic Ó Conaire's novel *Deoraíocht* in 1979 and Breandán Ó hEithir's novel *Lig Sinn i gCathú* in 1980, both translated for the stage by Macdara Ó Fatharta, as well as original works from Antoine Ó Flatharta, including *Gaeilgeoirí* in 1981, and *Imeachtaí na Saoirse* in 1983.

Although this period *was* dominated by stage adaptations, the adapted and original texts dealt with a variety of contemporary themes, including emigration, the relationship between church and state, the individual and the family, and the status of the Irish language itself. Antoine Ó Flatharta's stage work was especially interesting in this latter respect, pioneering the use of 'new' Irish on the stage – Irish that included newly-coined words to express contemporary phenomena – while in *Imeachtaí na Saoirse* he controversially included an entire scene in English. Ó Flatharta's interest in merging the contemporary realities of the Irish language with new modes of theatricality became a significant feature of the Irish language work that began to emerge in the Festival throughout the 1980s. In fact, by the late 1980s, Irish language theatre had largely moved away from the theatrical establishment at the Peacock Theatre and into more unconventional venues and more contemporary theatrical terrain. This move was spurred on by an emergent generation of new and exciting theatre directors and producers, including Ray Yeates (who now serves as the artistic director of Ballymun's Axis Theatre), and Fiach Mac Conghail (current director of the Abbey Theatre).

Irish language theatre during this period was invigorated by site-specific work, such as *Daoine ar an Dart*, written by Sean Ó Broin and produced nightly on the DART (Dublin's light-rail system) throughout the two-week period of the 1987 Dublin Theatre Festival. Meanwhile, Cathal Ó Searcaigh's play *Mairimid leis na Mistéirí* was produced at the Festival in 1988 as a special event in Christchurch Cathedral. Such work illustrates how Irish language theatre was engaging in the formal and thematic experimentation emerging both in new English-language theatre in Ireland and in the international touring productions that visited during the Dublin Theatre Festival.

The early 1990s, meanwhile, saw continued interest in Irish language theatre at the Festival, with Irish language plays being produced by various groups whose work was not exclusively Irish-language based: such companies as the Project Arts Centre, On the Bank Productions, and the short-lived City Centre venture. However, in the early 1990s, amateur drama groups began to supplement the Festival's Irish language programme, with up to three plays by various Irish language amateur drama groups being produced every year in a mini-festival at Coláiste Mhuire, Parnell Square, between 1990 and 1995. Unfortunately, as amateur involvement surged, professional productions of Irish language drama began to fall away from the Festival's repertoire.

In fact, the Amharchlann de hÍde production of Liam Ó Muirthile's lyrical poem *Tine Chnámh* at the Project Arts Centre in 1993, and Éilis Ní Dhuibhne's play *Milseog an tSamhraidh* at the Samuel Beckett Theatre in 1997, were the last two professional Irish language theatre productions at the Dublin Theatre Festival. Both were adventurous in their dramaturgical style. *Tine Chanmh*, under the direction of Michael Scott, used a surrealist theatrical style to complement the original poem's symbolism, while director Kathy McArdle created an imagistic production in her staging of Ní Dhuibhne's Irish-Welsh famine fairytale. Ní Dhuibhne's radical blend of two Celtic languages has since become a significant conceit for contemporary Irish language theatre, most notably in the work of Welsh theatre company Llwyfan Gogledd Cymru, whose productions

*Frongoch* and *Branwen*, which toured to Ireland in 2005 and 2006 respectively, used a blend of Welsh, Irish, and English.

In 1998, following the foundation of the Dublin Fringe Festival during the previous year, Irish language theatre was absorbed into the annual Festival celebrations as a fringe theatre event, and such companies as Blue Van Theatre Company and Aisteoirí Brennan maintained the tradition of organizing mini Irish-language theatre festivals under the rubric of the Dublin Fringe Festival.

Yet the Festival organizers' interest in Irish language theatre appeared to decline, until no Irish language theatre appeared at either of the major annual national theatre showcases, nor for that matter at the Abbey Theatre, where only three Irish language plays have been performed since 1995.[10] Significantly, for the Dublin Theatre Festival, the gradual disappearance of an Irish language remit happened in tandem with the increased globalized marketing remit of the Festival, including its key re-branding as a 'destination festival' and the re-assignment of the international label to the Festival in 2005 under the artistic directorship of Don Shipley.

In 2004, meanwhile, under the curatorship of Ray Yeates at Ballymun's Axis Theatre, an annual mini-festival of Irish language drama was reinstated at the Dublin Fringe Festival under the rubric of 'An Borradh Buan' ('Speaking in Tongues'). 'An Borradh Buan' was designed with the aim of 'bring(ing) together all the professional Irish Language Theatre Companies in Ireland to celebrate the development of Irish Language'.[11] Companies represented included Fíbín, Taibhdhearc na Gaillimhe, Aisling Ghéar, PÓC productions, and Aisteoirí Bulfin: companies which, according to one commentator, 'reflected the diversity of a theatrical scene that has been approaching something like rude health in recent years',[12] while their various productions featured everything from puppets to politics.

Discussing the significance of 'An Borradh Buan', festival director Ray Yeates stated that:

> With Irish-language theatre we're always on the fringe and are constantly asked to prove ourselves. There still exists a

cultural apartheid that views an Irish-language play as merely a vehicle to secure a grant. Lots of shows in English don't work, but when a show in Irish doesn't work everything is blamed, including the language itself. It's time we started to look at Irish-language drama as just theatre.[13]

As if to reinforce this commitment to an independent, rather than a tokenistic, Irish language theatre movement, 'An Borradh Buan' split from the Dublin Fringe Festival in 2006, in an effort to secure further its public identity as an exclusively Irish language enterprise. However, this move may have continued to contribute to the marginalization of Irish language drama within Irish theatre. Indeed, it seems noteworthy that no Irish language work was included in the play-reading programme for the fiftieth anniversary celebrations of the Dublin Theatre Festival, especially when the important archival work on the production history of Irish language theatre, being conducted by the Irish Theatre Institute, was reaching fruition at that time, recovering the scripts and production histories of many seminal Irish language dramas originally produced at the Festival.[14] It seems a particular pity when considered alongside the increased linguistic diversity of the Festival programme. In the fiftieth anniversary year alone, for example, the Festival scheduled three productions in Hungarian, all of which were surtitled for an English language audience, a standard technological intervention for touring foreign language work. The application of such live translation facilities to Irish language drama seems unlikely in the near future, with the post-colonial cultural frisson continuing to dominate contemporary discussions of the status of the Irish language. Yet perhaps it is in the context of cultural diversity fostered by internationally oriented organizations like the Dublin Theatre Festival that Irish language drama may find a less marginal status in the future.

---

[1] An Tóstal Festival's mission statement, taken from official website, 21 January 2008, www.antostalfestival.ie

[2] Alan Titley, 'Neither the Boghole nor Berlin: Drama in the Irish Language from Then Until Now', *Players and Painted Stage*, ed.

Christopher Fitz-Simon (Dublin: New Island Books, 2004), p. 115. Subsequent references are included parenthetically in the text.

3 See, for example, Paul Murphy, 'The Myth of Benightedness After the Irish Renaissance: the Drama of George Shiels', *Moving Worlds* 3, 1 (Winter 2003); Ian. R. Walsh, *The Irish Theatre Laboratory: A Study of Experimental Irish Drama in 1940s and Early 1950s (Unpublished PhD Thesis, Ireland: UCD, 2008)*; Clair Wills, *That Neutral Island, A Cultural History of Ireland During the Second World War* (London: Faber and Faber, 2007).

4 Christopher Morash, *A History of Irish Theatre: 1600-2000* (Cambridge: Cambridge University Press, 2002), p. 228.

5 *An Giall* was originally scheduled to open at An Damer in the final week of the Dublin Theatre Festival in May 1958. However, while the cancellation of the Festival celebrations delayed the premiere, *An Giall* opened at the theatre to widespread acclaim in June, 1958.

6 Titley, p. 114.

7 See James J. Blake, 'Irish-Language Theater in the 1990s: Slógadh to Teilifís na Gaeilge', *New Hibernia Review* (Summer 1999), p. 147-52.

8 Dublin Theatre Festival, Programme Note for *An Chúis in Aghaidh Íosa* by Diego Fabbri, translated by Liam Ó Bríain (Irish Theatre Archive).

9 Titley, p. 122.

10 Tom Mac Intyre's theatrical versions of *Caoineadh Airt Uí Laoghaire* (1998) and *Cúirt an Mheán Oíche* (1999) and an Irish language version of J.M. Synge's *Riders to the Sea* in 2004.

11 See http://www.axis-ballymun.ie/axis_all_areas

12 Sean Tadhg O Gairbhi, 'Thirsty for good stout and bad company', *The Irish Times* 27 September 2004, p. 13

13 Ibid.

14 At the time of the Irish Theatrical Diaspora conference in October 2007, research for the Irish language playography project was nearing completion. That section of the website was officially launched in October 2008. See http://www.irishplayography.com/

# 4 | Leonard's Progress: Hugh Leonard at the Dublin Theatre Festival

Emilie Pine

By any standards, Hugh Leonard has had an extraordinary dramatic career, penning twenty-five original full-length plays and nine adaptations or translations for the stage since 1954, in addition to credits as a screenwriter for television and film. At the Dublin Theatre Festival, Leonard has the distinction of having more plays produced than any other playwright, with eighteen original works and adaptations over the course of thirty-seven years. Indeed, if one looks at the record in this book of Irish plays premiering at the Festival, Leonard's name is a constant presence in the years between 1960 and 1985. Leonard also contributed to the Festival by becoming Programme Director in 1979, the same year that *Da* premiered (and the Pope visited Ireland). His play *Summer* (1974) received a rehearsed reading at the 2007 Dublin Theatre Festival, where it was directed by Patrick Mason with a very strong cast of Irish actors, including Susan Fitzgerald and Mark Lambert. Yet at the fiftieth anniversary he seems to have been remembered mostly as an aged godfather of Irish theatre, rather than a grand master.

The relative disappearance of Leonard from the Irish stage was marked by ten years of waning reviews, ill health, and thus fewer plays. His last new play, *Love in the Title*, was produced in 1999; he no longer writes his satiric 'log' for the *Sunday*

*Independent*; and, from an academic point of view, his work is
rarely studied in Irish theatre or literature courses. This decline
is seemingly confirmed by the reported rejection of his most
recently written play by the Abbey Theatre.[1] Whereas the plays
of his contemporaries Brian Friel and Tom Murphy seem to
accrue greater critical weight as they age, due in part to the
popularity of staged revivals and in part because they are taught
on school and university courses, Leonard's work seems to be
increasingly marginal. On the one hand, Leonard's body of work
has been consistently well received by audiences, and he has
been described as a 'major playwright of international
importance', yet on the other hand, despite these accolades,
Leonard is seldom seen as central to contemporary Irish
drama.[2] To explain this apparent paradox we must consider a
range of factors, first among them that Leonard's comic plays
and his choice to represent the domestic lives of the urban
middle class do not easily fit with an Irish critical preoccupation
with the deeper thoughts and emotions of Ireland. Leonard's
plays simply do not correspond to the dominantly realist or
naturalist context of plays that seek to represent the experiences
of colonialism, emigration, and the national love of storytelling
and masks. While Leonard's characters may indulge in nostalgia
for traditional Ireland, his plays seem to embody the fact that,
in reality, that kind of Ireland is truly out of date. Instead of
mapping Ireland's colonial past, Leonard's work for the theatre
represents modern Ireland in transition, caught between 'a new
life and new values' and the negotiations and betrayals that are
made necessary by that collision.[3] Reviewing Leonard's prose
memoir *Out After Dark* John Banville writes that 'The book is
funny, packed with stories and embarrassing incidents... a
splendid book, with an underlying seriousness the hasty reader
may miss'.[4] Banville's statement could stand as a well-judged
assessment of Leonard's dramatic work. This essay will revisit
that work in an attempt to be a less 'hasty' reader, to appreciate
the humour that runs through all Leonard's work, but also to
take account of the underlying seriousness.

Jack Keyes Byrne took the pen name of Hugh Leonard, after
a character from one of his plays, when he was first writing for
the Abbey but still working as a civil servant. For Leonard,

writing was an escape from the psychological monotony of work in the Land Commission; this is captured in his autobiography *Home Before Night*, in which he records his emotions after seeing Sean O'Casey's *Plough and the Stars*:

> The life that roared through the play itself had spilled over from the stage, sweeping him with it so that he would never again be content to just sit and watch and applaud like the rest of them. The thought burned him like a fever.[5]

Here there is the initial sense of defining himself in opposition to 'the rest of them', an apartness that would help drive him beyond passive consumption to active contribution. Most of all, there is the idea that the pulse of life is stronger on the stage than off it, that the energy of life is best experienced through the mediation of drama.

As well as offering an intellectual and emotional release, writing was also to become a financial and physical escape, once Leonard moved into screenwriting. In 1959, his work for television enabled him to leave the Civil Service and, eventually, to move to London and start making money as a professional writer. The actor David Kelly pays tribute to Leonard's writing for the British television screen and stage as having kickstarted many Irish actors' careers over the water, and making Irish characters if not quite respectable, then at least acceptable, to British audiences at a time when being Irish in England had a sense of stigma attached.[6]

In 1962, with the production of *Stephen D.* – a version of Joyce's autobiographical works *Stephen Hero* and *A Portrait of the Artist as a Young Man* – Leonard showed his talent for adaptation. Critically acclaimed, Leonard made Joyce not only accessible to theatre-goers but maintained the sense of experiment that defines Joyce's work, specifying in the directions a stage with split levels, and maintaining an impressionistic style and fragmentary plot. What is apparent in *Stephen D.* is not only Leonard's ability to deconstruct and adapt work for the stage, but also his capacity to do so with a level of innovation not otherwise on display in Irish theatre in the early 1960s: as Thomas Kilroy argues elsewhere in this book, the play 'marked a significant demarcation from what had gone before'. Perhaps what attracted Leonard to the Joyce project was the accord he felt with Joyce's rejection of 'the four great "F's" of Ireland: faith, fatherland, family and friendship'.[7] As for many writers, the work Leonard chooses for adaptation has certain affinities with his own, as the rejection of both patriotism and religion in Joyce's work is something that strongly courses through Leonard's also.

Leonard followed this success with two satiric plays that cut through the surface of the contemporary comedy of manners to comment on the shifting class structures of England and Ireland and, crucially, the moral vacuum at the heart of both. In *The Au Pair Man* (1968) Leonard turned his beam on the English class system where sexual favours can be exchanged for lessons in deportment, while in *The Patrick Pearse Motel* (1971) it is the turn of Irish sexual mores to be scrutinized. By this time, Leonard had moved back to Ireland, attracted by the tax-free status for artists, and he brought with him a love of farce, sharpened by recent productions of Feydeau on the London stage, in order to capture and caricature a type newly emerging in Ireland: the rich middle class. This new bourgeoisie superficially endorses the platitudes of patriotism and religion, yet also mercilessly, and without scruple, pursues material and sexual gain. While the comedy is farcical and the lines flippant, there is no mistaking Leonard's disdain for the new 'Quality'.

While presenting work on both the London stage and in Dublin, Leonard was also working with the Olney Theatre, Maryland, outside Washington, D.C. This relationship led him to write *Da* (1973), an autobiographical and somewhat experimental play, which brought Leonard not only the commercial success he was by now used to, but also critical approbation, sealed when the play garnered four Tony awards on Broadway. *Da* was a departure in terms of being a serious and personal play, and it put Leonard's work on a new level, bringing him a reputation for writing drama of substance as well as levity.

The play is set on the day of Charlie's father's funeral, yet when Charlie returns home, it is only to find that his father still sits in his old chair, taunting as well as haunting him. This is not the only element of experiment in the play, as Charlie is in conversation with both his dead father as well as with his younger self. As the critic Anthony Roche puts it, Leonard dramatizes the 'now and the then and brings the two into dialogue'. [8] This contrast brings into focus both the dreams of youth and the realities of old age, and the discrepancies between the two. The past is not so easily left behind and what the play seems to insist on is the necessity of confronting it, no easy task, while the project of resolution seems almost impossible. The autobiographical content of the play meant that Leonard was under public scrutiny now as a character as well as writer, and Charlie's situation may have been one way of Leonard working through his own return to Ireland. What also emerges from the play is the fact that Charlie – and therefore also Leonard – is adopted, something the writer had previously kept a 'dark secret'. [9] The insecurity of identity that comes across in so many of Leonard's plays is thus not the dislocation of national identity, the result of losing your native language and culture that is often foregrounded by other Irish playwrights, but the basic and fundamental dislocation of not knowing exactly who you come from, the fear that your original parent might at any moment appear and take you away from all that you know and understand as family. There is thus a bravery to *Da* that underscores the black humour of the play and makes it, perhaps, Leonard's most lasting play.

The bi-temporal stage device of *Da* is not merely a trope of this play but a motif of many of Leonard's most successful works from *Summer* (1974), Leonard's personal favourite among his plays, to *A Life* (1979), which follows some of the characters Leonard created in *Da*; the trope appears in *Moving* (1994), and in his most recent play *Love in the Title* (1999). What these plays share is not just the formal intrigue of showing more than one time frame; rather they coalesce into an exposition of how both small communities and families, as well as the larger community of Ireland, cope with social change. And in Leonard's work, this is where the politics are. Despite the fact that he claims to refuse to write issue plays – indeed as Christopher Murray has put it, Leonard rejects the idea of drama as social criticism at all – a strength of his best plays is that Leonard *does* speak to and about Ireland on a wider level. [10]

All the bi-temporal works are bent on showing how the past and present interact, throwing into relief where we are *now* in modern Ireland and where we have come from. And these are critiques that are surprisingly lasting, despite the socio-economic changes of the last fifteen to thirty years. Leonard lambastes the middle-class Irish for their blithe consumerism, the churning up of the Irish countryside for development, the compromising of dreams and ideals. We can hear in *Summer*, written in 1974, the same kinds of issues being raised by Irish social critics at the beginning of the twenty-first century, concerned that the Celtic Tiger has not in fact generated a prosperous and positive context for all. Indeed, as one of the play's characters says, 'instead of poverty we've got debts – that's progress', which is as easily applicable to current Irish society as it was in the 1970s.[11] In Act II of *Summer*, the teenagers have grown up, and one, Louise, is facing separation from her husband and the prospect of raising her child alone. Beyond the play's commentary on the vulgarity of wealth then, is a real portrait of how families change due to the pressures of personal as well as social and economic shifts. Again, these issues are brought into even greater focus by the changes of the Celtic Tiger period.

Indeed, the durability and persistence of Leonard's insights into the Dublin middle class go some way to question the idea that the cultural moment of the Celtic Tiger is a major break with the past. What Leonard's plays clearly demonstrate is that, although the Irish middle class has expanded, making it more visible, it is by no means a new phenomenon. This kind of commentary becomes even more pointed in the later play *Moving*, which records the shifts in Irish social life over the course of thirty years, from 1957 to 1987. The Noone family in each case is upgrading its house and lifestyle and, with its new, higher status, comes challenges to the integrity of the family as well as the wider social structure. While the pretensions of the Noone family are gently mocked, what is really pinpointed here is the increasing narrowness of social outlook. In 1987, John Turvey, the family's closest friend and a teacher in the local school, publicly acknowledges that he is gay, an act that alienates the whole community, including Ellie Noone, with a narrow-mindedness that her husband Tom struggles to understand:

**Ellie:** (*Simmering*) I mean, the cheek of him. Did he imagine that the town, all the kids' parents, that they'd thank him?

**Tom:** No, he thought they might be broad-minded.

**Ellie:** His mistake, then. (*Pause*) Do you mean that I'm not? Well, I beg to differ. I happen to think I am.

**Tom:** Sure you are. Just as long as whatever it is stays on the far side of that door.

**Ellie:** I never said I was a saint about it.

*Tom is about to speak*

Nor am I a devil, so don't make me out to be one. I don't care what John Turvey is or what he does or doesn't do. I'm not hard; I just want my peace and quiet. And my children are all I've got. The rest of it – the Mini, the holidays, the new house – they're the carrots that keep this donkey on the road. But no one, not you nor anyone like you, is taking from me the little I have left of those two. Now what you're going to do is this. You're going to tell my son to stay away from John Turvey.[12]

What Leonard does here is skilful. Ellie is part of the newly powerful and supposedly 'broad-minded' middle class. The disturbing aspect of this scene is just how reasonable Ellie sounds, merely wanting to safeguard her children and enjoy their innocence while she still can. The materialism that seems, on the face of it, to define Ellie is not definitive at all, and in dismissing this she seems to dismiss the easy judgements made about her character by the audience. Yet the price of her simple 'peace and quiet' is the demonization and exclusion of a former friend from her home and her son's life on the basis of his sexuality. Though set in the late 1980s, this is a play produced in the era of Mary Robinson, whose presidency is often taken to symbolize the increasing tolerance and open-mindedness of Irish society. But this play insists on the opposite; there is no great enlightenment accompanying greater wealth. This is the ugly, toxic side that is unashamedly there, Leonard implies, below the surface of the new 'quality' and the only promise for the future are their educated and unprejudiced children.

The idea that, along with the economic benefits of the Celtic Tiger, there quickly developed a liberalized social outlook, is thus debunked by Leonard with force. The representation of Irish culture that Leonard presents is consistently critical – Ireland is not at heart a liberal, forward-looking culture but is in fact always looking backwards, uncritically indulging its taste for parochialism and nostalgia. This comes through with cutting clarity in the early play *The Patrick Pearse Motel*, which features, among other highlights, rooms named for Irish patriots: The Robert Emmet Room, The Parnell Room, The Manchester Martyrs' Room and, lest we forget, The Famine Dining Room. This isn't just social satire of the bourgeoisie; it lampoons the whole concept of Irish republican nationalism and, beyond that, takes a shot at the full gallery of post-revolutionary Ireland: de Valera, the Catholic Church, and the tendency to glorify the past. The hyperbole of republican nationalism that Leonard spotlights in this early play is focussed on even more in *Kill* (1982), a clear political allegory, in which Mort Mongan is a sinister representative of the IRA. While the preface to the play clearly points out that it is 'a comedy, not a tract', Leonard also makes it clear that the play is aimed at 'harpooning' Irish 'indifference [towards] or partisanship on the side of the terrorists.'[13]

Leonard is critical of what he perceives as a blinkered and destructive republican nationalist vision of Ireland, and he does not hold back. Indeed, it would be out of character for him to be less than devastatingly caustic. Not only is Leonard determined to 'out' Irish attitudes towards the North and the 'three faces of post-revolutionary Ireland: the gunman-as-statesman; the new "Quality"; and the Church',[14] he is also bent on questioning the extent to which Irish theatre, indeed the Irish arts in general, foster some of the worst and most narrow concepts of Ireland and Irishness. Delivering a paper in 1988 under the title 'The Unimportance of Being Irish', Leonard protested against the isolationism of so much of Irish art, against what he termed the 'cultural apartheid' of thinking of drama in national terms first and artistic or human terms second, and he links the celebration of Irish identity in Irish writing to the activities of Irish terrorists in Northern Ireland.[15] And it is not just the art that Leonard critiques, but the 'parochial' attitude towards Irish writing of so many of its critics.[16] When 'a sense of nationality is the guiding factor in a discussion of art, one usually becomes aware of a society with a problem of identity, or with a culture that is as yet relatively unknown outside its frontiers.'[17] While the latter is not a problem for Irish culture, the implication is that in the late 1980s, despite over sixty years of independence, Ireland was still insecure in its identity.

Leonard's agenda is, ultimately, to write good plays and entertain an audience 'for a couple of hours'.[18] Yet there is also that 'underlying seriousness' of agenda, responding to the changes in the Irish social condition. As Leonard says:

> If Joyce could distil the events of one unremarkable day into literature, a lesser writer might validly make use of everyday life to depict a schizoid society caught between two worlds ... caught because we have been unable to make the transition. To survive, we must embrace a new life and new values, and yet to do so is a betrayal of the past.[19]

Though Leonard is careful to distinguish himself from Joyce, displaying his own particular insecurities perhaps, he is clear on the fractured nature of Irish society and the complex negotiations facing contemporary Ireland between the certainties of the past and an increasingly globalized future. This is at odds with Leonard's insistence elsewhere that he refuses to write plays that say 'Something' with a capital 'S'.[20] But as critics, we have the ability to reconcile these two elements: it is not an oxymoron that a playwright can both entertain and archive Irish society.

To read the press clippings concerning Leonard over the period of the last thirty years is to notice a shift in the critical view of both the plays and the playwright. In 1979 when *A Life* was the hit of the Dublin Theatre Festival – and after Brian Friel's *Faith Healer* had closed on Broadway with the faint whiff of failure – Leonard was deemed to be Ireland's leading

playwright, a master of 'devastating insight'.[21] Not only did he
manage to generate advance publicity and ticket sales – an
accolade in this particular year, when the Festival vied with the
visit of the Pope for public attention – but the critics piled on
the plaudits too. It is easy looking back to imagine a different
future for Leonard's critical reputation, one that involves lasting
acclaim and academic scholarship. But fifteen years later, it is
another story; Friel is the playwright of maturity and gravitas
while Leonard's farces have worn thin. In 1994, both Friel and
Leonard had plays opening within just nights of each other. But
where Friel's *Molly Sweeney* was greeted with strong reviews,
Leonard's double bill *Chamber Music* got much less favourable
press. Though Jocelyn Clarke noted the play's 'keen and
lacerating intelligence' the majority of the reviews gave the play,
particularly the first half about an unbreakable chamber pot, a
thorough, and perhaps deserved, mauling.[22] Of little
compensation must have been the positive *New York Times*
review of the play, which appreciated the humour but only
judged Leonard to be 'Ireland's most accomplished living
playwright, after Friel'.[23]

It is intriguing that as Ireland became more prosperous and
increasingly like the bourgeois caricatures that Leonard so often
presents us with, he became less popular as a playwright. While
no-one assumes that the main audience for a Friel play is made
up of nineteenth-century hedge school pupils, that kind of
assumption is often made about Leonard's audience, as if his
plays are only of value and interest to the demographic that he
represents on stage. Yet such plays as *Moving* tell us
uncomfortable truths about our families and our society. These
are stories about ourselves now, yet this is a play which seems
to have escaped any serious critical attention. And it raises the
question as to whether Irish critics are just not ready to take
comedy seriously, to consider it alongside the realist canon.
When interviewed in 1969, Leonard expressed an anxiety about
not being 'regarded even as an Irish writer anymore' because of
his place in the British 'scene'.[24] These anxieties seem to have
been quelled after his return home and the penning of some of
his classic plays; in a piece on the success of *A Life* at the
Festival in 1979 one reviewer commented that Leonard had 'at

last nailed the myth that the prophet is never received in his own country'.[25] But this reception has not endured.

Leonard's resolute rejection of republican nationalism and his mocking tone, combined with his love of farce and his appeal to 'Dublin's smoked salmon belt', may go some way towards explaining his marginal position in the Irish theatrical canon.[26] Yet many of Leonard's plays could stand within the canon. Director Joe Dowling argues that the production of Leonard's adaptation *Stephen D.* was one of the seminal moments in 1960s Irish theatre, along with Friel's *Philadelphia, Here I Come!* (1964). Indeed, it can be argued that in its focus on the psyche of a young man coming of age, preparing to emigrate and reject those 'four great "F"s' of Ireland, as well as in its staging, *Stephen D.* paved the way for Friel's work two years later. Because of this shared ability to reach audiences and to push at the boundaries of the Irish dramatic canon, Dowling argues that in the 1960s and 1970s Leonard and Friel stood as the two 'great, great men' of Irish playwriting.[27] And while it would be unproductive to labour the comparison with Friel, there are some striking similarities in their careers: not only do they make their critical breakthrough in the same decade, but two of their best-known plays, *Philadelphia* and *Da*, are about the conflict between father and son and utilize formal experimentation to convey the inner self of the son. Further, both playwrights have adapted work by others, both are popular in Ireland and abroad, particularly America, and the work of both writers seems rooted in distinctive places. But Friel's sense of place comes from the rural – Ballybeg – while Leonard's home place is Dalkey and the rich suburbs of Dublin. And, crucially, Leonard writes comedy. Though such critics as Fintan O'Toole have objected to the idea that Leonard, along with Bernard Farrell, are 'undervalued by Irish critics because they are funny', there is something to the argument, when O'Toole goes on to say that Leonard should emphasize the political satire and minimize the farce.[28] It is not just that farce is an underrated genre in Ireland, but also that over-the-top satire and farce do not fit with the Field Day-inflected idea of Irish theatre that has so dominated for nearly thirty years. Leonard's tone, aesthetic, and emphasis on the bourgeoisie do not accord

with the Irish peasant, or even Big House, version of Irishness
so beloved of critics and postcolonial scholars. Indeed, while
Leonard is mentioned in D.E.S. Maxwell's 'Introduction' to the
Contemporary Drama 1953-1986 section of *The Field Day
Anthology of Irish Writing*, none of his work is actually
anthologized.[29] The dependence of the Irish dramatic canon on
realist and naturalist works that address the national condition
and that lend themselves to being read allegorically, means that
writers like Leonard, as well as for example, many female
writers who focus on the domestic sphere, are simply not
considered serious or national in the same way. Yet in many
ways writers like Leonard, while recording the details of a
particular time or a class of Irish society, also reflect a general
humanity, which is what makes Leonard, if not a canonical
playwright then a wonderful Festival playwright.

Hugh Leonard has been inextricably bound up with the
history of Irish drama for over fifty years, producing
'quintessential Irish play[s]'.[30] Underneath the caustic wit there
is an intimate understanding of human nature that is the mark
of a master craftsman. And, crucially, there is an audience for
Leonard's plays that otherwise do not often go to the theatre.
Yet these two aspects of his career – his universalism and his
commercialism – are all too often praised with just a shade too
snide a tone, though they are exactly the qualities which make
him an ideal Festival playwright, if we imagine that the Festival
is about drama that engages across political and linguistic
boundaries. Indeed, in 1979, when Leonard presided as
Programme Director of the Festival, he argued that one of the
best elements of the international event was that it 'promotes an
awareness of Irish theatre abroad to people who only know us
for our three undisputed masterpieces: *Juno*, *The Plough* and
*The Playboy*'.[31] Thus in his role as Programme Director,
Leonard developed a 'policy' that was 'simple. I want to present
as many kinds of play as there are audiences', to respond to the
challenge of a 'catholic taste'.[32] And while I think this is a policy
that has stood the test of time at the Festival, perhaps it is time
to put it to good use when considering the canon of Irish drama.

1 Sara Keating, 'Frank views from a very "short fuse"', *The Irish Times* 24 November 2007. *Weekend Review*, p. 6.

2 Ned Chaillet, 'Hugh Leonard', *Contemporary Dramatists*, ed. D.L. Kirkpatrick, 4th edn (Chicago; London: St. James, 1988), p. 322.

3 Hugh Leonard, 'The Unimportance of Being Irish', *Irishness in a Changing Society*, The Princess Grace Irish Library (Gerrards Cross: Colin Smythe, 1988), p. 27.

4 John Banville, 'Review of *Out After Dark*', *Sunday Times*, quoted on book jacket, *Out After Dark* (London: Penguin, 1990).

5 Hugh Leonard, *Home Before Night* (London: Penguin, 1981), p. 159.

6 David Kelly interviewed by Seán Rocks for *Playwrights in Profile* (RTÉ broadcast, 23 March 2007).

7 Hugh Leonard, 'Production Note', *Stephen D.: A Play in Two Acts* (London and New York: Evans Plays, 1964).

8 Anthony Roche interviewed by Seán Rocks for *Playwrights in Profile*.

9 Hugh Leonard interviewed by Seán Rocks for *Playwrights in Profile*.

10 Christopher Murray, Review of *The Mask of Moriarty*, *Irish University Review* (Autumn/Winter 1988), p. 137.

11 Hugh Leonard, *Summer* in *Selected Plays of Hugh Leonard*, ed. S.F. Gallagher (Gerrards Cross: Colin Smythe, 1992), p. 246.

12 Hugh Leonard, *Moving* (London: Samuel French, 1995), pp. 76-77.

13 Hugh Leonard, Preface to *Kill*, *Selected Plays*, p. 380.

14 Hugh Leonard, 'Chamber Music', *Sunday Independent* 14 August 1994, p. 6L.

15 Leonard, 'The Unimportance of Being Irish', pp. 28-29.

16 Ibid., p. 19.

17 Ibid., p. 20.

18 Hugh Leonard, 'Introduction', *The Mask of Moriarty* (Dublin: Brophy Books, 1987), p. 16.

19 Leonard, 'The Unimportance of Being Irish', p. 27.

20 Leonard, 'Introduction', *The Mask of Moriarty*, p. 16.

21 David Nowlan, Review, *The Irish Times* 5 October 1979,

22 Jocelyn Clarke, 'Review of "Chamber Music"', *Sunday Tribune* 28 August 1994, p. B7.

23 David Richards, *New York Times*. Press Clippings at Abbey Theatre Archive.

[24] Hugh Leonard, interviewed by Des Hickey and Gus Smith, 'Leonard: Difficult to Say "No"', *A Paler Shade of Green* (London: Leslie Frewin Publishers, 1972), p. 198.

[25] Colm Cronin, Review, *Hibernia* 11 October 1979, Arts.

[26] Con Houlihan, 'Plumbing the Depths of Success', *Evening Press* 5 October 1979.

[27] Joe Dowling interviewed by Seán Rocks for *Playwrights in Profile*.

[28] Fintan O'Toole, Review of *Chamber Music*, 'Second Opinion', *The Irish Times* 13 September 1994, p. 8.

[29] D.E.S. Maxwell, Introduction, 'Contemporary Drama 1953-1986', *The Field Day Anthology of Irish Writing*, ed. Seamus Deane (Derry: Field Day; Cork: Cork University Press, 1991) p. 1139. Indeed, there is no comedy represented in this section, nor are any women playwrights included.

[30] Joe Dowling interviewed by Seán Rocks for *Playwrights in Profile*.

[31] Hugh Leonard, interviewed by John Boland, 'Prose & Cons', *Hibernia* 27 September 1979.

[32] Hugh Leonard, 'Unprofessional Conduct', *Evening Press* 28 September 1979, p. 10.

## 5 | Subjects of 'the machinery of citizenship': *The Death and Resurrection of Mr Roche* and *The Gentle Island* at the Dublin Theatre Festival

Shaun Richards

Interviewed in the mid-1990s, the lesbian writer Mary Dorcey reflected on the social and legislative changes in Ireland over the previous twenty years, and concluded: 'The Ireland I live in now is so far removed from the Ireland of twenty years ago it might be another country. And the Ireland of my childhood remembered from this perspective seems like another planet.'[1] One of her memories concerned her university-student brother informing the family that Oscar Wilde was homosexual, only for her mother to deny the slur: 'It was a British plot to disgrace him, like Parnell and Kitty O'Shea' (27). For, as noted by Kathryn Conrad:

> Homosexuality has troubled the notion of nationalism and 'Irishness'... Homosexuality in particular threatens the stability of the narrative of Nation: the very instability and specific historical contingency of the definition of homosexuality makes the category more fluid than most, and thus brings into question the fixity and coherence of all identity categories.[2]

And, to adapt David T. Evans's concept of 'the machinery of citizenship',[3] it was the role of the various institutional state apparatuses to ensure that what was produced was an identity in which, as David Norris caustically noted, to be Irish was 'to be white, heterosexual and Roman Catholic'.[4]

Article 41 of the 1937 Constitution of Ireland recognized 'the Family as the natural primary and fundamental unit group of Society' and located the woman's role as central because, through 'her life within the home, woman gives to the State a support without which the common good cannot be achieved'.[5] The male role is unspoken, assumed; but another 'cog' in the machinery of the fledgling nation-state, the Gaelic Athletic Association (G.A.A.), reveals that masculinity was equally fundamental. As made clear by Archbishop Croke's 1884 letter accepting the invitation to be a patron of the newly-formed movement, he despaired of an Ireland where one saw the 'modern young man who, arrayed in light attire, with parti-coloured cap on and racket in hand, is making his way, with or without a companion, to the tennis ground'. Instead, he embraced the ideals of the association which rejected England's 'effeminate follies' as these only led to laughter at Ireland's traditions by 'degenerate dandies', and instead encouraged 'youthful athletes' prepared to 'test each other's mettle' in games which are 'racy of the soil'.[6] The long-standing national centrality of the G.A.A. and its rejection of 'effeminate follies', is captured in Peter Lennon's 1968 film, *The Rocky Road to Dublin*, where the secretary of the G.A.A. speaks of the association attracting 'the best of Irish manhood', its role being to be 'the reservoir of Irish manhood' and to 'inject manhood' into the nation.[7]

Although described by Norris as 'the lingering shame of British imperial statute',[8] the law of 1861 (amended 1862) which stated that 'Whoever shall be convicted of the abominable crime of buggery, committed with mankind or with animal, shall be liable to be kept in penal servitude for life',[9] continued long into the life of the Irish state, which maintained, and in many ways strengthened, the absoluteness of the legally-permitted norms of sexual expression. Norris's long campaign to repeal this law culminated in his speech to the Dáil on 29 June 1993 which celebrated wiping the criminalization of homosexuality from the statute books and removing the legislation that had 'blighted the vulnerable youth of so many of our citizens with terror and shame'.[10]

The two plays with which I'm concerned, Thomas Kilroy's *The Death and Resurrection of Mr Roche* (1968) and Brian Friel's *The Gentle Island* (1971), in which homosexuality is integral to the plots, were performed in the Dublin Theatre Festivals of those years, both at the Olympia. However, I want initially to address the moment when they were next performed in Dublin: *The Gentle Island* in 1988 at the Peacock and *The Death and Resurrection of Mr Roche* in 1989 at the Abbey. This coincided with the culmination of Norris's campaign in 1988, when the European Court of Human Rights ruled in his favour and called on Ireland to end its violation of Article 8 of the Convention of Human Rights. The period between then and the law's final repeal in 1993 saw an upsurge of demand for sexual freedom and expression.[11]

This context helps us understand the comments made by Lance Pettit in 1989:

> Within the last two years Ireland's national theatre has staged two plays which deal centrally with the subject of homosexuality in Ireland. This simple fact is all the more pertinent when we consider that Friel's *The Gentle Island* (December 1988 at the Peacock) and Kilroy's *The Death and Resurrection of Mr Roche* (May 1989 at the Abbey) came in the aftermath of the Norris judgement at the European Court of Human Rights last October.[12]

The point Pettit makes most forcibly is that, despite this conjunction, '[m]ost reviews of the above two plays made only cursory reference to their gay context and none that I have come across attempted to address issues in the context of the above judgement or of the contribution these productions made to the debate about gay rights in Ireland'.[13] Pettit's discussion of the plays is informed, and correctly identifies the socially baffling fact that the reviews do not make any significant point about homosexuality: the reviewer of *The Gentle Island* for *Theatre Ireland* simply mentions 'two men from Dublin'.[14] But it is not as if reviewers were ignoring an aspect of the plays which the original productions had notably stressed. In a recent radio

interview, Niall Toibin, who played Kelly in the first production
of *Mr Roche*, recalled that the audience took a collective sharp
intake of breath when he delivered the line 'I let him handle
me'.[15] However, Clive Geraghty, who played Myles in the first
production, and Mr Roche in the second, states that 'the whole
anti-homosexual thing made far more impact on me this time
[the second production] ... than it had initially',[16] which suggests
that despite the audience reaction noted by Toibin,
homosexuality had not been a major issue in rehearsals for the
first production. Vincent Dowling's 'Director's Note' in the
programme for *The Gentle Island* in 1971 also provided no
sense of engaging with a socially-charged topic, informing the
audience that 'I just want you to enjoy the beautifully told story
of Brian Friel's and you can take out of it what comes to you'.[17]
And my communication with Shane Connaughton, who played
the character of the younger homosexual, Shane, in 1971, also
confirmed the lack of discussion about homosexuality. 'The
Irish theatre was still in its innocence that way', he commented;
indeed, 'I remember the first night Friel, Vincent Dowling and a
few others turned up wearing dress suits. Now that was camper
than anything going on up on stage'.[18] Reviews confirm the
extent to which the homosexuality was not a major source of
discussion; *The Irish Times* simply noted 'two teachers from
Dublin of homosexual persuasion'.[19] For these plays are not
centrally about homosexuality. And they are certainly not gay
plays in the sense of presenting a gay sensibility; they might
have been produced either side of the Stonewall riots of 1969
but they are far from presenting homosexuality as a socially and
sexually revolutionary stance. But this is not to say that they are
not controversially engaged in examining issues of sexuality and
national identity at the most troubling of levels.

The 1989 revival of *The Gentle Island* was directed by Frank
McGuinness, and it was the play's premiere in 1971 which, at
nineteen, was his first experience of theatre. That production,
he said, 'was a shock to my system and changed my life'.[20] Given
McGuinness's inability to speak to his family about his sexuality
because, as he said, 'that was a different world, a different
country',[21] the power of a play which featured a homosexual
couple is readily apparent, and in addition to directing that

1989 production he has written on the play in his essay in *The Cambridge Companion to Brian Friel*, describing it as, of all Friel's plays up to 1971, 'the most threatening, the most perplexing, the most far-sighted of all'.[22] The possible nature of that threat, however, is only clarified by his comments on *The Death and Resurrection of Mr Roche* which, he observed to Fintan O'Toole, was 'one of the hardest and uncompromising statements on heterosexuality in the Irish theatre'.[23] That insight is extended by his comment that it is 'fear of Roche's sexuality that acts as a camouflage for the true terror that binds the men into camaraderie. Terror of women, terror of difference, terror of change'.[24] For while Mr Roche's sexuality clearly antagonizes them and provides the pretext for the violence, this should not obscure the fact that it follows on from his judgement on the 'desolation' of 'this debauch' with its 'Waste, withering, joylessness' (38).

*The Irish Times* advert for the first production of Kilroy's play in October 1968 states that it was the drama of 'The adventures and misadventures of a group of men drawn from different walks of life' and makes no reference to homosexuality. This conspicuous absence was echoed in Seamus Kelly's review of the play which ran under the heading: 'Cold light of truth on the frustrations of aging bachelors'. But this captures, in large part, the play's import. Noting, but not dwelling, on the fact that Kelly has had 'some sort of homosexual fumble with Mr Roche' the review addresses the fact that the dramatic focus is on what it terms the men's 'arid and squalid' lives.[25] This sense of direct engagement with the harsh realities of contemporary society is exactly what Kilroy had already advocated in an article of 1959. Above all, he said, the worst defect of contemporary Irish dramatists was that they were 'inclined to shirk the painful, sometimes tragic problems of a modern Ireland which is undergoing considerable social and ideological stress'.[26] A little later than Kilroy, but simultaneous with the first productions of both plays, Friel was interviewed in *The Irish Times* in 1970 when, in response to the question as to how he would like to see his work developing, he said: 'I would like to write a play that would capture the peculiar spiritual, and indeed material, flux that this country is in at the moment'.[27] Clearly, both playwrights at this relatively early stage in their careers were committed to a theatre which, in Kilroy's words, would stage 'conflicting, topical, social issues'.[28]

Both plays are 'Time – the present', in other words that of late 1960s-early 1970s Ireland, and while the geographical spectrum, Dublin to Donegal, suggests difference, they are remarkably similar in dramatic structure as both feature the entry of homosexual 'otherness' into worlds which are already suffering dislocating stresses of varying kinds: the mass emigration which opens *The Gentle Island* or the ritual of the drunken Saturday night in *Mr Roche*. But Ireland, according to Myles in *Mr Roche*, 'is on the move ... On the up and up. For those that are on the move, that is',[29] and while his crass success ethic is seen to be shallow and fraudulent, it is 'modernity' in all its manifestations which is destabilizing these societies. 'Are youse yanks?' is Sarah's early question to Peter and Shane in *The Gentle Island*, a question she follows up with her reminiscence of her time working as a chambermaid on the Isle of Man: 'In the eight weeks I was in Douglas I was at fifty-one dances. I wore out three pairs of shoes. I never had a time like it.'[30] This is a world which promises materialism and pleasure, and while Myles's belief that he is 'One of the top seven per cent. The executives. The boys on the button.' (20) is a delusion, he does signal to a world other than that occupied by Kelly who has lived in his flat since 'I moved in here fifteen years ago when I came up from the country with the Junior Ex' (20). Whether it is the slothful suburban somnambulism of Kelly, or the crumbling patriarchal kingdom of Manus, these are male worlds threatened by change, one which is centrally sexual.

The agents of destabilization are Mr Roche, 'aged between forty and fifty', whose entry accompanied by Kevin, 'an anaemic young man in his twenties' (8), prefigures that of Peter, 'a plump balding middle-aged man' with Shane, 'twenty years younger' (25), in *The Gentle Island*. The extent to which Peter and Shane are a couple is clearly established, while that of Mr Roche and Kevin is only hinted at obliquely as the other men at Kelly's impromptu party try to force Roche into the toilet where Kevin is being sick. 'Into his lover-boy, into's stable, into's stable' (30), chants Kelly, followed, *'fretfully'*, by the comment:

'It's his own look out if anything happens to him. The young lad I mean. It'd serve him right with the company he keeps' (32). However the fact that the real threat is from the group, rather than Mr Roche, is made manifest when the men force him into the 'holy-hole', the cellar, in which he dies.

While the play changes in Act 2 to a nominal comedy in which the violent and disquieting homophobia which led to Roche's death is replaced by attempts to dispose of his body, followed by his Act 3 resurrection, it also contains the clearest articulation of the play's central theme. 'You're sick, Kelly, you're all sick' declares Seamus, directly identifying that illness with immobility: 'Why haven't you changed? Why haven't you changed even a little?' (52). But he is as unable to cope with change as Kelly is unable to embrace it; and for both it is to do with the actuality of women who are clearly intruding into a world of self-contained, self-satisfied masculinity: Seamus's despair at his wife – 'She surrounds me with the same things. Same talk. Same tears. I need a break' (51) – and Kelly's bachelor-rejection of women's 'skittering and giggling' (54). What has been lost in this change, which is signalled by, but extends far beyond, a move from rural to urban, is a world of certainties:

> **Kelly**: Walking to the parish church for Midnight Mass with white frost on the roads and ice in the drains. They like that, the young brothers. Standing in the chapel yard. The cut of my suit. My white shirt. It was a sort of white Christmas ... All clean collars and long, white candles (53).

And at the heart of that world was the stable point of the father; the fulcrum of this rooted, rural existence:

> **Kelly**: (*continuing heatedly*): And when the auld fellow would sit at the top of the table, his elbows planked down in front of him, and all of us around waiting for one of the girls to lift the hot potatoes. And a big fire roaring up the kitchen chimney. That was a natural place to live in, boy, whatever you may say about its appearance (56).

It's this same image of male power and centrality which marks the opening of *The Gentle Island* as Manus, 'in his sixties, well made, still enormously powerful' (11), sits on his 'throne', the powerless immobility of his position captured in the fact that this is actually a seat from a long-wrecked aircraft.

In *Mr Roche* the key admission is Kelly's acknowledgment to Seamus that 'I let him handle me', followed by the lines: 'I used to have very strict views. I mean the first night I knew what it all meant was one night they laughed at him in Murray's. It was far from my head that I was going to be implicated with the like of him. The horror of it all is it's so simple' (60). And that 'simple' fact of homosexuality existing within the dominant masculine domain is there too in *The Gentle Island*, in Philly: 'Unlike his father and his brother he is lightly built. And unlike all the other islanders he talks quietly' (19). This could be taken as an invitation to play the part as effete, but rather it stresses the 'otherness' contained within the island – and before the entry of the strangers: a clear opposition to the aggressive masculinity of Manus and Joe and one by which they are clearly threatened. Just as it is Kelly, who let Roche 'handle' him, who is the most virulent in his antipathy – 'the very idea of it makes me sick. The very idea of it makes me want to puke' (59) – so it is Manus, whose masculinity and lineage is challenged by Philly, 'the apple of your blind eye' in Sarah's words, whose virulence is the greatest in *The Gentle Island*:

> **Manus:** It's them – them queers! I should have killed the two of them when I had them! What we had wasn't much but what there was decent and wholesome! And they blighted us! They cankered us! They blackened the bud that was beginning to grow again! My curse on them! My curse of hell on the two of them! *Agus marbhfháisc orthu* – an early shroud on them! (72)

But the shots which shatter Shane's spine are fired by Sarah. Manus, for all his wrath, collapsing into a succession of 'I – I – I – I – ' (8). Reminiscent as it is of Gar's 'I don't know. I – I –I – don't know' of *Philadelphia, Here I Come!* there is a dormant self-knowledge in Manus's inability to fire.[31] When Joe asks him 'Was it you or her? ... Shot him' (70), his response, 'When the time came I – I –I – ' (70), with the absent but implied 'couldn't', is an expression of his subconscious knowledge that such an act would also be to 'kill' Philly by rejecting his son's 'other' reality. The play closes, however, in his refusal to acknowledge, at any conscious level, this understanding of his son's otherness, stressing to Sarah how, in the darkness of the boathouse where she claimed to have seen Philly 'doing for the tramp what he couldn't do for me' (61), that 'it's so dark in that yon place you could imagine anything' (74). Manus, then, effectively refuses to acknowledge the reality of Philly's sexuality, and the final stage direction, 'fade to black', with its evocation of the final stage directions of *Translations*, suggests the demise of the kingdom which cannot embrace that truth. Kelly, too, is unable to accept the otherness of the resurrected Mr Roche, still wishing to be 'rid of your man' (74). Mr Roche's resurrection and occupancy of Kelly's flat could be read, simply, as a return of the repressed. But this is more to do with redemption than revenge. Mr Roche's return with Kevin and the Medical Student is described as being in a *'mood of delirious revelry'* (69), and his *'priest-like'* (72) evocation of a changed world, 'Breaking up into light. Breaking up into life ... Breaking up over the roof-tops into particles of silver and gold,' in which *'the tone should shift radically from all that has gone before'* (72-3), clearly suggests that this is literally the dawn of a new day; an opportunity for change which is shunned by Kelly. In closing on the inability to embrace 'the other', both plays dramatize, in Kilroy's words, the 'failure to achieve a wholeness of community in the Irish experience'.[32]

What then unites both plays is their engagement with 'hegemonic masculinity':

> Hegemonic masculinity was not assumed to be normal in the statistical sense; only a minority of men might enact it. But it was certainly normative. It embodied the currently most honored way of being a man, it required all other men to position themselves in relation to it, and ideologically legitimated the global subordination of women to men.[33]

The specific resonance of this reference with *Mr Roche* is that Kilroy's original impetus for the play was a story he had heard while a student in Dublin concerning 'the beating up of a female prostitute', as mentioned elsewhere in this book. However, the

play 'would not come into focus' and it was only when he
changed the victim of male violence to the homosexual Mr
Roche that he found that 'the play wrote itself in a couple of
weeks.' Along with references to Mr Roche as 'whore', what has
been most clearly retained from the original idea to the finished
play is what Fintan O'Toole noted in his review of the 1989
production: 'Mr Roche's homosexuality is there to make the
"normal" maleness of the other characters visible. And with this
light shone on it, we can see it as troubled, insecure, full of
mistrust, terror and sheer downright misogyny.'[34] And it is the
violence which underpins this uncertain male identity that is
the thematic concern of both *Mr Roche* and *The Gentle Island*.

Lynne Segal's linking of what she termed 'the late-Victorian
storm-troopers of a new aggressive masculinity' with the
expansion of British colonization chimes in with 'hegemonic
masculinity' as it developed in Ireland during the same period.[35]
Ashis Nandy's study of the definition of masculinity within the
context of colonized India led to the formulation of the concept
of 'hyper-masculinity', an exaggerated performance of
masculinity which could counter suggestions that the colonized
were effeminate and so necessarily, within the sexual codes of
the time, legitimately subordinate.[36] Based as it was on an
exaggerated masculinity as a means of self-defence as much as
self-definition, any threats to that hegemony were to be
violently resisted. This is most starkly expressed in the Irish
context in Tom Murphy's *A Whistle in the Dark* (1961), which
laid bare the hollowness of patriarchal power as a compensation
for inferiority in a modern Ireland where social class has
replaced colonial power. Dada's bluster is exposed by his eldest
son, Michael, whose emigration to England and marriage to a
local girl tests the aggressive masculinity the father has
encouraged in his sons. When, in the play's closing moments,
the youngest son, Des, taunts Michael as 'The mouse! Couldn't
command a woman even!' the values and hierarchies of
hegemonic masculinity are clearly delineated.[37] And, to adopt
the observations of R. W. Connell, whose work has largely
defined this concept:

> In the dynamics of hegemony in contemporary Western masculinity, the relation between heterosexual and homosexual men is central, carrying a heavy symbolic freight. To many people, homosexuality is a negation of masculinity, and homosexual men must be effeminate. [38]

As the homosexual does not even claim to desire to 'command a woman' then the threat to the behavioural norms of hegemonic masculinity is even greater. In this sense, as observed by Jonathan Dollimore, homophobia 'helps secure a coerced identity and social organization; homophobia enforces the heterosexual norm by policing its boundaries'.[39] Hence the virulence of Manus's rejection of 'them queers', Kelly's abuse, *'near hysterically'*, of Mr Roche as a 'Dirty, filthy pervert" (28), and Myles, whose physical and verbal assault on Mr Roche – '(*Whips behind and catches Mr Roche about the chest*) Are you wearing your bra tonight, Agatha?' (38) – masks the fact that his probably fictitious 'randy women' (66) come second to 'The Mammy' who will have his breakfast 'nice and ready for me by the time I get home.' (74).

Nandy's concept of hyper-masculinity makes clear why, following Dollimore, Irish nationalism was 'committed to policing not only the actual geographic borders and literal or legally defined aliens, but symbolic and ideological boundaries (both internal and external) between the normal and the abnormal, the healthy and sick, the conforming and the deviant'.[40] *The Death and Resurrection of Mr Roche* and *The Gentle Island* are of a moment when those borders and boundaries, both literal and symbolic, were becoming porous as new ideas and images, new values and cultural expressions were entering Irish social and cultural discourse. They stand, then, not so much as expressions or explorations of homosexuality *per se*, but as public engagements with one of the founding faiths of the state: hegemonic masculinity and its subsequent contemporary discontents.

---

[1] Interview with Mary Dorcey, *Lesbian and Gay Visions of Ireland: Towards the Twenty-first Century*, eds Íde O'Carroll and Eoin

Collins (London: Cassell, 1995), p. 25. Subsequent reference appears parenthetically in the text.

[2] Kathryn Conrad, 'Queer Treasons: Homosexuality and Irish National Identity', *Cultural Studies*, 15, 1 (2001), p. 125.

[3] David T. Evans, *Sexual Citizenship: The Material Construction of Sexualities* (London: Routledge, 1993), p. 5.

[4] David Norris, 'Homosexual People and the Christian Churches in Ireland', *The Crane Bag*, 5, 2 (1981), p. 31.

[5] Constitution of Ireland – Bunreacht Na hÉireann. http://www.constitution.ie/reports/ConstitutionofIreland/pdf

[6] See http://multitext.ucc.ie/d/Archbishop_Croke_the_GAA_November_1884

[7] *The Rocky Road to Dublin*, directed by Peter Lennon (1968). DVD, Irish Film Institute, 2005.

[8] David Norris, 'Criminal Law (Sexual Offences) Bill 1993, Second Stage Speech, 29 June 1993', *Lesbian and Gay Visions of Ireland: Towards the Twenty-first Century*, p. 14.

[9] Cited in Kieran Rose, *Diverse Communities: The Evolution of Gay and Lesbian* Politics (Cork: Cork University Press, 1994), p. 74.

[10] Ibid, p. 23.

[11] See Rose, pp. 9-59.

[12] Lance Pettitt, 'Gay Fiction – 2', *Graph*, 7 (1989-90), p. 13.

[13] Ibid.

[14] Sean Moffat. 'The Gentle Island', *Theatre Ireland* 18 (1989), p. 48.

[15] Seán Rocks, *Playwrights in Profile: Series 1*, RTÉ Radio 1, 4 March 2007.

[16] See Rocks.

[17] Vincent Dowling, 'Director's Note on *The Gentle Island*', Olympia Theatre programme for *The Gentle Island*, (commenced Tuesday, 30 November 1971), np.

[18] e-mail communication with Shane Connaughton, 3/08/2007. I'm particularly grateful to Shane Connaughton for sharing these recollections and for the copy of the programme for the original production of *The Gentle Island*.

[19] *The Irish Times*, 13 December 1971.

[20] 'The healing touch', interview with Frank McGuinness by Joe Jackson, the *Irish Independent* 21 April 2002.

[21] Ibid.

22 Frank McGuinness, 'Surviving the 1960s: three plays', *The Cambridge Companion to Brian Friel*, ed. Anthony Roche (Cambridge: Cambridge University Press, 2006), p. 27.

23 Fintan O'Toole, *Critical Moments: Fintan O'Toole on Modern Irish Theatre*, eds Julia Furay and Redmond O'Hanlon (Dublin: Carysfort Press, 2003), p. 217.

24 Frank McGuinness, 'The Catholic Mind and Modern Irish Theatre', unpublished lecture. I'm especially grateful to Frank McGuinness for his correspondence on the play and for making a copy of his lecture available.

25 Seamus Kelly, 'Cold light of truth on the frustrations of aging bachelors', *The Irish Times* 8 October 1968.

26 Thomas Kilroy, 'Groundwork for an Irish Theatre', *Studies* 48 (1959), p. 195.

27 Fergus Linehan, 'The Future of Irish Drama: A discussion between Fergus Linehan, Hugh Leonard, John B. Keane and Brian Friel', *The Irish Times* 12 February 1970.

28 Kilroy, p. 192.

29 Thomas Kilroy, *The Death and Resurrection of Mr Roche* (London: Faber and Faber, 1969), p. 19. All subsequent references are cited in the text.

30 Brian Friel, *The Gentle Island* (Dublin: The Gallery Press, 1973), p. 29. All subsequent references are cited in the text.

31 Brian Friel, *Philadelphia, Here I Come! Selected Plays of Brian Friel* (London: Faber and Faber, 1984), p. 99.

32 Thomas Kilroy, 'The Irish Writer: Self and Society, 1950-80', *Literature and the Changing Ireland*, ed. Peter Connolly (Gerrards Cross: Colin Smythe, 1982), p. 181.

33 R.W. Connell and James R. Messerschmidt, 'Hegemonic Masculinity. Rethinking the Concept', *Gender and Society*, 19, 6 (2005), p. 832.

34 O'Toole, p. 217.

35 Lynne Segal, *Slow Motion: Changing Men, Changing Masculinities* (London: Virago, 1990), p. 107.

36 Ashis Nandy, *The Intimate Enemy: Loss and Recovery of Self Under Colonialism* (Delhi: Oxford University Press, 1983), pp. 7-10.

37 Thomas Murphy, *A Whistle in the Dark* (Dublin: The Gallery Press, 1984), p. 74.

---

38 R.W. Connell, 'A Very Straight Gay: Masculinity, Homosexual Experience, and the Dynamics of Gender', *Americomman Sociological Review*, 57, 6 (1992), p. 736.

39 Jonathan Dollimore, *Sexual Dissidence, Augustine to Wilde, Freud to Foucault* (Oxford: Clarendon Press, 1991), p. 245

40 Dollimore, p. 236.

# 6 | West Meets East: Russian Productions at the Dublin Theatre Festival, 1957-2006

Ros Dixon

Between 1957 and 2006, the Dublin Theatre Festival featured two productions with Irish casts directed by Russians, seven by performers from Russia or former Soviet states, two of Shakespeare plays with Russian casts, five of Russian plays performed by Irish companies, and five of adaptations of Russian texts.[1] I have space here to refer, and even so in no great detail, to only six of these; but they illustrate changes in Irish perceptions of Russian theatre, as well as changes in that theatre's complex history over the period, a history I shall broadly and briefly sketch.[2]

From the mid 1930s the brutally repressive regime of Stalin saw the silencing and annihilation of such leading figures of the Russian avant-garde as Vsevolod Meyerhold, and the theatre suffered from the dictates of Socialist Realism. Experimentation in form was repressed, and the use of overtly theatrical techniques condemned. The patriotism engendered by the approach of World War II and Stalin's openly Russo-centric, chauvinist policies led, moreover, not only to a consolidation and canonization of Russian history, culture and literature, but also to a demand for what was to become, in effect, a national theatre. As a result, the performance history of the Moscow Art Theatre (MAT) was deliberately distorted to support the notion that it had always belonged to a realist tradition, and those of its productions deemed to conform to this idea were promoted as models to be copied.[3]

The death of Stalin in 1953 produced a rejuvenation of Soviet theatre, encouraged by the relatively liberal policies of Khrushchev's Thaw.[4] A relaxation of the censorship laws led to the publication of new translations of the works of previously proscribed foreign writers. The Party's new, more open policy was manifest also in 'posthumous rehabilitations' of native Russian writers and artists whose work had been suppressed. This new policy significantly included the rehabilitation of Meyerhold, initiating a process of re-discovery and salvage that would eventually result in the publication of two volumes of his collected letters, speeches, and theoretical writings.[5] Access to his ideas and to those of such innovators as Brecht, led to a phenomenon known as 'new theatricalism'. This provided the impetus for a new generation of directors to develop their own distinctive approaches by fusing Stanislavsky's theories with a more consciously theatrical style.

But in 1964 the Thaw came to an end. Khrushchev was ousted and replaced by Leonid Brezhnev, whose government brought about changes in cultural policy aimed at crushing dissidence. Under his regime attempts were made to stifle the theatre once more. Thus practitioners, though not subjected to the horrors of the Stalinist years, were harassed and censored and saw their work banned. Playwrights were encouraged to write ideologically appropriate plays, such as the so-called 'industrial' dramas that extolled the heroic virtues of factory workers. Censorship (including self-censorship), and the imposition of such strictures led to a relative dearth of high-quality contemporary plays.[6] In the late 1960s, however, and throughout the *zastoi* (stagnation) of the 1970s, several directors (most notably Anatoly Efros) began to produce Russian classics. The works of such writers as Chekhov and Gogol, less subject to censorship than modern plays, were open to multiple interpretations and allowed for indirect comment on current concerns. Other directors, like Yury Lyubimov in his adaptations of prose works at Moscow's Taganka, evaded the censor by becoming masters of so-called 'Aesopian language', criticizing through verbal hints and scenic metaphors the abuses of the Soviet system, and thus giving public voice to private dissent. Nevertheless all theatre was state controlled, and until the early 1980s many directors were not allowed to travel outside Russia.[7] The only productions permitted to be shown in the West were those that conformed by and large to the 'blueprint' of the MAT. These included the first three productions that I shall discuss — Chekhov plays staged by Soviet directors heavily indebted to the style of Stanislavsky.

In 1968 Maria Knebel directed an Irish cast in a production of *The Cherry Orchard* at the Abbey. Knebel had trained under Stanislavsky, had played Charlotta in the 1920s in a revival of his original 1904 production of *The Cherry Orchard*, and had directed the play at the Soviet Army Theatre in Moscow in 1965. That production, the one in Dublin, and indeed her techniques in rehearsal were all heavily influenced by Stanislavsky's approach. She later published a full and illuminating account of her time in Dublin.[8] Accustomed to lengthy rehearsal periods, she was shocked at the prospect of having to produce so complex a play in the space of a single month, and initially found her cast alarmingly laid-back.[9] She was soon impressed, however, by their enthusiasm and readiness to work ten-hour days.[10] They too at first were fazed by, but then responded to, her Stanislavskian exploration of psychology and use of improvisation. Though indebted to Stanislavsky's, her production was by no means a carbon copy of his, in particular in the setting. Stanislavsky had added a wealth of naturalistic detail, and of off-stage sound effects. These had been much criticized by some contemporaries, including Meyerhold, who maintained that the orchard and the old life it represents were expressed in Chekhov's play in an openly symbolic way.[11] This idea had been central to the setting for Knebel's Moscow production, now recreated on the Abbey stage. There was no attempt at a physical representation of the orchard; the set consisted instead of a semi-opaque shroud of floating drapes around the stage, intended to evoke not its presence but a memory of its existence and its spiritual essence. Siobhán McKenna, who played Ranevskaya, was initially alarmed at this subversion of traditional expectations, but Knebel explained

that in her view the loss of the orchard was not so much actual
as metaphorical.

> It seems to me that in his last plays Chekhov understood very
> well what it means to lose something infinitely beloved. Each
> of us has lost and will lose our own 'cherry orchard'. Each of
> us is trying to hold on to it. The moment when you lose 'the
> cherry orchard', you might think you lose everything. But
> ahead lies a life, a thousand times richer than any loss.[12]

In the rehearsal process Knebel explored those themes that
resonated most with her Irish cast.[13] They discussed the role of
the home and hearth in Irish social interaction, the importance
to Irish people of possessing one's own home, and the sorrow
felt at its loss. But for the cast such ideas of ownership were less
important than the broader notion of a homeland – a place
which the young must abandon but which remains the site of
childhood memories, and to which the exile feels compelled to
return.[14] Such notions were central to Knebel's Irish production,
but were not imposed on Chekhov's play; they evolved instead
from an exploration of it. Knebel made no attempt to create on
stage a specifically Irish world. On the contrary she was
concerned to present an authentic image of Russia. This led to a
minor contretemps which was both amusing and revealing in
respect of preconceptions. The Abbey props department
presented Knebel with that most common signifier of all things
Russian — a samovar — and they were very disappointed when
she politely but quite categorically rejected this 'unnecessary
piece of local colour', remarking that the script itself called for a
coffee pot.[15] Knebel's production was greeted enthusiastically;
she herself was fêted in the Irish press.[16] But one commentator,
Seamus Kelly, expressed some dissatisfaction with her
traditional approach; he thought that the production would
have made a greater impression had the action been translated
to an Irish idiom and context. Though he praised the high
standards of the performance of the ensemble in general and of
McKenna and Cyril Cusack (as Gayev) in particular, he
described Knebel's production as a fine piece of 'theatrical
archaeological digging' and as a 'beautiful and faithful period

reproduction of the play as it was originally played by Olga Knippur' (*sic*).[17]

In 1978 Vladimir Monakhov was invited to direct *Uncle Vanya* at the Abbey. Monakhov's approach was if anything more indebted to tradition than Knebel's. On meeting his cast the director advised them all to read Stanislavsky's *My Life in Art*, and his approach in rehearsals demonstrated a painstaking concern for detail.[18] His *Uncle Vanya* opened with a slow fade of the houselights, three minutes of a lilting soundtrack of birdsong, and continued at a meandering, gentle pace towards a closing note of sad despair. *The Irish Times* reviewer David Nowlan praised the production's technical finesse, Bronwen Casson's set and delightful costumes, and declared it a 'triumph'.[19] In truth, however, it offered little new. But then in Russia Monakhov was only ever regarded as a jobbing director whose work was solid but unstartling. The scant comment in the Russian press on his visit to Dublin focussed almost exclusively on his suitability as a representative of Soviet culture, and the trip may well have been a kind of prize, for loyal service, to a director whose work was unlikely to stir controversy abroad.[20]

Monakhov's visit to Dublin was low-key in comparison to the excitement generated by the visit in 1989 of the MAT itself. Their *Seagull*, directed by Oleg Yefremov and performed in Russian, was the must-see, centrepiece production of the Theatre Festival that year.[21] That production, however, which was eight years old and which had not been performed in Russia for over a year, was again relatively traditional (though less so than the two discussed above), especially in view of Yefremov's previous career. Though trained as an actor at its school in the late 1940s, Yefremov had become increasingly dissatisfied with the state of the MAT at that time. Concerned to re-create what he saw as the true legacy of Stanislavsky, he had imitated that pioneer by establishing his own affiliated studio. This had soon become a separate company, the Sovremennik (Contemporary), and rapidly gained a reputation as a crucible for new Soviet writing.[22] His final work there in 1970 when he was appointed to rescue the MAT itself from its creative crisis — a tough task, given its huge and demoralized staff and a heavily bureaucratic administration, and one in which he enjoyed only limited success — had been a production of *The Seagull*, which Russian critics have often contrasted with the later one seen in Dublin.

According to Tatiana Shakh-Azizova, Yefremov's *Seagull* in 1970 had much in common with several Russian productions of Chekhov plays in the 1960s, all characterized by 'thorough objectivity'.[23] By this she meant that the sympathetic identification with his characters that had provided the pathos of previous productions had been replaced by dispassionate enquiry that exposed rather than concealed their weaknesses. In Yefremov's production Treplev had been the only character treated sympathetically while the selfish indifference of the others to his plight – even when in Act II he shot himself before their very eyes – had been offered up for the audience's censure. As Smeliansky later recalled, the characters had stopped hearing or listening to one another, and instead squabbled aggressively and struck attitudes but failed to act.[24] In this, he maintained, the production had expressed a loss of 'the common ideal', the ideological confusion and sense of disillusionment felt by many of the Soviet intelligentsia as Khruschev's Thaw came to an end. But the production had also signalled a decisive break from the traditional stage naturalism of the MAT. In several productions of the time, detailed and architecturally accurate interiors and the beauties of the Russian countryside had been replaced by starkly unromantic, even harsh settings, and at the Sovremmenik there was no enchanted lake; instead the keen angler Trigorin dug worms for bait in a flower-bed centre-stage.[25]

But between his first *Seagull* and his second in 1980 Yefremov's approach had changed. He now suggested that the single-mindedness of 'sweeping directorial interpretations of Chekhov kill something in him' and that the way to discover the real secret of his (or any writer's) work lay instead in allowing actors freer rein.[26] Thus in 1980 the characters were no longer harshly judged, but approached with greater understanding and compassion. They were not, however, idealized. On the contrary, according to G. Brodskaya, the actors revealed their faults, but also played them as painfully aware of these, and in this very awareness revealed their humanity.[27] For Konstantin

Rudnitsky, Yefremov's broader, more even-handed approach softened the dramatic conflict but also restored a 'polyphonic aspect' absent from some modern interpretations.[28] According to Smeliansky the political themes of 1970 were replaced in 1980 by motifs of reconciliation, understanding and forgiveness.[29] Yefremov also explored, moreover, the concept that a transcendent nature alters the scale of human conflicts.[30]

This idea was reflected in Valery Levental's visually stunning set, which had a delicately ephemeral and cinematic quality. It consisted of a series of light, moveable gauzes, which by deliberately merging shadowy interior and leafy exterior spaces generated a sense of the characters living in the midst of nature.[31] In Rudnitsky's description, a wide expanse between upstage and downstage allowed two or three figures to be isolated in close-up, before flowing back into the shadows and general chatter as another couple came into focus.[32] The centrepiece of the design was a gazebo that could glide back and forth and was used for various purposes, including the performance of the play-within-the-play in Act I. But Yefremov also broke with the tradition of a break after the second of the play's four acts, making the first three one long 'half', followed by the interval and the last. For this Levental's magical scenery disappeared, leaving a gloomy dark space surrounded by black drapes. For Brodskaya, this created a cold and empty atmosphere that matched the apocalyptic vision of Treplev's play in Act I.[33] But she also described a new finale, added by Yefremov, in which Nina stood once more on the gazebo-cum-stage and repeated her lines from that act. The repetition of Treplev's words after his death underscored, in Brodskaya's view, Yefremov's belief in the redemptive power of theatre.[34]

Reviewing what was essentially the same 1980 production in Dublin in 1989, Fintan O'Toole was particularly impressed by Yefremov's treatment of the drama as a treatise on the relationship of art to life.[35] For him the gazebo's movement during the performance of Treplev's play produced an extraordinary effect. As it slid forward the on-stage audience retreated, turning the real audience into Treplev's spectators. The dividing line between stage and auditorium was violated, forcing the Abbey theatre-goers not merely to consider but to

experience directly Chekhov's central questions: What is
reality? And what play? O'Toole also interpreted Yefremov's
ending rather as Brodskaya had, suggesting that it was another
point at which art and life came together in a kind of unity, and
that in giving Treplev's play an afterlife there was a moment of
subtle, albeit rueful, hope.[36] Nowlan admired the quality of the
ensemble playing and intensity of the actors' performances, and
the careful creation and maintenance of a lyrical mood.[37] He
suggested too that there was no escaping the sense of history
aroused by watching the MAT perform *The Seagull*, because
this was the play that both actually and symbolically
represented the essence of that theatre itself. In an interview in
*The Irish Times* Yefremov defended his choice to tour not a
contemporary work but a classic, remarking that Chekhov was a
playwright for our times as well as his own.[38] Nevertheless, as
we have seen, the MAT production was not new, and the
decision to bring it to Dublin, though it fulfilled audience
expectations, was a predictable, even conservative one.[39]

Yefremov's decision to 'play it safe' is perhaps explained by
the fact that the MAT had only recently emerged from a major
crisis, during which his position as Artistic Director had been
directly challenged, and which had resulted in the splitting of
the theatre into two entirely separate companies.[40] That crisis
had been caused at least in part by sweeping changes being
made at the time to the organization of Soviet theatres. In 1987,
in anticipation of a law introduced in 1989, and initially as a
kind of experiment, state control was lifted and responsibility
for running theatres was put into the hands not of Party
apparatchiks but of elected artistic councils of practitioners. But
this resulted in major disagreements and power struggles, not
only at the MAT but at several other leading theatres.[41] The
difficulties they faced mirrored the political turmoil and social
chaos that accompanied the collapse of the Soviet Union, and
were exacerbated both by restrictions in state funding and by
the financial instability that accompanied the economic reforms
initiated under *perestroika*.

*Perestroika* (restructuring) was concomitant with the motor
for change in social and cultural spheres: *Glasnost*. Often
translated as 'openness', this literally means 'giving voice', and

implied not only exposure of the secrets of the past but also discussion of the severe social problems of the present.[42] It might have been expected to have prompted the writing of a host of new plays on previously taboo topics, but in fact the theatre was slow and indeed cautious in its response. On the one hand a general sense of confusion and suspicion was felt at the time by Russians; they had seen in the past the reversal of liberal reforms. On the other, such an expectation demonstrated too a misunderstanding of the special place that theatre had occupied in Soviet society. When ideas once expressed, albeit often covertly, from the stage, could begin to be articulated in the press and even to much larger television audiences, theatre ceased (except in some rare cases) to have a special function as a forum of debate.[43]

Although the political turmoil and financial hardship of the early 1990s brought severe difficulties to long-established theatres, for others adversity and social upheaval acted as a creative spur. There was a proliferation of small experimental theatres, formed not as in the past by state decree 'from above', but from the grassroots. Having low overheads, they could secure sponsorship from the burgeoning business community, and with the lifting of travel restrictions began to tour to the West, bringing work that challenged audiences' traditional expectations. One such company was the dance theatre troupe Derevo, founded in Leningrad in 1988, by a former underground rock musician Anton Adasinsky. In 1994 Derevo provided Dublin Theatre Festival audiences with their first opportunity to see a very different type of Russian performance. *The Rider*, played with remarkable physical dexterity by just four performers, eschewed all narrative logic and was described by one critic as 'a crazy-paving of incident, music, mime, acrobatics, clowning — often hilarious, often captivatingly lyrical, but often puzzling, obscure, even horrible'.[44]

Adasinsky had been trained by and performed with the clown Slava Polunin who, though very popular in Russia, having hosted his own television programme, had first achieved international notoriety in 1989 when he led a convoy of clowns, The Peace Caravan, through Eastern Europe. In 1996 he delighted Dublin audiences with *Snowshow*, a magical and

surreal tale of man's helplessness before the elements. In the
1990s, touring proved a good way of generating funds for many
cash-strapped Russian companies, though it also led to
resentment back home and to charges that theatre was being
made only for export. In the last decade Polunin has played
*Snowshow* all over the world, while Derevo, having acquired a
kind of cult following with audiences across Europe, are now
based not in Russia, but in Dresden.

But in recent times no Russian company has toured quite so
widely or as extensively as the Maly theatre of St Petersburg,
under the artistic direction of Lev Dodin. In 1998 they brought
Alexander Galin's *Stars in the Morning Sky* to the Dublin
Theatre Festival. Written in 1987, this play, described as a
modern-day *Lower Depths*, is set on the outskirts of Moscow
and takes place during the 1980 Olympics. With the world's
focus trained on Russia's capital, its streets have been
deliberately cleansed of such embarrassing human debris as
beggars, drunks, drug addicts, and prostitutes. Locked up out of
sight in a dilapidated barracks are four ladies of the night,
whose personal stories form the backbone of the play. It suffers
from some weak characterization and is overly sentimental, but
is remarkable in representing what we have seen was
comparatively rare in theatre of its time: a direct response to
*Glasnost*.[45]

*Stars in the Morning Sky* toured widely, and critics were
astounded by the cohesion and dynamism of the Maly theatre
ensemble. Dodin's company was (indeed is) a remarkable
institution. When many long established companies were
beginning to fall apart, Dodin set about creating a new one.
Today, supported by a huge investment from an oil magnate
Vadim Somov, the Maly's staff numbers over 200, of whom
sixty-four are actors, and few companies in the world are as
tightly knit or as exclusively focussed on working permanently
together.[46] Though critical of some of Stanislavsky's
methodology, Dodin draws on his ideas. But in the opinion of
Maria Shevtsova he fuses these with the techniques of
Meyerhold, by encouraging actors to play their internal
emotions outwardly, with a strong sense of fantasy and self-
awareness that generates humour and ironic self-reflection

regarding the material performed.[47] The fusion of inner conviction with self-conscious theatricality lends the Maly's work a startling freshness which, when they first performed in the West, was much admired for its novelty. The theatre has made this its own distinctive style, but as noted above the melding of these two approaches (often erroneously seen as opposites), is not in itself new.

No foreign director has enjoyed as much direct contact with the Russian theatre as Declan Donnellan, who in 2004 brought a memorably exuberant all-male Russian *Twelfth Night* to the Festival. Donnellan's collaboration with Russian actors is indicative of the kind of interaction now possible between the West and the East. The break-up of the Soviet Union has provided access to a wealth of theatre practices not just from Russia, but from several former Soviet states, and indeed from the whole former Eastern bloc. In recent years at the Theatre Festival audiences have seen work as diverse as that of the anarchic AKHE from St. Petersburg and the stunningly evocative and moving *Battle of Stalingrad* by the Georgian puppeteer Rezo Gabridze. In 2005 Vilnius City Theatre brought us *Romeo and Juliet* set in a pizza parlour, and in 2006 the Omsk State Theatre presented a startlingly new interpretation of Gorky's *Vacationers*.

Theatre is now a global affair, and over its fifty years the Dublin Theatre Festival has often aimed to be, and has increasingly evolved into, a showcase for both Irish and international talent. There were no Russian companies or directors in 2007, the Festival's fiftieth anniversary, but in a much changed Ireland, in a ever-changing world, we should not be surprised that devotees of her still best-loved playwright could enjoy his work either as a home grown *Uncle Vanya* at the Gate, or in *Ivanov* and *The Seagull* in Hungarian at the O'Reilly and at the Project Arts Centre.[48]

---

[1] The Russian directors were Maria Knebel (*The Cherry Orchard*, Abbey Theatre, 1968) and Vladimir Monakhov (*Uncle Vanya*, Abbey Theatre, 1978). The seven productions staged by performers or companies from Russia or former Soviet states were: The Moscow Art Theatre (directed by Oleg Yefremov, *The Seagull*, Abbey Theatre, 1989), Derevo (*The Rider*, 1994), Slava Polunin

(*Snowshow*, The Gaiety Theatre, 1996), The Maly Theatre (directed by Lev Dodin, *Stars in the Morning Sky*, The Gaiety Theatre, 1998), Rezo Gabriadze Puppet Theatre (Georgia) (*The Battle of Stalingrad*, Samuel Beckett Centre, 2005), AKHE (*White Cabin*, Project Arts Centre, 2005), and Omsk State Drama Theatre (*The Vacationers*, The Gaiety Theatre, 2006). The productions of Shakespeare (performed in Russian) were Chekhov International Theatre Festival (directed by Declan Donnellan, *Twelfth Night*, Olympia Theatre, 2004), and Vilnius City Theatre (Lithuania) (*Romeo and Juliet*, The Gaiety Theatre, 2005). The Russian plays by English and Irish companies were the following: *Old World* by Aleksei Arbuzov (translated by Ariadne Nicolaeff, Eblana Theatre, 1977), *The Proposal* by Anton Chekhov, (directed by Andy Hinds, Players' Theatre, 1977), *The Seagull* by Thomas Kilroy (after Chekhov) (The Gate Theatre, 1981), *The Successful Woman* by Aleksei Arbuzov (Focus Theatre, 1983), *Uncle Vanya*, a version by Brian Friel (The Gate Theatre, 1998). Finally the stage adaptations of Russian texts were *The Kreutzer Sonata*, an adaptation of Leo Tolstoy's novella (The Pike Theatre, 1960), *The Inspector* or *The Man from Brussels* (based on Nikolai Gogol, by Eamon Morrissey, The Gate Theatre, 1975), *Diary of a Madman*, adapted from Gogol by Tim McDonnell (Project Arts Centre, 1987), *The Inspector*, an adaptation from Gogol, (Footsbarn Travelling Theatre, Iveagh Gardens, 2000), and *The Yalta Game*, Brian Friel's version of Chekhov's short story, *Lady With a Lap Dog* (The Gate Theatre, 2001). In addition, in 1991, as well as its Autumn programme, The Dublin Theatre Festival presented three plays, billed as a 'Soviet Week', as part of the Mayday to Bloomsday Festival during Dublin's tenure as 'European City of Culture'. The information above has been compiled from research of newspaper advertisements and reviews in the relevant years and of the Dublin Theatre Festival archives. These are incomplete and therefore the list while accurate may not be exhaustive.

[2] This paper is part of a larger research project that includes a study of the impact on Irish theatre of the plays of Anton Chekhov — productions, translations, adaptations and influences — with particular emphasis on how Irish dramatists have attempted to adapt these works to a specifically Irish context. The project is funded in part by a grant from the Irish Research Council for the Humanities and Social Sciences.

Note on the transliteration of Russian names. In the notes for references to texts published in Russian the transliteration system of the Library of Congress has been used. There are, however,

names of persons, plays and theatres which may now be deemed to
have been standardized in English according to a different system
and this standardized form is used in the following instances:
Alexander, Anatoly, Charlotta, Gayev, Gorky, Lyubimov, Maly,
Maria, Meyerhold, Ranevskaya, Stanislavsky, Vanya, Yury,
Yefremov, Yermolova. Though not consistent with a single system
other names have been anglicized to forms the present author
believes are more familiar to non-specialist readers. These are:
Adasinsky, Aleksei, Bolshoi, Brodskaya, Fevralsky, Nikolai,
Rudnitsky, Smeliansky, Tverskoi, Tverskaya, Valery. In addition the
conventional indicator of a 'soft sign' (a single inverted comma) has
been omitted from words in the main text but retained in references
in the notes. After a first full reference to the Moscow Art Theatre
the abbreviation MAT (not MXAT or MKhAT) is used.

3 A typical example of how Stanislavsky's legacy was reinterpreted and
distorted to suit Socialist Realist principles is N. Abalkin, *Sistema
stanislavskogo i sovetskii teatr* (Moscow: Iskusstvo, 1950).

4 The so-called Thaw was a period that lasted for approximately a
decade from the early 1950s. It was not a revolutionary movement
and should not be regarded as a return to the artistic freedoms that
had characterized the immediate post-Revolutionary period, nor
can it be seen to have been governed by a coherent programme on
the part of the Communist Party with the concerted aim of greater
liberalization. Instead policy was frequently determined by
Khrushchev's strategy of appeasement of the conservative and
liberal factions in the artistic and literary world, and also governed
by pragmatic responses to events beyond the borders of the Soviet
Union. In general, however, despite the unpredictable nature of
many of Khrushchev's decisions, and although the initial
enthusiasm of the intelligentsia for the Thaw was tempered
somewhat by 're-freezes', a spirit of optimism persisted until the
early 1960s.

5 Meyerhold was officially rehabilitated by the Military Board of the
Soviet Supreme Court in 1955. The first study of his work appeared
in 1960, and was followed by a series of reminiscences by his pupils
and others who had worked with him. Alexander Fevralsky, one of
his former assistants, edited the collection of his writings published
in 1968, and the following year Konstantin Rudnitsky published in
Russian *Meyerhold the Director* (Moscow: Nauka, 1969), the first
major critical study of his work. The facts and circumstances of his
arrest and execution in 1940 remained obscure until the early
1990s. For a more detailed account of these, see Edward Braun,

'Meyerhold: the Final Act', *New Theatre Quarterly* 33 (February 1993), pp. 3-15.

6 Unpublished scripts were sent to *Glavlit*, the main organ of literary censorship, which had wide-ranging powers of control over all printed matter and could 'recommend' the elimination from a work of any material deemed ideologically suspect before allowing the play to be produced. Government officials then monitored the rehearsal process, and also viewed the production at the final dress rehearsals before it opened. They could make mandatory requests for omissions and additions before issuing a licence permitting public performances, at which the theatre was required to reserve two seats (no further back than the fourth row) for censors, who could thus ensure that lines were not changed. The reality of censorship in the former Soviet Union was rather more complex than this brief outline implies. On the one hand, it was complicated by such issues as self-censorship and permitted dissent. On the other the fact that policy on political issues was frequently determined by external events and therefore subject to change could mean that censors themselves were not always sure what was permissible and were afraid to act without guidance. Such 'grey areas' could on occasion be exploited to a theatre's advantage. For further discussion, see R. Conquest, *The Politics of Ideas in the USSR* (London: The Bodley Head, 1967).

7 From 1953 control of the theatres was under the Ministry of Culture. It received directives from the Council of Ministers and the Secretary for Ideology of the Central Committee of the Communist Party, but in turn delegated direct responsibility for most theatres in Moscow and Leningrad to their respective City Council Executive Committees. These Committees, through various sub-sections, controlled the budgets both for the general administration of theatres and for individual productions. The Party could also exert control over the theatres through its local district committees, and the larger theatres had internal systems of control. Indeed most had their own party organizations. These cells were responsible for education programmes among the staff, such as lectures in Marxist-Leninist ideology, and in accordance with the remit of a given theatre were instrumental in organising performances for specific groups. Theatres were therefore an integral part of a wider political network. All theatres also had their own artistic councils which, chaired by an Administrative Director (appointed by the Ministry), were made up of actors, theatre critics, and other theatre practitioners, and functioned as advisory bodies to Artistic Directors in the matter of the selection and production of plays.

8 Mariia Knebel', "'Vishnevyi sad" v Irlandii', *Teatr* (May 1969), pp. 158-66. Knebel also wrote about her experiences in Ireland in the following: Mariia Knebel', 'Dublin: Ebbi-teatr', *Sovetskaia kul'tura* 7 January 1969, p. 3.

9 Knebel', *Teatr*, p. 163.

10 Ibid.

11 Letter to Chekhov. V. E. Meierkhol'd, *Stat'i, pis'ma, rechi, besedy: 1891-1917* (Moscow: Iskusstvo, 1968), pp. 84-86. See also: 'The Naturalistic Theatre and The Theatre of Mood', *Meyerhold on Theatre*, ed. and trans. Edward Braun (London: Eyre Methuen, 1969), pp. 28-33.

12 Knebel', *Teatr*, p. 162. See also: Mariia Knebel', *Vsia zhizn*, 2nd ed. (Moscow: Iskusstvo, 1993) p. 570.

13 Knebel', *Teatr*, p. 164.

14 Ibid.

15 Ibid.

16 See: 'Henry Kelly Talks to Madame Maria Knebel', *The Irish Times* 3 October 1968, p. 6, and 'Producer Speaks of Abbey Skill', *The Irish Times* 10 October 1968, p. 10.

17 Seamus Kelly, 'Chekhov's classic as in Russia', *The Irish Times* 9 October 1968, p. 10.

18 M. Korotkov, 'Irlandiia znaet Chekhova', *Sovetskaia kul'tura* 5 December 1978, p. 3. For an account of Monakhov's rehearsals at the Abbey see: David Nowlan, '"Uncle Vanya" at the Abbey', *The Irish Times* 26 September 1978, Arts, p. 8.

19 David Nowlan, 'Uncle Vanya Opens at the Abbey', *The Irish Times* 5 October 1978, p. 10.

20 L. Bodolazov, 'Veter stranstvii', *Sovetskaia kul'tura* 22 January 1982, p. 3.

21 Fergus Linehan, 'Take heart, theatre lovers, the circus is in town', *The Irish Times* 16 September 1989: Weekend, p. 3.

22 For an account in English of the rise (and fall) of Yefremov's Sovremmenik, see: Anatoly Smeliansky, *The Russian theatre after Stalin*, trans. Patrick Miles (Cambridge: Cambridge University Press, 1999), pp. 16-30.

23 T.K. Shakh-Azizova, 'Dolgaia zhizn' traditsii', *Chekhovskie chteniia v Ialte*, eds Kuleshov et al. (Moscow: Kniga, 1976), p. 25.

---

[24] Anatoly Smeliansky, 'Chekhov at the Moscow Art Theatre', *The Cambridge Companion to Chekhov*, eds Vera Gottlieb and Paul Allain (Cambridge: Cambridge University Press, 2000), p. 33.

[25] Ibid.

[26] Oleg Yefremov, 'A Path to Chekhov', *Chekhov on the British Stage*, ed. and trans. Patrick Miles (Cambridge: Cambridge University Press, 1993), pp. 131-32.

[27] G. Brodskaia, 'Chekhov v khudozhestvennom teatre 1970-kh godov', *Chekhov i teatral'noe iskusstvo*, eds A. Al'tshuller et al. (Leningrad: LGITMiK, 1985), pp. 190-91.

[28] K. Rudnitskii, 'Vremia i mesto', *Klassika i sovremennost'* (Moscow: Nauka, 1987), p. 210.

[29] Smeliansky, 'Chekhov', p. 35.

[30] Ibid.

[31] Ibid.

[32] K. Rudnitskii, p. 210. See also Laurence Senelick, *The Chekhov Theatre* (Cambridge: Cambridge University Press, 1997), p. 231.

[33] Brodskaia, p. 193.

[34] Brodskaia, pp. 193-94.

[35] Fintan O'Toole, 'A brilliantly disturbing theatrical coup', *The Irish Times* 23 September 1989: Weekend, p. 5.

[36] Ibid.

[37] David Nowlan, 'Moscow Art theatre in "The Seagull" at the Abbey', *The Irish Times* 21 September 1989, p. 12.

[38] Paddy Woodworth, 'Chekhov and the Moscow Art today', *The Irish Times* 16 September 1989: Weekend, p. 5.

[39] The MAT tour was a reciprocal gesture. In February 1988 the Abbey had toured to Leningrad and Moscow. In marked contrast to the decision made at the MAT, the Abbey had taken, not as expected of our National Theatre, an Irish classic, but rather two modern plays: John B. Keane's *The Field* and Tom Mac Intyre's *The Great Hunger*. Taking Mac Intyre's experimental work had generated considerable controversy in the Irish press, and had been regarded by some as a misguided choice for foreign audiences; others had defended it, suggesting it demonstrated that the Abbey's repertoire was not mired in tradition but instead progressive and challenging. For details see Conor O'Cleary, 'Choice of play splits Abbey company ', *The Irish Times* 12 February 1988, p. 11; Conor O'Cleary, 'Choice of Abbey play defended', *The Irish Times* 17 February 1988,

p. 13; and David Nowlan, 'The Leningrad choices', *The Irish Times* 18 February 1988, p. 14.

[40] Conor O'Cleary, 'Democracy brings crisis to Russian theatre', *The Irish Times* 8 February 1988, p. 12. One company was led by Yefremov and the other by the actress Tatiana Doronina, At the time of the split the MAT had two separate main stages. In 1973, to celebrate its seventy-fifth anniversary, a new building with a huge, cavernous stage and auditorium had been constructed on Tverskoi Boulevard. But an older theatre, off Tverskaya, which had been part of the MAT since 1902 was still in use. Yefremov relinquished control of the newer building to Doronina. In 1932 the MAT had been named in honour of Gorky and Doronina's theatre retained this name. Yefremov moved his company to the older building, and named it after Chekhov.

[41] The year 1989 also witnessed the break up of the Yermolova theatre; later in 1993 after a protracted and bitter court battle the Taganka also split in two, and in 1995, after years of talk and rumour, controversial director Yury Grigorovich was ousted from the Bolshoi.

[42] Maria Shevtsova, *Dodin and the Maly Drama Theatre* (London: Routledge, 2004), pp. 10-12.

[43] For further discussion of the effects of political change on the theatre of this period, see: Mikhail Shvidkoi, 'The Effect of *Glasnost*: Soviet Theater from 1985 to 1989', *Theater* 3 (Fall 1989), pp. 7-20.

[44] Ismene Brown, 'Absolute Clowns', *The Daily Telegraph* 16 January 2001, p. 23.

[45] Shevtsova, *Dodin*, p. 13.

[46] These figures are taken from Shevtsova, *Dodin*, p. 8. Her illuminating book is the most authoritative account of Dodin's work in English.

[47] Maria Shevtsova, 'Lev Dodin' *Fifty Key Directors*, eds Shomit Mitter and Maria Shevtsova (Abingdon: Routledge, 2005), p. 203.

[48] The *Uncle Vanya* was a new production of Brian Friel's version of the play, first performed at the Gate for the Dublin Theatre Festival in 1998. The Hungarian companies Katona József and Krétakör brought the productions of *Ivanov* and *The Seagull*, respectively.

# 7 | Tom Murphy's *The Sanctuary Lamp* at the Dublin Theatre Festival, 1975 and 2001

Alexandra Poulain

> It seems to me that the real play must be regarded as what goes on in the mind of the audience. What, therefore, a play is about depends entirely on who is listening to it. *Denis Johnston.*[1]

When *The Sanctuary Lamp* opened at the Abbey during the 1975 Dublin Theatre Festival, part of the audience were shocked by the violence of one character's ferocious attacks on the Catholic clergy. It did not help that Francisco's angry diatribe was issued from the pulpit, in a strikingly realistic reconstitution of a church. A controversy broke out over what one commentator called 'the most anticlerical Irish play ever staged by Ireland's national theatre', prompting several reviewers to evoke, somewhat exaggeratedly, the rows which had erupted over *The Playboy of the Western World* and *The Plough and the Stars*.[2] A quarter of a century later, *The Sanctuary Lamp* was revived in the Peacock Theatre as part of the 'Murphy season' which was one of the highlights of the 2001 Festival. In a quasi-secularized Ireland that had become bitterly disillusioned after revelations of clerical abuse, Francisco's rants against the 'Furies', as he calls the Jesuits who strove to indoctrinate him as a child, could not have caused much indignation. Judging by the warm reactions with which the play was greeted, however, it had lost nothing of its actuality – rather, in Lynne Parker's production, it had started to resonate differently, reaching beyond the polemical issue of anticlericalism to unravel a tale of despair and redemption in a godless age. This, then, is a paper about the mutual interaction between a play and the context in which it is performed; it is about how a truly great play, when brought to life by a perceptive artistic team, will evolve and mutate to deploy its vision according to the priorities and values of the day.

In a 1971 essay published in the Catholic periodical *Christus Rex*, Monsignor Jeremiah Newman had reflected upon the changes that entry into the EEC would signify for Ireland. The country, he predicted, would need to construct

> a culture that will be considerably secular yet without losing our religious persuasions. Our beliefs, it is true, will be less structurally supported, less sociologically conditioned, but they will also be more personal. Our religious vocations will be less institutionally funnelled, less conditioned by employment possibilities, but they will be all the more consciously elected for that.[3]

Changes were certainly underway by the mid-1970s, with vocations to the priesthood declining steadily, and new attitudes emerging towards religious practice among that portion of the population that had been most exposed to modernizing influences. Terence Brown writes that 'religious belief, particularly among the well-educated young, had begun to be experienced less as an all-embracing reality within which life must be ordered and as an immutable aspect of Irish national identity than as a personal expression of individual commitments and values'.[4] Yet such changes as there were had not yet affected the vast majority of the population, who continued to practise their faith within Church institutions. Thus, in 1973-74, ninety percent of the Catholic population declared they attended mass at least once a week.[5] In that context, it is easy to imagine that *The Sanctuary Lamp*, with its vitriolic denunciation of institutionalized religion, must have come as a shock.

The play premiered on 7 October 1975 and, in spite of a successful opening night, trouble soon erupted. There were hisses and loud walk-outs, and various manifestations of hostility during performances (on one occasion Harry's question, 'What's that got to do with us?' was reportedly answered by a voice from the audience, 'That's what we're wondering too!'[6]), and the Abbey received a deluge of telephoned and written complaints. One spectator wrote in outrage to the *Irish Independent*:

> Considering that as a race we take justifiable pride in the retention of our Faith and of the Mass in spite of countless years of imperialistic and satanic pressures, one cannot be expected to excuse this attempt at ridicule simply on the grounds that it is a dramatic episode on the Abbey stage. Neither can we be expected to swallow our traditional sensitivities because the author's name is Murphy.[7]

For that particular spectator, religion was undoubtedly still, in Brown's words, 'an immutable aspect of Irish national identity'. And 'traditional sensitivities' may have been exacerbated at that particular time since, rather unfortunately, the opening of *The Sanctuary Lamp* turned out to coincide with the canonization (on 10 October 1975) of Oliver Plunkett, martyr of English persecution, and the first new Irish saint for almost seven hundred years.

Faced with such reactions, the Abbey and Festival boards decided to hold an after-show public discussion of the play on 10 October, featuring playwright Father Desmond Forristal, Andy O'Mahony, drama critic Sean Page, and Peadar Lamb, who played the Monsignor. Murphy himself watched the proceedings from the control box, but took no part in the debate. One unexpected attendant was President Ó Dálaigh , an enlightened theatre-goer and an Abbey trustee, who got on stage at the beginning of the session and famously declared that 'the play ranks in the first three of the great plays of this theatre: *The Playboy of the Western World*, *Juno and the Peacock*, and *The Sanctuary Lamp*'.[8] 'It was very flattering to me', Murphy

comments, 'but it killed the debate. Had he gone instead of
staying throughout, there might have been better chances for
people expressing their wishes.'⁹ As it was, the discussion
veered into what one reporter called a '"we love Tom" seminar,
and dare you say anything about him'. 'At the end of the
discussion', the reporter continued, 'when a rather rural lady
expressed her opinion of the play as a "jumble of words" and
such goings-on would not happen in an Irish church, she was
rather savagely sneered at by the host of religious and
irreligious liberals present'.¹⁰

Murphy rather deplored the incident; in fact, although he
claims he had not anticipated hostile reactions, he says 'it would
have been better for the play if it had been *more* controversial –
if hundreds of people, half the audience, all the audience had
walked out every night'. This is an interesting formulation,
because it suggests that a play is not quite finished, even at the
term of the staging process, until it has had an impact upon its
audience – a claim since then popularized by Reception
theorists. Murphy's anger with the Catholic clergy was voiced
with such unprecedented rage that in 1975 this aspect of the
play seems to have overshadowed its wider implications, which
might have emerged if a larger-scale public controversy had
occurred. Still, a significant part of the spectators (among them
the enthusiastic Ó Dálaigh) sensed that the play also had a
vision – though Murphy might have been too much ahead of his
time, politically as well as theatrically, for it to blossom fully just
then. In fact, the play anticipates the change in attitudes to
religion which was just beginning to occur in Irish society, and
questions the capacity of institutionalized religion to cater for
individual quests for transcendence. In the years which followed
the sensational premiere of *The Sanctuary Lamp*, other plays
with similar preoccupations were to appear on the Irish stage.
In his *History of Irish Theatre*, Christopher Morash yokes
together Murphy's *The Sanctuary Lamp*, Kilroy's *Talbot's Box*
(1977), and Friel's *Faith Healer* (1979), and regards them as 'a
trilogy by different hands'. 'All three', he writes, 'attempt to
reconfigure Christian (and more specifically, Catholic) faith
outside of the limits of institutionalized religion; and all three
do so by creating theatrical forms whose breaks with stage

realism signal a wider change in society as a whole.'[11] The new theatrical language that Murphy explores in *The Sanctuary Lamp* is rooted in the equivalence which the play postulates between church and theatre.

In the original production, directed by Jonathan Hales and designed by Bronwen Casson, the Abbey stage had been turned into a gigantic old church, complete with pews, confessionals, pulpit and altar, and marble pillars soaring up. The stage was plunged in gloom, which the faint glimmer of the sanctuary lamp hardly diminished. Actors looked dwarfed, and many commentators at the time pointed out the sense of loneliness and emptiness emanating from the stage, ironically questioning the notion of a 'holy presence' which the sanctuary lamp is supposed to symbolize. Entering a familiar theatre and finding oneself in a church must have come as a shock to the original audience; Murphy adds further provocation by using a rundown, soulless church as an obvious metonym of the dilapidated state of the ecclesiastical institution to which it belongs – the Roman Catholic Church.

However, the equivalence created between theatre and church works both ways: while the church is exposed as a purely theatrical matrix of desacralized signs, the play reasserts the transformative power of theatre as sacred ritual. In its original version, the play opens with two brief scenes outside the church (Harry dancing in imitation of his daughter Teresa at night and begging). Scene Three then transports us into the church, where a young guitar-swinging curate delivers an appalling sermon, cracking jokes and calling out to the congregation in the manner of a stand-up comedian. The trope of the play within the play efficiently exposes the ritual of the Mass as a profane spectacle of 'pure' entertainment devoid of any spiritual dimension. The process of demystification continues (or begins, in the revised version where the character of the curate has been suppressed) as the Monsignor, having offered the Jewish Harry a job as church clerk, proceeds to show him round the place to instruct him in his new duties. The Monsignor actually takes Harry and us behind the scenes, and lays bare the very mundane mechanisms that keep the holy spectacle going – most importantly, the candle of the sanctuary lamp which must be replaced every twenty-four hours for the 'mystery' of the holy presence to endure. The scene is an exercise in Brechtian alienation, showing what is normally hidden and forcing us to recognize the holy rituals of the Catholic Church for what they are – merely a show at the theatre. That Harry used to be a performer in the circus makes him particularly well suited to the job, despite the incongruity of his religious background. When the Monsignor leaves and Harry is left alone in the church, exposure of the mystery of the Holy Presence as mystification (or Holy Absence) takes a different turn with that most bizarre – and poignant – of dramatic forms, a dialogue with only one interlocutor. Job-like in the desert of his solitude, Harry turns to the lamp and strikes up a 'conversation' with God, unravelling his tale of betrayed love and friendship for the benefit of an ever-silent deity. The mood here is tragic rather than sardonic, as Harry's questions and pleas are left hanging in the air. God's silence is what sends Harry on his 'long night's journey into day', as Murphy puts it.

When the idea for *The Sanctuary Lamp* started to emerge, Murphy read widely on religion, magic, occultism, and so on. He says one significant source for the play was William James's series of lectures on *The Varieties of Religious Experience*, which he gave at the University of Edinburgh in 1901-2. In lectures VI and VII, jointly entitled 'The Sick Soul', James analyses the morbid temperament he terms 'religious melancholy' – a form of such extreme pessimism that it can only be relieved by religious conversion, or 'second birth'. 'The completest religions', he concludes, 'would therefore seem to be those in which the pessimistic elements are best developed. Buddhism, of course, and Christianity are the best known to us of these. They are essentially religions of deliverance: the man must die to an unreal life before he can be born into the real life.'[12] 'Deliverance', or 'conversion' (an individual experience which may also happen outside institutionalized religions) is the object of a further lecture; James is obviously fascinated with the phenomenon, and argues that 'what is attained is often an altogether new level of spiritual vitality, a relatively heroic level, in which impossible things have become possible, and new energies and endurances are shown'.[13] 'To make the impossible possible' is of course JPW's definition of 'dynamatology' in Murphy's *The Gigli Concert*. Put together, those two quotations in fact spell out the dramatic syntax of some of Murphy's greatest plays – *The Morning After Optimism* (1971), *The Sanctuary Lamp*, *The Gigli Concert* (1983), and *Too Late for Logic* (1989). In those four plays, the (invariably male) protagonist descends into the abyss of despair and self-contempt and re-emerges into a new world, 'in which impossible things have become possible'. James kills his fairy-tale brother Edmund; JPW sings 'like Gigli'; Christopher replays the initial scene of his suicide and comes out 'undead'; and, in *The Sanctuary Lamp*, Harry lifts the massive pulpit which he had previously found too heavy for him – this time with Francisco in it.

Of course James's vision of religious conversion is given a twist, as Harry's 'deliverance' and 'relatively heroic' per-formance with the pulpit are by no means attributable to a sudden revelation of God's goodness. What Harry discovers instead is that he must live with his share of guilt, in a world where God, whether or not He exists, has obviously chosen to keep a low profile. In fact, 'conversion' is treated objectively, theatrically: the 'new world' is not just for newly enlightened individuals to see; it is really brought about on the stage – a world of theatrical possibility, declaring the old rules of stage realism obsolete. Theological questions are left in suspense, but a new 'spiritual vitality' has clearly been released by the end of the play, which enables Maudie, Harry, and Francisco to re-create a sense of communality and, in the case of the two men, to envisage a future together.[14] While the weary rituals of Catholicism are exposed as mere theatricals, a new kind of ritualistic theatre is thus invented onstage – a magical theatre such as Craig and Artaud had dreamed of, turning the stage into a sacred space again.

Departing from the old world and taking a leap into the unknown is precisely what Ireland in 1975 was preparing to do. The play anticipates the rapid process of secularization the country was about to undergo, with a significant part of the population distancing themselves from the institution of the Catholic Church – a process considerably accelerated in the

1990s by the revelation of a series of sexual scandals involving
Catholic priests, which followed one another in rapid
succession. So when in 2001 it was decided to include *The
Sanctuary Lamp* in the group of six Murphy plays that were to
be revived at the Abbey as homage to the playwright, the play's
angry denunciation of the hypocrisy and destructiveness of the
clergy might have sounded like old news. It did not, partly
because of the rise of fundamentalist movements and beliefs
worldwide, a phenomenon from which Ireland is no longer
isolated. The Catholic Church may be a 'dying horse', as
Francisco has it, but the pervasive control it sought to exert over
individual minds and bodies is by no means a thing of the past
(especially as regards women today). Lynne Parker's directorial
choices also tended to understate the Catholic specificity of the
play's setting, by making the church a more abstract location
than it had been in the original production. This was partly due
to the difficulty of turning the small, low-ceilinged Peacock
Theatre into a church, especially as all the shows alternating in
the Peacock for the Murphy season were to be played in
traverse. Parker used an element of sound-design to produce a
slight echo and evoke the acoustics inside a church, keeping the
set as bare as possible, and using only a lighting effect to
suggest the stained-glass window. Besides, she asked composer
Helene Montague to create a score for the play, which was
played live on piano and clarinet, introducing an unfamiliar
element in the recognisable church-like atmosphere. Parker
comments that 'the sound of the woodwind gave it a slightly
Greek feeling',[15] detaching the play from its Catholic context and
giving more resonance to the subtext of Greek tragedy.

Part of the enduring appeal and actuality of the play comes
from its use of a double referential system – Christian and
Greek. Fintan O'Toole has brilliantly elucidated its complex
network of structural and thematic borrowings from *The
Oresteia*; Francisco may rant against the 'coonics' as the
corrupters of the spirit of Christianity, but he speaks of 'the
Gods' in the plural (as in 'Who's going to forgive the Gods?'),
evoking those distant deities of Greek mythology who dally with
human beings and then forget all about them. Against this
'Greek' backdrop, the Catholic church in which the play is set

becomes slightly dislocated – an empty space dedicated to the worship of an absent deity, waiting to be reconverted into a theatre.

Another crucial difference from the original production was that in Parker's staging, both Maudie and Harry were played English, and only Francisco was identifiable as Irish. This is in fact in keeping with Murphy's script, which gives Harry and Maudie recognisably English intonations and phrases, thus suggesting that the play may be set in England (where Murphy had spent most of the 1960s); however, in the original production all three protagonists had been played Irish, for convenience's sake, and this must have further incensed those who had felt that the play was attacking the Irish clergy. In Parker's production, Maudie and Harry's Englishness tended to dissociate the play from a specifically Irish locus. Thus, performed as it was in an Ireland considerably estranged from the Catholic Church and its clergy, the play resonated less as anticlerical tract than as an invitation to seek spiritual fulfilment outside institutionalized religion.

*The Sanctuary Lamp* changed considerably between its 1975 and 2001 productions. While the emotion which came across most powerfully in the original production was anger, in the latter the satirical mood was balanced by the sense of tragic desperation which Murphy makes the paradoxical agency of renewal. Between 1975 and 2001, the script of *The Sanctuary Lamp* underwent substantial revision, in accordance with Murphy's habit of constantly rewriting his plays, and of course each new production reinterpreted and recreated the play anew. However, the transforming and maturing process of a play does not end with deliberate artistic intervention. Keir Elam has argued against the French linguist George Mounin's description of the actor-audience transaction as a 'non-communicational, one-directional flux of information, from active performer to passive spectator': 'Not only are the audience's signals, in any vital form of theatre, an essential contribution to the formation and reception of the performance text – and indeed various post-war performers and directors such as the Becks and Richard Schechner have extended the bounds of the performance to include the audience explicitly – but the spectator, by virtue of his very patronage of the performance, can be said to initiate the communicative circuit (his arrival and readiness being, as it were, the preliminary signals which provoke the performers into action).'[16] A piece of genuinely 'vital' theatre – such as *The Sanctuary Lamp*, with its plasticity, its capacity to reshape in the minds of successive audiences and to generate a variety of meanings – will indeed be appropriated and remodelled by the culture and the moment in which it is performed, as much as it will contribute to remodel them.

---

[1] Denis Johnston, A Note On What Happened, about the first American production of *The Old Lady Says 'No!'* 1929.

[2] Seamus Kelly, 'Theatre Festival First Nights', *The Irish Times* 8 October 1975, p. 10.

[3] Jeremiah Newman, 'Ireland in the Eighties: Our Responsibility', Christus Rex, 25, 3 (1971), p. 181. Quoted in Terence Brown, *Ireland, A Social and Cultural History, 1922-2002* (London: Harper Perennial, 1981; 2004), p. 287.

[4] Brown, p. 289.

[5] Ibid.

[6] Reported in 'Kevin O'Connor at Dublin Theatre Festival', *The Stage and Television Today* 23 October 1975, p. 19.

[7] *Irish Independent* 15 October 1975.

[8] 'President's praise for Tom's play', *The Sunday Press* 12 October 1975, p. 11.

[9] Tom Murphy, in conversation with the author.

[10] Noel Pearson, 'Theatre Festival was worthwhile', *Evening Press* 18 October 1975.

[11] Christopher Morash, *A History of Irish Theatre, 1601-2000* (Cambridge: Cambridge University Press, 2002), p. 249.

[12] William James, *The Varieties of Religious Experience, A Study in Human Nature (1902)* (New York: Penguin Books, 1982), p. 165.

[13] James, p. 241.

[14] Cf. Shaun Richards's 'Response' to my paper 'Fable and Vision: *The Morning After Optimism* and *The Sanctuary Lamp*', *Talking About Tom Murphy* ed. Nicholas Grene (Dublin: Carysfort Press, 2002), pp. 63-65.

[15] Lynne Parker, in conversation with the author.

[16] Keir Elam, *The Semiotics of Theatre* (London : Routledge (1980) 2002), p. 30.

# 8 | Patrick Mason: A Director's Festival Golden Fish

Cathy Leeney

In *There Are No Secrets*, Peter Brook explains his idea of fishing and theatre:

> Think of a fisherman making a net. ... He draws his thread, he ties the knots, enclosing emptiness with forms whose exact shapes correspond to exact functions. Then the net is thrown into the water, it is dragged to and fro, with the tide, against the tide, in many complex patterns. A fish is caught, an inedible fish, or a common fish good for stewing, maybe a fish of many colours, or a rare fish, or a poisonous fish, or at moments of grace a golden fish. ... In the theatre, those who tie the knots are also responsible for the quality of the moment that is ultimately caught in their net... the fisherman by his action of tying knots influences the quality of the fish that land in his net.[1]

Patrick Mason is one of the major architects of Irish theatre performance over the past thirty years. As a director, and as Artistic Director over two terms at the Abbey Theatre, he is and has been an inspirational collaborator with the foremost playwrights, actors, and designers, who have together created the canon of Irish performance in that period.

To speak of a director as an architect associates performance with space, the literal space of the theatre, the imagined space inhabited by the play, the imaginative space in the minds of audiences, and the space of memory, where one reflects on and re-imagines the impact of theatre. I have tried to centre this paper on some of the spaces, and moments created in those spaces, that Mason has been responsible for over thirty years in the Dublin Theatre Festival, moments whose validation is documentation and memory, and whose vitality in recollection is enduring. His creative skills  have sustained a pre-eminent contribution to the Festival's reputation for new Irish writing.

How does one write a history of a director's work, particularly a director who does not set out self-consciously to promote a singular vision with an ensemble of actors? Patrick Mason has undoubtedly been highly influential through his work, but he has also been catholic in his theatrical ambitions and achievements. He has worked internationally, although his key productions are deeply embedded in Irish theatre. Unlike an architect, Mason has no buildings standing to substantiate his concepts and creativity. Perhaps then he is more shape-changer than architect, more a Prospero than a Solness.

Peggy Phelan proposes that '[p]erformance is the art form which most fully understands the generative possibilities of disappearance'.[2] She goes on to point out that as soon as you try to capture performance, to document it and tie it down, it becomes something else: a DVD, an analysis, a memory, a review, an archive. These are signposts to the work. Here I am looking to documentary images and to memory as signposts. The image in performance strikes in the moment. It roots itself, and with the benefit of distance and reflection can grow to reveal connections that were obscured at closer quarters. Thus, a director's individual projects and ventures, considered over time, coalesce into a shape, a network of spaces and images, collaboratively created, that energize not only theatrical culture and tradition, but also the imaginary of audiences. In Mason's case, this shaping has to do with theatrical style and the stream in his work of reflexivity or reflection on the process of representation itself. Mason has also worked to broaden the context of Irish theatre, its connections across cultures and histories in Europe and internationally, its collaborative sophistication and professionalism.

A director's collaborative skills have been a key element for Mason, who himself prefers the word 'producing' because, as he has said: 'you are leading something out or bringing through a group of very disparate talents from writer to actor to designer to lighting designer'.3 Besides his modesty, this comment reflects Mason's understanding of the meshed contributions of a creative team. His collaborations have been with leading practitioners in all roles. He is renowned for his work with actors, and design collaborators include the most eminent names in the field, while his record with the work of living playwrights attests to his skills in diplomacy, perhaps, as well as his linguistic, dramaturgical, and performance insights. The directing/design teamwork of Mason and Vaněk predominates here and constitutes a key Festival achievement.

Given the issues of a reflexive theatrical style and collaboration, how then might one consider the role of the director over time? Peter Brook offers the idea of 'form'. He redefines the word to be something mutable, linked with life and thus subject to life's laws: '[t]here is no form, beginning with ourselves, that is not subject to the fundamental law of the universe, that of disappearance' (50). Brook makes the link with the Hindu concept of 'sphota'; 'between the unmanifest and the manifest,' he writes, 'there is a flow of formless energies, and at certain moments there are kinds of explosions which correspond to this term' (50). This idea of putting into form can be called a birth, an 'incarnation'. It is the director who leads this collaborative process, the putting into form. Brook explains that:

> When one puts on a play, inevitably at the beginning, it has no form, it is just words on paper or ideas. The event is the shaping of the form. What one calls the work is the search for the right form (51).

The Dublin Theatre Festival productions that Patrick Mason has directed are almost all of new writing (whether original play texts or new translations), although he also is known for accomplished revivals of classic plays, where he has capitalized on his deep understanding of theatre history and stagecraft, and his sensitivity to dramatic language. For the Festival, Mason's credits for new writing are gasp-inducing. In conversation with Colm O'Briain, Mason describes a germinal period of working with playwright Tom Mac Intyre; he directed six of Mac Intyre's plays at the Peacock Theatre, including *The Great Hunger* (1983) and *Rise Up Lovely Sweeney* (for the Festival in 1985). He notes how 'the intensity and energy of that contact ... jolted me out of a more literal, realist kind of reading of text into a far more emblematic, symbolic reading of text and action' (320).

From the beginning, Mason's work was theatrically complex and reflexive. The year of his first Mac Intyre production, 1977, also saw his Festival production of Thomas Kilroy's *Talbot's Box* at the Peacock, a case in point. The 'box' of Kilroy's title, in the stage directions '*a primitive, enclosed space, part prison, part sanctuary, part acting space*' was brilliantly realized in Wendy Shea's design.4 In Mason's staging there was a layered awareness of Matt Talbot's spiritual journey as metonymic of the audience's aesthetic and imaginative experience of the play. Talbot's room is the room of theatre; there, alone, Matt Talbot denies the world, but the world is returned to him re-born. Kilroy dramatizes the invasion of this space by the demands of social justice and history. The resilience of Talbot's spiritual *via negativa* was embodied in Mason's production by actor John Molloy when Matt Talbot explains:

> The way to God was by giving up them that's nearest to me [...] But then I discovered something strange [...] having given all up, it was all given back to me, but different, y'know what I mean. All the world and the people in the world came back to me in my own room. But everything in place. Nothing twisted and broken as it is in this world. Everything straight as a piece of good timber, without warp (23).

This moment in performance, which still resonates in my memory, opened the idea of 'the onset of the image', in the phenomenological sense. Gaston Bachelard, in his classic book *The Poetics of Space*, proposes that 'consideration of the onset of the image in an individual consciousness can help us to restore the subjectivity of images and to measure their fullness, their strength and their transubjectivity'.5 In his fascination with spaces and their role in materializing images, Bachelard was 'conscious of doing pioneering work in turning to the "images of matter"'.6 Theatrical images are perhaps the apotheosis of materialization. They occur within the house of the theatre, and lead us back to Bachelard's idea of the house as 'a nest for dreaming, a shelter for imagining'.[7] In performance, the starting point of the image is absolutely material, made up of space, the stuff of costume and setting, the fabric of design shapes, yet paradoxically these materials may initiate an explosion of energy, such as Kilroy's idea of Matt Talbot's room as a site of imagined renewal, repair, and recovery of the world, no less. Amidst the flow of the action, Mason and Shea created in the production a collaborative image of Talbot's vision through belief (to which Talbot returns, incidentally, at the end of the play), while also materializing powerfully for the audience, the stage and auditorium as 'a nest for dreaming and a shelter for imagining' (Bachelard, p. viii).

The memory of this began the process I am suggesting: a tracking of the director's work through images in performance spaces, and through materialized forms that Mason has collaboratively made, where something was both captured and also released: an inward movement towards refuge and intensification, and at the same time, an outward energy of nexus, change, and possibility. The 'to and fro' aspect of this emerges as key, reflecting Brook's description of small explosions: energy flows into the performance space, through action, physicality, language. At certain moments in the language, or through patterns of action, energy explodes outwards, connecting the audience into the performance.

Transformability of the space enables this movement, so that scenography is a channel here. Stage spaces that accommodate transformation in their mutable limits, their provisionality, their self-conscious theatricality and porousness, seem to characterize or be associated with the phenomenon, where an encounter occurs between the fiction on stage, and the imagination of the audience. As Mason himself describes the phenomenological impact: 'I am ... for the specificity and intensity of theatre ... I want works of power ... movements of power, gestures of power, I want presence' (325).

In 1988 Mason directed Ibsen's *Peer Gynt* at the Gate Theatre, in a new translation by Frank McGuinness. This production presented the action through the idea of Peer's room as the imaginative ground, a space that transforms to reflect his mythic/epic adventure towards his vocation as an artist. In the design of Joe Vaněk (and with a cast numbering twenty-four, including the director Joe Dowling playing the name character) we saw a claustrophobic attic space, over which loured a curved wood slatted ceiling, painted with clouds, as if Peer Gynt were trapped under the roll-top desk of Ibsen, and determined to escape. Under this buckling cloudscape, snow gave way to a scarlet Moroccan heat, which in turn became the psychic crucible of a lunatic asylum and, finally, Peer's Shadow forces his confrontation with self. Mason and Vaněk's concept for this cradled platform was to transform it through texture and colour into the mind landscape of the artist, from whitened canvas, to green cotton sward, to red silk, and finally the reflective obsessional black of plastic sheeting. The production won a Harvey's award, and marks Mason's collaborations with Vaněk and with playwright Frank McGuinness dating back to *The Factory Girls* (1982) and *Observe the Sons of Ulster Marching Towards the Somme* (1985).

But in Dublin Theatre Festival terms, Ibsen's quest play was preceded by *Innocence* in 1986, again at the Gate Theatre. McGuinness dedicated that treatment of the life of artist Caravaggio to Patrick Mason. Set in 1606, in a wrecked Vatican palace and in the back streets of Rome, the play twists time and space around a day of murder, hauntings, betrayal, and the violent energy and longing of Caravaggio, to see the world fully, to live in the image in paint. Joe Vaněk designed, and the stage became a moving canvas of references to Caravaggio's paintings, his compositions, emotional uses of colour, an animal sense of physicality and chiaroscuro. The stage was lit by Mick Hughes, predominantly using cross-lighting from the left side, thus creating an extraordinary depth of field, contrasting glowing flesh with shadow. The life of the artist was a blazing and painful flare soon to be swallowed by darkness.[8]

Garrett Keogh played Michelangelo Merisi Caravaggio in one of his best performances yet. The image of his pale hands, flickering in the light, aiming paint brush or dagger to immortalize or to kill, was staged by Mason with rough, chaotic, and bewildering vitality.[9] *Innocence* is a flawed masterpiece.

Reading it now, it shows, perhaps, too much of its author. Mason confronted how McGuinness ambitiously pursues the dramatization of the passion of seeing: the violence of embodiment, its spirit greedy for life and death, recklessly desiring regardless of its incarnated vulnerability. The performance began with the fall of a black curtain, revealing the ruined palace behind, as if a veil had been torn from our eyes, and we would have to see, to see as if life depended on it. Through Joe Vaněk's anachronistic design choices in costume and stage objects, history was broken open, inviting the audience to think beyond the museum past, and into the present moment.

At this point, and arising out of Ibsen's *Peer Gynt* and McGuinness's *Innocence*, a further theme in Mason's work begins to emerge – a challenge to the limits of Ireland's isolation, and a creation of theatrical forms resistant to the parochial, the materialistic, and the narrowly national. In his Festival production record this is wholly evident, as Mason has produced Orton and Ibsen, Murphy and Barry, Chekhov, Kilroy and Carr, Mac Intyre, McGuinness, Farrell, Leonard, and Friel.

Having begun the 1990s caught up in the wild success of Friel's *Dancing at Lughnasa*, Mason brought Sebastian Barry's *The Only True History of Lizzie Finn* to the Abbey main stage for the 1995 Festival. The play is an extraordinary one, and I will mention only one aspect of it here: how its scenic environment, with huge ambition, allows insight into landscape, the natural world, and the human love affair with all that that means, while homesickness, loss and isolation underlie a tenuous proposal: to carry home on your back, and to look for it in the faces you love. Joe Vaněk again designed, presenting a self-consciously theatrical space where the various performances of Lizzie and Jellie Jane's lives played out. The big house was represented in miniature in this theatrical landscape, a charming model, lit from within, and as appealing as any miniature. It allowed the audience to consider reflexively how theatre has romanticized the Big House, and to distance themselves from the scenes enacted within its putative walls. The image is nostalgic, yet suggests how its burdensome mortality may be overcome, when we see it nested within the frame of the ancient midden, the seashore, and the hills beyond. The narrowness of its confinements, of class, of history, of loss, are laid gently aside in the play, in favour of Lizzie's impulse towards the dance, the open road, and a way through beyond the old categories. As in other plays by Barry, *Lizzie Finn* complicates ideas of Irishness until it is only something that hurt and that will be left behind; and the play did this through and with a metaphor of performance as identity, of theatre as a space where the present wins a victory over a punishing past.

Vaněk's use of horizontal timber fencing in *Lizzie Finn* creates a provisional border within which a number of frames are placed. Images from late nineteenth-century advertising created the music hall setting within the onstage proscenium arch in the first part of the play, while iconic objects such as the military uniforms of Robert's dead brothers, sculptural on tailor's dummies, hovered above the men's desolate family house. Later, a linked image of timber slats, but now resembling a fragile stockade, surrounded the kitchen in McGuinness's *Dolly West's Kitchen*, at the Abbey Theatre in 1999. In both Barry's and McGuinness's plays the movement from indoors to outdoors is central to the action. Set in Donegal in the Emergency, *Dolly West* places Ireland amidst a larger catastrophe. The overwhelming events of World War II, represented in the form of smoke, gunfire, and explosions just offstage, infiltrated the nurturing kitchen and the dream-space of the garden and shore. Thus, neutral Ireland and Donegal were implicated in the wider concerns of Europe and the world. The stage energy dissolved this separation, and the distance between fiction and imagination. The movement outwards is made explicit in Dolly's speech at the end of Act I. The stage directions specify '*the evening light turns blue and gold*', and Donna Dent, playing Dolly, described her visit to Ravenna to see the sixth century mosaics in the churches there:

> A procession of men and women. They were white and blue and gold, walking towards their God, and it was the walking that was their glory, for that made them human still in this life, this life that I believe in. I believe in Ravenna. I

remember it. I came home to Ireland, so I could remember it
... I think it's my life's purpose to say I saw it.[10]

The image of potentiality, of spaciousness shattered the archetypal trope of Irish theatre, the kitchen.

The quality of daring in Mason's productions of new writing was matched textually with Marina Carr's *By the Bog of Cats* in 1998. As the title implies, place is at the heart of the play, and Hester's attachment to the Bog is clear from the opening when she enters the wintry expanse of the stage hauling the dead body of a black swan. Olwen Fouéré has written eloquently about her role as Hester, and of her immediate and intense identification with the character. Fouéré describes how Mason supported the huge emotional investment she made in each performance, and offers a rare insight into the skills of the director in the creative process of drawing out a performance of genius.[11]

The setting for this Abbey staging was created by Monica Frawley. An epic, painterly, and exposed quality characterized the scene; and all of the action, even including the wedding scene in Act II, took place on the stepped levels of the bog, against a sky-scape from Tintoretto or Jack Yeats.[12] Enrica Cerquoni has written in detail about the staging of this play and its spatial implications. Here I only wish to mark the almost agoraphobic openness of this blasted heath, where anything may happen, and extreme things do. Yet Hester's love for and knowledge of the Bog of Cats is deeply tied to her longing for her mother, and to her fierce love for her young daughter – these are the piercing moments in her inevitable journey towards death. Mason and Frawley created a powerful image in the production of a stage space belonging to a woman, expressive of her passion, her reality, and her desire. This would be remarkable on any stage, but on the Abbey stage it was and remains a revelation.

Almost finally, and to make the circle, Mason in 1997 returned to the work of Thomas Kilroy, with *The Secret Fall of Constance Wilde*, which he directed at the Abbey Theatre for that Festival. The visual impact of this production is a watershed and arose out of Kilroy's text, Vaněk's design, Nick

Chelton's lighting, and Mason's direction. Its abstraction, its borrowing of conventions from ritualized theatre, and from the architectural spaces, and shadow and light of Edward Gordon Craig freight it as a performance that asserted and celebrated every anti-realist impulse of the Abbey Theatre.

As a leader and collaborator, as a maker of images, materialized in performance, and in bringing into form a vast range of new writing, Patrick Mason has made a history. In his Dublin Theatre Festival work, he has found and offered audiences new relationships between language, image, and action that work. The Mason productions I have not had space even to mention include Kilroy's *The Seagull* in 1981 and Leonard's *Kill* in 1982; in 1983, Tom Murphy's *The Gigli Concert*; *Rise Up Lovely Sweeney* by Mac Intyre and *Baglady/Ladybag* by McGuinness in 1985; Stewart Parker's *Pentecost* in 1986; Murphy's 1989 play *Too Late for Logic*; and Friel's *Performances* in 2003.

In this (re)collection of some of the forms, or as Brook would have it, 'explosions' created by Mason in collaboration with theatre artists, where the onset of images was conjured out of the materiality of the stage, and now recalled to mind, perhaps it is possible to glimpse some few of Mason's Festival golden fish: 'the fisherman works, care and meaning are present in every flick of the finger' (84). Through his collaborations with playwrights, designers, and performers, he has succeeded in producing for Festival audiences 'from very concrete elements, a relationship that works' (63).

---

[1] Peter Brook, *There Are No Secrets: Thoughts on Acting and Theatre* (London: Methuen, 1993), p. 84

[2] Peggy Phelan, *Unmarked: The Politics of Performance* (London: Routledge, 1993), p. 27

[3] Patrick Mason in Conversation with Colm O'Briain, *Theatre Talk* (Dublin: Carysfort Press, 2001), pp. 319-30, (p. 320).

[4] Thomas Kilroy, *Talbot's Box* (Oldcastle: Gallery Books, 1979), p. 9

[5] Gaston Bachelard, *The Poetics of Space*, trans. Maria Jolas (Boston, Mass.: Beacon Press, 1994), p. xix.

[6] Etienne Gilson, Foreword to 1964 edition, *The Poetics of Space*, pp. xi-xiv, (xiii).

[7] John R. Stilgoe, Foreword to 1994 edition, *The Poetics of Space*, pp. vii-x, (viii).

[8] Joe Vaněk, Interview with the author, Dublin, 8 September 2007

[9] Vaněk described how the design and lighting worked together to re-shape itself in response to Keogh's hand movements, which he performed down stage, dominating the image morphing behind him. Vaněk, 8 September 2007.

[10] Frank McGuinness, *Dolly West's Kitchen, Plays 2* (London: Faber, 2002), pp. 218-19.

[11] Olwen Fouéré, 'Journeys in Performance: On Playing in *The Mai* and *By the Bog of Cats'*,*The Theatre of Marina Carr: 'before rules was made'*, eds Cathy Leeney and Anna McMullan (Dublin: Carysfort Press, 2003), pp. 160-71, (p.166)

[12] See Amelia Stein's photographs in *The Theatre of Marina Carr*, Illustrations 9-12.

# 9 | In-dependency: Rough Magic and the Dublin Theatre Festival

Tanya Dean

Speaking about Ireland's contribution to international theatre at a symposium during the first Dublin Theatre Festival in 1957, Ernest Blythe articulated the challenge and the potential facing both the fledgling Festival and Irish theatre as a whole: how to foster a distinct and uniquely Irish theatre that would be heard globally:

> I think that if Ireland and the Irish theatre were to give any contribution to the international theatre, it would have to be true to itself by giving something that was distinctive because it has roots in our national personality. It is particularly necessary that we be true to ourselves and that we try to draw on whatever richness there is in Irish life, because of the impoverishment that occurred through the cultural apostasy of the 19<sup>th</sup> century.[1]

The Dublin Theatre Festival has served as a valuable platform for evaluating Irish theatre in an international context; it has provided an opportunity for production companies to position themselves on the international playing field; and it offers Irish audiences an annual opportunity to compare and contrast homegrown companies to non-Irish imports. It also provides an opportunity for production companies – particularly independent companies – to benefit from an alliance with a well-known and well-marketed theatrical event. Rough Magic, as an important independent Irish theatre company, is a prime example of how the evolution of the Dublin Theatre Festival and the emergence of the independent Irish theatre scene are intimately intertwined, with each fostering the development of the other in a symbiotic relationship.

Even prior to Rough Magic's first official affiliation with the Dublin Theatre Festival, it was clear that the two shared common aspirations in terms of offering exciting international work to Irish audiences. Rough Magic marked their foundation as a company in 1984 with determined ambition, making their professional debut with not just one production but a whole season that ran from July to September 1984 in Players Theatre, Trinity College Dublin. They produced *The Big House* by Brendan Behan, *Talbot's Box* by Thomas Kilroy, *Thirst* by Myles na Gopaleen, and *Fanshen* by David Hare. This opening season, combining work by both Irish and international playwrights, was an early example of how Rough Magic's artistic goals would mirror and complement those of the Dublin Theatre Festival, which also set out to produce Irish and international work under one banner. Speaking about the genesis of Rough Magic, Artistic Director Lynne Parker explained that

> the first key personnel, I suppose, were Declan Hughes and myself. We had the notion while we were at college, because we'd had such a wonderful time doing plays in Players Theatre in Trinity, that we wanted to continue working this way. I suppose the other important thing was that there was no other option if you wanted to work in theatre. The Abbey had just sort of closed down its director training programme and there was no opening at all at the Gate ... I suppose that's why there was such a proliferation of independent companies in the early 1980s, because people were really thrown on their own resources.[2]

Rough Magic quickly established themselves as a hardworking and innovative young company that was keen to provide an alternative to the existing Irish theatrical repertoire. In an artistic policy document prepared for the Arts Council in 1984, they stated that theatre should be a means of communication, a popular medium and a lively art. Our choice of play – in the main, English and American work – is made not in ignorance or neglect of Irish writing, but because of the upbringing and education our generation has had; an education coloured by countless television images, an upbringing divorced from interdependent closely-knit community life. The former has fostered an Anglo-American cultural vocabulary while the latter has alienated us from any real sense of Irishness of the 'the Irish way of life.[3]

This desire to bring a taste of international theatre to Irish audiences was reflected in Rough Magic's early repertoire, with Irish premieres of work by such playwrights as David Mamet (*Sexual Perversity in Chicago*, Project Arts Centre, 1984), Stephen Berkoff (*Decadence*, Players Theatre, 1984), and Caryl Churchill (*Top Girls*, Project Arts Centre, 1984). Irish audiences already benefited annually from the short, intense burst of international theatre work courtesy of the Dublin Theatre Festival, but now Rough Magic was looking to build upon that groundwork by including international work in the year-round Irish season. However, by clearly articulating their passion for developing an international repertoire, Rough Magic were not classifying themselves as being *opposed* to Irish work; rather, they were keen to clarify their intention only to produce plays that they felt were relevant to the contemporary cultural climate – a goal that did not necessarily exclude Irish work. 'We hope to produce Irish writing also', they stated. 'However, we can only really do this if we feel it does relate to us and to our potential audience. It would be a sham for us to attempt peasant theatre. That is a part of our culture our experience does not include.'[4]

It is unclear whether Rough Magic were reacting against the early 1980s theatrical repertoire in Dublin (which, at that time, did not involve the production of a large number of so-called 'peasant plays') or a perceived general emphasis historically in Ireland on 'peasant theatre'. But the young company were definite in their aims: they wished to bring international work to Irish audiences, and would explore work by Irish writers if it was relevant to the current generation of theatre-goers.

The young company strove to delineate their position as an independent company operating outside the centre of the professional Irish theatre scene. In 1988, Fintan O'Toole noted that small independent companies were actually central to the Irish theatre economy:

> The small companies in Ireland aren't a 'fringe'; they are the core of activity. In funding terms, everyone except the Gate and the Abbey is fringe in Ireland. Even well-known and relatively long-established companies like Druid and Rough Magic have the kind of funding that in other countries would mark them as experimental extras ... These aren't the frills – they're the essential material of the patchwork.[5]

The factors marking the Abbey and Gate Theatres as 'Establishment' were relatively high levels of funding, historical precedent, reputation and, to a certain extent, the physical presence of the buildings themselves. Independent theatre companies generally started up with low finance levels and without the benefit of a fixed performance space; often the catalyst for the foundation of an independent company was the desire to pursue a specific artistic programming policy or to react against a cultural, social, or political trend. Despite their (now) central position on the Irish theatre scene, Rough Magic have always defined themselves as operating outside of the 'Establishment'. Lynne Parker states that she 'would be quite shocked if people were to start considering an independent theatre company as an institution. I actually don't believe that any theatre should become an institution, and it does so at its peril. We have to work just as hard as we ever did, and that's a good thing.'[6]

In the years since its foundation, Rough Magic has become a fundamental part of the Irish and Dublin theatre scene, a role highlighted by increased levels of Arts Council funding which in recent years has been exceeded only by Druid, the Gate, the Abbey, and the Dublin Theatre Festival itself. Yet despite this success and their receipt of greater funding than most other Irish theatre companies, Rough Magic continue to emphasize their independent status, resisting the mantle of 'Establishment'. So how does Rough Magic's independence relate to their long-standing association with a major establishment like the Dublin Theatre Festival?

Casting a critical eye over the relationship between the Dublin Theatre Festival and independent Irish theatre companies in her 1993 article, 'Shop Window or Closed Shop', *The Irish Times* journalist Victoria White noted that

> The Dublin Theatre Festival has become a Great White Hope for Irish independent theatre companies ... In a better world, the Dublin Theatre Festival would represent a crest in the city's theatrical graph as an opportunity to see some foreign shows, and a showcase for the best of Irish theatre. In practice, for many Irish independent theatre companies, the two-week festival can often represent one of a couple of chances in the course of the year, or even the only chance, to get a show on.[7]

White's comments highlight a number of important features of Rough Magic's relationship to the Dublin Theatre Festival. The benefits of participation in the Festival for an independent company like Rough Magic are manifold: a raised profile, the possibility of additional funding for their productions, the prestige of being involved in a major theatre festival, and the potential to arrange touring and/or to achieve international recognition. Of course, participation in the Dublin Theatre Festival does not guarantee success. For independent companies, presenting a Festival production involves specific dangers and calculated risks. There is always the threat for the company of being overshadowed – that its production may be passed over by audiences during a concentrated period of dedicated theatregoing. And in order to be viable, a production must have the flexibility to be revived and perhaps toured post-Festival: the one or two week Festival run is unlikely to be sufficiently long to recoup costs. There is also the issue of whether a company compromises its independence for the sake of inclusion in the institution of the Festival. The temporary incorporation into a large Festival means that the smaller company and their artistic output will at least superficially be aligned and associated with the ethos of the dominant force of the Festival for its duration. Does affiliation with a large-scale Festival damage the autonomy of a smaller company?

The answer to that question is quite complex. On the one hand, companies obviously benefit from involvement with the Festival. And in the Irish context, it must be considered that no matter how independent the company, it is still nearly impossible to be independent 'on your own', so to speak. In the Irish theatre economy, companies still rely heavily on funding in order to stage work; that often means that programming must combine artistic vision with a shrewd eye on what projects are likely to be favoured by funding bodies such as the Arts Council when it is time to allocate the limited annual grant resources. Also important is that most independent companies are operating without a dedicated theatre base, and so must foster positive relationships with receiving venues in order to obtain a space to perform. In this context, the Dublin Theatre Festival can represent a valuable ally to independent companies, rather than a dominating force. In fact, the Festival has traditionally been heavily dependent on the individual programming ambitions of a relatively small pool of theatre companies to yield a rich and varied programme, particularly in terms of a national contribution. For that reason, fostering strong and mutually beneficial relationships with independent theatre companies has long been a productive programming tactic for the Festival. Increased Arts Council funding and lucrative sponsorship deals in recent years have given the Festival more financial clout, but it still gives contributing Irish companies, if not *carte blanche*, than at least a strong degree of autonomy in production programming. This means that companies can still exert their independence and individuality when programming artistic output for a Festival context. In terms of Festival programming, independent companies like Rough Magic were traditionally seen as contributing a more subversive, 'fringy' element to the Irish section of the Dublin Theatre Festival (as opposed to the more august presentations by the Gate and Abbey).

Rough Magic first entered the Festival only a year after their official launch as a company, and their listing in the 1985 Dublin Theatre Festival programme proudly boasts the fledgling company's successes since their inception, with a catalogue of achievements that already featured ten evening shows (including seven Irish premieres), three lunchtime shows, an Arts Council Establishment Grant, and a regional tour of their productions of *Top Girls* and *Sexual Perversity in Chicago*.[8] While this is a strong résumé for any company still in its relative infancy, it is nevertheless impressive that such a young company was offered a slot in the country's largest theatre festival. This was the beginning of an enduring relationship between Rough Magic and the Dublin Theatre Festival. In the early years of that relationship, Rough Magic's focus on primarily (but not exclusively) producing international works and breaking away from the Irish canon can be observed. For their first Festival offering in 1985, the company produced a vibrant and farcical version of Brecht's *The Caucasian Chalk Circle*, playing at Project Arts Centre (aside from the occasional appearance in such venues as the Samuel Beckett Centre and the Tivoli Theatre, the Project was to be the venue for most of Rough Magic's Festival productions). The production (directed by Declan Hughes) was played out amidst a set (designed by Lynne Parker) featuring swings, a climbing frame, a seesaw, and a roundabout. *The Irish Times* described it as 'a delectable farrago of class war', and stated that 'Rough Magic has brought some dramatic magic to the Dublin Theatre Festival, and maybe also to Brecht's original text'.[9] This is a key example of how the Dublin Theatre Festival helped Rough Magic to boost their profile and be considered in a larger theatrical context (both nationally and internationally). However, the positive reactions to Rough Magic's first experience with Dublin Theatre Festival did not guarantee a longer run for the production: following the end of the Festival, attendance for *The Caucasian Chalk Circle* dipped and never recovered.

Emboldened by this positive first Festival experience, Rough Magic managed to contribute a production for each year of the Dublin Theatre Festival throughout the remainder of the 1980s. The year 1986 saw their production of Wycherley's *The Country Wife* (directed by Lynne Parker). In their Festival Programme listing, the company again showed a willingness to go against existing conventions:

It is customary to treat Restoration comedy as a vehicle for
fancy dress which is little more than naughtily chic.
Wycherley is a serious playwright, so such treatment would
impoverish and emasculate this savage comedy of passions.
Rough Magic's production of *The Country Wife* will approach
the characters on their own terms – as creatures, not only of
flesh but of blood.[10]

This statement of intent seemed to offer an alternative to the
more traditional painterly Restoration stagings from companies
like the Gate. In 1987, Rough Magic presented O'Casey's *The
Silver Tassie*, directed by Declan Hughes. This was an
uncharacteristic move into the Irish theatrical canon; however,
it is perhaps fitting that their production was by an Irish
playwright with a similarly independent spirit: the original
rejection by the Abbey in 1928 of *The Silver Tassie* (combined
with the furore surrounding *The Plough and The Stars*)
confirmed O'Casey in his exile in England.

In 1988 Rough Magic made the bold move of presenting two
productions in the Festival, simultaneously remaining true to
their passion for international work whilst breaking new ground
in a growing commitment to producing new Irish playwrights.
*Serious Money*, Caryl Churchill's scathing look at morals,
money, and murder in the British stock market (directed by
Lynne Parker), marked a return to international productions,
whereas Donal O'Kelly's one-man show *Bat the Father, Rabbit
the Son* (directed by Declan Hughes) was the company's first
Festival production of an original work by an Irish playwright.
Both benefited from their inclusion in the Festival: *Serious
Money* enjoyed an extended post-Festival run at the Olympia
(transferring from the Project), and *Bat the Father* later toured
to Britain, the U.S. and Australia. This is a perfect example of
the potential value of the Festival acting as a springboard to
longer production runs and international touring for
independent companies like Rough Magic. The 1980s were
rounded out by a production of Timberlake Wertenbaker's *Our
Country's Good* in 1989 (directed by Declan Hughes), appearing
just one year after the play's world premiere in the Royal Court
Theatre, London: demonstration of the Festival and Rough

Magic's shared passion for presenting international theatre to Irish audiences and helping Ireland to keep pace with global developments in the theatre.

Rough Magic's Festival presentations during the 1990s saw an increased emphasis on new Irish work, as the company moved their focus away from their original emphasis on international theatre. Founding member Declan Hughes began to concentrate his energies on playwriting rather than directing, and had an exceptionally strong debut with the 1990 Festival production, *I Can't Get Started* (directed by Lynne Parker), a fictional account of the relationship between mystery writer Dashiell Hammett (author of *The Maltese Falcon*) and playwright and memoirist Lillian Hellman, who met in the 1930s. *I Can't Get Started* was given exceptionally strong praise by David Nowlan in his somewhat negative overview of the year's Festival, 'Playwrights' Failure Casts Gloom on Festival' (in which he decided that the 1990 Dublin Theatre Festival must 'be accounted below par'). 'It is many years since there has been so accomplished a first play by a new Irish writer,' wrote Nowlan, suggesting that 'if this festival is to be remembered over the years to come it will surely be for Mr Hughes's auspicious dramatic debut'.[11]

Building on this positive start to the 1990s, Rough Magic further developed their affiliation with the Festival to provide a platform for productions highlighting home-grown writing talent, with yet another Hughes play lauded during a Festival that was regarded as disappointing in 1991. Their 'excellent' production of Hughes's *Digging for Fire* (directed by Lynne Parker) was classed as the 'single exception, in writing, acting and direction' in a 'succession of disappointing new Irish plays' by Paddy Woodworth in *The Irish Times*.[12] The year 1992 brought with it another double-bill on the Festival, with Arthur Riordan's anarchic de Valera-impersonating farce, *The Emergency Session* (directed by Declan Hughes), and Donal O'Kelly's *The Dogs* (directed by Lynne Parker) both playing at the Project. However, there was a sense this time that the double-billing left the company stretched too thinly to really shine: *The Dogs*, for instance, was described as 'a curate's egg'.[13]

In 1993, the company focused their energies on an elaborate production of William Congreve's *The Way of The World* (directed by Lynne Parker), setting the intricate Restoration intrigues in a sleek, 1930s-style cocktail bar to resounding success ('a hit, a palpable hit,' cried Gerry Colgan[14]). 1994 was the year of *Hidden Charges*, another Arthur Riordan piece (directed by Lynne Parker). For both the 1995 and 1996 Dublin Theatre Festivals, Rough Magic revived works by Stewart Parker (Lynne Parker's uncle): 1995 was the year of *Pentecost*; while in 1996, the IRA's ceasefire came to an end and the presentation of Parker's *Northern Star* acquired a special contemporary relevance.

*Boomtown*, Rough Magic's 'low farce' production for the 1999 Dublin Theatre Festival (performed in a specially constructed temporary auditorium on Meeting House Square, Temple Bar), was a significantly less than triumphant return to the Festival for the company following a two-year hiatus. The company struggled in their attempt to find a theatrical voice to represent and speak to an Irish society on the cusp of a new millennium. In *Irish Theatre Magazine*, Brian Singleton expressed his distaste for the sleazy style of the production: 'Homefare in the main festival, however, plummeted to new depths as evidenced in Rough Magic's base-comic *Boomtown*,' he wrote. 'The scaffolding arena specially constructed in Meeting House Square, Temple Bar may leave no traces after its dismantling, but the play's sordid, *Viz*-comic style will take longer to be eradicated from our memories.'[15] Rosita Boland summed up aptly: 'The ill-judged *Boomtown*, however, received the sort of reviews everyone in theatre has nightmares about: definitely more Black Magic than the Rough Magic we've become used to.'[16]

Following the ill-fated *Boomtown*, Rough Magic took another break from the Dublin Theatre Festival, this time for a lengthier gap of four years. However, the strong ties between the Festival and Rough Magic were not severed during this period: Lynne Parker stepped aside from the independent company to direct three non-Rough Magic productions for the Festival. All three productions were by Irish playwrights, and all three were produced at the Abbey: *Down the Line* by Paul

Mercier in the Peacock in 2000, *The Sanctuary Lamp* by Tom Murphy in the Peacock in 2001 (discussed further by Alexandra Poulain elsewhere in this volume), and *The Shape of Metal* by Thomas Kilroy on the Abbey's mainstage in 2003.

Rough Magic's contributions to the Dublin Theatre Festival in the twenty-first century have placed an emphasis on new Irish work, a marked development from their original determined preference for the international. 2004 marked a strong return with the colourful new musical *Improbable Frequency* by Arthur Riordan and Bell Helicopter (the musical duo Conor Kelly and Sam Park). It could be argued that *Improbable Frequency* is the model of a successful independent production for the Dublin Theatre Festival. Not only did Rough Magic's 'wilfully, gleefully, dynamically different' musical enjoy a successful two-week Festival run, it proved itself as adept at the marathon as the sprint: a successful transfer to the Abbey for a six-week run in 2004 was followed by a national and international tour (including a critically acclaimed run in the Traverse theatre during the 2006 Edinburgh Festival).[17] 2005 was another notable absence for Rough Magic from the Dublin Theatre Festival, especially since the Festival programme did not include a production of any major new Irish plays in this year. Rough Magic sought to remedy that omission in 2006 with their production of Rosemary Jenkinson's *The Bonefire* (directed by Lynne Parker), a much more aggressive and darkly humorous look at sectarian violence in the North than the eloquent hopefulness of the Stewart Parker productions of the 1990s. The reviews were mixed: 'while [Jenkinson's] first play's extreme take on extremism largely fails to make any dramatic impact – or indeed to make any sense – some of the barbed dialogue around the sitting-room sofa is undeniably, albeit unbelievably, sharp-witted', stated Peter Crawley.[18] The previous international success of *Improbable Frequency* seems to have emboldened Rough Magic into touring their 2007 production *Is This About Sex?* by Christian O'Reilly (directed by Lynne Parker) to Edinburgh in August, rather than producing it in the Dublin Theatre Festival first. However, a three-week run in the Edinburgh Fringe Festival followed by dates in Galway and Cork gathered decidedly mixed reviews that did not noticeably improve with the Dublin run. *Irish Theatre Magazine* observed shrewdly that '*Is This About Sex* is a production that is, and will be, popular with audiences if not critics: a comic-romance that occasionally manages to hit below the belt.'[19] Mary Leland (reviewing the production's run in Cork) agreed: 'The great disappointment of this production is that the play seems to have drifted past director Lynne Parker. No energy has been invested and nothing is generated. Whatever potential it may have had is allowed dribble into impotence.'[20] Grant announcements from the government body Culture Ireland in 2008 indicate that Rough Magic have gone back to safer bets, with funding procured to facilitate a further tour of *Improbable Frequency* to the 59E59 Theatre in New York.

The official demarcation of the Dublin Fringe Festival from the Dublin Theatre Festival in 1995 marked a sea change in programming, as an official avenue for more experimental work became available. Some companies still felt that to produce a show for the Fringe after producing for the Dublin Theatre Festival would be retroactive, but Rough Magic were quick to adapt to the possibilities of regularly navigating both Festivals. While Rough Magic still tends to devote 'proper' productions to the Dublin Theatre Festival, they have taken advantage of the Fringe as a space for experimentation, with events like public play readings, such as the *Down Stage Under* staged readings of contemporary Australian plays in the 2004 Fringe. More recently, Rough Magic has focused on the Fringe as an outlet for their SEEDS mentoring programme. This allows the company to provide the mentorees (in playwriting, production, design and direction) with the chance to be involved in a Fringe Festival production, without forcing the company to commit the resources needed for a full-blown Dublin Theatre Festival production. The Rough Magic SEEDS production of Camus' *Caligula* (translated by David Greig) in the 2007 Dublin Fringe Festival even garnered two *Irish Times* Theatre Awards nominations for Best Production and Best Costume Design respectively: rare for a Fringe production, doubly unusual for a production created as part of an artistic mentoring project. That production was then 'promoted' into the main Festival in 2008.

Straddling these two festivals has allowed Rough Magic to re-affirm their status as an independent company, whilst continuing to maintain their own theatrical output.

Rough Magic's catalogue of Festival productions since 1985 has showed a marked evolution of the company, from their earlier determination to introduce Irish audiences to international work, to the recent string of Festival productions promoting new Irish writing. The association with the Dublin Theatre Festival has been profitable, allowing both sides to demonstrate their shared interests in international and new work. Rough Magic has moved from its origins as a small fringe ensemble to its current status as one of the leading Irish theatre companies, but the continuing evolution of the company's Dublin Theatre Festival output contrasts interestingly with its affiliation with the Fringe Festival. And the Dublin Theatre Festival benefits greatly from an ally that offers the best of both worlds: national and international, independent and reputable.

---

[1] Ernest Blythe, 'Ireland's Contribution to World Theatre', *The Irish Times* Monday 27 May 1957, p. 16.

[2] Lilian Chambers et al. (eds), 'Lynne Parker in Conversation with Loughlin Deegan', *Theatre Talk: Voices of Irish Theatre Practitioners* (Dublin: Carysfort Press, 2001), p. 393.

[3] Quoted by David Nowlan in 'Why International Plays Help Irish Writing', *The Irish Times* 2 May 1985, p. 10.

[4] Ibid.

[5] Fintan O'Toole, 'When Survival Depends on the Luck of the Draw', *The Irish Times* 5 November 1988, p. 25.

[6] Peter Crawley, 'The Rough Guide to Growing New Talent', *The Irish Times* 11 February 2004, p. 6.

[7] Victoria White, 'Shop Window or Closed Shop', *The Irish Times* 1 October 1993, p. 14.

[8] 1985 Dublin Theatre Festival programme (courtesy of the Dublin Theatre Festival programme archives), p. 32.

[9] David Nowlan, '*The Caucasian Chalk Circle* at the Project', *The Irish Times* 3 October 1985, p. 12.

[10] 1986 Dublin Theatre Festival programme (courtesy of the Dublin Theatre Festival programme archives).

[11] David Nowlan, 'Playwrights' Failure Casts Gloom on Festival', *The Irish Times* 18 October 1990, p. 8.

[12] Paddy Woodworth, 'A Light Shining Through the Chaos', *The Irish Times* 26 October 1991, p. 32.

[13] Gerry Colgan 'Review of *The Dogs*', *The Irish Times* 15 October 1992, p. 8.

[14] Gerry Colgan, 'Oh, What a Lovely War', *The Irish Times* 14 October 1993, p. 12.

[15] Brian Singleton, 'Festival Fallout', *Irish Theatre Magazine*, 1, 4, (autumn/winter 1999), p. 13.

[16] Rosita Boland, 'Theatre Festival Ups and Downs', *The Irish Times* 21 October 1999, p. 18.

[17] Belinda McKeon, 'Taking Up Where Synge Left Off', *The Irish Times* 29 September 2004, p. 14.

[18] Peter Crawley, 'Review of *The Bonefire*', *The Irish Times* 2 October 2006, p. 12.

[19] Matthew Harrison 'Dublin Theatre Festival Reviews', *Irish Theatre Magazine* online. http://www.irishtheatremagazine.ie/home/dublintheatrefestivalIT AS.htm

[20] Mary Leland, 'Review of *Is This About Sex?*', *The Irish Times* 12 September, p. 2.

# 10 | Festivals National and International: The Beckett Festival

On its fiftieth anniversary, it is helpful to recall that the Dublin Theatre Festival is an important part of that great cultural shift in modern Irish culture from an entirely national consciousness to an entirely international one. Christopher Morash places the Festival in the socio-economic context of the 1950s, the context of 'accelerated modernisation of [Ireland's] late twentieth-century life' by citing the shift from An Tóstal to the Dublin Theatre Festival and the contemporary influence of T.K. Whitaker's *Economic Development* report.[1] To fully represent the modernization in question, we can also cite the creation in the 1950s of Bord Fáilte, Aer Lingus, the Industrial Development Authority, and Irish membership in the United Nations. Suggestive coincidences representing performing arts include the creation of the Wexford Opera Festival and the destruction of the original Abbey Theatre building, both at the outset of the decade, in 1951. Morash quotes President Sean T. O'Kelly on the idea of An Tóstal as commemorating 'the progress made in the cultural, social, and economic spheres in the relatively short time since we won our national independence in this part of the country' and also the founder Brendan Smith soon after on the 'original idea' of the Dublin Theatre Festival as becoming international by programming 'two-thirds Irish contributions ... and one-third foreign

contributions'.[2] The subsequent cultural 'progress' that O'Kelly
evoked accelerated for the remainder of the century. The course
of progress by end of century would result in what Fintan
O'Toole described as 'the paradox of the Republic in the
aftermath of the British Empire: its national independence is
underwritten by transnational corporations and by a supra-
national European Union. Its sovereignty is a power that can be
exercised mostly by giving it up.'[3]

Another part of the same phenomenon, or the paradox, was
Samuel Beckett's work. Contemporary with the decade of
movement from An Tóstal to Dublin Theatre Festival, Beckett's
work, slow in movement from page to production, opened as *En
Attendant Godot* in Paris in 1953, as *Waiting for Godot* in
London in 1955, and as *Fin de Partie* at the Royal Court in
London in the inaugural year of the Dublin Festival. The
complexity of Irishness and foreignness could not have been
more complete. Nor was the interaction solely a British-French
one. In the inaugural year of the Festival, his mime *Acte sans
Paroles* was performed under the French title in London and
Paris by Deryck Mendel. In the second year of the Dublin
Festival, Mendel planned to perform it at the 'Dublin
*International* Theatre Festival'. Unhappy over objections by
Irish cultural conservatives to Sean O'Casey's *The Drums of
Father Ned* and to a stage adaptation of Joyce's *Ulysses*, Beckett
responded with an action that is well remembered but in terms
that are not. He wrote to Alan Simpson, producer of *Godot* in
Dublin and eager for more importations from the world stage,
'[a]fter the revolting boycott of Joyce and O'Casey I don't want
to have anything to do with the Dublin Theatre "Festival"'. The
sarcastic quotes were his. Further, he wrote to Carolyn Swift,
co-producer with Simpson of the Pike Theatre, 'I am
withdrawing altogether. As long as such conditions prevail in
Ireland I do not wish my work to be performed there, either in
festivals or outside them'.[4]

What made Beckett so unhappy with the Irish conception of
'festival' and why did he find festival programming, at least in
Ireland, less than exceptional? This seems worth considering in
terms of the mid-century, because by the end of century his
work was produced as  the Beckett Theatre Festival, and not just

in Dublin, but transnationally in New York and London as well. Plainly, at mid-century, Beckett derided the Dublin representation of festival in theatre as insufficiently modernized if productions could be censored by the conditions that prevailed in Ireland in the first half of the century. Whatever quotas for 'contributions' the founders set, he found the 1958 vision excessively Irish and insufficiently international in value. This is interesting because, despite his own contempt for 'festival', the Beckett Festival that opened in a greatly changed and European Union city, Dublin, in 1991, would attempt, at least, to renationalize the work as 'the Irish Beckett'. The Beckett Festival may seem remote from the Dublin Theatre Festival over its fifty-year history. The Beckett Festival, unlike the Dublin Theatre Festival, is an occasional and not an annual event. It is grounded in a playwright's work rather than national capital. It is also a moveable fest and lives in many places including but not limited to Dublin. However, the idea of the Beckett Festival and its history helps to illustrate in small form some of the strongest characteristics of the Dublin Theatre Festival and its many imitators. The Beckett Festival of 1991 in Dublin and of 1996 in New York City, both versions of the Gate Theatre program developed by Michael Colgan, are exemplary instances of performing arts festival, of the conception of the Dublin Theatre Festival itself, and of a kind of cultural activity even more urgent in our time than in 1957.

That probably sounds like quite a lot to extract from the playwright associated in festival publicity with ideas like 'nothing is more real than nothing'. But it is the festival context of Beckett's work that provokes it. Colgan said of the festival format and the Dublin-New York transfer, 'It's the same plays, but different audiences'.[5] It is more than that. It is the same works, the different audiences, newly sited with all the figurative values of spatial relocation, and in new and different temporal contexts. The festival format – Dublin, Beckett, and otherwise – are perfect instances of what the literary critic Pascale Casanova, in *The World Republic of Letters*, has called 'the unification of international space [proceeding] for the most part through rivalries between national fields'. Casanova's interesting thesis is that after the rise of cultural nationalism, 'literary space has come to be structured, and lastingly so, according to ... the relative degree of autonomy enjoyed by each national space'.[6] As that degree of autonomy declines, without disappearing entirely, the enterprise becomes more like O'Toole's sense of the transnational. Casanova's work is not a rehash of the critique of literary nationalism. Instead, it points to the obvious disparity of national identity with literary practice, to the 'Irish Paradigm' of negotiating nationalism and internationalism as emblematic, and to James Joyce and Samuel Beckett as exemplary figures of the rivalries of nationalism and internationalism. Nothing could be more exemplary of her sense of rivalries and complex relations than Brendan Smith's 'original idea' of programming by proportions of Irish and 'foreign'.

Festivals and performing arts are proudly messy, or at least characteristic in practice of values other than 'autonomy'. Hence no better format than festival to stage the complex relations, rather than mutually exclusive alternatives, of nationalism and internationalism that Casanova postulates: 'the literary world needs to be seen, then, as the product of antagonistic forces rather than as the result of a linear and gradually increasing tendency to autonomy'.[7] The exceptional festival qualities of compressed scheduling of performances and invitation to audiences to over-indulge, or at least to exceed theatre-going habits, heightens the antagonisms and colliding contexts. In less theoretic form, we can say that the format fulfils the ambition expressed in a Dublin Theatre Festival press release on its twenty-fifth anniversary, in 1983, or at midpoint between its first year and its fiftieth: 'Both feast and celebration: a feast of international shows and a celebration of the creative talents of Irish artists.'[8]

The long history of festival is the story of antagonisms rivalling tendencies toward autonomies. Bakhtin is one of the best-known anatomists of the festival of spontaneous and satirical carnivals in the Rabelaisian sense. For Bakhtin, ideally so in Renaissance culture, 'in folk festivities of the carnival type', 'a boundless world of humorous forms and manifestations opposed the official and serious tone of medieval ecclesiastical and feudal culture'.[9] Sad to say, the world of humour has become less boundless in the modern world, but for Bahktin, Victor Turner, Johan Huizinga, and many others, theatre remains one of the legacies of the boundless in however diminished form. Inevitably, as humour waned, commerce waxed. As Christopher Morash puts it, An Tóstal and then the Dublin Theatre Festival were 'part of the dawning recognition that culture could be more than just the spirit of a nation; it could also be its bankroll'.[10] The commercial, rather than oppositional, stance must have been at least part of Beckett's contempt for the Irish notion of 'festival' in 1958.

In contemporary incarnations, arts festivals, Irish or other, are all either quite designed to communicate cultural formations or, if not, unintentionally to repeat them. The host of the Beckett Festival in 1996 at Lincoln Center in New York City was John Rockwell, a wonderful critic as well as an impresario of performing arts. He boasted in the official program of following the tradition of festival models from ancient city state festivals like the Olympic Games, medieval liturgical ones, the nineteenth-century European celebrations of composers like Bach and Wagner, and what Rockwell called the 'Crystal Palace Handel blowouts'.[11] Later, more modern cultural formations served as festival themes, such as nation in the case of Salzburg, and it should not surprise us that such a trend coincided with the rise of Fascism before World War II. Rockwell's point has been put in more dour form by social scientists such as Stanley Waterman. In a journal optimistically named *Progress in Human Geography*, Waterman wrote a very highly cited analysis of festival data (1,266 festivals in Europe in 1994) verifying that 'there are tensions between festival as art and festival as culture', concurring with others on the diminished degrees of anarchy common to contemporary times, and concluding that 'a successful festival involves the active processing of culture'.[12] So among the many antagonisms of festival format is that between the order imposed on culture and the rivalries allowed to erupt even in controlled festival form. Both the Dublin and the New York Beckett Festivals were very successful by any measure, including both critical and commercial, and so their most interesting dimension is exactly what they actively processed and what erupted on its own.

The Beckett Festival at the Gate Theatre in 1991 processed ideas about Beckett and Ireland. It was a production of the Gate Theatre, Trinity College, and Radio Telefís Éireann. The additional sponsoring entities included Aer Lingus and the Arts Council. The Board of Directors of the Festival was entirely Irish. The foyer of the Gate Theatre, where the Beckett performances were staged, exhibited the photos from Eoin O'Brien's *The Beckett Country*. One of the innovations of the program was Irish casts, notably Barry McGovern, Johnny Murphy, Alan Stanford, David Kelly, Fionnuala Flanagan, Stephen Rea, and others. The cultural message was reappropriation of the French existentialist as the Irish writer. That much had all the indicators of reduction of performance art to tourist commodity. But against the Irish cast Colgan's truly festive innovation was importation of contrastingly European directors, especially Antoni Libera and Walter Asmus, which admitted at least a degree of antagonisms and subversion of autonomy. The Irish Beckett was very much part of the temporal context of the time, but the Beckett Festival did not accept that uncritically. The accompanying lecture proceedings included presentations on Beckett such as 'A Dubliner at Heart', but they also featured an international cast of speakers, including Jean Martin of the original Paris *Godot* production. The Festival is often remembered as an independent, discrete event, but it was in fact a part of the Dublin Theatre Festival, or a Festival within the Festival, allowing for colliding contexts. A full disclosure of all sponsors reveals the small but significant roles of the British Council, the French Cultural Institute, and the Goethe Institute. Further, the Beckett Festival within the Dublin Theatre Festival was just part of the Dublin transnational role in 1991 as the European City of Culture for that year, or an emblem of city culture among European ones and in the midst of international cultures.

One very interesting part of the Festival was an analysis by James Mays, who has written influentially on Beckett and Ireland, and who, in Dublin, in a Gate Festival, despite the commercial interests, seemed to reconsider the whole notion of an Irish Beckett. He appropriately enough took to task my book called *The Irish Beckett*, part of the 1991 phenomenon, for

stopping my account of the writer 'when it gets interesting',[13]
that is, when later in life Beckett started writing in French and
became an international figure much more like the one studied
by Pascale Casanova, more antagonistic and less autonomous.
Putting Beckett in the Gate Theatre and casting his works with
fairly familiar Irish actors impressed Mays not with the Irish
Beckett but with the 'loss in converting the writing back into the
material it was produced from'.[14] For Mays, and for many
others, including myself, the result of, as Colgan put it, 'the
same plays', with the Irish cast, the international directors, and
the transnational Irish context, was complex and not reductive.
The American visitor Claudia Harris summed up the effect:
'certainly, some of the attraction of the Festival was
experiencing the craft of the Irish actors ... but in the end the
Festival's merit remained with Beckett'.[15] What was truly festive
was the complexity of it all, and not the tourist commodity of it
all, and that is an admirable and prescient platform for festive
complexity.

The American restaging of the same programme followed all
these principles on a larger scale, as might be expected by a
transfer from Dublin to New York and the Gate Theatre to
Lincoln Center. The transfer was of the same nineteen works, in
the same directorial designs, with only minor cast changes, and
none of them leads. Rockwell boasted that 'our festival
epitomizes and expands the synergy of companies and arts
forms'.[16] It certainly expanded the scale of festival within
festival by setting the Beckett works in the context of a Merce
Cunningham Festival, a Morton Feldman celebration, a world
premiere by the British Théâtre de Complicité, and the New
York debut of the Vietnamese Thang Long Water Puppet
Theatre. One advance in New York of internationalism over
Dublin's was that the Dublin configuration of Irish cast,
international directors, and *Irish* audience (or at least audience
in Ireland) was in New York raised to Irish cast, international
directors, and *international* audience (or at least one foreign to
the Gate Theatre).

The effect of this context could have been to fit Beckett
snugly into that very familiar niche in American theatre of
stereotypical, and intentionally so, Irish products, dramatic,

literary, musical, and consumer. The Irish casts rather emphasized the mugging and the brogues for the Americans, as they have for the rest of the twentieth century. However, oddly enough, the effect seemed to be the reverse, to introduce and then to reject the Irish Beckett, somewhat as James Mays had five years before. Among the most literate of the writers, as opposed to critics, of the Festival was Louis Menand. Provoked by the idea he thought evident in pre-production publicity, that '*this*, with Irish actors and the respectful mentions in the Playbill notes of what "Sam" would have wanted, was the genuine thing', Menand found instead that the works superseded the association with the Gate Theatre, Dublin, and Irish authenticity. To find a concrete theme or identification, he wrote, 'is to exchange a fortune of emptiness for a dime's worth of concreteness'.[17] That rather confirms Mays's disappointment at the 'loss in converting the writing back into the material it was produced from'. In New York, that rejection of an authoritatively Irish Beckett was even stronger among the critics. Martin Washburn in the *Village Voice*, no purist journal then or now, called 'the Gate Theatre attempt to reclaim Beckett as Irish [as] understandable', but he then decried the richness of diction and the effort toward a specific 'canonization' of Beckett's work as Irish or as anything else in particular. [18]

It feels a little inappropriate to over-intellectualize the festive and its celebratory, somewhat chaotic dynamic. There was no shortage of commentary in New York of audiences flocking to Beckett by limo and by rollerblade and collecting official Beckett T-shirts. Nor was there any shortage of keen attention and praise for the by this point very practised performances. Both Colgan in Dublin and Rockwell in New York avidly embraced the tourist trade usually shunned, or at least verbally so, by less festive and more purist performance contexts. But a challenging point about Beckett and performance was established and replicated five years later: in a genuinely international context of festivals within festivals, a particular claim, the Irish Beckett, was introduced, analyzed, resisted, and dissolved. By the time the Beckett Festival had its third incarnation, at the Barbican in 1999, without the broader surrounding festival or cultural city framework, the issue of the nationality and internationality of

Beckett had pretty much disappeared, thus diminishing the provocation and the stimulation. Barry McGovern told the press, with 'a certain defensiveness', that 'I'd rather see a good Japanese production of Godot than a bad Irish one'.[19] However 'good' the play was at the Barbican in 1999, the context was poorer for lack of colliding visions and antagonisms.

All of which reiterates and reaffirms the premise and mission of the Dublin Theatre Festival as stated at mid-point in its fifty-year history: 'a feast of international shows and a celebration of the creative talents of Irish artists'. The Festival is the local and the global meeting in a single complex, compressed event. The Festival is an event capable of representing 'rivalries', as the literature critic Pacale Casanova called them, and not merely autonomous categories. The Festival is an event capable of representing 'cultural formations', as the social scientist Stanley Waterman called them, without reducing them to easily transmitted messages. These festival qualities are not always the case. Many festivals become monolithic: Bayreuth is a prominent example today of a festival attempting to restore festive conditions in place of excessively policed ones.

The Beckett and the Dublin Theatre Festivals have succeeded where others have not. It is particularly timely, I think, that the rivalries and formations associated with the Beckett Festivals about nation in an international context occurred during the 1990s, when Ireland was trying to determine its own identity in the post-Cold War context of small nations in a globalized world. Before the word entered common usage, the Beckett and the Dublin Theatre Festivals were 'transnational', or exemplified by interconnectivity of nations rather than the bilateral, controlled relations suggested by 'international' or 'world powers'. The word and the concept comes to us from the American social thinker and antiwar activist Randolph Bourne, who conceived it in the early twentieth century in the context of World War I, immigration patterns, American xenophobia, and the imperative of an international engagement he described as 'cosmopolitan enterprise', all of which have twenty-first century equivalents. In 'Trans-National America' Bourne conceptualized the erosion of 'premature and sentimental nationalism' and its replacement by 'a vivid consciousness of the new ideal'.[20] That suggests the resistance to the Irish Beckett, for Men and 'a dime's worth of concreteness', and desire for a much more Beckettian emptiness, neither of which would be as compelling without the other. The new ideal can be as complex and as vivid as the chaotic social interactions Bakhtin located in Rabelais. The pith of festival sense was isolated best by John Rockwell when he wrote about the Beckett Theatre Festival in New York in 1996 that 'our festival epitomizes and expands the synergy of companies and art forms'.[21] That he did, with Colgan, with Beckett festivals in the context of Dublin and Lincoln Center festivals, with an appropriate amount of cultural and performative disorder, which expanded cultural formations rather than restricting them, and in that achieved the vivid consciousness of festival.

[1] Christopher Morash, *A History of Irish Theatre 1601-2000* (Cambridge: Cambridge UP, 2002), p. 209.

[2] Ibid. pp. 209-210.

[3] Fintan O'Toole, *The Ex-Isle of Ireland* (Dublin: New Island Books, 1997), p. 20.

[4] James Knowlson, *Damned to Fame: The Life of Samuel Beckett* (New York: Simon and Schuster, 1996), p. 401.

[5] Alan Riding, 'Finding New Audiences for Alienation', *New York Times* 11 June 2000, p. 24.

[6] Pascale Casanova, *The World Republic of Letters* (Cambridge: Harvard UP, 2004), p. 109.

[7] Ibid.

[8] Dublin Theatre Festival, clippings, Billy Rose Theatre Collection, New York Public Library.

[9] Mikhail Bakhtin, *Rabelais and His World*, trans. Hélène Iswolsky (Bloomington, IN: Indiana University Press, 1984), p. 4.

[10] Morash, p. 210.

[11] John Rockwell, 'Festivals: Lincoln Center Festival Program Book, July 1996', *Outsider: John Rockwell on the Arts 1967-2006* (New York: Limelight Books, 2006), p. 351.

[12] Stanley Waterman, 'Carnivals for Elites? The Cultural Politics of Arts Festivals', *Progress in Human Geography* 22.1 (1998), pp. 61-62.

[13] J.C.C. Mays, 'Irish Beckett, A Borderline Instance', in *Beckett, Dublin*, ed. S.E. Wilmer (Dublin: Lilliput Press, 1992), pp. 133-46.

[14] Mays, p. 145.

[15] Claudia Harris, 'The Beckett Festival,' *Theatre Journal* 44.3 (1992), p. 407.

[16] Rockwell, p. 352.

[17] Louis Menand, 'Now What I Wonder Do I Mean by That?' *Slate Magazine* 20 August 1996, http://samuel-beckett.net/theater.html.

[18] Martin Washburn, 'Alive and Well', *Village Voice* 20 August 1996, p. 78.

[19] 'Theatre: There was This Irishman', *Independent* 1 September 1999, http://findarticles.com/p/articles/mi_qn4158/is_19990901/ai_n1 4248245

[20] Randolph Bourne, 'Trans-National America', *Atlantic Monthly* (July 1916) (January 31, 2008): http://www.swarthmore.edu/SocSci/rbannis1/AIH19th/Bourne.ht ml

[21] Rockwell, p. 351.

## 11 | From Ex Libris to Ex Machina: Two Shakespearean Case Studies at the Dublin Theatre Festival

Carmen Szabó

During the first decades of the Dublin Theatre Festival, Shakespeare's plays appeared only sporadically in the programme. However, from the 1980s onwards, Shakespeare entered the space of the Festival with a bang, with multiple venues producing what critics (using a rather salad-like metaphor) termed 'Shakespeare made fresh'. The 1980s were marked by Maciek Reszczynski's production with his Kilkenny-based Theatre Unlimited of *The Murder of Gonzago* (after Shakespeare's *Hamlet*) in 1986; Declan Donnellan's *Twelfth Night* with Cheek by Jowl appeared in the same year, and the Royal Shakespeare Company visited with *Hamlet* in 1988. The 1990s saw the return of Cheek by Jowl with *As you Like It*; the Schiller Theater of Berlin visited with their version of *Macbeth*; and Footsbarn's celebrated *Midsummer Night's Dream* was produced in the fairytale setting of the Iveagh Gardens off Harcourt Street. The new century brought a multitude of *Hamlets*, among them a Royal National Theatre production directed by John Caird, and a cabaret-style interpretation of the play by Calixto Bieito and the Birmingham Repertory Theatre. There was also a new *Macbeth* by Blue Raincoat directed by Niall Henry, and Declan Donnellan's *Othello* and *Twelfth Night*. For the purpose of this article, from the flurry of Shakespearean

productions, I will focus on two productions of *Hamlet* – by
Robert Lepage and Conall Morrison – that provided a fresh
approach to the play, both of them presenting a memorable
postmodern – and perhaps post-human – perspective on reality
within the framework of the Festival.

In 1997, the Dublin Theatre Festival hosted Robert Lepage's
*Elsinore*, the production arriving to Dublin's Gaiety Theatre
after a fairly successful run at London's Royal National Theatre,
and notorious (lack of) presence at the Edinburgh Festival. The
Dublin run of *Elsinore* marked not only a sea change in the
status of the production, which then continued at festivals in
New York and Ottawa, but also presented Irish audiences with a
new actor, Peter Darling, taking over from Lepage. The
production was devised at La Caserne Dalhousie, the multimedia creative centre built in Québec City for Lepage and his
company Ex Machina. The French language version, *Elseneur*,
premiered in Montréal in November 1995, but the English
version, *Elsinore*, was staged more often, playing to and with
the elite audiences that attended theatre festivals in Europe and
North America. *Elsinore* was a production intended for the
stages of international festivals. It did not incorporate the
linguistic, racial, ethnic, and political undertones that defined
previous productions by Lepage, such as the devised *Tectonic
Plates* (1988-1990) or Shakespeare's *A Midsummer Night's
Dream* (1992). *Elsinore* responds primarily to Lepage's
conception of theatre as play, as never completed work in
progress. The cuts and mixes that he applied to the Shakespearean text do not surprise through radicalism, but rather
through familiarity. Lepage played with the ability of the
audiences to recognize, and/or fail to recognize, one of the
world's most canonical plays. Richard Paul Knowles observes
that in *Elsinore* Lepage 'is less concerned with adapting,
interpreting or producing *Hamlet* than with the ways in which
the play's words and iconography have entered contemporary
discourse'.[1] Before Peter Darling took over, Lepage's assumed
English accent during the performance (closer to the RSC
standard way of speaking Shakespeare's lines than his own
French-Canadian accent) conveyed a neutral tone (much
criticized, both by audiences and by London theatre critics like

Michael Billington and Alastair Macaulay) but also played with the expectations of the audience who were awaiting an 'ethnic' *Hamlet*. The process of play also relates to Lepage's relationship with the text of *Hamlet*. After numerous changes to the text used in the production (later published as the 'Darling version' in the *Canadian Theatre Review*) and to the structure of the production itself, the opening scene '*The castle at Elsinore. A platform before the battlements*', followed the modern editions of the play and situated *Elsinore* firmly within the frame of canonical, mediated texts of Shakespeare's play.[2]

The space that embraces play is characterized mainly by potentiality. This space, be it Peter Brook's 'empty space' or *Star Trek's* holodeck, encourages the players to engage in an activity that, at times, undermines the traditional readings of theatricality both in text and in performance. Elsinore is such a space. It is interesting to note that in the original text, Hamlet's description of Denmark and implicitly Elsinore as 'a prison' (*Hamlet*, II, ii, 242) seems to bracket it off from the 'infinite space' (II, ii, 254) of imagination; however, the performative capacity of such a space is unlimited. The reflective microcosm of Elsinore allows a comparison with Jeremy Bentham's *Panopticon*, the perfect prison – later discussed by Michel Foucault, with its central observation tower.[3] Hamlet takes up the role of the observer and manipulator of the actions that are about to unfold on stage. He becomes the playwright, the creator of the rules that define the game of life and death initiated by the first appearance of the Ghost. Not only does he change the play-within-a play, *The Murder of Gonzago* – 'We'll ha't to-morrow night. You could, for a need, study a speech of some dozen or sixteen lines which I would set down and insert in't, could you not?' (II, ii, 534-536) – but also by 'putting on this confusion' (III, I, 2), he is the *perpetuum mobile* that pushes forward the action on stage.

In *Hamlet*, the excitement of play, the fun that normally generates and supports the play acts, is exchanged for the danger of dark play. Hamlet is the only one who knows the rules of the game and one may suggest that the prolonged action of the play – the eternal question of why Hamlet does not kill Claudius when he sees him praying – can be related to the rules

of dark play and the feeling of flow that emerges as a result. The
player loses himself or herself in the action, so that awareness of
anything other than the game disappears. This total
involvement in the game/play can also explain the continuous
philosophical problems that Hamlet faces in his soliloquies. As
Mihaly Csikszentmihalyi notes in *Beyond Boredom and
Anxiety*, in the flow state

> action follows upon action according to an internal logic that
> seems to need no conscious intervention by the actor. He
> experiences it as a unified flowing from one moment to the
> next, in which he is in control of his actions, and in which
> there is little distinction between self and environment,
> between stimulus and response, or between past, present and
> future.[4]

Hamlet's experience of flow justifies the game of uncovering
Claudius as old Hamlet's killer; and above all, it justifies the
completion of each step towards the tragic denouement. The
rules are not about violence *per se* – killing Claudius as soon as
possible – but more about creating another type of game with
words and tongue, that 'most miraculous organ' (II, ii, 589).
Indeed, Hamlet the player keeps questioning the rules of his
game and his position in it.

In his long soliloquy at the end of Act 2, Hamlet tries to
understand his lack of action by comparing himself to the actor,
usually defined in play theory as a second degree player – a
player 'twice removed' or, as discussed later in this essay, 'not
not' the character he/she is interpreting:

> O, what a rogue and peasant slave am I!
> Is it not monstrous that this player here,
> But in a fiction, in a dream of passion,
> Could force his soul so to his own conceit
> That from her working all his visage wann'd;
> Tears in his eyes, distraction in's aspect,
> A broken voice, and his whole function suiting
> With forms to his conceit? And all for nothing! [...]
> Yet I,
> A dull and muddy-mettl'd rascal, peak,

Like John-a-dreams, unpregnant of my cause,
And can say nothing (*Hamlet*, II, ii, 543-563)

At the end of the speech, Hamlet reiterates that 'The play's the thing', that the game is important and obeying its rules is what will solve the apparent confusion of the present. Thus, Hamlet's madness is not only 'put on' but most importantly it is part of the game. As Laertes notes, 'on [Hamlet's] choice depends/The sanity and health of this whole state' (I, ii, 20-21). The game has to be rightly conducted and completed as Denmark's transformation from decay to growth depends on it. Within the framework of 'dark play', associated with tragedy in performance analysis, Hamlet constructs the game, puts on *The Murder of Gonzago*, observes the reaction of Claudius, and 'wins' by unmasking the King as the killer of his father. Metatheatre is used to reinforce the frame of 'dark play'. The role-playing – Hamlet's madness, Polonius's 'spy games', the play-within-a-play – all are elements that define the tragic ending. In dark play, sometimes even the conscious players are not certain if they are playing or not. They are sucked into the action and what begins as a game can quickly get out of control. With Hamlet, the structure of 'dark play' is present from the very beginning. He creates the play of words as a way around violence, a way to express aggression without doing harm. The danger of dark play however is always present and it escalates towards Claudius's poisoning of the foils and of the Queen's drink, thus breaking the rules of the game and causing a deadly ending.

Accordingly, the textual possibilities towards play and playing become Lepage's tools for rendering *Elsinore*'s non-representational staging. The production is detached from the text and starts a life of its own, resembling M. Mitchell Waldrop's description of a DIY universe:

> What would happen if we could somehow reproduce the conditions of Big Bang in the modern universe? More precisely, what would happen if a sample of matter were somehow compressed into a tiny region of ultrahigh density and temperature – say 1024 K? In one solution, for example, the outside universe simply crushes the hot region into a

standard black hole. However, there is a much more
interesting solution in which the hot region does indeed
inflate – but in a totally different direction that is
perpendicular to ordinary space and time. It becomes a kind
of aneurysm bulging outward from the side of our familiar
universe. In fact, it quickly pinches off and becomes a
separate universe of its own ... This newborn cosmos could
then expand to a scale of billions of light-years, producing
galaxies, stars, planets and even life.[5]

The 'play' principle ruling Lepage's universe in *Elsinore* is
ranging from the 'free-play' described by Jacques Derrida as
'lying beyond stable, centred structures',[6] making them
untenable and decentred; to the 'dark, subversive or deep play'
that Jeremy Bentham discussed in his *The Theory of
Legislation* as 'playing with fire' or 'getting away with murder'.[7]

The ruling aura of the principle of play appears from the very
title of the production. *Elsinore* was chosen not only because, as
Lepage himself asserted in a conversation with Richard Eyre in
January 1997, he was 'too chicken to call it *Hamlet*',[8] but also
because this is not *Hamlet*. However, using Richard
Schechner's double negation, it is also 'not not' *Hamlet*.
*Elsinore*, the name, defines the structural makeup of the
production. The focus is not only on the main character of
Hamlet, who, in a DIY universe ruled by fragmentation and
deconstruction is dead anyway; but on the space that frames the
postmodern 'death of the subject'. Lepage is interested in the
internal scaffolding of the play, in understanding, or at least
trying to understand how *Hamlet* – seen as both text and
character – is constructed.

The production creates an atmosphere that reflects George
Duhamel's observation about avant-garde art and the
emergence of visual technology: 'I can no longer think what I
want to think. My thoughts have been replaced by moving
images'.[9] Techno-art defines *Elsinore*. Lepage plays not only
with Shakespeare's text, rearranging the pieces of the puzzle in
a collage that resists linearity and clarity, but also with his giant
technological toys trying to discover how to do theatre using
technology. He takes the text apart and puts it back together in

ways that challenge the audience's imagination. The infinite play of signification is enjoyed by Lepage both visually and verbally, *Elsinore* becoming a play about playing, or, as Lepage himself put it, 'a statement of the playfulness of *Hamlet*'[10].

A one-man show – a term which is yet again played with, given that there is a body double involved in the production – *Elsinore* opens in the middle of *Hamlet* with the 'To be or not to be' monologue. Hamlet allows his mind to exhaust moving images that trigger a game of dice overseen by both Lepage playing the director Ex Machina and the god – or maybe more appropriately the ghost – in the machine.

The hyper-technological set of *Elsinore* is described by Andy Lavender as:

> the monolith: a plane surface held at its four corners by industrial wires connected to a set of motors. Thus the monolith could be lifted horizontally, tilted backwards and forwards, stood upright, and flipped through a plane of 180 degrees. It could be floor, wall or roof, and present its front or its back to the audience.[11]

Lepage usually referred to it as 'the machine'. This *perpetuum mobile* or *perpetuum lude* framed the actor's moves in a game that had very strict rules. Darling had to position himself on the exact spot at the exact time in order to keep the machinery playing, also being engaged in a sort of 'dark play', running the chance of being crushed by the monolith. This positioning was also determining for the smooth continuation of the metamorphoses of role-play. One particular scene, Ophelia's death, clearly encapsulates not only the play of bodily changes but also the astonishing use of simple technology. Knowles describes it as follows:

> the actor (Peter Darling) entered as Gertrude, stage right, in a stiff, gilded dress, and delivered Gertrude's Act 4 Scene 4 speech straight, and effectively, in front of the curtain. At the end of the speech, the dress broke away from the actor like the encrustation from a pupa, and Ophelia emerged embryonic in a flimsy white undergown, partially open at the chest to reveal the male body beneath...

After Ophelia's songs from Act IV, scene 5, the actor-as-Ophelia crossed the centre stage and lay down on a vast blue cloth, his arms crossed, as the stage mechanism rose, presenting a rectangular, coffin-shaped opening at its centre, into which the body seemed to sink engulfed by the drapery that slid into the grave-like opening to enshroud her. As the machinery lifted, the same actor, as Hamlet, emerged from beneath it, completing the metamorphoses.[12]

Lepage's 'playful machine' – which could appear a contradiction in terms – gave rise to a whole series of critical observations, centred mainly around issues of decontextualization reinforced by the production's staging within the 'placelessness' of international festivals. For many, the game seemed to have gone too far, *Elsinore* becoming a chest of toys which many critics described as multimedia and theatrical tricks of hidden cameras, microphones, and projection devices. However, the main problem behind the majority of the critical remarks is a continuous search for meaning and structure, for a comprehensible dramatic whole. If this is not obvious to the naked eye, then it means that *Elsinore* involves disorder and disharmony as opposed to the order and harmony of the cohesive whole. *Elsinore* resists these binaries and without trying to argue for the already clichéd space of between and betwixt or liminality – which Victor Turner managed to turn into yet another binary of liminal/liminoid[13] – Lepage's *Elsinore* is rather a continuum of experimentation, of playing games at different levels and even managing to engage critics into a game of 'dark play'. When Peter Darling states at the very beginning of the production that 'The play is the thing', play here does not refer to the written text of Shakespeare's *Hamlet* as a dramatic *totum*. On the contrary, it refers to play as process, as fragmentation and almost childlike curiosity for finding what is hidden behind the meaningful mechanism. The cut-and-paste jumbling of the Shakespearean text moves away from trying to make sense of the play's totality and towards a space that seems to be continuous anarchy with the touch of Lepage in the background, harnessing the machine of the set, the actor-machine, and the text-machine.

The year 2005 brought a new version of Shakespeare's *Hamlet* as a joint venture of the Lyric Theatre in Belfast and the Abbey Theatre in Dublin, under the direction of Conall Morrison. The production became a 'landmark moment for Irish Theatre', as Fiach Mac Conghail and Paula McFetridge noted in the programme, because it was the first ever collaboration between the two theatre companies. Morrison's *Hamlet* is remarkable for its attempt to discuss the problematics of the Shakespearean play in a vision that blended technology, installation, and performance art. The programme to the production becomes a kaleidoscope of artistic quotes reflecting the position of Patrick O'Kane's Hamlet as an artist marked by what Joseph Beuys interprets as the need to complete, through art, 'the transformation from a sick world to a healthy one'. Hamlet is not the victim of a playmaker as Lepage's is but the playmaker himself. He becomes a voyeur, an observer, using modern surveillance devices to control and direct the action on stage. Many filmic sequences are used by Morrison, Hamlet becoming not only a director on stage but also a filmmaker, reminding one of Michael Almereyda's big-screen version of *Hamlet* (2000) starring Ethan Hawke in the title role.

The striking resemblance between O'Kane's Hamlet and the figure of Joseph Beuys reinforces the close relationship between performance/installation art – Beuys's 'actions', and theatre within the boundaries of this production. Joseph Beuys discusses the issue of artistic 'action' from the point of view of responsibility and the creation of a 'beautiful' which surpasses the expectations of the audience.[14] He refuses to give in to the attempts of the masses to perpetuate themselves with images of beauty, images that can only remind one of the familiar and which fail to initiate any thought but that of pleasure in the comfortable and accepted. This becomes the creed of the postmodern artist as underlined by Jean-Francois Lyotard who discussed the responsibility of the artist thus in 'Answering the Question: What Is Postmodernism':

> Those who refuse to re-examine the rules of art pursue
> successful careers in mass conformism by communicating, by

means of the 'correct rules,' the endemic desire for reality
with objects and situations capable of gratifying it.[15]

Morrison's Hamlet refuses conformism and the accepted
images of beauty, challenging not only the Irish political
realities (both North and South) embedded in the production at
different stages, but also the more universal problems of
identity and existence posed by a postmodern world order.
Hamlet creates a world of video images and camcorder
projections in a continuous search for what Beuys terms the
'social sculpture'. The search for this construct happens within
the inner stratum of the production with Hamlet facing both the
political crisis of his society and the personal crisis of the
intellectual existing between 'being' and 'non-being'. Also,
Morrison's direction reinforces the attempt to shape this
production of *Hamlet* as 'social sculpture'. Beyond the social
and political references of what the programme notes refer to as
the 'country's endemic political corruption and systematic
religious violence' and 'the southern suits and northern bigots',
*Hamlet* investigates the position of the individual in a highly
technological world. The video camera and the projections do
not seem to be imposed from the outside but, on the contrary,
become part of Hamlet. This constitutes the main difference
between Lepage's version of *Hamlet* and Morrison's production.
In *Elsinore* the technology, the machine at the centre of the
production, aided the detachment of the piece and moved it
towards 'a play' with the canon and the audiences. However,
Conall Morrison's *Hamlet* attempted to present the Festival
audiences with the complex political and social issues (which go
beyond Ireland, North and South) that the individual faces
within the frame of a new, post-human, age.

The fractured individual or the subject here is not dead as in
Frederic Jameson's version of postmodern reality, but
transformed into what Donna Haraway describes as 'the
cyborg'. Haraway's definition of the cyborg is quoted in the
show programme: it is a 'cybernetic organism, a hybrid of
machine and organism, a creature of social reality as well as a
creature of fiction'. She states that:

> By the late twentieth century, our time, a mythic time, we are
> all chimeras, theorized and fabricated hybrids of machine
> and organism; in short, we are cyborgs. The cyborg is our
> ontology; it gives us our politics. The cyborg is a condensed
> image of both imagination and material reality, the two
> joined centres structuring any possibility of historical
> transformation. In the traditions of 'Western' science and
> politics – the tradition of racist, male-dominant capitalism;
> the tradition of progress; the tradition of the appropriation of
> nature as resource for the productions of culture; the
> tradition of reproduction of the self from the reflections of
> the other – the relation between organism and machine has
> been a border war. The stakes in the border war have been
> the     territories     of     production,     reproduction,     and
> imagination.[16]

Hamlet is such a dual individual who, through a Beuysian
resistance in the face of 'the tradition of reproduction of the self
from the reflections of the other', engages his 'machine self' in
'terminating' the hypocritical political world around him. The
issue of duality also determines the extremely interesting
relationship established, through visual (and technological)
poetry, between Hamlet and the ghost of his father. Old
Hamlet's ghost appears to him on a video-screen and the
paternal image is later implanted on the hero's naked chest,
providing an effective doubling and intimacy.

However, Hamlet is also defined by rupture, following
Haraway's description of the 'cyborg' as 'no longer structured by
the polarity of public and private', defined as technological
poles based partly on a revolution of social relations in the
oikos, the household. His anger is directed against the
household of Elsinore, represented for example by an extremely
bloody and violent 'mousetrap' but also against the knowledge
that there is no hope for regenerating that household. He
knows, as does the cyborg, that there is no dream of community
on the model of the organic family; there is no creation of a
perfect whole because there is no previous knowledge of such a
construct. The image of the social sculpture and the lack of hope
for achieving a cohesive whole clash in Morrison's Hamlet,

opening up numerous questions about the position of the individual – if there is such a philosophical construct – and the fractures caused by the technological short circuits.

The two productions discussed above mark not only the integration of hybrid, technological theatre within the framework of the Dublin Theatre Festival, but also project the future of the Festival as a panel that comprises multiple varieties of visual cultures, including in 2007 installation art pieces, giving the impression of being born out of Isaac Asimov's 'Robot Dreams'.

---

[1] Richard Paul Knowles, 'Reading *Elsinore*: The Ghost and the Machine', *Canadian Theatre Review*, 3 (Summer 2002), pp. 87-88

[2] This description of place for 1.1 was first introduced by Edward Capell in his 1768 edition of *Mr. William Shakespeare, his Comedies, Histories and Tragedies*, continued by Edmond Malone in his 1790 edition of *The Plays and Poems of William Shakespeare* and present in many editions of the play well into the twentieth century.

[3] See Michel Foucault, *Discipline and Punish: The Birth of the Prison* (New York: Vintage Books, 1979).

[4] Mihaly Csikszentmihalyi, *Beyond Boredom and Anxiety* (Michigan: Jossey-Bass Publishers, 1975), pp. 35-36.

[5] M. Mitchell Waldrop, 'Do-It-Yourself Universes', *Science* (1987), pp. 845-46

[6] Jacques Derrida, *Writing and Difference* (Chicago: University of Chicago Press, 1978), p. 280.

[7] For a performative analysis of Bentham's 'theory of legislation', see Clifford Geertz, *The Interpretation of Cultures* (Ann Arbor: University of Michigan Press, 1973).

[8] Robert Lepage in an interview with Richard Eyre, 10 January 1997, the Lyttelton Theatre. Accessed on 23 January. Available on http://www.nationaltheatre.org.uk/?lid=2627

[9] In Walter Benjamin, 'The Work of Art in the Age of Mechanical Reproduction', *Illuminations* (New York: Schocken Books, 1969), p. 238.

[10] Lepage and Eyre.

[11] Andy Lavender, *Hamlet in Pieces* (London: Nick Hern, 2001), p. 97.

[12] Richard Paul Knowles, 'From Dream to Machine: Peter Brook, Robert Lepage, and the Contemporary Shakespearean Director as

(Post)Modernist', *Theatre Journal* (Baltimore: Johns Hopkins University Press, 1998), p. 202.

[13] See Victor Turner, *The Anthropology of Performance* (Baltimore: Johns Hopkins University Press, 1988).

[14] See Joseph Beuys, *What is Art?* (London: Clairview, 2004).

[15] Jean-Francois Lyotard, *The Lyotard Reader* (Oxford: Basil Blackwell, 1989), p. 246.

[16] Donna Harraway, *Simians, Cyborgs and Women: the Reinvention of Nature* (London: Free Association, 1991), p. 198.

# 12 | An Antipodean Epic: *Cloudstreet* at the Dublin Theatre Festival

Peter Kuch

Although *Cloudstreet*, an adaptation by Nick Enright and Justin Monjo from the Australian novelist Tim Winton's award-winning blockbuster novel of the same name, was barely eighteen months old when it opened as a major attraction at the Dublin Theatre Festival in 1999, it had already been staged with great success in Sydney, Perth, Melbourne, Adelaide, Zurich, and London by Company B Belvoir, an innovative company under the direction of Neil Armfield that had been formed in 1984 when some 600 arts, entertainment, and media professionals and ardent supporters of the theatre had banded together to save the Nimrod Theatre building in Belvoir Street, Surry Hills, Sydney, from demolition. Dublin Theatre Festival audiences were therefore at the considerable advantage of seeing an indisputably 'new' play by an established company in the process of securing an international reputation in which the original cast were able to draw on a rich history of recent performance. Perhaps alluding to its co-operative origins, an advance notice in *The Irish Times* promised Festival audiences a 'company [that was] an example of live theatre at its most powerful and inclusive, where actors, directors, writers, musicians, and designers combine talents to present a theatrical experience of extraordinary quality'.[1] This paper will touch on some of the 'dangers' and 'delights' of that history — in part to trace the evolution of the version that was staged in Dublin; in part to examine some of the risks of cross-cultural performance, particularly as they manifested themselves in Abbey and Druid productions at Australian Theatre/Arts Festivals; and in part to provide a context for speculating about the universal appeal of the play.

To mention *Cloudstreet* in conversation to theatre-goers in either Sydney or Dublin is to invoke a ready smile and an enthusiastic account of a great night at the theatre. What was it about this sprawling, gutsy, raw epic of two families that impressed national and international audiences as quintessentially Australian? What was its universal appeal? And how did a play succeed so triumphantly as theatre when its characters and plot, with unimaginative staging, bad direction, or poor acting could so readily have degenerated into a sentimental proscenium-arch soap opera, a version of *Neighbours* on the boards?[2]

*Cloudstreet* premiered at the Sydney Festival on 3 January 1998. By then the novel, published in May 1991, had won a wide and devoted Australian readership. Encompassing the years 1943 to 1963, the novel traces the lives, fortunes and interaction of two families, the feckless Pickles and the bible-toting Lambs, fated by tragedy to share a rambling history-haunted house, No 1 Cloudstreet, in a working-class suburb of Perth, Western Australia. For the Lambs the tragedy involves their son Fish, the most promising of their five children, who is brain damaged as a nine year-old when he is accidentally trapped under a prawn net; for the Pickles, it involves Sam, husband to Dolly and father to Rose, who loses his hand in an industrial accident. Around Fish Lamb, who functions as an *idiot savant*, circle his elder brother Quick, guilt-ridden by his failure to prevent the accident; his mother Oriel, a thin, prim woman who loses her faith; and his father Lester, a doggedly cheerful, well-intentioned good man. The Pickles, the promiscuous Dolly, and the fortune-hunting but ill-starred Sam, are defined in terms of one another and their long-suffering daughter Rose, who discovers in Fish Lamb someone at once more perceptive and more vulnerable than herself. Shadowing both families is the larger tragedy of colonial Australia, for No 1 Cloudstreet is both haunted by a young aboriginal suicide, one of the 'fallen' girls who had been forcefully kept there to save her for Christ, and casually ignored by an old aboriginal man, representative of black Australia's incomprehension at white Australia's racism.

Devotees of the novel who booked for the opening night must have wondered how such an epic work could be adapted for the stage; but the production was extremely fortunate in its director, cast, crew, and venue. The adapted *Cloudstreet* is after all a three-act play of 102 scenes that runs for three hours and fifty minutes with two intervals, demands a cast of at least fourteen to perform some forty-seven parts, requires 100 costumes, takes in twenty years of events between the end of World War II and the mid-1960s, and has settings that range from suburban Perth to the Australian outback.[3] As one critic laconically observed: 'It makes *Hamlet* look like a haiku'.[4] Yet, within days of its opening, the Box Office was able to report eighty percent of capacity sold, while the cast and crew were able to bask in reviews that were as enthusiastic as they were laudatory.[5] By Tuesday 4 January, Rachel Healy, the General manager, was quoted in the *Sydney Morning Herald* as saying: 'There was already some discussion about whether *Cloudstreet* would launch Company B onto the international stage, and after opening night I feel even more certain of that'.[6]

Several factors contributed to this success. The first was the choice of venue, a large shed adjacent to Pier 9 at Darling Harbour. This cavernous space, with pre-assembled seating for 550, gave Neil Armfield, a highly experienced director, sufficient space to evoke the amplitude of the play, while his decision to use lighting effects and drapes enabled him to apportion the space when he needed to evoke the confines of domesticity.[7] Having actors enter through drapes between scenes also enabled him to elicit, as one critic observed, a sense of the play being rehearsed even while it was being performed.[8] The feeling of improvisation these seemingly unrehearsed entrances and exits created not only chimed with the ramshackle, piecemeal experiences of the characters as they sought to find meaning in their lives, but it also generated a momentum that drove the plot and characters from situation to situation. And technically, it gave Armfield a way of configuring and reconfiguring scenes to solve any problems with acoustics peculiar to the venue. Props were kept to a minimum and were constructed to be highly portable — a table, a bed, several chairs, a few planks, a small boat — the bare essentials at once suggesting the reduced circumstances of the characters and reinforcing the sense that each triumph and each crisis was merely provisional, simply part of a larger narrative whose trajectory would eventually disclose itself.

Not premiering the play in a purpose-built theatre meant that the Sydney production initially faced some special problems. For the first eight of their scheduled nine weeks of rehearsals a large ship with a noisy generator was berthed at Pier 9 and was only moved just prior to opening night after some 'high level negotiations.'[9] Then, on opening night itself, a heavy downpour of rain on the tin roof of the shed — a quintessentially Australian sound — rendered whole speeches of the dialogue inaudible.[10] But again, the flexibility of the space allowed Armfield and the actors to devise strategies to mitigate if not overcome such eventualities. It was as if the performance space was plastic to the needs of the performance and not, as is so often the case, particularly with festival theatre, of the performance having to adapt itself to an inflexible performance space.

Several Abbey and Druid tours of Australia have suffered as a result of this problem, the most notable being the 2004 Abbey centenary tour of *The Gigli Concert* to Brisbane which got lost in the desolate vastnesses of the Suncorp stage,[11] and the 1988 Druid *Playboy* at the York Theatre in Sydney, where the large angled stage, set back from the audience, made it difficult for patrons to appreciate the subtleties of the acting.[12] Those productions that have succeeded are ones where the performance space chimed with the choreography of the play, such as Patrick Mason's 1991-2 Abbey Theatre production of *Dancing at Lughnasa* which toured Melbourne, Sydney, and Perth where the large stages of the state capital city theatres, for the most part designed for late nineteenth-century musicals with all their broad effects and spectacle, suited the size of the cast and the dynamics of the plot; or those productions such as Patrick Mason's Abbey Theatre production of *The Well of the*

*Saints* for the 1995 Perth Festival of the Arts where the large stage of His Majesty's Theatre was effectively expanded to reinforce the mood of isolation that pervades the play.[13]

With *Cloudstreet* travelling to Perth, and then to Melbourne, and then to Adelaide, immediately after its Sydney premiere, Armfield was able to use the strengths and weaknesses of the various performance spaces to explore different aspects of the play. Undoubtedly the most dramatic variations came with scene 102, the final scene of the play, where Fish Lamb secures his brother Quick's tacit permission to return to the very element that has robbed him of his reason.

> *Riverbank. The LAMB and PICKLES families make their picnic. The BLACK MAN is there. FISH watches, then heads for the water. QUICK tries to stop him, but lets him go.*
>
> **Fish**: I know my story for just long enough to see how [far] we've come, how we've all battled in the same corridor that time makes for us, and I'm Fish Lamb for those seconds it takes to die, as long as it takes to drink the river, as long as it took to tell you all this, and then my walls are tipping and I burst into the moon, sun and stars of who I truly am. Being Fish Lamb. Perfectly. Always. Everyplace. Me.
>
> He's gone into the water. **Quick** lets him go.
>
> Curtain[14]

In Sydney and in Perth, where the venues were beside water, Dan Riley, who played Fish, simply ran out the back of the performance space and leapt into the water — in Sydney, into the Harbour; in Perth, into the Swan River. As one of the cast observed: 'that was pretty breathtaking for the audience'.[15] In Melbourne, the ending was dramatized as a receding shadow, as the shadow in all its forms, especially Sam Pickles' metaphor for 'luck' ('the Shifty Shadow of God'), is one of the dominant symbols in the play. Staging the final scene in this way not only linked it to the opening scene but also linked both opening and closing scenes to the history of the house that is narrated in

Scene 8 by the Black Man, a spokesperson/witness for the dispossession of Aboriginals.[16] To stage this scene Armfield used a backcloth to create the effect of a shadow puppet theatre, with those of the cast not on stage dancing the death of the young aboriginal women for whom *Cloudstreet* had become, as a consequence of misguided white middle-class philanthropy, a prison rather than a refuge.[17] In Adelaide, where the Company was obliged to work with a proscenium stage, Armfield chose one of the metaphors from the final scene and contrived to make it appear that there was a wall falling in. While these different ways of staging the ending could simply be characterized as skilful direction, as exploring and exploiting the boundaries of the venue, each ending in effect reads back into the actions and the characters to its own distinctive interpretation of the entire work.

A *Cloudstreet* that ends in shadows becomes a play about luck, and about the way fortune and misfortune shape family and community. As Sam Pickles ruefully reminds his daughter Rose when she suggests to him that he should refrain from gambling on the horses until his 'luck changes': 'Luck don't change, Love. It moves'.[18] To end the play with elongated shadows is to imply that the 'luck' that has brought everyone to that point in their lives will continue to remain with both the Pickles and the Lambs. This was an ending that the Company was to use in Zurich, London, and at the Dublin Theatre Festival, where the *Cloudstreet* was staged in the SFX Theatre.[19]

A *Cloudstreet* that ends with the apparent collapse of Fish's wall, however, becomes a play about dissolution, about the failure of the *idiot savant* to sustain his view of what has taken place over the previous twenty years. Similarly, a *Cloudstreet* that ends with Fish throwing himself into the river, a place Oriel has forbidden him to frequent since his near drowning so traumatized him that it turned him into a 'slowbo',[20] becomes a play about the self-destruction of a damaged life, and a damaged life that lacks the resilience of the other damaged lives he has spent nearly three-and-a-half hours commenting on and observing.

This is not to say that shadows make *Cloudstreet* a comedy while a collapsed wall and a suicide render it a tragedy; but it is to argue that a shadowed ending implies that all will turn out well for Quick and Rose, that Sam will persist with his attempts to 'pick a winning streak', that Oriel's return to the house will be permanent, and that the ghosts of the displaced aborigines, exorcized by the birth of Rose's baby, will be forever placated. In such a production Fish retains his role of *idiot savant*, his individual tragedy merely being subsumed into the ebb and flow of fortune and misfortune that has not only brought both families into proximity with one another but has also been the capricious force provoking that interplay of character and circumstance that has generated the plot. However, a *Cloudstreet* that ends with the metaphorical collapse of Fish or his enacted suicide not only calls into question his status as a reliable narrator and the veracity of his narrative, but it also implies that Australian society has little room for the marginalized, that the mentally disadvantaged and the displaced indigenous should banish themselves or be banished. All the actors in such a production will interpret and perform their roles very differently from a production that ends with shadows.

But it was not only the fact that the Sydney production ended with Fish leaping into the harbour while the Dublin Theatre Festival production ended with elongated shadows that meant the two audiences saw different plays; it was also the case that the Perth, Melbourne, Adelaide, Zurich, and London productions, all taking place within eighteen months, gave the lighting, sound, and special effects crews, and the actors, who for the most part also doubled as scene shifters, a significant opportunity to refine their work. As Armfield explained to a journalist just prior to bringing the production to Dublin: 'It now has a simpler, more physicalized approach towards storytelling ... finding a theatrical language for mystical encounters and drowning and boats flying and miracles'.[21] One critic, who saw both the Sydney premiere and the production prior to the Dublin Theatre Festival, observed:

> The *Cloudstreet* that is playing in London is not the same *Cloudstreet* that opened in Sydney to packed audiences early last year; but is refined, polished, and far more developed. ...

> [S]pecial mention must go to the sound design. Stage effects
> managed by the actors, live music and recorded sound all
> work in harmonious accord to create an epic world of rivers,
> beaches, stars and homes.[22]

Despite the different endings of the Sydney, Perth,
Melbourne, and Adelaide productions eliciting different
interpretations, the play was greeted with enthusiasm
everywhere it was staged, an unusual reaction in that
Melbourne audiences do not always endorse the taste of
Sydney, Adelaide, or Perth's, or *vice versa*. So what was it about
*Cloudstreet* that appealed to local audiences as quintessentially
Australian; and what were the 'dangers' and 'delights' of
bringing such a quintessentially Australian play to Ireland?
That approximately twenty percent of the Australian population
has a traceable Irish heritage does not guarantee that success in
Australia will be matched by success in Ireland, even though the
two countries' shared heritage is acknowledged in the play when
Lester forcefully reminds Sam when he requests 'somethin
special to mark the occasion' that there aren't any Australian
songs — 'they're all Irish.'[23]

The Abbey's 2004 production of *The Gigli Concert* at the
Suncorp Theatre in Brisbane offers a case in point. As Nigel
Munro-Wallis, the most perceptive of the Australian critics
attending the performance, observed on ABC 621:

> while many in Brisbane claim the Irish connection, there are
> few who actually understand in any depth the complex
> psyche of that nation in its recent context. ... even though the
> story is relatively easy to follow, the nuances of the language
> and the cultural references ... are difficult for Australian
> audiences ... Of course the Irish speak English, and of course
> Queensland has strong Irish connections, but we have grown
> apart and this play serves to illustrate that. ... It was all quite
> brilliant but ... perhaps just a little too far removed for
> Brisbane audiences.[24]

Similarly Ben Barnes's decision to put a bowler hat on Adolphus
Grigson and encourage the actor to speak with a Northern
accent as a comment on the Irish politics of the day drew stern

criticism from Fintan O'Toole when *The Shadow of a Gunman* opened in Dublin prior to coming to the 1990 Adelaide Festival of the Arts. In Adelaide however this piece of political comment went entirely unremarked by the critics, even though Ben Barnes had signalled to the Australian Press that he intended to make a political comment. Not all the cultural and political references/allusions of national theatre travel equally well.

So what was it about *Cloudstreet* that resonated with Australians and appealed to audiences in Ireland, that did travel remarkably well? Much of the appeal, I suspect, had to do with when the novel was written and the play performed, and the extent to which the play in particular articulated feelings that were widely shared in both countries. The novel was begun in 1987 and published in 1991, while the play had its Australian premiere in 1998 and its Irish premiere in 1999. In Australia the novel created an audience for the play, while their appearance, almost a decade apart, chimed with a significant shift in the 1990s from nostalgia for what Australia once was, to debate about the ways Australia should image itself to the rest of the world. *Cloudstreet* the novel did not sell widely in Ireland, even though it was a finalist for the Booker Prize, but the play was performed at a time when Australia and Australian culture were featuring in the Irish media,[25] and when many middle-class Irish people, like many middle-class Australians, seeing the ways their lives, cities and countryside had been ravaged by the greed of the 1980s, were beginning to look back with deepening nostalgia to the Ireland and Australia of their childhood. In Australia, *Cloudstreet* the novel was a rebuttal of the corporate property worlds of Bond Corporation, Laurie Connell, and Western Australia Inc., while *Cloudstreet* the play chimed with an image Australia wished to present of itself at the 2000 Olympic Games, and with images that had already found wide appeal in TV soap operas like *Neighbours* and *Home and Away* and films like *Crocodile Dundee* (1986), *The Year My Voice Broke* (1987), *Strictly Ballroom* (1992), *The Nostradamus Kid* (1992), *Muriel's Wedding* (1994), *The Adventures of Priscilla, Queen of the Desert* (1994), *Shine* (1996), and *The Castle* (1997).[26] What *Cloudstreet* shared with all of these was an air of insouciance, a way of showing how innocence could emerge from experience untainted by cynicism, a confidence in the authenticity of its own emotions, and an unashamed delight in the robustness of the Australian vernacular.

Tim Winton, who wrote much of the novel while he was living with his family in Paris and who finished it on the Greek island of Hydra, told Neil Armfield when they visited Perth and Freemantle together in preparation for the play's premiere, that *Cloudstreet*

> began out of an impulse ... to visit all the places around the [Swan] river and Perth that were sacred to the history of his family – places that confirmed his identity because of the family stories that stayed there. 'They were nearly all gone', Tim said. 'Knocked down, rebuilt, dug up, concreted over, eradicated. We're going to have nothing to pass on to our children but the sky', Tim said. 'No sense of place or the growing inherited sense of culture that gathers around a city or a particular physical environment. The memory is being lost, and without that memory there is ultimately no civilisation. Why is it that in Australia places often don't even last a generation before they get rubbed out and started again? Why this insecurity? Are we so fearful of the past that we keep breaking it up and covering it over?'[27]

Like Joyce with 1904 Dublin, Winton knew he had to leave Perth in order to keep it with him. Like Joyce, Winton has a keen ear for the fruity richness of the vernacular. As Max Cullen, a highly experienced Australian actor who played the role of Sam Pickles in the Australian, Swiss, English, and Irish productions remarked to a London journalist: 'Tim has a very good ear for the vernacular. He must have listened to his grandparents. ... We are hearing words we haven't heard for generations.'[28] *Cloudstreet* is as Australian as

> barrel down the hill like mad bastards; we're done, kids, we're cactus; two thousand quid down the dunny; Quick's looking blue; don't be a whacker; mind if I tag along; pennies, zacks, and deeners; like he's just found a mullet in his shorts.[29]

And like Joyce's *Ulysses*, Winton's *Cloudstreet* appealed because of its generous, inclusive celebration of the quotidian, of the individual and the particular; because of its epic scale; and because of the way it showed people negotiating the full range of human experience –birth, death, physical and mental illness, addiction, friendship, love, sex, betrayal, guilt, religion, marriage, parenthood, families, relatives, neighbours, nationality, ethnicity, and personal, familial, and national histories. Also, like Joyce's *Ulysses*, Winton's *Cloudstreet* appealed because of its honesty about contemporary social, cultural, and political mores, prejudice and in particular about history. As Penelope Dening, writing in *The Irish Times* a fortnight before the play opened in Dublin, observed of both the novel's and the play's exploration of issues that in her own experience had all too often been met with silence or an averted gaze:

I first read *Cloudstreet* when I returned from Australia earlier this year and it touched and moved me in its exploration of the nature of love, friendship and pain in a way that my time in Australia had not. I thought it an unfathomable place, with Australians proud of the future but dismissive, if not actually silent, about the past. Questions about an individual's antecedents, or even general historical discussion, proved an easy way to end a conversation, *ditto* anything to do with aboriginals. ... Towns turn their faces away from the land and face inwards towards each other, in a wagon-train mentality. ... Those few people interested in preventing the destruction of 19th century heritage are hard put to raise either money or interest.[30]

But Winton is unlike Joyce, though like many Australian novelists, poets and dramatists, in his desire to see the quotidian disrupted, rendered slantwise, by the transcendental. As one critic quipped: 'For *Cloudstreet* — imagine *Neighbours* taken over by the writing team of John Steinbeck and Gabriel Garcia Marquez'.[31] Despite its laconic secularism, its harsh landscape, its bravura scepticism, and its crass materiality, Australia hungers for some form of existential revelation – witness the poetry of Christopher Brennan, of John Shaw Neilson, of Judith Wright, of Kenneth Slessor; Henry Handel Richardson's *The Fortunes of Richard Mahoney*, Randolph

Stow's *Tourmaline*, and *To the Islands*; Patrick White's *The Aunt's Story, Voss, The Tree of Man, The Vivisector*, and *Riders in the Chariot*; and to switch genres and to exchange the past for the present, the closing scene of Nick Cave's *The Proposition*. If the void of this continent that is still deemed *terra nullius* is to be filled it seems to need to be filled by realigning the ordinary, setting it at odds with itself.

Finally, while it is arguable that *Cloudstreet* appealed to Irish audiences because of the popularity of *Neighbours* and *Home and Away*; because of the curiosity aroused about Australia as it marketed itself for the 2000 Olympics; because of the vigour of its vernacular speech; and because of the deeply-rooted, innocent albeit conservative larrikinism celebrated in contemporary Australian film; it is also arguable that *Cloudstreet* appealed to a people who had experienced the emotional complexities of dislocation through diaspora. It appealed because the play expresses an unresolved tension in Winton's own work, and I suspect an unresolved tension in the minds of many in the audience. Winton is deeply ambivalent about nostalgia. On the one hand he can talk passionately about the way the places that he knew best changed utterly in the '80s.

> I grew up in Scarborough, a colony of holiday shacks that gradually grew into a lower middle-class community with modern housing, and an easygoing atmosphere. Like all Western Australians we were absurdly proud of our white beaches and unpretentious coastal culture ... The 80s, though, brought a new twist. The traditional league of gentlemen who ran the place from the Terrace were shoved aside by the new school of spivs. Suddenly government was in business and business was in government.[32]

And he can also affirm: 'My fiction, my stories have their roots in nostalgia.'[33] On the other hand, however, he has been adamant that he 'didn't write *Cloudstreet* out of nostalgia, because you can get sentimental about what you never knew. I wrote it out of a sense of diminution, an ache of absence.'[34] *Cloudstreet* appeals because it is simultaneously about what we have lost, what we imagine we have lost, and what in a perverse way we wish we had lost.

In the event Dublin audiences and critics were almost unanimous in their praise. Angela Long in *The Irish Times* reported that the play 'deserves the term "phenomenon"' and that there were 'looks of elation' on the faces of the audience 'on Saturday night around 10 pm, when a full house gave the 14-member ensemble a standing ovation after a five-hour performance'.[35] David Nowlan, writing for the same paper, remarked that while 'the acting is occasionally uneven' it was 'always invested with energy and commitment'. 'If the rest of the company will forgive', he added, 'the performance of Daniel Wyllie as Fish Lamb must be singled out as an act of high art, astonishing energy and sustained determination. But everyone contributed mightily to the creation of theatrical magic.'[36] Jocelyn Clarke in the *Sunday Tribune* was equally laudatory: 'Combining exquisite stagecraft with extraordinary per-formances *Cloudstreet* is an ambitious and affecting piece of theatre, which manages to tell an epic story — not only of two families but also of a community and a nation – without ever losing sight of the domestic, particularly in its astonishing warmth and humanity.'[37] Sophie Gorman, reviewing the opening performance in the *Irish Independent* not only praised the acting, singling out Mr Lamb (John Gaden) and Mr Pickles (Max Cullen) for special mention, but also observed that though the 'predominantly off-white set design may be sparse … it is impressively versatile. It portrays the inside of the characters' minds. As every emotion is exposed in this portrait of impoverished post-war Australian family life, there is a universal humanity that traverses time and location barriers.'[38] The one dissenting voice was Mary Carr's in the *Evening Herald,* who grudgingly allowed that while 'this epic story of two Australian families' is not 'actually bad or boring' 'it's just that it washes over the audience in the same bland way as any sentimental and emotionally manipulative saga that aims to leave nothing to the imagination'.[39] However, not even her own paper agreed with her, for *Cloudstreet* received *The Evening Herald* Theatre Award for the best International Production of the Festival. Accepting it from Jim Sheridan, Neil Armfield, the director, described Dublin 'as the happiest venue of our tour',[40] feelings that were evidently reciprocated by many in Dublin with newspapers a week later still describing *Cloudstreet* as 'the hit of the Festival'[41] and a year later as 'wonderful'.[42]

---

[1] Penelope Dening, 'Stormy Weather', *The Irish Times*, eircom Dublin Theatre Festival Supplement, 25 September 1999, p. 1.

[2] Several of the London critics drew a comparison with *Neighbours*; for example, Nick Awde, *The Stage* 23 September 1999, p. 4: 'The bare plot is one of simple, strange folk and their offspring — a sort of *Tobacco Road* populated by *Neighbours* via *One Hundred Years of Solitude.*'

[3] Anon., *The Age*, Metro Arts 6 January 1998, p. 7: 'The advance publicity ballyhoos the four-and-a-half-hour-long Cloudstreet, featuring 15 actors, 50 characters, and about 100 costumes as 'the Australian theatre event of the decade'. Along with *The Leenane Trilogy*, a must-see of the festival.'

[4] Alix Buscovic, '*Cloudstreet*: Riverside Studios', *What's On* 22 September 1999.

[5] Joyce Morgan, 'Cloud's Silver Lining', *Sydney Morning Herald* 6 January 1998, p. 29.

[6] Rachel Healy, 'Sydney Festival '98', Summer Arts, *Sydney Morning Herald* 4 January 1998, p. 29.

[7] Some critics say the drapes were made from calico, some say muslin.

[8] John McCallum, 'Epic experience overflows with human spirit', *The Australian* 6 January 1998, p. 9.

[9] Joyce Morgan, 'Cloud's Silver Lining', *Sydney Morning Herald* Tuesday 6 January 1998, p. 29.

[10] Ibid.

[11] *The Gigli Concert*, Nigel Munro-Wallis at the Brisbane Festival, 612 ABC Brisbane, 3 September 2004, accessed at http://www.abc.net.au/Brisbane/stories/s1195785.htm

[12] Ann Nugent, 'Joys and Sorrows Made Real', *The Canberra Times* 12 January 1988, p. 11: 'I think the York Theatre space, larger, angled and with a greater distance between the stage and the audience is not as sympathetic to the Druid's acting as in Belvoir Street where the actors and the audience are close, almost face to face.'

[13] Chris McLeod, 'Saints be Praised', Arts Today, *The West Australian* 2 March 1995, p. 8: 'The great shroud-like curtain of Monica Frawley's set broods behind the actors like an inescapable entrance to some desolate country of the spirit.'

[14] *Cloudstreet*: Adapted by Nick Enright and Justin Monjo from the novel by Tim Winton (1999; Sydney: Currency Press in association

with Company B. Belvoir and Black Swan Theatre, 2004), p. 122.
Hereafter *Cloudstreet*.

[15] Gareth Gorman, 'Max Cullen: Every cloud has a silver lining', 7
September 1999, unidentified and presently untraced newspaper
clipping in Company B archive.

[16] *Cloudstreet*, pp. 9-10.

[17] Ibid.

[18] Ibid., p. 8.

[19] 'A Tasty Drop of McGuinness', *The Daily Mail* 8 October 1999, p. 12.

[20] Ibid.

[21] Quoted in David Benedict, 'Trains and Boats and Planes', *The
Independent* 8 September 1999, p. 21.

[22] Nick Pugwail, '*Cloudstreet*', *L.A.M.* 28 September 1999, p. 27.

[23] *Cloudstreet*, p. 117. For evidence to the contrary, see *The Reedy
River Songbook*, eds David E Millis and John Meredith (Sydney:
New Theatre, 1954).

[24] *The Gigli Concert*, Nigel Munro-Wallis at the Brisbane Festival, 612
ABC Brisbane, Tuesday 3 September 2004, accessed at
http://www.abc.net.au/Brisbane/stories/s1195785.htm

[25] The decade also marked a number of treaties between Ireland and
Australia, indicative of the growing relationship between the two
countries. Treaty on Extradition between Ireland and Australia,
Dublin 2 Sept 1985, enacted 1991; Agreement between Ireland and
Australia on Social Security, Canberra, 8 April 1991, enacted 1993;
Agreement on Medical treatment for Temporary visitors between
Ireland and Australia, done at Dublin on 12 September 1997,
entered into force 25 May 1998, enacted 2000. See N.C. Fleming
and Alan O'Day, eds, *The Longman Handbook of Modern Irish
History Since 1800* (Harlow: Pearson Education Limited, 2005),
pp. 670-77.

[26] *Neighbours* is sold to over forty Broadcasters in over sixty countries
with the show now averaging more than 120 million viewers every
day. *Neighbours* is also broadcast every evening on Republic of
Ireland state TV station RTÉ Two at 5:30 p.m., and is repeated the
following morning at around 7.00 am on RTÉ One. These episodes
are at the same pace as the episodes shown on BBC, but are not the
BBC version. RTÉ purchase the show directly from Australia and
broadcast the unedited Australian version with full closing credits.
Irish films such as *My Left Foot* (1989), *The Commitments* (1991),
*The Crying Game* (1992), *In the Name of the Father* (1993),

*Michael Collins* (1996), *The Boxer* (1997), *Waking Ned Devine* (1999), and *Angela's Ashes* (1999) have been widely screened in Australia, while TV soaps such as *Ballykissangel* (from 1996) and the sitcom *Father Ted* (from 1995) enjoy good ratings. [Italics]

27 Neil Armfield, 'Director's Note', eircom *Dublin Theatre Festival Booklet*, p. 3.

28 'Fiona Clancy speaks to Max Cullen on the eve of the play's debut', *TNT Magazine*.

29 *Cloudstreet*, pp: 4, 6, 10, 14 22, 23, 23, 32.

30 Penelope Dening, 'Stormy Weather', *The Irish Times*, eircom Dublin Theatre Festival Supplement, 25 September, 1999, p. 1.

31 Penelope Dening, 'Stormy Weather', *The Irish Times*, eircom Dublin Theatre Festival Supplement, 25 September, 1999, p. 1.

32 Salhia Ben-Messahel, *Mind the Country: Tim Winton's Fiction* (Perth: University of Western Australia Press, 2006), pp. 18-19.

33 Ibid., p. 79.

34 Ibid., p. 8.

35 Angela Long, 'Aussie marathon dazzles the Irish', *The Irish Times* 11 October 1999, p.13.

36 David Nowlan, 'Cloudstreet SFX Theatre', *The Irish Times* 11 October 1999, p. 13.

37 Jocelyn Clarke, 'Calling the Shots', *Sunday Tribune* 3 October 1999, p. 12.

38 Sophie Gorman, 'Family epic with magical touch', *Irish Independent* 11 October 1999, p. 16.

39 Mary Carr, 'It's Not Up My Street', *The Evening Herald* 11 October 1999, p. 22.

40 Anon, 'Awards for Dublin Theatre Festival Presented', *The Irish Times* 20 October 1999, p. 5.

41 Rosita Boland, 'Front Row', *The Irish Times* 21 October 1999, p. 18; and *The Irish Times* 28 October 1999, p.14.

42 Gerry Colgan, 'Reviews the eircom Dublin Theatre Festival 2000', *The Irish Times* 6 October 2000, p. 13.

## 13 | 'Bogland Parodies': The Midlands Setting in Marina Carr and Fabulous Beast Dance Theatre

Lisa Fitzpatrick

Since the mid-1990s, the Dublin Theatre Festival has presented a range of new and revived Irish work with roots in folk belief, legend, and mythology. These have included Marina Carr's *By the Bog of Cats* and *Ariel* in 1998 and 2002 respectively; Druid Theatre Company's production of John B. Keane's *Sharon's Grave* and Fabulous Beast's *Giselle* in 2003; *The Dandy Dolls* by George Fitzmaurice, directed by Conall Morrison at the Peacock in 2004; and Fabulous Beast's productions of *The Bull* in 2005 and *James Son of James* in 2007, which were co-produced with the Barbican in London. In addition to those listed, multiple productions that are similarly based in legend or ancient epic were staged in mainstream theatres or produced by established companies during that time. Examples include Vincent Woods's *A Cry from Heaven*, based on the *Deirdre* legend and staged at the Abbey in 2003; Macnas's production of *The Táin* in 1992; and the range of translations and adaptations of ancient Greek tragedies for the contemporary Irish stage.

The use of folk belief and legend in these productions ranges from such plays as *Sharon's Grave*, which incorporate figures from folklore into otherwise naturalistic dramas; to *Giselle*, which adapts a classical ballet that was itself originally based on Central European folklore; to palimpsestic reinterpretations of earlier material, sometimes from other genres, such as *By the*

*Bog of Cats, Ariel,* and *The Story of the Bull.* The variety of work includes new scripts, contemporary reinterpretations by directors and actors of earlier works, and collaborative creations like the work of Fabulous Beast Theatre Company. Yet despite this variety of approach, what these productions have in common is their transformation of original material for performance before a contemporary audience – and, indeed, for performance before an international audience, where it is at least possible that the reception of the work will be shaped by its national provenance. The international audience is composed both of those who travel to the Festival, and of those who see the work later, on tour.

Within Ireland, given the status of the Dublin Theatre Festival as a showcase for the best Irish work alongside work from the international stage, the choice of material provokes questions about its function in a globalized, post-industrial economy. This essay explores these questions in relation to work by Marina Carr and Michael Keegan-Dolan of Fabulous Beast, which uses the Irish midlands as the dramatic setting. Both artists may be said to have created 'Midlands Trilogies' of work that can stand alone but which are linked by recurrent themes, images, and conflicts. The main emphasis is on four Dublin Theatre Festival productions that explicitly feature the natural landscape on stage: Carr's *By the Bog of Cats,* and Fabulous Beast's trilogy. The essay examines the transformation of the original material through the use of the grotesque, and then considers the resulting representations as part of a dialogue about contemporary Irish society. Although the work all premiered at the Festival, the significance of the Festival in their creation and production varies. Fabulous Beast's first production, *Giselle,* premiered in Dublin and later toured to the Barbican. The Barbican's co-commissioning of the later works – *The Bull* and *James Son of James* – therefore exemplifies the role of the Festival in the promotion of new work by Irish companies. In the case of Carr, the Festival's role is arguably less important, since the selection of her work for production seems primarily to have been part of a process of canonization, and a testament to her status as Ireland's premiere woman dramatist. However, by programming these new works with productions of earlier, canonical plays, the Festival facilitates a dialogue about Ireland's changing society.

It is significant that these representations of contemporary Ireland are set in the midlands, a space that was largely ignored until recently as a locus for dramatic action. As a fictional dramatic space, the midlands have historically been less significant in Irish theatre than either Dublin or the west of Ireland. From Ballybeg to Mayo, and from the Aran Islands to Kerry, the west of Ireland has conventionally represented authentic Ireland, particularly in the peasant play genre and also in the contemporary theatre. Even McDonagh's parodic and violent anti-pastoral comedies are set in the west, simultaneously reinforcing and parodying its ubiquity. Christopher Morash notes that the cottage-kitchen set, the conventional design for plays set in the west, was first used by the Irish Literary Theatre in 1901 for Hyde's *Casadh an tSúgáin*. The company had re-used it sixteen times by 1911, and 'by the middle of the twentieth century it would be embarrassingly ubiquitous,' states Morash.[1] Both implicit and explicit representations of the west of Ireland as a site of authentic and uncorrupted Irishness, in theatrical representation and in nationalist discourse, are well documented.[2] The other iconic setting is the Dublin tenement which, as Grene writes, is not very different dramaturgically from the rural settings of the earlier plays: 'The box-set which enclosed the space of the country cottage could be, and no doubt was, reused with a minimum of adaptation to make up the one room on view in O'Casey's first two tenement plays.'[3] The representation of the Dublin tenements was received as authentic, Grene argues, because of the topicality of the events depicted in the Dublin Trilogy, and because O'Casey was generally believed to have emerged from the tenements himself, and so was understood to be recording lived experience (155). Regardless of authenticity, the Dublin setting functions as a recognizable image of urban Ireland and a counterpoint to the rural West.

And yet, though the midlands region has rarely been represented on the Irish stage, it is the ubiquitous Irish landscape. As bogland, it is an iconic space that signifies Ireland to an international audience. It is a colonial trope – many of the derogatory names for Irish people reference the bogs – and in colloquial speech to say someone is from the bogs is similarly to dismiss them as uncivilized and unsophisticated. The work of Fabulous Beast and Carr both play upon this sense of the midlands bog as a savage place. Yet the bogland is also celebrated in culture and literature as a characteristic geographic feature of the country and a preserver of its ancient, and recent, history. Heaney's bog poems, adapted by Big Telly Theatre Company in 2007 into five short plays titled *Bog People*, address the power of the bog both to preserve and destroy. Although neither the plays nor the poems make the point explicitly, the motif of corpses found in the bog inevitably recalls the violence in Northern Ireland, the disappeared, and the grief of the bereaved.

Yet despite the iconicity of the setting, the performances exhibit a grotesque savagery which limits the possibility for spectators to engage with the productions as nostalgic evocations of a lost golden age, or as innocent pastoral images of rural life. While this is also true of revivals of earlier plays, like the dystopia in Druid's productions of Keane, more radical shifts in representation are apparent in these contemporary midlands dramas. For example, there is no sense in which Druid's production of John B. Keane's plays arouses a longing for the Ireland of the 1950s or 1960s; on the contrary, *Sharon's Grave* evoked the harshness of life at that time through the bare domestic interior of the set and the desperation with which the characters struggle for ownership of pitifully meagre possessions. Most powerfully, however, it is evoked in Frankie McCafferty's performance of Dinzee Conlee's maimed body, and in the harsh, staccato rhythm of the voices and the awkward eroticism of Peader's expression of his love for Trassie. These characters struggle with life, grasping at every shard of happiness and comfort. Yet, with the exception of Dinzee, they maintain a pitiful dignity in the midst of their poverty. This is less true of the midlands plays discussed here: in the work of Carr and Keegan-Dolan, the characters are sometimes identified with marginalized communities (Carr's characters are often descended from 'Tinkers'), and are always physically, psychologically, or morally deformed. Both artists represent characters who are lame, dumb, one-eyed, and despairing, as well as lecherous, venal, greedy, and murderous. These characters do not often suffer the hardships of Keane's characters; more often, they are self-made wealthy businessmen and women, and their impoverishment is spiritual and moral rather than material.

Joe Cleary writes:

> The woebegone midland settings to be found in Carr's plays ... ostensibly recall the old naturalist drama, but her characters are so extravagantly crazy, repressed and demented that what we get is a grand guignol version of naturalism ... the new neo-naturalism [post-1990], would seem to signal that one of the fundamental literary paradigms of post-independence culture is now finally breaking up. But if this is so, then the once dominant naturalist aesthetic is not displaced by some entirely new aesthetic agenda: instead, the old naturalism is denaturalized by pushing its content and conventions to violent or kitschy extremes.4

For Cleary, the naturalist aesthetic in Ireland, which is still apparent in revivals of Keane and Synge, historically offered a mode of social critique that was imbued with a 'strong sense of post-revolutionary disenchantment' yet which desired 'normalization, not radical transformation' (141-2). The work of the post-revolutionary playwrights no longer sought utopia, but a feasible strategy for progress in the new and impoverished state. If, as Cleary argues, the new neo-naturalist aesthetic signals the breaking up of literary paradigms, it would seem to be offering a more despairing form of social critique, one where the moments of joy and celebration are carnivalesque or even destructive. Meanwhile the ceremonies and rituals that formerly underpinned social stability are reimagined as comical and grotesque. Witness the wedding in *By the Bog of Cats* which has four women dressed in white: the bride herself, her jilted rival, the groom's illegitimate daughter, and his mother. The essence of the marriage ritual is the conjoining of one man and one woman in a mutually monogamous relationship intended to produce a new family, intended as a stable and stabilizing social structure, through a ceremony that has both religious and legal status. That notion is challenged, however, by the appearance on stage of a very different vision of the contemporary family that is both unstable and destabilizing, and that originates, and ends, in death.

The landscape of the bog is often represented aurally and diegetically in the work of Marina Carr, yet apart from *By the Bog of Cats* it is only occasionally evoked visually on stage. In the original production of *The Mai* (1994), Kathy Strachan's design emphasized an interior space and the water beyond its windows to give visual expression to the dramatic setting, while in the 1996 premiere of *Portia Coughlan* Kandis Cook's design was an expressionistic, painted backdrop depicting distorted faces of the community with props to suggest the different dramatic spaces and a downstage area designated as the riverbank. Frank Conway's design for *Ariel* was a stylized domestic interior, into which the surrounding landscape intrudes only once: in Act 2, in an expressionistic scene when the central character is suddenly lost in the horror he has created. However, as discussed by Cathy Leeney elsewhere in this book, the first production of *By the Bog of Cats* used the setting of the bog for all of the performance, although the text suggests at least partially cultivated spaces near Hester's caravan.

The bog setting is signalled by the play's title; in the dialogue; in the accents of the characters which are suggested in the written text and concretized in performance, and in the set: a steppe of black and white frozen bogland, built on different levels. The minimal use of props and furniture maintains the oneiric quality of the piece, as does the shifting, hallucinogenic landscape of the bog communicated through the dialogue. It is a watery landscape, a liminal space that is neither lake nor dry land, populated with grotesques. This watery quality, shared with Fabulous Beast's trilogy, recalls Frye's mythoi of the seasons, specifically the mythos of Winter: irony and satire. He describes irony and satire structurally as a parody of romance, and as an attempt to give form to the 'mythical patterns of experience ... the shifting patterns and ambiguities of un-idealized existence'.[5] Speaking of water, he writes that it 'traditionally belongs to a realm of existence below human life, the state of chaos or dissolution which follows ordinary death, or the reduction to the inorganic. Hence the soul frequently crosses water or sinks into it at death' (146). Frye links certain kinds of irony, characterized by a sense of futility and of nightmare, to the demonic, and one of the central themes of demonic imagery is parody.

In using the term 'parody', which often has connotations of humour, I refer to Linda Hutcheon's definition of 'the paradoxes of parody' as 'signalling ironic difference at the heart of similarity and as an authorized transgression of convention' requiring investigation 'by a doubled model that combined the semiotic with the formally intertextual'.[6] Using Hutcheon's definition, I propose that Carr parodies the genre of classical tragedy in *By the Bog of Cats* and *Ariel*, successfully in the case of the former, but unsuccessfully in the latter. The locus for this parodic engagement with Aristotle's prescription for tragedy is the bog – the watery and shifting dramatic space where things are not as they seem; as one of the characters says, 'ya know this auld bog, always shiftin' and changin' and coddin' the eye'.[7] Similarly, the watery landscapes of *The Bull* and *James Son of James* in particular, attest to the parodic adaptation of both the heroic *Táin* and the Christ story. In both, the instability of the landscape is made visible on stage through mud that covers the floor in *The Bull*, and the water revealed beneath the floorboards in *James*. Like *By the Bog of Cats*, these texts engage with core texts of Irish and Western culture respectively.

In *Revolution in Poetic Language*, Julia Kristeva defines intertextuality as the 'transposition of one (or several) sign system(s) into another ... it specifies that the passage from one signifying system to another demands a new articulation of the thetic – of enunciative and denotative positionality'.[8] She continues:

> If one grants that every signifying practice is a field of transpositions of various signifying systems (an intertextuality), one then understands that its 'place' of enunciation and its denoted 'object' are never single,

complete, and identical to themselves, but always plural, shattered, capable of being tabulated (60).

Read thus, Marina Carr's play *By the Bog of Cats* can be seen to transpose the myth of Medea (with reference also to Dido and Aeneas) and Euripides' classical tragedy, onto a drama which explores the psychological journeys of Irish women through a representation of the social and cultural landscape of contemporary Ireland.[9] But this play, though finally tragic, incorporates elements explicitly excluded from the Aristotelian definition of tragedy, carnivalizing not only Euripides' version of the myth (its Ur-Text), but the very genre to which it belongs.

> Tragedy, then, is an imitation of an action that is serious, complete, and of a certain magnitude; in language embellished with each kind of artistic ornament ... in the form of action, not of narrative; through pity and fear effecting the proper purgation of those emotions ... [the character] is that of a man who is not eminently good and just, yet whose misfortune is brought about not by vice or depravity, but by some error or frailty. He must be one who is highly renowned and prosperous.[10]

I have quoted Aristotle at length to draw attention to Carr's subversive fulfilment of his prescriptions. *By the Bog of Cats* imitates an action that is of a certain magnitude: Hester Swane's murder of her only child and of herself. The tragedy is in the form of the action, and revolves around characters who are, in a sense, 'renowned and prosperous' — yet only by the standards of the Bog. Carthage is a subsistence farmer. Xavier Cassidy, Carr's counterpart to Creon, is a brutal incestuous small-time landowner, whose power is strictly local. They are piddling heroes. Hester Swane herself is no better than she should be: an uneducated, dispossessed woman; a fratricide; mother of an illegitimate and half-neglected child; an alcoholic. The Catwoman tells her that 'not everywan knows the price of wrong. You do and it's the best thing about ya *and there's not much in ya I'd praise*' (276, emphasis added). This construction of character parodies Aristotle's prescriptions, even as it fulfils them. Tragic language is 'language into which rhythm, "harmony", and song enter' (Aristotle: 10/VI), and characters' speech is a masterful blend of local pleasure in metaphor, vivid imagery, and casual profanity, with a baroque sheen borrowed from classical myth. This vivid language is further embellished with song: Carr includes two which are to be sung at points during the play, both of them eerie, sinister mockeries of the folksong. Yet Carr's mimetic reproduction of the Midlands dialect mocks the received concept of civilized, standard English, just as Hester, the central character, mimics Medea, Barbarian Princess, granddaughter of the Sun, in both her actions and in her construction. Hester is presented as 'Barbarian' through her tinker blood which, tellingly, she inherits from her mother, the source of contamination and despair.

However, Carr's text not only subverts, in its mimicry of classical conventions. It also satirizes, introducing elements which are unsuitable for the noble world of ancient tragedy. These grotesqueries and comic exchanges further set the action within the mythos of Winter, the mythos of satire. The blind seer Tiresias is replaced with the figure of the Catwoman, a blind seer who eats live mice. 'If ya could see yourself and the mouse fur growin' out of your teeth', Hester tells her in disgust; Catwoman replies, 'I need mice the way you need whiskey' (273). This seer undermines the concept of Fate, telling Hester that she can escape, if she will: 'There's ways round curses. Curses only have the power ya allow them' (276). And the function of the chorus is largely performed by a hodge-podge of eccentrics, who include Carthage's vitriolic mother, the lascivious and irreverent Father Willow, and the forlorn ghost of Joseph Swane.

The grotesque aspect of Carr's work has been discussed by a number of critics, including Victor Merriman in his essay, 'Decolonisation Postponed: The Theatre of Tiger Trash'. Merriman criticizes Carr for locating her female protagonists at the Nature side of the Reason/Nature dialectic and argues that she presents marginalized characters – Travellers and an economic underclass – for the entertainment of the middle class theatre audience.[11] It can be argued, however, that Carr's plays present a grotesque reflection of contemporary Ireland, and that the audience are intended to see, not their 'Other', but themselves. This grotesque aesthetic is most successful when used to subvert heroic or classical genres, as in *By the Bog of Cats* or *The Bull*. Even more extravagantly in the work of Fabulous Beast, the middle class audience see themselves in monstrous shape, bloated on the Celtic Tiger and over-whelmingly engaged in a display of ostentatious consumption. In contrast, Carr's later play *Ariel*, which arguably attempted instead a democratization of classical tragedy in its adaptation of the *Oresteia* to contemporary Ireland, was not well received by critics. Similarly in Keegan-Dolan's oeuvre, the most successful of his productions for the Dublin Theatre Festival have been *Giselle* in 2003 and *The Bull* in 2005, both of which adapted pre-existing texts to represent violent dramatic worlds inhabited by monstrous characters. These make use of cross-gender casting to engage playfully with gender signifiers such as costume, hair, and material physicality.

The midlands in Keegan-Dolan's work is a flat, featureless space which also, in *Giselle*, suggests the American prairies through the use of cowboy boots as a key item of costume, and a steer's skull which is one of the few props used in the production. Stage right is a telegraph pole on which Giselle's father perches for most of the performance. The telegraph pole signifies the possibility of communication with the outside world, the world from which some of the characters enter − such as Albrecht, the bisexual dancing teacher from Bratislava whom Giselle loves. In *James Son of James*, the landscape is again represented by a flat stage, with the water beneath the boards revealed at various points. In conjunction with the skeletal building site that forms the main visual focus of the set, and which suggests something unfinished − and, since it topples at the end, precarious − the instability of land which floats above water signifies the unfixed, in-flux nature of the dramatic world. The set is read quite differently by different critics, though in each case as suggestive of instability. Helen Meany, writing for *The Guardian*, describes it as representing 'Ireland's precarious property boom ... still under construction in the opening scene',[12] while Judith Mackrell, reviewing the piece from the Barbican, sees it as a 'huge wooden cut-out house' that 'serves as an ingenious series of locations'.[13] The idea of a cut-out house, a house that no longer functions as a closed, private space or a space of security but that instead exposes its contents and occupants to the threatening external world, may be read as a comment on recent shifts in Irish culture and identity, particularly when set against the 'embarrassingly ubiquitous'[14] naturalistic box-set of the country kitchen. While exposing its occupants to the outside world, this set also allows that world in. In the traditional space associated in performance with the stable, monogamous Irish family of the peasant plays, or even of McDonagh's comedies, this skeleton is home to a multicultural, multilinguistic, multiracial cast. It is, therefore, permeated by the outside world, even though it is situated in an iconic Irish landscape. It may be read extra-nationally as a comment on the shared experience of postmodern, post-industrial economies as they adjust to multicultural, shifting populations. However, a more cynical reading would suggest that the multiculturalism of the work is shallow and largely visual and aural; the structures and norms operational in Irish society, and in theatrical production and promotion, are largely unchanged.

Keegan-Dolan's most extraordinary engagement with the midlands landscape, however, is to be seen in *The Bull*, his adaptation of *Táin Bó Cuailgne*. Fintan O'Toole's review praises this show as 'the first great piece of theatre about the new hyped-up twenty-first century Ireland'. He describes it as

> a hilarious new Irish comedy, a scintillating new satire on Celtic Tiger Ireland, a profound reflection on the continuing resonance of Irish mythology, a raw, fast-paced Irish crime thriller, a vastly impressive exercise in avant-garde physical theatre, a quirky new Irish musical, and even a new post-*Riverdance* Irish dancing show.

It involves the performers in the extraordinary virtuoso feat of dancing in clay, as the stage is covered in a layer of earth which is saturated with water over the course of the performance to create muck. This presents the spectator with a visual and aural representation of the bog in which the characters live, and which the dancers must negotiate in performance.

Violence in Carr's work is represented through language and accent, and through the mutilation evident in the characters' bodies (one-eyed Stacia and lame Raphael in *Portia Coughlan*; the blind Catwoman and the broken Caroline in *By the Bog of Cats*). It is evident in the characters' psychological torment, most noticeably in the presentation of the unmothered and unmothering female protagonists. In Keegan-Dolan's work, the violence is visceral, physically enacted on stage, and reiterated in the difficulty and enforced violence of dancing in mud. *The Bull* imagines Queen Maeve and her husband Ailill as Maeve and Alan Fogarty, Dublin millionaires. Maeve has invested in a dance show titled *Celtic Bitch*, a parodic representation of *Riverdance*, whose title aptly characterizes the Ireland represented here: crude, amoral, frantic, and bawdy. Its lead dancer is her lover, but he has 'fucked' his knees and his career is suffering. She goes in pursuit of the Bull, which belongs to a family of psychopathic Midlands builders called Cullen; but they are not about to part with it, not for all the ranch-style bungalows in the commuter belt. In its representation of sex and murder, it puts onto the stage a carnivalesque feast of all that lurked beneath the surface of conservative Catholic Ireland. The characters are smothered in plastic bags, hacked with sléans and axes, and beaten in the mud. Played by Olwen Fouéré, Maeve is sexually voracious, coupling violently with a number of the male characters and leading the naked Milos Galko, who plays her bull terrier, around on a leash. Her age positions her unequivocally as sexually powerful and dominant. Where a younger actress might have been reduced to a pretty body displayed on stage to the spectatorial gaze, Fouéré's ferocity and the contrast between the body of the older woman and those of the younger male actors lends the representation a kind of sexual potency that is rarely attributed to women on the Irish stage and that unsettles normative gender stereotypes.

Although the action is based on the plot of the *Táin*, Keegan-Dolan's production erases the heroism, self-sacrifice, and nobility of the epic poem, and reduces the characters' motivations to self-serving greed and the urge to satisfy their carnal appetites. In place of epic, we find a soap opera of adultery and murder and a postmodern kitsch rendition of traditional culture in the show *Celtic Bitch*. The piece offers a strange combination of cultural heritage, multicultural cast, and mass media storyline, and it is presumably this mix of 'old' and 'new' Irelands that O'Toole welcomes so enthusiastically in his review. Like *James Son of James*, *The Bull* resonates with audiences who are not familiar with the source material. Judith Mackrell's review of the Barbican performances provides little information about the *Táin*, other than to describe it as a '12th-century Irish epic … about two families and their long feud over a prize bull.' However, she describes the production as a 'ruthlessly comic anatomisation of greed, stupidity and corruption as the two families… are slaughtered in a deliriously accelerating torrent of tribal bloodlust'. The comic and outrageous murders and the 'swipes the show takes at modern Ireland: the Church, Michael Flatley, consumer and celebrity culture surreally and savagely lampooned' offer the London audience, unfamiliar with the legend, a way to access the material. The reference to 'tribal bloodlust' may sit uncomfortably with contemporary Ireland's sense of itself, post-Ceasefire. But the popular culture references and soap opera storylines in Fabulous Beast's work undoubtedly address an international audience and ease the play's transition across cultural boundaries. This is work that, despite its local resonance, is designed to travel. Keegan-Dolan's interview with Susan Conley in the programme makes clear that he wishes to reject 'diddley-eye' versions of the *Táin* to focus instead on 'the dynamic or the psychology of the power struggle'.[15]

*The Bull* presents its audience with a cast of bizarre and misshapen characters who are that audience in distorted portraiture: business people, builders, dancers, nurses, housewives, mothers, and fathers. It offers a savagely ironic representation, not of a violent and debased underclass, but of the new glitterati. In addressing a native audience, the play reads like a furious rejection of the politically and economically repressive past, and, as unlovely as they are, the characters' frenzied pursuit of wealth and sex is also a vast rage to possess all that the world has to offer. This greed attests to what has gone before: not a lost golden age of simplicity, but a time when it was difficult to scrape a living and when all the wealth that

Maeve and Alan can now access was beyond imagination. In these ironic comedies, the laughter comes from the cruel infliction of pain on the victim and from the overwhelming experience of witnessing greater and greater acts of violence; but there is pathos in the refusal to contemplate the past. In that sense, these productions engage in dialogue with works like *Sharon's Grave*, the Synge cycle, and *The Dandy Dolls*, with the grim contemporary productions providing a contrast and a background to the lurid present.

The bogland setting complicates the rejection of history. The physical representation of the bog on stage ties the characters to the land through a visual reference to that most immediately recognizable Irish landscape. As the performers struggle to move and dance in clay the audience are presented with a metaphor of the power of history and the difficulty of escaping it: the characters are literally spattered with it. As in Heaney's poetry, the bog functions as a space of remembrance, a preservative of history and of past life. The 'new Irish' – the Slavic, African, and Italian dancers with the company – are similarly dashed with the landscape and incorporated into it, although disappointingly, their presence does not seem to offer any commentary. They are simply present, in the bog, but are largely incidental. Their presence is a by-product of the economic boom.

The bogland setting in these works, particularly in *By the Bog of Cats* and *The Bull* where it is visually and aurally represented on stage, gives a physical expression to the shifting and uncertain nature of the dramatic world. The watery landscape of the bog shown in the frozen steppe of the bog of cats, the muck and the skeletal house, comments on the characters' embeddedness in their site of origin and on its inescapability. In the shifting and unstable landscape, despite the characters' oddly moving fear of history, they are haunted by ghosts, wilis, and their own actions: they reject the past, but it laps beneath the floor of the stage or spatters their bodies, constantly threatening to swallow them up. Although these plays, as Cleary argues, signal cultural change by denaturalizing naturalism (99), using psychological, verbal, and physical violence, kitsch, and the grotesque to create monstrous visions of contemporary Ireland, they continue to speak to their society's enduring relationship to history. In a dialogue that the Dublin Theatre Festival programming has facilitated during the past decade, these plays engage with contemporary productions of earlier, naturalistic texts, while also forming part of a body of new work that draws upon myth, legend, and folklore to adapt traditional material for contemporary society.

---

[1] Christopher Morash, *A History of Irish Theatre 1601-2000* (Cambridge: Cambridge University Press, 2002), p. 121.

[2] See for example the debates of the Gaelic League, the journalism of D.P. Moran, documentation on the *Playboy* riots in Grene's *The Politics of Irish Drama*, Pilkington's *Theatre and State in Twentieth Century Ireland*, and Ferriter's *The Transformation of Ireland 1900-2000*.

[3] Nicholas Grene, *The Politics of Irish Drama* (Cambridge: Cambridge University Press, 1999), p. 132. The subsequent reference appears parenthetically in the text.

[4] Joe Cleary, *Outrageous Fortune: Capital and Culture in Modern Ireland* (Dublin: Field Day Publications, 2007), pp. 99-100. The subsequent reference appears parenthetically in the text.

[5] Northrop Frye, *Anatomy of Criticism* (Princeton and Oxford: Princeton University Press, 1957; 2000), p. 223. The subsequent reference appears parenthetically in the text.

[6] Linda Hutcheon, *The Poetics of Postmodernism* (New York and London: Routledge, 1988). p. x

[7] Marina Carr, *By the Bog of Cats, Plays 1* (London: Faber and Faber, 1999), p. 267. Subsequent references appear parenthetically in the text.

[8] Julia Kristeva, *Revolution in Poetic Language* (New York: Columbia University Press, 1984), pp. 59-60. The subsequent reference appears parenthetically in the text.

[9] 'Psychological journeys' is a phrase used by Victoria White in her newspaper article, 'Women Writers Finally Take Centre Stage' *The Irish Times* 15 October 1998.

[10] Aristotle, *Poetics*, trans. S.H. Butcher (New York: Dover Publications, 1997) pp. 14 and 23.

[11] Victor Merriman, 'The Theatre of Tiger Trash' *Irish University Review* 29. 2  Autumn/Winter 1999, p. 317.

[12] Helen Meany, 'James Son of James' *The Guardian* 5 October 2007.

[13] Judith Mackrell, 'Fabulous Beast' *The Guardian* 7 February 2008.

[14] Christopher Morash, ibid., p.121.

[15] 'The Fabulous Beast Within: Michael Keegan-Dolan in conversation with Susan Conley.' Programme, *The Story of the Bull*, Dublin Theatre Festival 2005.

# 14 | The Dublin Theatre Festival: Social and Cultural Contexts

Fintan O'Toole

[This is an edited transcript of a talk given by Fintan O'Toole during the Irish Theatrical Diaspora Conference at the 2007 Dublin Theatre Festival.]

I want to talk about how we can relate the Dublin Theatre Festival both to Irish society over the last fifty years, and to Irish theatre generally. It's important to start with the way in which the Festival outgrew and to some extent contradicted its own origins. It's worth putting that into the context of what the grand narrative of the late 1950s was in Ireland, and to consider how the Festival was originally intended to reflect that grand narrative.

That narrative involved facing up to the inadequacies of Irish nationalism as a political and economic construct. Lemass and Whitaker, with their 1958 Programme for Economic Expansion, implicitly admitted that the foundation of the state as an autarchic entity had failed. They did not accept that the foundation of the state *itself* had failed, but that Ireland could no longer exist as an entity that was self-sufficient, as it had been imagined in the 1930s.

Part of that project necessitated a degree of cultural self-reflection. This involved trying to make the case that the core of the nationalist project was not economic but cultural – that, essentially, what nationalism involved was the maintenance and sustaining of an independent Irish *identity*. It didn't really matter what the economics of the situation were; it was no longer important to express our sense of a monolithic and independent Irish cultural identity through an economics of self-sufficiency. The logic of breaking this link between self-sufficiency and national identity was that, in Marxist terms, there was no impact of the base on the superstructure – that economics could change many things, but that it would not change Irish culture. Ireland could move from an economic model that involved high tariff-barriers and was relatively isolated, to a new model that we would now call globalization (though the phrase wasn't used in that sense at the time) but this change could be made without fundamental cultural consequences. Or, if there *were* cultural consequences, they would be essentially conservative. The intention was to reanimate the economy in a way that was aimed primarily at ending emigration, and which would (paradoxically) open Ireland up to the world economically, in order to allow it to become a more enclosed space – politically, socially, and culturally.

It's important to remember that in the 1950s the Catholic Church (for example) was one of the great forces arguing for change, because it saw how the economic consequences of an autarchic philosophy were playing themselves out: we were seeing the deconstruction of the Irish family, of Irish rural society, of the very conservative values that the Church supported itself. This was a cultural moment when it was felt that Ireland could change everything about itself, and the result would be conservative; it could fundamentally alter the way in which its society and economic system were organized, and those changes would only make us culturally more like ourselves.

This idea was I think expressed most vividly by the author of the entire policy, T.K. Whitaker, the great Secretary of the Department of Finance whose Programme for Economic Expansion is one of the most important cultural texts of the 1950s, as well as being one of the most important economic and political texts of the period. Whitaker once wrote about what the new Ireland was going to be like, and what was going to happen in this modernizing process. He described having visited German monasteries that were founded by Irish monks in the early Middle Ages, and seeing in them images of Irish saints and German saints side by side. He thought that this is what the Irish future was going to be like: instead of having some kind of anarchic change in the social structure, we would just add a couple of international Catholic saints to our collection of Irish Catholic saints. The metaphor he applied was that we would have a bit of German efficiency and productivity co-existing with Irish virtues, within the same imagined cultural structures that had been there from the beginning.

The foundation of the Dublin Theatre Festival was a direct response to that impulse; it came out of that mode of imagining how a stable culture could go hand-in-hand with the big economic changes that were taking place at the time. It imagined the Festival as a cultural version of the economic modernization project: you would take a resource (in this case culture) and export it or sell it. Culture would become part of the tourist industry and acquire a productive capacity in economic terms; and it would therefore help to underpin and to some extent demonstrate to the rest of the world the process of economic modernization going on in Ireland at the time. It's a perfectly comprehensible and, in some ways, quite logical way of thinking about the purpose of the Festival in its early years.

As you know, however, the contradictions of that project were immediately evident. There was *The Rose Tattoo* case in the first Festival in 1957, and then the cancellation of the 1958 Festival after the clash with Archbishop John Charles McQuaid over the proposed productions of Joyce and O'Casey. Those conflicts had the enormous benefit of demonstrating from the very beginning that the founding ideas of the Festival weren't feasible: they demonstrated that the Festival was actually promoting a form of Irish culture that did *not* have the stabilizing conservative capacity that Irish culture was imagined as having.

Irish theatre in the 1950s was itself a conflicted zone. It's very easy to look back and say that, prior to the 1950s, Irish theatre was very conservative. It certainly was, but the maintenance of that conservatism was a full time job: it was extraordinarily difficult in the 1950s to retain the idea that Irish theatre presented an acceptable version of Ireland to Irish people, never mind to the rest of the world. It's not accidental that much of the 1950s is characterized, really for the first time, by the importation of the state censorship which applied to written literature into the dramatic sphere. It wasn't legislative censorship, but self-censorship, and all the sharper, therefore, and more damaging. These are the years when the only badge of merit for an Irish playwright was rejection by the Abbey. When the Abbey was celebrating its centenary in 2004, I half-jokingly urged that they should do a season of plays that they had rejected; it might have been a lot better than the season of plays that they actually did. It is worth reminding ourselves that almost every single interesting play of that period was rejected by the theatre – and the few that somehow did get through, like John Murphy's *The Country Boy* (1959), were met with responses which didn't at all mirror their quality. Brendan Behan was rejected; John B. Keane was rejected; Tom Murphy was rejected. There was an impulse within the Irish theatre that was questioning, critical, and is in some way destructive of the old certainties, but unofficial censorship had been so effective in blocking this impulse that no-one realized that allowing Irish writers to put on their plays would give it release.

A very simple example is Tom Murphy's great play *A Whistle in the Dark* (1961). Ernest Blythe's rejection of that play for the Abbey was quite vicious: instead of the standard letter of rejection from the theatre, he sent one saying 'there are no such people in Ireland as are represented in your play'. Implicit in the period of the Festival's beginning was a conflict between an official version of what Ireland was supposed to be, and what you were actually going to see if you put these plays on. In hindsight, therefore, it seems inevitable that the initial project of the Festival – as a nice little earner, a showcase for the rest of the world of how civilized we were – was unlikely to be fulfilled. The influence of the Festival was evident not just in terms of how it presented a wider set of theatrical images to an Irish audience. It also put pressure on the Irish state by the almost accidental validation of a set of energies which were not intended to be validated.

It would have been rather pleasant for official Ireland if the 1958 Festival non-event had become permanent, if the implicit tensions had become so obvious that people said that they should cancel the Festival entirely: all it was going to involve was making a show of ourselves 'in front of the foreigners'. That, in fact, is what actually happened in 1958: the 1958 Festival was arguably one of the most brilliant Dublin Theatre Festivals ever staged, since it said an enormous amount about Irish culture, Irish society, and Ireland's relationship to the rest of the world. It was not accidental, for example, that one of the spurs for the state's action against the Pike's production of *The Rose Tattoo* was a review in the London *Times* which stated in passing that a condom had been dropped on stage. If this had appeared in *The Irish Times*, they perhaps wouldn't have bothered objecting: the fact that this was internationally recorded as happening in Dublin may well have been one of the factors behind the case.

You could say, therefore, that the Festival was by force of circumstance addressing itself both inwards and outwards, and both upwards and downwards. It was addressing theatre audiences (as of course it was supposed to do), but it was also implicitly addressing the state, forcing the state to acknowledge that there was a cultural space in which unpleasant things could happen and could be discussed, and in which unpleasant images could be shown. Understanding that helps you to understand why historically the Festival had an impact that was disproportionate to its economic strength. In international terms it was a relatively small and very poorly resourced Festival, making the importance it acquired all the more remarkable.

One of the major effects of the Festival was gradually to alter the programming of the main Irish theatres. The need to put on a play for the Festival had an impact on what the mainstream Irish theatres would do each year. So it is in the Festival that we first hear the voice of Hugh Leonard, beginning to become very adventurous in what he's doing theatrically with *Stephen D.* (1962) – a kind of response in itself to the fact that a previous adaptation of Joyce had brought the 1958 Festival down. You find Friel's *Philadelphia, Here I Come!* in 1964, with its fundamental questioning of some of the main co-ordinates of Irish culture: space, exile, family, generational relationships, even the Irish personality. Friel's play acts out the idea that there is such a severe division between our public image of ourselves and our private realities, that you have to have two people playing one young Irish person. This was itself a profound statement of the tensions in the culture between what people knew to be true and what was acceptable to say, between the face that was shown to the rest of the world and the face that we show to ourselves. The exploration of sexuality and of family tensions was also evident in Eugene McCabe's *The King of the Castle* (1964). Then there was Thomas Kilroy's *The Death and Resurrection of Mr Roche* in 1968. Frank McGuinness expressed it best when he said that play isn't about homosexuality but heterosexuality: that by putting a gay man on stage you problematize Irish heterosexuality. That play had a fundamental power, using the idea of difference as the grit for an exploration of the psychological and cultural tensions within that group of Irish men.

Tom Murphy's *Famine* was also significant. It was the first time Murphy had an Irish premiere since the one-act amateur play *On the Outside* appeared in 1959, and he returned from London to Ireland in 1968 in the context of the Festival. As I have said, his previous great play *A Whistle in the Dark* had been condemned by Blythe not only because it misrepresented people living in Ireland – the Irish of the play, of course, aren't living in Ireland but in Coventry – but also because of its treatment of violence. Official culture responded to it as a play that let us down in front of the foreigners: it was being performed in the West End, and was portraying us as a bunch of savages. This is what makes the return of Murphy with *Famine* in the 1968 Festival so important.

*Famine* itself is an extraordinary representation of the power of international theatrical modes to explore fundamental historical issues within the Irish psyche and within the Irish culture that emerged from the Famine. *Famine* is not a play about the Great Famine, although it's set in that period – it's a play about what the experience of going through a famine does to the collective psychology of a nation, about why we are we so afraid, why we are so ungenerous as a consequence. What's striking about *Famine* when you look at it now is that it embodies in both form and content the idea that Irish theatre is an international entity. *Famine* is the first Irish play to take up from Eugene O'Neill's *Long Day's Journey into Night* the question of what happens to people when they go through hunger. At the same time, in its form it's using a Brechtian expressionist mode to explore not just the surface of Irish society, but the very deepest wellsprings of what is wrong with us. Thus *Famine* embodied a very different version of what the Festival could achieve. Instead of the original impulse to show the world how wonderful we were, it presented a play that in the most intimate way used the international mode to explore the very deepest intimacies of the Irish psyche – putting a very different kind of German saint side by side with our Irish saints. So by the late 1960s, the remit of the Festival had reversed itself completely.

I would suggest that this is a useful way of looking at how the Festival operated, even though it is obviously very crude and leaves out all sorts of distinctions. Rather than the Festival being a showcase for Irish theatre – or just some kind of caesura, a big punctuating event in the theatre going on all the time with some international stuff thrown in to make it even bigger – something much more profound was happening. Irish theatre, Irish audiences, and certainly Irish playwrights, were seeing the Festival itself as a context in which you could do *more*, in which you could present work raising fundamental questions not just about Irish culture as it had been, but also about an emerging Irish cultural project. It's striking that within a decade of the foundation of the Festival, the important new Irish plays being produced in it are subverting the idea with which the Festival started – that you could change everything but not affect the underlying culture. What the Festival is increasingly saying is that the culture itself is the problem – who we are, who we think we are, how our official versions of ourselves relate to the everyday lives of real Irish people – these questions not only will be affected by change, but they *need* to be affected by change.

This represents a tension within the grand narrative of Irish modernization. On the one side, there is that idea that economic change is possible without cultural change, and on the other side there are the playwrights, declaring in effect that all other change is immaterial if cultural changes do not happen. You can change your economic circumstances, they are saying, but unless you undertake a cultural or even a spiritual process of engagement with the secrets of Irish society – its internal tensions, the lies we tell ourselves – then you are missing the point of change. There's a contest between a political version of modernization and a cultural version of modernization, the legislators and the 'unacknowledged legislators' in direct conflict. The political narrative continues to maintain that everything is fine: it's getting better, we've never had it so good, there's a boom going on. At the same time, there is a cultural narrative heavily concentrated on theatre – not exclusive to theatre but finding its sharpest expression in that medium – claiming the space of modernization for the writers, because the tensions in the system have opened up an empty space to be filled by the dramatization of fundamental personal conflicts.

The Festival work of Murphy, Kilroy, Friel, and many others at this time significantly explores the idea of sexuality as basic to Irish society. Running through many of these plays is a very direct attack on the tenet of the Constitution by which the fundamental unit of Irish society is the nuclear family. This idea is challenged from many angles and from different voices in Irish theatre in the 1960s by a desire to look closely at what the Irish family is and how it operates. In fact, you almost never find a conventional Irish family in any of these plays. What you get instead are extraordinary presentations of the domestic space being invaded by images of death, hatred, and violence, with all sorts of other undercurrents. *Philadelphia, Here I Come!* is one example in which the Irish mother – the core of the entire Irish system – just disappears. Running all through that work is a sense that the family space is at once an intimate personal space and a political space.

Such a perception relates to a new international understanding, signalled in the events of 1968 and the emergence of feminism, that the personal *is* political. In the Irish case that slogan is literally true, because the official version of the society is founded specifically on notions about personal behaviour, about gender roles, about the way in which the family operates as a building block for Irish society. Consequently playwrights are in a position to argue that the family comprehends everything. If you are dealing with economics, you have to deal with the family: emigration means that you cannot have your nuclear family because its nucleus is splitting, and its electrons buzzing off around the world. Sexuality itself is something that we have (ironically) attempted to keep away from the family, as though the family could be a non-sexual unit. The whole area of sexual tension and sexual ignorance underlying Irish life, which has never been properly acknowledged can only express itself in violence and conflict. This too is an underlying theme running through so much of the Festival work of the 1960s.

In the 1970s and 1980s, the international dimension of the Festival becomes more important as a direct result of the questions raised by 1960s Irish theatre. The focus on sexuality, the family, and gender means that formal questions in the theatre are no longer *just* formal questions. If personal issues are not just personal but are also about politics and society, so as the Festival develops, the questions about sexuality are no longer just national questions, and it's no longer possible to confine them within the terms of the well-made naturalistic Irish play. Hence an awareness of the body raises formal questions about theatre and theatricality, about how people move and express themselves on stage.

By the early 1980s, the single dominant image in Irish public and political life has become the body. Two major psychodramas are being played out in Ireland at this time. The first is the H-Block hunger strikes, where excrement is a weapon, where starvation of the body itself is a political weapon and a political battleground, where the whole idea of the use of the body to alter political reality has gone far beyond deconstructionist texts and has become the site for terrible political tensions in both parts of Ireland, in Britain, and echoing throughout the world. Simultaneously running is the other great psychodrama about abortion. In the run-up to the 'pro-life' referendum designed to introduce a clause proscribing abortion into the Irish Constitution, we have the emergence of a political discourse which is not dominated by economics and trade unions and government decisions, but by fallopian tubes, ectopic pregnancies, embryos, and zygotes. Specific aspects of reproduction, the body, and the control of the body, have become part of the mainstream political discourse.

It could therefore be argued that, as art so often does, the Irish theatre of the 1960s prefigured the way physicality itself became a major battleground for a whole set of tensions in Irish history concerned with the control of Irish women and the idea of what it was to be Irish. Even though they might have seemed to be about very different things, the hunger strikes and the abortion referendum were linked very closely in being attempts to assert an Irish identity. The hunger strikes were of course part of a larger narrative about Irish nationalism and Irish separatism, but it's important to remember that a key part of the abortion argument was also about our being different, distinguishing ourselves from other people, maintaining that we did not have to follow the lead of the rest of the world. The Pope's visit in 1979 provided the impetus for an attempted return to the 1950s, an effort to pretend that the forces unleashed by the globalizing project of Whitaker and Lemass were still containable, and that we could still, as in the 1950s, assert a distinctive, separate, and autarchic Irish identity.

You could say, then, that in the late 1970s and early 1980s Festival, we were almost back to where we had started. We were back with questions about whether there was a culturally distinctive Irish identity that could support a culturally distinctive Ireland, standing out against cosmopolitanism, internationalism, and globalization, the forces seen to be extraneous to Ireland. In that context, one of the reasons for the power of international theatre in Ireland was its language of the body, a language that had not been fully explored by the Irish literary theatre of the 1960s.

The production style in Irish theatre by the time that I was starting to go to the theatre in the 1970s was still highly conservative. The actor and the theatrical space were still essentially there to allow us to hear the words of the playwright; the production was acted out in the service of the content of the play. International styles brought in the sense that theatre actually does *two* things, often at the same time. It could give a unified sense of what's happening on stage, but it could give complex and contradictory senses of the one event, simultaneously verbal and visual. One might be to do with language and the other with the body, but the way the two interacted was very potent.

Clearly it wasn't only the Festival that created this in Irish theatre. If you look at the great Garry Hynes Druid productions of *The Playboy of the Western World* from the late 1970s and early 1980s, their shocking physicality was organic. It didn't come directly from the experience of the Festival or of international productions; it picked up on influences already present in the culture. I think that when influence happens, it occurs because it relates to something that's emergent anyway. You never really have an influence if what you're doing is completely unconnected to the thing that you're *trying* to influence: you have an influence when you help to articulate or catalyze forces that are already present. That's what the Festival did in the early 1980s.

1981 was the year that I became aware of this. With the visit of companies like the Wroclaw Contemporary Theatre from Poland (who came to the Festival in 1981 and 1982) you could see Irish audiences being profoundly disturbed by what they were seeing, but profoundly engaged too. They realized that theatre could function in a largely non-verbal and physical way, using image, movement, and light. This has a profound effect on audiences. I remember strongly at the time that practitioners were also talking about these developments: you could actually overhear conversations between actors and director about how interesting these productions were. There was a real sense of a connection being made.

That connection we can now see was influential in terms of theatre form, but it also had deeper resonances for the culture itself. In terms of the development of theatrical form in Ireland, it's significant that quite a number of our actors started going off to study with Marcel Marceau and Jacques Lecoq: that was a very conscious and deliberate response to seeing their techniques at the Festival. There was also a trickledown effect, with Irish productions showing greater attention to movement, greater awareness of space. Over the 1980s, Irish audiences became less tolerant of productions that didn't show that attention; so the visual awareness of Irish audiences was changing too. This appeared very directly with Tom Mac Intyre's experiments with Patrick Mason and Tom Hickey at the Peacock throughout those years, showed the possibility of a very different kind of theatre. Making those shows was a collaboration between Mason and Mac Intyre that used Tom Hickey's body as the text for what they were doing. Some of those productions were successful; some weren't; but more important than whether they worked individually was the fact that they were making a statement about how the body could be used.

One of the interesting things about this was that, paradoxically, shows coming out of the Festival began to relate themselves back to some of the misconceptions from the 1950s – and began to make some of those misconceptions seem oddly true. For instance, the idea that you could change everything about Ireland but preserve its culture had been blown away successfully throughout the 1960s and 1970s. What came back in the 1980s was a sense that, although you couldn't preserve the culture, you can attempt to ask what it was, to understand it, and to start to engage with the body of inherited Irish culture in theatrical terms. So over this period we started to see re-engagement with classic Irish texts. There was the re-evaluation of Synge: people said we can actually start 'doing Synge' now. There were also James Flannery's Yeats Festivals at the Peacock. They had mixed levels of success, but they at least tried to use techniques and ideas from an international context for plays from our own national canon that nobody had succeeded in staging in Ireland. This was also true for the Mac Intyre projects, most of which used traditional texts by writers like Patrick Kavanagh and Jonathan Swift. So there was a re-engagement with the literary tradition of Irish identity. To some extent, one paradoxical echo of the 1950s could be heard, because there was a sense in which the more internationalized Irish theatre was becoming, the better it was able to be an Irish theatre.

There is a further paradox in this view of the way the Festival has functioned: it has in fact been so successful that some of its success is now invisible. In the first place, the notion that economic change can happen without cultural change is one that we no longer would even consider to be serious. Secondly, physicality and non-verbal communication have become so much part of the mainstream in theatre, that we no longer see the development of these techniques as a function of international influence. Finally, we might say that these forces have been so profoundly influential and successful that we're faced with a reversal of the question from the 1950s. The question then was whether we could have massive economic change and massive engagement with globalization without that having any cultural effect. The question now is this: can we have any cultural identity at all, in what is now the most globalized society in the world?

# PART TWO: MEMOIRS AND PRODUCTIONS

# 1 | An Tóstal and the First Dublin Theatre Festival: a Personal Memoir

Christopher Fitz-Simon

> In the City of Dublin, at no distant date,
> We resolved on a Tóstal – a sort of a fête –
> In the culture of Europe we wished to take part
> So we made it a feast of theatrical art!
> Tooralay, tooraloo,
> And we got a few bob from the Fáilte Bórd too...

The 'no distant date' was in fact May of 1957. The piece of doggerel verse was written a few weeks later by Mr R.B.D. French, Reader in English at Trinity College, Dublin, who was also a closet satirist. I performed his *Ballad of the Rose Tattoo* in the Dublin University Players' intimate revue, an annual event which, significantly, first attracted the Dublin theatregoing public through the forbidding front gate of TCD and led to the Players Theatre becoming a recognized fringe venue for the city rather than a place of purely student entertainment.

An Tóstal was a nationwide festival of cultural and sporting events, subtitled *Ireland At Home*, which had been devised in 1953 by An Bórd Fáilte, the Irish Tourist Board, in an effort to attract visitors from abroad, more especially people of Irish descent in the United States who might be encouraged to seek familial roots in parts of the country that hitherto might not have received a fair share of tourists. The organization of these activities caused much excitement and not a little controversy in hundreds of centres. In Waterford it was said that the person employed by the Local Authority to collect door-to-door subscriptions achieved a sum which exactly covered the salary he was paid for his endeavours without anything left over to support the actual event. In Drumshanbo, Co. Leitrim a programme of outdoor *ceilidhe* dancing and singing – an *aeríocht* – on a tract of waste ground was backed by a celebratory bonfire comprised of dozens of discarded motor-tyres, creating smoke of such density that it became difficult to appreciate the subtlety of footwork in the jigs, reels and hornpipes performed by ringleted village maidens, and the chief *sean-nós* vocalist had to be led to the chemist's shop to gargle his throat. In Drogheda, a pageant representing the arrival in Ireland of St Patrick was performed by local amateurs with, as guest artist, the celebrated Birkenhead-born actor Anew McMaster in the role of the Apostle of Ireland.

As McMaster disembarked from a replica Viking longboat, a splendid figure in white robes and an emerald-green bishop's mitre, members of the assembled quayside audience fell to their knees – hardly the reaction of the people of A.D. 432. The saint and his attendant monks then proceeded to the Hill of Tara by motor-coach, where the conversion of the High King, Laoghaire, was enacted; here again it was difficult to discern the performers, though on this occasion it was due to the fall of night. Yet such was the acknowledged success of this site-specific performance it was decided to stage something similar the following year to a wider public. Micheál Mac Liammóir was engaged to write the script for *The Pageant of St Patrick* which Hilton Edwards was to direct in Croke Park. I auditioned and was cast in the very minor role of Cianán of Duleek at £10 to cover rehearsals and six performances.

The Archbishop of Dublin John Charles McQuaid was said to be keen to promote seemly leisure activities in the large parishes that were growing up in the south-west of the city. Drimnagh had become the most populous parish in Europe, and it was in the community hall there that rehearsals took place with members of the local confraternity and sodality as crowd extras: a thousand persons gladly gave their services without payment. Hilton Edwards remarked, *sotto voce,* that he was sure they would participate magnificently at the first performance but he doubted if they'd trouble to turn up after that; and so it was that the number of druids, soothsayers, warriors, shepherds, slaves and persons of noble birth dwindled nightly, leaving a somewhat bare arena.

The Dublin theatres co-operated with the Tóstal Council in return for publicity for their productions. In the Tóstal's first year, 1953, Edwards and Mac Liammóir gave the Irish *première* of Christopher Fry's verse drama *A Sleep of Prisoners* – the verse was described by Harold Hobson, the English theatre critic, as 'sliced, spiced prose' – set in a church in wartime France, as part of a double bill that included Yeats's *The Countess Cathleen*, at the Gate Theatre. There was speculation that in the former play Mac Liammóir would make a holy show of himself because he would hardly manage the part of the Cockney soldier with any credibility; but his gossipy detractors were discountenanced, for the body-language of the character, and more especially the accent, seemed absolutely authentic: what a truly versatile actor he surely was after all! In the Yeats, as the poet Aleel, he interpolated several early lyrics including *The Song of Wandering Aengus* in order, it was generally surmised, to demonstrate his real talent, which was for verse-speaking in the mode of his native wood-notes wild. It would be another fifty years before the truth would emerge: Mac Liammóir was born and brought up in the very milieu of the London tommy in *A Sleep of Prisoners,* and the bucolic Irish accent of Aleel the poet was a stage postulation.

The Abbey acknowledged the first Tóstal with a revival of Lennox Robinson's *The Whiteheaded Boy,* this time with the young actor Rae Mac an Aili in the name part, and a new comic opera by Gearóid Mac an Bhua, *An Fear a Phós Balbhán.* This double-bill made for a remarkably long evening.

The Tóstal Council did contribute to the cost of Our Lady's Choral Society's presentation of the Salzburg *Everyman,* a translated version of Hoffmannstahl's *Jedermann,* at the Capitol Theatre, in order to allow the engagement of the

Austrian director Ernst Lothar. A remarkably strong cast was assembled for the principal roles – Christopher Casson in the name part, Coralie Carmichael as his mother, Ginette Waddell as the Courtesan, Helena Hughes as Good Deeds, Fred Johnson as Death and Maurice O'Brien – the most 'stylish' Irish actor of the mid-twentieth century – as the Devil. This was generally acknowledged to be the major theatrical success of the Tóstal.

Four years and three pageants passed during which members of the theatre community muttered about the almost negligible financial assistance provided by the Tóstal Council in support of their efforts. The view was put forward that a Theatre Festival, separate from An Tóstal, should be their aim. Years later the actor and director Shelagh Richards claimed that this was her idea, but it was the theatrical entrepreneur Brendan Smith who put the idea into action and it was he who was instrumental in obtaining a subsidy from An Bord Fáilte, the Arts Council having refused to contribute to such an outlandish scheme. The Bórd also continued to support its own creation, An Tóstal, which gradually evaporated throughout the country though it left enduring progeny such as the International Choral Festival and the Film Festival in Cork, the Light Operatic Festival in Waterford, and the Tidy Towns Competition. Wexford Festival Opera was also sustained by Bórd Fáilte for many years, the Arts Council initially failing to appreciate the significance of this annual event. The only place where An Tóstal continues in its original form to this day is Drumshanbo.

In Dublin, a Theatre Festival Council was formed. Brendan Smith was appointed Director. He was also a playwright and theatre manager, and he ran the Brendan Smith Academy of Acting situated, as the advertisement stated, 'over Hipps, Gentleman's Outfitters', in South Great George's Street. It was from this address that the Dublin International Theatre Festival was at first administered. Its programme was announced for May, following the now distinctly moribund Tóstal in April, the relationship and nomenclature of the two festivals confusing everybody.

I happened to be Chairman of the Dublin University Players at the time and was busily promoting myself to the managers of the profession to which I aspired. These were Hilton Edwards at the Gate – who was kind enough to pretend that he recognized me from the *Pageant of St Patrick*; Godfrey Quigley who ran the Globe Theatre Company; Alan Simpson and Carolyn Swift at the Pike Theatre Club – the most adventurous management of the day; and Ernest Blythe at the Abbey (I need not have bothered there). One back-door *entrée* was to enrol as a volunteer helper. I prepared a speech to say how useful I would be to the Théâtre National Populaire during its visit to the Olympia Theatre – I had in fact been transfixed with excitement by their production of Molière's *Don Juan* at the Palais de Chaillot while I was in Paris in a temporary tutorial capacity earlier in the year. I knocked on Mr Smith's door without an appointment and was surprised to find that I had no difficulty in being taken on, for he appeared to believe my assurances that I had (fairly) fluent French and so there was no need for me to emphasize my interest in 'Le TNP', which would be presenting Jean Vilar's new productions of *Le Faiseur* and *Le Malade Imaginaire* in the Festival.

Jean Vilar, a tall aquiline man in his forties, was the most admired actor-director in the French theatre. He was famous for having founded the Avignon Festival where his innovative productions of Bibbiena, Clavel, Montherlant, and Maulnier were presented. The idea behind the TNP was the creation of a theatre where 'les gens du peuple' could enjoy the international classics of all periods – Brecht, Büchner, Corneille, Chekhov, Eliot, Kleist, Marivaux, Shakespeare – in great numbers at low prices. The Palais de Chaillot seated 2,700 people; 'scenery' was rarely used on its immense stage, the visual impact being achieved by lighting, movement, by superb costumes, and by the mesmeric presence of the leading actors of the day – Gérard Philipe, Georges Wilson, Maria Casarès, the comedian Daniel Sorano, and Vilar himself. This was in total contrast to what was seen on the two stages of the Comédie Française, where the French masterpieces of the seventeenth and eighteenth centuries were seen in fussy declamatory productions that had not changed much since the nineteenth.

I asked for M. Vilar at the Olympia stage door. It was Sunday, and the TNP company was setting up. I was directed through an evil-smelling subterranean corridor from which I emerged in the grubby orchestra-pit. Vilar and another man were conversing in the gloom. I had last seen him resplendent in a cream and gold suit with an immense white ruff on the grand stage of the Palais de Chaillot. Here he was wearing a coloured shirt and flannel trousers under the stage in a confined space where, it seemed, old music-stands had come to die. It was immediately clear that he was in consultation with his stage-director and that they were not at all pleased with their surroundings. 'Affreux!' was the word Vilar used for the flimsy-looking forestage that had been built out over the pit at his request. (It was one of his precepts that a pit created a barrier between performers and public – 'a play is not an opera', he had been reported as saying, his musicians appearing in the productions as part of the *mise-en-scène*). I introduced myself and was asked to find Mr Smith.

Vilar had also requested additional lighting that was clearly considered unnecessary by the Olympia staff – why couldn't he leave the stage as it was and use the footlights? Brendan Smith appeared, looking harassed, and said that everything Monsieur Vilar required would be supplied by the Olympia management – over which, he hastened to add, he had no jurisdiction. M. Vilar looked perplexed. 'But there is an agreement!' he declared in beautifully modulated English. On account of the inevitable delay I was asked to take some of the actors for a walk and we went to see the ducks in St Stephen's Green. Georges Wilson thought it would be pleasant to sit on deck chairs for a bit, but I had no money on me and he graciously paid the tuppence that the Corporation charged.

Back at the theatre all was frenzy. It appeared that never, on their worst provincial tours, had the TNP come across such a scruffy and ill-equipped *salle-de-théâtre*. Vilar's aristocratic disdain was not well taken by the sulky Olympia stage staff who murmured among themselves about making a complaint to their Union, but they evidently found they had no real grounds to do so. Vilar's team stripped the stage while the members of the No 7 Branch of the ITGWU watched from the shadows. The leader of the Olympia orchestra was dismayed because she had taken a great deal of trouble to find some suitable French pieces to perform during the intervals – a romping selection from

*L'Arlésienne,* she thought would be nice, and she would herself play the *Méditation* from *Thaïs* – but no pit, no orchestra. She wondered if they would be paid for doing nothing. (Perhaps they were not.)

I knew from working in Players and at the Pike Theatre Club that what looked like chaos coming up to 8 pm on opening night would suddenly be transformed into a silent brooding scene of expectation with dim lights, the curtain lowered. M. Vilar eschewed the curtain, so the stage had to be ready by 7.30, and it was. Chaos of a different kind was manifest elsewhere. There was to be an official Franco-Hibernian ceremony prior to the performance. Someone from the Alliance Française had hung a French tricolour from the stage-left box where the Ambassador was to sit but no Irish tricolour to match it on stage-right had been found. I was sent to Hector Grey's to buy a flag, and though I selected the largest it made very little impact opposite the swathes of red, blue and white; in fact, it looked as if someone had left it behind after a boxing match. No sooner had I delivered the flag than I was sent to Radio Eireann (on the top floor of the GPO) to borrow a disc of *La Marseillaise.* Brendan Smith himself took possession of the record, which he clutched in his hand while welcoming the Lord Mayor of Dublin, Councillor Robert Briscoe, T.D., and members of his party at the stage door.

I thought this an odd procedure. In my own very limited experience, distinguished patrons were introduced to the actors after the performance rather than before. I mentioned to Mr Smith that perhaps it would be more appropriate if the Lord Mayor were first conducted to his box, and introduced to the actors later when everyone would be more *relaxed,* but Mr Smith hissed that this had been arranged with the Lord Mayor's office *months* ago and he led the visitors up the concrete stairs to the dressing-rooms. Because I had been engaged as a speaker of French I was told to knock on the first door and announce the Lord Mayor of Dublin. I arrived at the door of the largest dressing-room, which I thought was used mainly by male actors in minor roles, knocked, opened it, and revealed a number of ladies and gentlemen in various stages of Second Empire undress. 'Messieurs, Mesdames!', I croaked, 'Je veux vous présenter Monsieur le Maire de la Cité de Dublin!'

The players looked mildly surprised as they assisted each other into chemises and long frilly drawers without any appearance of haste. Mr Briscoe bowed graciously from the threshold but did not enter the room, averting his eyes. He then withdrew and Mr Smith led him off by means of dingy corridors and staircases to his box. I closed the door on the scene of *déshabille*. I could hear raucous laughter from inside but, unfortunately, none of the words. The record of *La Marseilleise* was played and everyone stood up but when the spotlight was turned on the stage-right box there was no one in it, for the Ambassador had got lost on one of the Olympia's labyrinthine spiral staircases.

*Le Faiseur* (a *faiseur* is a mixture of a fixer and a bluffer) was an original play by Balzac – most of his stage works are adaptations of his own novels – produced posthumously in 1851 as *Mercadet le Faiseur*. It was hardly known in mid-twentieth-century France and therefore not known at all in Ireland. It turned out to be something in the nature of a boulevard comedy, though rather darker in tone than most plays in that genre. Monsieur Mercadet appeared to be a Figaro-like character, but in his case the accumulation of money was the chief motif. Daniel Sorano was on stage throughout, keeping the audience entertained by Mercadet's abrasive wit and by his unceasing stratagems for confusing his creditors. The *doyen* of these was a Monsieur Godeau, in debt to Mercadet for 1,500 francs. Godeau was always expected, but never arrived. The Pike Theatre Club had recently given the first production in Ireland of *Waiting for Godot,* but the coincidence of the names of the elusive Monsieur Godeau/Godot was not remarked upon either as a promotional ploy for the production or as a piece of pseudo-literary intelligence.

Vilar may have tampered judiciously with the text in order to build up the leading role, which Sorano performed with admirable finesse. The audience at the Olympia was sparse, eked out with Leaving Certificate students who were certainly not studying this obscure play but whose teachers probably thought – correctly – that they would hear the French language spoken with exemplary clarity. Houses for *Le Malade Imaginaire* were a great improvement. Vilar's production emphasized Molière at his rudest – one Dublin headmistress was heard to say she was sorry she had brought her pupils, but it is likely that they enjoyed the show immensely. A chorus of medics pranced around at a graduation ceremony brandishing outsize syringes that can only have been intended for irrigation *per anum,* while engaging in expertly choreographed lewd gestures. It may have dawned upon the only Irish management which regularly produced the plays of Molière, Longford Productions, that Molière's characters are middle to lower class, for they had always been presented on the Dublin stage as simpering, fan-fluttering members of the aristocracy, or at least gentry, dressed in extraordinarily elaborate court clothes, the thinking presumably inspired by the fact that because Molière's troupe was patronized by Louis XI and frequently performed at his court the only possible dress should be the extreme fashions of the period – but, as Vilar's production emphasized, Argan, Monsieur Diafoirus and Toinette exist socially many miles from Versailles.

If the visit of the TNP was a real coup for Brendan Smith, so was that of the Royal Ballet, which had never been to Ireland before. Anton Dolin's London Festival Ballet made annual two-week visits to the Gaiety Theatre so the standard classical repertoire was familiar, but not the big story-ballets which were only known to us from the music and the reputation. The Royal Ballet which, under Ninette de Valois, had recently been reconstituted from the Sadlers Wells Ballet, would have been much too large an ensemble for the Gaiety stage and orchestra pit, but it was ideally suited to the Theatre Royal, normally a cine-variety house. Some doubts had been expressed in the press about the likelihood of the Dublin public filling almost 4,000 seats each evening for six nights for such a *recherché* offering as *Lac des Cygnes* (as it was advertised), but fill them they did. I had some difficulty convincing the box office management that my status as Voluntary Helper entitled me to a ticket, but an unsold seat was found in the uppermost of the three circles from where the vast stage looked like a small television screen. Nevertheless, the effect was magical.

There had been much publicity to the effect that Miss de Valois was of course Miss Idris Stannus from Blessington, and there were reminiscences concerning her time at the Abbey Theatre, when she ran the School of Ballet. My grandmother, an inveterate theatre-goer and a former honorary-secretary of the United Arts Club under the presidency of William Butler Yeats, said that Miss de Valois had worked very hard, but it was difficult for her travelling from London every week and many of the Abbey dancers were big lumps of girls who should never have been allowed near a stage, and as she had great difficulty in persuading any men to join the class it wasn't much of a ballet!

Undoubtedly one of the chief reasons for the tremendous public response to *Swan Lake* was the presence of Margot Fonteyn as Odette-Odile and Michael Somes as the Prince. Such consummate artistry and expertise had never been seen before in any form of ballet or dance in Ireland. Miss de Valois arrived by taxi for the opening and ascended the marble staircase of the Theatre Royal as if she were, indeed, royalty. There appeared to be nobody to greet her, and when she approached the entrance to the dress circle the doorman asked for her ticket. 'Oh, I didn't know I needed one!' said de Valois with a wry smile. 'Sorry, Missus', said the doorman, 'but no one gets in here without a ticket!' Mr Louis Elliman, the theatre's proprietor, suddenly appeared and shrivelled his doorman with a glance. Miss de Valois was far too composed even to have noticed the slight.

The Abbey produced *The Playboy of the Western World* and *Juno and the Paycock*. The Gate, equally predictably, produced *The Old Lady Says 'No!'* I had always wanted to see Denis Johnston's play, having read Micheál Mac Liammóir's breathless description of its first production in 1929 which had suddenly and unexpectedly placed the year-old Dublin Gate Theatre on the international map amid critical cries concerning the way in which the Gate had so rapidly replaced the Abbey in terms of innovative writing. (It had definitely replaced the Abbey in terms of imaginative staging.) Mac Liammóir had created the role of the Speaker/Robert Emmet and in the part had found his apotheosis both as actor and as Irishman. The company had subsequently performed *The Old Lady Says 'No!'*

– at once a poetic evocation of romantic Ireland, a raging satire on the Free State, and a wildly revolutionary Expressionist dance-drama – in London and New York, and had revived it over the years at least six times in Dublin, but I had never seen it. I was mistrustful of Mac Liammóir's reminiscence, for his autobiography *All for Hecuba*, highly enjoyable as it was, bore all the marks of the narcissistic thespian. Furthermore, as Emmett had died for Ireland at the age of twenty-four and the actor portraying him was now fifty-nine admitting to forty-five, I bought my two-and-sixpenny ticket to the Gate in a spirit of callow scepticism.

Within a very few minutes of the opening my misgivings were confounded, for the leading role was clearly not meant to be a character of flesh and blood and therefore endowed with all the appropriate propensities for ageing and feeling, but a Figure: an embodiment, perhaps, of an Ireland that 'the poets have imagined, terrible and gay'. If anything, it appeared, the part was better if played by an elderly actor going through a routine, achieving pathos through simplification, and somehow achieving ecstasy by means of well-tried tricks. Several people of my parents' generation had told me how impressed they had been by the first production of the play, and how *new* it had seemed then, and here was I, twenty-seven years later, finding myself confounded into having to agree with their antiquated opinions, and recognizing that if the play still had the glint of newness surrounding it, that was because nothing much that was innovative had happened in the Irish theatre over the intervening years.

In its publicity, the Festival had made much of the fact that for the first time since 'the split' the two Gate companies were coming together to reproduce the theatre's earliest success. The Gate had been founded by Edwards and Mac Liammóir but they had soon discovered that they could not survive financially without subsidy and this was provided by the philanthropic Edward, seventh Earl of Longford. To their gradually increasing dismay they found that he, as chairman, was becoming all too influential in the artistic direction of the company, and while on tour in Mediterranean countries in 1936 the partners were shocked to learn that he was casting Gate productions at home without consultation and even presenting them in London. There was the inevitable parting of the ways, after which Longford Productions occupied the theatre for six months of the year and Edwards-Mac Liammóir Productions for the other six. The proposed subsidy from the Festival Council for the revival of *The Old Lady Says 'No!'* as everyone well knew, was the reason for this dramatic rapprochement. It was widely – and, as it later turned out, correctly – rumoured that Hilton Edwards would direct whichever of two plays suggested was approved by the Council; if it was to be *Dr Faustus* (which Lord Longford favoured) Aidan Grennell would play the title role opposite Mac Liammóir's Mephistopheles; if it was to be *The Old Lady Says 'No!'* (the partners' preference) Iris Lawler, Longford Productions leading lady, would play Sara Curran and Mac Liammóir would repeat his celebrated Speaker/Emmet. When the decision was announced it was further rumoured that Mr Mac Liammóir was not on speaking terms with Miss Lawler, but if this were the case it was not apparent to those of us who were carefully watching out for instances of upstaging and other slights. The production was a triumph for the organizers of the Theatre Festival as a politico-theatrical coup, and for the two companies as a brilliant recreation of 1920s Expressionist art.

I had wondered if it would have been worth my while auditioning for a small part in the much-heralded production of Tennessee Williams's *The Rose Tattoo,* which had not yet been staged outside the United States. I had appeared in plays at the Pike Theatre Club, but now final exams were looming and as theatre is a very *visible* activity I decided that if I were observed by one of my lecturers, however heavily disguised as a Sicilian navvy, it might be considered that I was not being attentive enough to the Old French and Middle English texts that were considered essential for a Moderatorship in Modern Languages. Behind-the-scenes work in the Festival was much less conspicuous. And so it was that I was not involved in the series of events that led to the arrest of the producer of *The Rose Tattoo,* Alan Simpson, for purportedly presenting 'for gain an indecent and profane performance' – save in my joining the crowd of supporters who gathered each night in Herbert Lane after it was reported that the police were endeavouring to close the play.

As celebrated by R.B.D. French in his ballad for the Players' intimate revue, *The Rose Tattoo* had been welcomed when Alan Simpson proposed it for inclusion in the Festival programme:

> So the Festival Council remarked in reply
> 'If we put on this play we'll be wiping the eye
> Of London and Paris and Moscow, we hear,
> So go on, me brave Alan, and have your prem-eer!'
> Tooraloo, tooralay,
> And they gave him some money to put on the play...

The Pike production turned out to be the critical hit of the Festival. Foreign as well as local reviewers were greatly taken by the substance of the piece, by the manner in which the teeming life of a downtown immigrant section of American society was vividly brought to life on the tiny Pike stage, and by the performance of Anna Manahan in the leading role of Serifina.

> When the overseas critics arrived at a trot,
> They wrote that this show was the best of the lot;
> Said Hobson, 'Be damn, but the play stands alone
> For its ethical values and deep moral tone!'
> Tooralay, tooraloo,
> And the Dublin ones though it was 'Wondherful too!'

I bought a standing-room ticket for the night on which Carolyn Swift unwisely read in the juvenile part because Kate Binchy had had to leave the production, her father being a member of the judiciary and all sorts of legal and familial complications would have ensued had she not; yet – I remember thinking – surely someone with a figure approaching that of the slim Miss Binchy could have been chosen, for Miss Swift was crammed into the costume with the help of safety pins and laces, and one could not keep one's eyes from straying to this garment as pins popped and laces strained. In the Festival Club each night members of the cast regaled us with the latest incident that endangered the freedom of theatrical managements to present plays that added to one's understanding of what the *cognoscenti* of that decade was calling 'the human condition':

Then out from the wings stepped a big Civic Guard.
He said, 'Tis immoral! – or so I have heard –
'Tis so shockin' obscene there's no question of bail',
So they clipped on the handcuffs and took Alan to jail!
Tooraloo, tooralay,
To the Bridewell he went for producing the play...

Since then, the story of the *Rose Tattoo cause-célèbre* has
been widely re-run, most notably in Alan Simpson's book
*Beckett, Behan and a Theatre in Dublin,* in Gerard Whelan and
Carolyn Swift's *Spiked,* and in Jocelyn Clarke's beautifully
crafted rehearsed reading *The Case of the Rose Tattoo* in the
2007 Theatre Festival. Though the mysterious forces that
unsuccessfully attempted to close the production certainly did
irreparable damage to the Pike Theatre Club (and also, most
sadly, to Alan and Carolyn Simpson's marriage due to the
enormous personal pressures exerted by that most public of
trials), it is worth mentioning that the perception at the time
among the sector of society of which I, my fellow students, and
most theatre people were a part, was that it was all a lot of
silliness and not worth the steam generated in the press. It was
all so absurd!

Certainly we did not appreciate that had Alan Simpson not
been discharged by District Justice Cathal O'Flynn after over a
year of delays and postponements, a repressive and reactionary
era would undoubtedly have begun, exceedingly dangerous for
freedom of expression not only in the Irish theatre but in
Ireland as a whole. In this country we had never had to endure
official dramatic censorship, for the Lord Chamberlain's remit
did not extend to Ireland, and the Censorship of Publications
Act of 1929 did not cover stage performance. Alan Simpson was
the first person in the history of the State to stand accused of
producing a performance alleged to be 'indecent and obscene
and profane'; had he been convicted, a period of intense
puritanical zeal would certainly have ensued and (who knows?)
an extreme form of official theatrical censorship introduced.

But that did not happen. The silliness continued for just one
more year, during which Archbishop McQuaid refused to say a
votive Mass for the second Theatre Festival because a play by

Sean O'Casey was to be included in the programme. The spineless members of the Festival Council lost their heads and the Festival was cancelled. This was unacceptable absurdity beyond all absurdities. From that date a turning-point could be identified that led, within a very few years, to the much more open-minded attitude for which the present generation may be grateful.

Of course we were not aware of these implications at the time. As for me, when I learned of the second Festival's cancellation I was on the road with the Canadian Players on a nationwide tour in a programme of plays that a new regime in Ireland – had it been established – might have dismissed as immoral and obscene, by the bawdy Shakespeare and the subversive Shaw.

Tooraloo, tooralay...

# Production History Part One: 1957–1970

## About the Production History

For ease of reading, the production history is divided into four parts, each concluding at a significant year in the Festival's history. The first part runs up to 1970, which was one of the three years in which the Festival did not take place. The second section runs up to 1984, when, again, the Festival did not take place (the other year in which there was no Festival was 1958). The third part finishes in 1994, which was the year before the Dublin Fringe Festival began. The final section runs from 1995 to 2008, the most recent year for which details were available.

We have included details of all performances staged as part of the DTF – not just theatre, but also stand-up comedy, ballet, opera, mime, puppetry, recitals, live music, and so on. We have not included information about ancillary events, such as conferences, critics' forums, rehearsed readings, or social events like the garden party that took place at the inaugural Festival.

Since 1957, some theatres (notably the Abbey and the Gate) have programmed shows that ran simultaneously with the Festival, but were not necessarily programmed by the Festival Director. Furthermore, throughout the Festival's history, there have always been shows that present themselves as part of an official or unofficial 'fringe' – which means that, again, they may not have been programmed by the Festival Director. And finally, the DTF has often included smaller festivals, such as the 1991 Beckett Festival, or the numerous Children's Seasons. We have not included listings of shows that appeared in the Dublin Fringe Festival from 1995 onwards, but our policy in all other cases has been to include any shows that were staged during the same period as the Dublin Theatre Festival, unless those shows were self-evidently *not* part of the programme.

All information is listed alphabetically, in the following format:

> Title of Play/Performance. Name of Author. Production company (where appropriate). Venue. Name of Director (where appropriate).

When alphabetizing play titles, we have not included definite and indefinite articles in any language. Hence *The Playboy of the Western World* appears under 'P'; *An Giall* is listed under 'G'; *Le Faiseur* appears under 'F', and so on.

The names of some venues, companies, and writers vary slightly in programme listings from one year to another. For clarity, we have chosen the name most frequently used, and applied it consistently. Hence, for example, we use the title 'Barabbas... The Company' rather than 'Barabbas', though both forms are used; and we use 'An Damer' rather than 'The Damer Hall', though again both forms are used. Similarly, we use 'Tom Murphy' throughout the history, although he was sometimes referred to as 'Thomas Murphy'.

The information in this list was compiled from a variety of sources. We initially worked from lists that were prepared by the DTF itself. We have used many other publications and resources, including the following: the standard histories of the Abbey Theatre (by Christopher Fitz-Simon, Hugh Hunt, Michael O'Neill, and others, supplemented by material on the theatre's website, www.abbeytheatre.ie); the digital archives of *The Irish Times* and the *Irish Independent*; the Irish Playography; and the standard histories of Irish theatre since the 1950s (especially by Christopher Morash and Robert Hogan). Readers who wish to know more about any of the Irish plays listed in this production history may access details about most of them on www.irishplayography.com That website also provides a full list of all new plays that were produced by the DTF.

# Dublin International Theatre Festival 1957

13–26 May

*Aida* by Giuseppe Verdi. Dublin Grand Opera Society at the Gaiety Theatre. Conductor: Franco Patane.

*The Barber of Seville* by Gioachino Rossini. Dublin Grand Opera Society at the Gaiety Theatre. Conductor: Giuseppe Morelli.

*Checkmate* by Arthur Bliss and *Birthday Offering* by Frederick Ashton. Royal Ballet at the Theatre Royal. Directed and choreographed by Ninette de Valois. *Cúirt an Mheán Oíche* by Brian Merriman. An Compántas. Pocket Theatre.

*Le Faiseur* by Honoré de Balzac. Théâtre National Populaire at the Olympia Theatre. Directed by Jean Vilar.

*The Gilla Rua* by Kenneth Reddin. Studio Theatre Club. Directed by Fergus Cogley.

*The Importance of Being Earnest* by Oscar Wilde. Olympia Theatre. Directed by Michael MacOwan.

International Folk Dance Festival. The National Stadium.

*Irish Festival Singers* at Philips Concert Hall.

*Juno and The Paycock* by Sean O'Casey. Abbey Theatre. Directed by Ria Mooney.

*Le Lac Des Cygnes* by Pyotr Ilyich Tchaikovsky. Royal Ballet at the Theatre Royal. Directed and choreographed by Ninette de Valois.

*Madame Butterfly* by Giacomo Puccini. Dublin Grand Opera Society at the Gaiety Theatre. Conductor: Franco Patane.

*La Malade Imaginaire* by J-B.P. Molière. Théâtre National Populaire at the Olympia Theatre. Directed by Jean Vilar.

*The Old Lady Says No!* by Denis Johnston. Hilton Edwards and Micheál Mac Liammóir Productions and Longford Productions at the Gate Theatre. Directed by Hilton Edwards.

*The Playboy of the Western World* by J.M. Synge. Abbey Theatre. Golden Jubilee Production. Directed by Ria Mooney.

*An Pósadh* by Douglas Hyde. Abbey Theatre. Directed by Tomás Mac Anna.

*The Rose Tattoo* by Tennessee Williams. Pike Theatre. Directed by Alan Simpson.

A Season of Yeats's Plays: The Land of Heart's Desire, At the Hawk's Well, Purgatory, the Shadowy Waters, The Dreaming of the Bones,

The Cat and the Moon, and The Unicorn from the Stars by W.B. Yeats. Globe Theatre. Directed by Jim Fitzgerald.

*The Shadow* by John Cranko, *Symphonic Variations* by Frederick Ashton and *Ballet Imperial* by George Balanchine. Royal Ballet at the Theatre Royal. Directed by Ninette de Valois.

*Les Sylphides*, music by Frédéric Chopin orchestrated by Alexander Glazunov. The Royal Ballet at the Theatre Royal. Directed and choreographed by Ninette de Valois.

## Dublin International Theatre Festival 1958

This Festival was to have featured plays by Samuel Beckett, *The Drums of Father Ned* by Sean O'Casey, and an adaptation of Joyce's *Ulysses* by Alan McClelland. It was officially 'postponed' following objections to the inclusion of this 'obscene' and 'objectionable' material by Archbishop John Charles McQuaid.

## Dublin International Theatre Festival 1959

14–26 September

*The Death of Cuchulain* by WB Yeats and *Oedipus at Colonus*. Lyric Players at Dagg Hall. Directed by Mary O'Malley.

*Deirdre of the Sorrows* by J.M. Synge. Liffey Theatre and the Eblana Theatre. Directed by Tony Page.

*The Dreaming Dust* by Denis Johnston. Louis Elliman in association with Edwards-Mac Liammóir Productions at the Gaiety Theatre. Directed by Hilton Edwards.

*For Humans Only* by Lotte Goslar Company. Accompanied by *Quatre Barbus*. Olympia Theatre. Directed by Lotte Goslar.

*The Good Natured Man* by Oliver Goldsmith. Lord Longford Productions at the Gate Theatre. Directed by Dan O'Connell.

*Harlequinade* by Riccardo Drigo *and The Dying Swan* by Camille Saint-Saëns. London Festival Ballet with London Philharmonic Orchestra. Theatre Royal. Performed by Alicia Markova. Artistic Director: Anton Dolin.

*The Hogarth Puppets*. Olympia Theatre. Directed, conceived, and performed by Jan Russell and Ann Hogarth.

*Inquisition* by Diego Fabbri. Translated from Italian by Carolyn Swift. Pike Theatre. Directed by Alan Simpson.

*Lady Spider* by Donagh McDonagh. Orion Productions at the Gas Company Theatre. Directed by Jim Fitzgerald.

*Landscape With Figures* by Cecil Beaton. Olympia Theatre. Directed by Douglas Seale.

*Leave it to the Doctor* by Anne Daly. Abbey Theatre. Directed by Ria Mooney.

*Necropolis* by Roger McShane. Lantern Theatre Club. Directed by Roger McShane.

*Orson Welles at Midnight*. Solo Recital at the Gaiety.

*The Simpleton of the Unexpected Isles* by G.B. Shaw. Globe Theatre Company at the Gaiety Theatre. Directed by Godfrey Quigley.

*Súgán Sneachta* by Máiréad Ní Ghráda. Abbey Theatre. Directed by Tomás Mac Anna.

*Swan Lake* by Pyotr Ilyich Tchaikovsky and *Don Quixote* by Ludwig Minkus. London Festival Ballet with London Philharmonic Orchestra at the Theatre Royal. Artistic Director: Anton Dolin.

*Symphony For Fun* by Don Gillis and *London Morning* by Noel Coward. London Festival Ballet with London Philharmonic Orchestra at the Theatre Royal. Artistic Director: Anton Dolin.

## Dublin International Theatre Festival 1960

12–25 September

*Hassan* by James Elroy Flecker. Belgrade Theatre Trust (Coventry) at the Olympia Theatre. Directed by Basil Dean.

*The Highest House on the Mountain* by John B. Keane. Orion Productions at the Gas Company Theatre. Directed by Barry Cassin.

*An Ideal Husband* by Oscar Wilde. Longford Productions at the Gate Theatre. Directed by Christopher Casson.

*The Importance of Being Oscar* by Micheál Mac Liammóir. Edwards-Mac Liammóir Productions at the Gaiety Theatre. Directed by Hilton Edwards.

*The Kreutzer Sonata* by Leo Tolstoy, adapted by Roderick Lovell and Hannah Watt. Pike Theatre. Directed by Louis Lentin.

*Macbeth* by William Shakespeare. Old Vic Company at the Olympia Theatre. Directed by Michael Benthall.

*Mourn the Ivy Leaf* by G.P. Gallivan. Globe Theatre/Liffey Theatre Productions at the Eblana Theatre. Directed by Godfrey Quigley.

*The Playboy of the Western World* by J.M. Synge. Gaiety Theatre. Directed by Shelagh Richards.

*The Scatterin'* by James McKenna. Pike Theatre Productions at the Abbey Lecture Hall. Directed by Alan Simpson and Carolyn Swift.

*The Song of the Anvil* by Bryan MacMahon. Abbey Theatre. Directed by Ria Mooney.

*Spailpín, a Rúin* by Seán MacRéamoinn. An Damer. With music by Sean Ó Riada. Directed by Frank Dermody.

*The Voices of Doolin* by Walter Macken. Cyril Cusack Productions at the Gaiety Theatre. Directed by Jim Fitzgerald.

*A Walk on the Water* by Hugh Leonard. Globe Theatre/Liffey Theatre at the Eblana Theatre. Directed by Jim Fitzgerald and Godfrey Quigley.

## Dublin International Theatre Festival 1961

10–24 September

*All the World's a Stage* (Shakespearean scenes/speeches) by William Shakespeare. Dagg Hall. Performed by Jack Aronson and Mary Rose McMaster.

*Brand* by Henrik Ibsen. Lyric Players Theatre at Dagg Hall. Directed by Mary O'Malley.

*L'École des Femmes* by J-B.P. Molière and *L'École des Mères* by P. Marivaux. Compagnie de Rigault at the Olympia Theatre. Directed by Jean de Rigault.

*The Hour Glass, The Dreaming of the Bones,* and *The Player Queen* by W.B. Yeats. Lyric Players Theatre at Dagg Hall. Directed by Mary O'Malley.

*Monsieur Chasse* by G. Feydeau. Compagnie de Rigault (Paris) at the Olympia Theatre. Directed by Jean de Rigault.

*Mrs. Warren's Profession* by G.B. Shaw. Dublin Festival Company at the Gaiety Theatre. Directed by Gerard Healy.

*No More in Dust* by John B. Keane. Orion Productions at the Gas Company Theatre. Directed by Barry Cassin.

*North City Traffic Straight Ahead* by James Douglas. Pike Theatre Productions at the Gaiety Theatre. Directed by Alan Simpson.

*The Passion of Peter Ginty* by Hugh Leonard. Gemini Productions at the Gate Theatre. Directed by Godfrey Quigley.

*Plays in the Abbey Tradition* (revivals of plays in repertoire, including Richard Johnson's *The Evidence I Shall Give,* Lennox Robinson's *Whiteheaded Boy,* Louis D'Alton's *This Other Eden,* and the premiere of Tomás Coffey's *The Long Sorrow*, which was directed by Tomás Mac Anna). Abbey Theatre.

*Scéal ar Phádraig* by Seán Ó Tuama. An Damer. With music by Sean Ó Riada. Directed by Tomás Mac Anna.

*Slings and Arrows* by Fergus Linehan. Gate Theatre. Directed by Lelia Doolin.

*Saint Joan of the Stockyards* by Bertolt Brecht. Edwards-Mac Liammóir Productions at the Gaiety Theatre. Directed by Hilton Edwards.

*The Temptation of Mr. O* by Cyril Cusack (after Kafka's *The Trial*). Cyril Cusack Productions at the Olympia Theatre. Directed by Tomás Mac Anna.

*Teresa of Avila* by Hugh Ross Williamson. Olympia Theatre. Directed by Norman Marshall.

Triple Bill: *A Night Out* by Harold Pinter, *Barnstable* by James Saunders, and *Soldiers from the War Returning* by David Campton. Caravel Productions (London) at the Gate Theatre. Directed by Lelia Blake.

*The Voice of Shem* by Mary Manning (adapted from Joyce's *Finnegans Wake*). Libra at the Eblana Theatre. Directed by Louis Lentin.

## Dublin Theatre Festival 1962

24 September–7 October

The American Dance Company at the Shelbourne Ballroom. Directed by Richard Graham.

*And Him Stretched* by Patrick Galvin. Orion at the Eblana Theatre. Directed by Barry Cassin.

*The Apricot Season* by Aldo Nikolaj. Translated from Italian by Terence Butler. Olympia Theatre. Directed by Allan Davis.

*Cabaret of Savagery and Delight*. Excerpts from Brecht, performed by Agnes Bernelle. Grafton Cinema.

*The Cave Dwellers* by William Saroyan. Arch Productions at Dagg Hall. Directed by Marie Conmee.

*Courtship Through the Ages* by Shirley Smith and Peter O'Shaughnessy. St Anthony's Theatre.

*Cúirt an Mheán Oíche* adapted by Eoghan Ó Tuairisc. An Damer. Directed by Tomás Mac Anna.

*Dossers* by William J. Murdock. Dublin Stage Company at the Pike. Directed by Bill Skinner.

*Fiesta Citana.* Spanish Gypsy Company at the Gaiety Theatre.

*Fursey* by Fergus Linehan, adapted from the novel *The Unfortunate Fursey* by Murvyn Wall. Gaiety Theatre. Directed by Alan Simpson.

*A Jew Called Sammy* by John McCann. Abbey Theatre. Directed by Tomás Mac Anna.

*Little City* by Seamus Byrne. Gemini Productions at the Gate Theatre. Directed by Barry Cassin.

*Long Day's Journey Into Night* by Eugene O'Neill. Abbey Theatre. Directed by Frank Dermody.

*Murder in the Cathedral* by T. S. Eliot. St Patrick's Cathedral. Directed by Nora Lever.

*One Actor – Nine Voices.* Richard Morris with excerpts from Shakespeare at the Studio Theatre.

*Othello* by William Shakespeare. Edwards-Mac Liammóir Productions. Gaiety Theatre. Directed by Hilton Edwards.

*Pictures in the Hallway* by Sean O'Casey. Adapted for stage reading by Paul Shyre. The Olympia Theatre. Directed by Peter Duiguid.

*The Pinedus Affair* by Paolo Levi. Art Theatre Productions at Father Matthew Hall. Directed by Louis Lentin.

*Stephen D.* by Hugh Leonard. Gemini Productions at the Gate Theatre. Directed by Jim Fitzgerald.

*A Touch of the Poet* by Eugene O'Neill. Tennent Productions at the Olympia Theatre. Directed by Toby Robertson

*Waiting for Godot* by Samuel Beckett. Portora Royal School at the Pocket Theatre.

*A Whisper in God's Ear* by Sam Birnkrant. Gas Company Theatre.


## Dublin Theatre Festival 1963

24 September–6 October

*The Big Finish* by Gerry Simpson. New Theatre Productions at the Irish Life Theatre. Directed by Frank J. Bailey

*Carrie* by Wesley Burrowes, Michael Coffey, and James Douglas. Olympia Theatre. Directed by Peter Collinson.

*The Coach with the Six Insides: Characters from James Joyce's Finnegans Wake* by Jean Erdman. Jean Erdman Company at the Eblana Theatre. Directed by Jean Erdman.

*Dublin One* by Hugh Leonard. Gemini Productions at the Gate Theatre. Directed by Barry Cassin.

*Dúchas*, an adaptation of *Roots* by Arnold Wesker. Translated into Irish by Pádraig Ó Gaora. An Damer. Directed by Séamus Páircéir.

*Happy Days* by Samuel Beckett. Envoy Productions at the Eblana Theatre. Directed by John Beary.

*Inquiry at Lisieux* by Marcelle Maurette. Translated by Chloe Gibson and Adrian Vale. Olympia Theatre. Directed by Chloe Gibson.

*The Last P.M.* by Conor Farrington. Edwards-Mac Liammóir Productions at the Gate Theatre. Directed by Hilton Edwards.

*A Little Winter Love* by Alun Owen. Gaiety Theatre. Directed by Godfrey Quigley.

*The Man from Clare* by J.B. Keane. Abbey Theatre. Directed by Frank Dermody.

*Moytura* by Padraic Colum and *The Tinker's Wedding* by J.M. Synge. Romar Productions at the Pike Theatre. Directed by Liam Miller.

*The Poker Session* by Hugh Leonard. Gemini Productions at the Gate Theatre. Directed by Jim Fitzgerald.

*Stella* by Conor Farrington. Edwards-Mac Liammóir Productions at the Gaiety Theatre. Directed by Hilton Edwards

*The Successor* by Reinhard Raffalt. Translated from German by Stephen Vass. Abbey Theatre. Directed by Frank Dermody.

*The Tin Soldier* by Arthur Johansson and Once Upon Eternity by William Finnan. John Molloy at Dagg Hall.

## Dublin Theatre Festival 1964

21 September–4 October

*Ages of Man* by John Gielgud. Recital of passages from Shakespeare. Abbey Theatre.

*Cu-Cu, Jug-Jug, Pu-We* by Wesley Burrowes (script and lyrics). M. P. Productions at the Irish Life Theatre. Directed by Michael Bogdin.

*Do You Know the Milky Way?* by Karl Wittlinger. Vulcan-Nimara Productions at the Eblana Theatre. Directed by Michael Lindsay-Hogg.

*The Eye of a Stranger* by Adrian Vale. Javelin Productions at the Eblana Theatre. Directed by Jim Fitzgerald.

*The Forests of the Night* by Arnold Sundgaard. Taurus productions at the Irish Life Theatre. Directed by Louis Lentin.

*The Ice Goddess* by James Douglas. Orion Productions at the Gate Theatre. Directed by Laurence Bourne.

*The King of the Castle* by Eugene McCabe. Gemini Productions at the Gaiety Theatre. Directed by Godfrey Quigley.

*Laurette* by Stanley Young. Laurette Productions at the Olympia Theatre. Directed by Albert Marre.

*The Lunatic, the Lover and the Poet* by John Gielgud, after Shakespeare. Dagg Hall.

*Philadelphia, Here I Come!* by Brian Friel. Elliman, Edwards-Mac Liammóir Productions at the Gaiety Theatre. Directed by Hilton Edwards.

*Sir Buccaneer* by Henry Morgan and G.P. Gallivan. Envoy Productions at the Olympia Theatre. Directed by George Meredith.

*The Wooing of Duvessa* by M.J. Molloy. Abbey Theatre. Directed by Frank Dermody.

*You Never Can Tell* by G.B. Shaw. Edwards-Mac Liammóir Productions at the Gate Theatre. Directed by Chloe Gibson.

## Dublin Theatre Festival 1965

20 September–3 October

*Bior* by Diarmuid Ó Súilleabháin. An Damer. Directed by Edward Golden.

*Campobasso* by G.P. Gallivan. Premier Productions at the Irish Life Theatre. Directed by Frank J. Bailey.

*Dearest Dracula* by Margaret Hill, Charlotte Moore, Jack Murdoch, Fran Landsman, and Joyce Adcock. Olympia Theatre. Directed by Gordon Caleb.

*Deirdre* by W.B. Yeats. Abbey Theatre. Special Centenary Performance.

*Gallows Humour* by Jack Richardson. City Film Corporation in association with DTF at the Olympia Theatre. Directed by Joseph Strick.

*The Game* by Alun Owen. York Promotions at the Gaiety Theatre. Directed by Godfrey Quigley.

*Gone Tomorrow* by Tom Coffey. Gemini Productions at the Gate Theatre. Directed by Barry Cassin.

*Hogan's Goat* by William Alfred. Olympia Theatre. Directed by Louis Lentin

*The Life of Galileo* by Bertolt Brecht. Abbey Theatre. Directed by Tomás Mac Anna

*Little Malcolm and his Struggle Against the Eunuchs* by David Halliwell. Gaiety Theatre. Directed by Patrick Dromgoole.

*Muses with Milligan* by Spike Milligan. Abbey Theatre.

*Not with a Bang* by Kevin Casey. Elmar Productions at the Eblana Theatre. Directed by Laurence Bourne.

*One Man's Show*. Peter Bridge Productions in association with DTF. Eblana Theatre. Directed by Larry Adler

*Talking about Yeats* by Micheál Mac Liammóir. Shelbourne Rooms. Directed by Hilton Edwards.

*When the Saints Go Cycling In* by Hugh Leonard, an adaptation of Flann O'Brien's *The Dalkey Archive*. Gemini Productions at the Gate Theatre. Directed by Denis Carey.

## Dublin Theatre Festival 1966

3–16 October

*All Gods Die On Friday* by Michael McDonnell. Eblana Theatre. Directed by Sean Cotter.

*Breakdown* by Eugene McCabe. Gate Theatre. Directed by Chloe Gibson.

*Cemented with Love* by Sam Thompson, adapted for the stage by Tomás Mac Anna. Gemini Productions at the Gaiety Theatre. Directed by Barry Cassin.

*Dylan* by Sidney Michaels in association with Jack Aranson. Gaiety Theatre. Directed by Jim Fitzgerald and Jack Aranson.

*Hogan's Goat* by William Alfred. Olympia Theatre. Directed by Louis Lentin.

*Hughie* by Eugene O'Neill. Eblana Theatre. Directed by Sean Cotter.

*Jack and Jill and After* by Angela Vale and John Molloy. Gas Company Theatre.

*Love and a Bottle* by George Farquhar. Gate Theatre. Directed by William Chappell.

*Mick and Mick* by Hugh Leonard. Gemini Productions at the Olympia Theatre. Directed by Guy Verney.

*One For The Grave* by Louis MacNeice. Abbey Theatre. Directed by Frank Dermody.

*Out of Africa: A Dramatic Recital* from the novel by Karen Blixen. Irish Life Theatre. Directed by Maria Corvin.

*A Quick One 'Ere-And Out The Other* by Terence Brady and Michael Bogdanov. Bradov Productions at the Eblana Theatre. Directed by Michael Bogdanov.

*Tycoon* by Seán Ó hEidirsceoil. An Damer. Directed by Noel Ó Briain.

## Dublin Theatre Festival 1967

2–15 October

*Antigone* by Sophocles. The Living Theatre of America at the Olympia Theatre. Directed by Julian Beck.

*A Beckett Evening*. Abbey Theatre. Directed by Jack McGowran.

*Borstal Boy* adapted from Brendan Behan's memoir by Frank McMahon. Abbey Theatre. Directed by Tomás Mac Anna.

*A Brecht Evening*. Abbey Theatre. Directed and performed by Agnes Bernelle.

*Faill an Bhfeart* by Séamus O'Neill. Peacock Theatre Directed by Tomás O Muircheada.

*Frankenstein* by Oscar Lewenstein. The Living Theatre of America at the Olympia Theatre. Directed by Julian Beck.

*The Goose* by Alun Owen. York Productions at the Gate Theatre. Directed by Alun Owen.

*Gustaf and His Ensemble Puppet Theatre*. Produced by the Embassy of the Federal Republic of Germany. Peacock Theatre.

*The Invincibles* by Frank O'Connor and Hugh Hunt. Abbey Theatre. Directed by Hugh Hunt.

*Iúdás Iscariot agus a Bhean* by Seán Ó Tuama. An Damer. Directed by Noel Ó Briain.

*Laugh But Listen Well* by William Cappell and William Morrison. Gaiety Theatre. Directed by William Cappell.

*The Noon-Day Devil* by Maurice Davin Power. Eblana Theatre. Directed by Michael Bogdanov.

*O'Flaherty VC* by G.B. Shaw and *The Words Upon the Window Pane* by W.B. Yeats. Tideway Productions at the Gaiety Theatre. Directed by Sean Cotter.

*The Order of Melchizedek* by Críostóir Ó Floinn. Gemini Productions at the Gate Theatre. Directed by Keith Darvill.

*The Quick and The Dead* by Hugh Leonard. Gemini Productions at the Olympia Theatre. Directed by Barry Cassin.

*The Zoo Story* by Edward Albee and *Please Break the Glass Gently* by Michael Judge. Eblana Theatre. Directed by Michael Bogdanov.


## Dublin Theatre Festival 1968

30 September–12 October

*After the Fall* by Arthur Miller. Gaiety Theatre. Directed by Ray McAnally.

*The Anniversary* by Bill MacIllwraith. Gemini Productions at the Gate Theatre. Directed by Frank Bailey.

*The Au Pair Man* by Hugh Leonard. Gate Theatre. Directed by Ted Kotcheff.

The Black Theatre of Prague. Olympia Theatre.

*The Cherry Orchard* by Anton Chekhov in a version by Michael Frayn. Abbey Theatre. Directed by Maria Knebel.

*The Colleen Bawn* by Dion Boucicault. Gaiety Theatre. Directed by Frank J. Bailey.

*The Countess Cathleen* by W.B. Yeats and *The Second Kiss* by Austin Clarke. The Peacock Theatre.

*The Death and Resurrection of Mr. Roche* by Thomas Kilroy. Olympia Theatre. Directed by Jim Fitzgerald.

*Famine* by Tom Murphy. Abbey Theatre. Directed by Tomás Mac Anna.

*The Fisherman and His Soul*, adapted from the work of Oscar Wilde by Frank Kelly. Dagg Hall. Directed by Eugene Lambert.

*An Giall* by Brendan Behan. The Peacock Theatre. Directed by Frank Dermody.

*Gunna Cam Agus Slabhra Óir* by Seán Ó Tuama. An Damer. Directed by Noel Ó Briain.

*Old and New*. A recital by Grainne Yeats. Peacock Theatre.

*The Orphans* by Tom Murphy. Gemini Productions at the Gate Theatre. Directed by Vincent Dowling.

*Passes in The Night* by Kevin P. Grattan. Lantern Theatre Club. Directed by Patrick Funge.

The Playboy of the Western World by J.M. Synge. Abbey Theatre.

*She Stoops to Conquer* by Oliver Goldsmith. Castletown House. Directed by Dominic Roche.

*Smock Alley* by Maureen Charlton. Castletown House. Directed by Martin Dempsey

*The Stronger* by August Strindberg translated by Edith and Warner Oland. Peacock Theatre. Directed by Frank Dermody.

*The Tailor and Ansty* by Eric Cross. The Peacock Theatre. Directed by Tomás Ó Murchú.

*Watershed* by G.P. Gallivan. Eblana Theatre. Directed by Roland Jaquarello.

*You in Your Small Corner* by Wesley Burrowes. Four Courts Hotel. Directed by Noel MacMahon.

## Dublin Theatre Festival 1969

29 September–11 October

*The Assassin* by John Boyd. Gaiety Theatre. Directed by Bill Bryden.

*The Barracks*, adapted by Hugh Leonard from the novel by John McGahern. Gemini Productions at the Olympia Theatre. Directed by Tomás Mac Anna.

*The Crying Room* by Patrick Gilligan. Eblana Theatre. Directed by Frank J. Bailey.

*The Dandy Dolls* by George Fitzmaurice. Abbey Theatre. Directed by Hugh Hunt.

*The Dublin Woman* by Dominic O'Reilly. Shelbourne Rooms. Directed by Marie Keane.

*The Immortal Husband* by James Merrill. Artists Theatre of New York at the Gate Theatre. Directed by Herbert Machz and John Bernard Myers.

*In the Summerhouse* by Jane Bowles. Artists Theatre of America at the Gate Theatre. Directed by Herbert Machz and John Bernard Myers.

*Is Glas iad na Cnuic* (*The Far Off Hills*) by Lennox Robinson. Peacock Theatre.

*John Synge Comes Next* by Maurice Good. Player Wills Theatre. Directed by Maurice Good.

*Juno and The Paycock* by Sean O'Casey. The Abbey Theatre. Directed by Vincent Dowling.

*King Herod Explains* by Conor Cruise O'Brien. Gate Theatre. Directed by Hilton Edwards

*The Liar* by Micheál Mac Liammóir. The Gate Theatre. Directed by Hilton Edwards.

*Man and Superman* by G.B. Shaw. The Gaiety Theatre. Directed by Nat Brenner.

*Mr. Handel's Visit to Dublin* by Maurice Davin Power. Nora Lever Productions at St. Patrick's Cathedral.

*The Mullingar Recruits* by George Farquhar. Period Productions at the Olympia Theatre. Directed by Dominic Roche.

*On the Rocks* by G.B. Shaw. The Gaiety Theatre. Directed by Frith Banbury.

*Opium* by Roc Brynner. Commonwealth United Entertainments at the Player Wills Theatre. Directed by Roc Brynner.

*Part of the Main* by Grace Butt. Eblana Theatre. Directed by Desmond Perry.

*Swift* by Eugene McCabe. The Abbey Theatre. Directed by Rhona Woodcock.

*A Tale After School* by James Douglas. Eblana Theatre. Directed by Frank J. Bailey.

*An t-Údar I nGleic* by Labhrás Mac Brádaigh. An Damer. Directed by Seán Ó Briain.

*The Weaver's Grave* by Seamas O Kelly, adapted by Mícheál Ó hAodha. Peacock Theatre. Directed by Seán Cotter.

*The Well of the Saints* by J.M. Synge. Abbey Theatre. Directed by Hugh Hunt.


## 1970 – Festival postponed until 1971

# 2 | Dublin Theatre Festival: 1984–1989

Lewis Clohessy

## Finding the Money

The footsteps on the rickety stairs to the Dublin Theatre Festival office sounded unusually slow and heavy. As he rounded the corner into my room, the gloomy expression on Phelim Donlon's face confirmed that he was the bearer of bad news – the worst possible news for the 1986 Theatre Festival.

It was only a matter of weeks since Phelim, Drama Officer of the Arts Council and a staunch supporter of the Festival, had sent me a letter on behalf of the Council expressing that body's enormous satisfaction with the success of the 1985 event. Now, as he wearily explained, the Council's chronic financial situation, arising from inadequate government funding, meant that a decision had had to be taken to suspend grant-aid for 1986 to a number of the Council's regular clients. Because of the seasonal nature of Festivals, grant-aid to these events had been identified by the Arts Council as being less vital to the continuing life of the arts in Ireland than support for permanent institutions and individual artists. Accordingly, to ensure the necessary support for priority areas, the Council axe was now about to be wielded on the necks of the Wexford Opera, Cork Choral, and Dublin Theatre Festivals.

For the Dublin Festival, the Arts Council action seemed particularly cruel: the Festival had come back to vibrant life in 1985, having (for only the second time in its history) failed to

mount an event in the previous year. The appointment of the
Festival's dynamic Programme Director, Michael Colgan, to the
position of Director of the Gate Theatre in late 1983, coupled
with the obviously declining energies of the Festival's founder
and long-time Director, Brendan Smith, and the Festival's
fragile financial state, had all contributed to the decision, taken
on my recommendation as Arts Council-nominated consultant
to the Festival, not to proceed with a 1984 event.

The 1985 Festival was, therefore, of huge significance to all
who loved and supported the event (such commitment dating,
in my own case, from the stunning theatrical experience of
*Stephen D.* in 1962). It was proof that the event could survive
major organizational change, financial difficulties, and a serious
break in continuity to re-emerge as Dublin's premier arts
Festival. The 1985 revival's 'resounding success' (the verdict of
Dr David Nowlan, theatre critic of *The Irish Times*) convinced
many of us that the Festival's future was secure. The Arts
Council's decision in early 1986, however, showed that
conviction to be questionable.

Deprived of a major funding pillar, the prognosis for the
event seemed bleak. However, to my great pleasure and relief,
the Council of the Dublin Theatre Festival, when advised of the
withdrawal of Arts Council funding, immediately decided that
the 1986 event must go ahead. This was an extremely brave
decision in the context of the mid-1980s, when, to say the least,
the general economic situation was grim. It was decided,
nonetheless, that a special fundraising campaign, directed at the
Dublin business community, should be undertaken to make up
as much of the deficit as was possible in the limited time
available. The determination and resolve of the Festival
Chairman, Dr Tim O'Driscoll, was crucial in this regard.

Tim, one of the great Irish 'nation-shapers', a renaissance-
style figure in the fields of industry, tourism, heritage, and
diplomacy, was precisely the type of person to have at one's side
in a crisis such as that faced by the Festival in 1986. He
immediately set to work persuading, with great success, his
many business contacts to contribute generously to the rescue
fund for the event. No less active in the campaign was Tim's
wife, Elizabeth, who, entirely on her own initiative and as an

admitted 'long shot', telephoned Tony O'Reilly to seek emergency funding for the Festival from the Ireland Funds.

This time, the footsteps on the Festival office stairs were rapid and light: they were those of Máirtín McCullough, Dublin representative of the Ireland Funds and, with consummate irony, Chairman of the Arts Council. Máirtín brought wonderful news: the Ireland Funds, in emergency session, had agreed to support the Irish arts festivals, in view of their importance to the cultural life of the country. It was agreed that the announcement of the Ireland Funds grants to the festivals would be made at a press conference at the Dublin Theatre Festival office.

In the meantime, possessed of the knowledge of the lifesaving grant, I appeared on a television programme dealing with the subject of arts funding and was roundly castigated by the Arts Editor of *The Irish Times*, who was, in fairness, unaware at that stage of the Ireland Funds intervention, for not taking the opportunity of a television appearance to bring the Festival down in a blaze of public glory, thereby illustrating the wretched level of government support for the Arts Council! In another of the ironies which surround the history of the Dublin Theatre Festival, the Arts Editor's son (Fergus Linehan) subsequently became a successor of mine as Festival Director.

Thanks to the timely and generous support of the Ireland Funds and to the greatly enhanced funding response from the corporate sector, the 1986 Dublin Theatre Festival went ahead, was warmly received critically, attracted large attendances and even returned a modest profit. I believed then and remain of the opinion that, if that year's Festival had failed to take place, the event would have died – two missing Festivals in three years would have been terminal.

It may seem odd that, in recounting my experiences at the helm of a major cultural event, I have devoted so much initial space to the finances of the organization and so little to the artistic content of the five Festivals of which I was Director. The fact is that, from beginning to end of the 1980s, the period of the Festival's history with which I am most familiar, the viability of the Festival was never guaranteed (Michael Colgan aptly described the gruelling annual process of seeking funds for the Festival as 'fighting the same old battles') and, even in years when the Arts Council was fully 'on board' in regard to funding, enormous amounts of time and energy had to be expended on the uncertain process of raising sufficient funds to complement box office receipts and grant aid, with a view to presenting a Festival of acknowledged international standard.

This uncertainty inevitably hung over every artistic decision made by the Festival, perhaps most strikingly in the case of one of the theatrical masterpieces of the 1980s, Peter Brook's three-part presentation of the *Mahabharata*, based on the ancient Indian sacred book. The production in its entirety was available to our Festival in 1985 but at an asking price of £90,000, not including travel and accommodation. While vigorous fundraising brought us to within £20,000 of the asking price, the remaining gap was too great to bridge without jeopardizing the continuing viability of the Festival. We were therefore forced to relinquish what would, without argument, have been one of the most significant presentations ever at a Dublin Theatre Festival, together with the pledges of sponsorship for the production received up to that point.

To illustrate our heavy dependence on fundraising, I can give a noteworthy example. In my report to the Festival Council on the 1988 Dublin Millennium Festival, the fourth and largest of the events under my stewardship, I noted that the turnover of close to £600,000 was made up of approximately one-third each of box office receipts, grant aid (Arts Council, Dublin Millennium Committee, British Council, Dublin City and County Councils, and Bord Fáilte) and commercial sponsorship/Festival patronage. Since direct expenditure on Festival productions that year amounted to nearly £400,000 (fourteen shows being presented and fully funded by the Festival, with another thirteen receiving financial support), the importance of fundraising during that period of the Festival's life is abundantly clear. This importance was all the greater because, in effect, during the 1980s, the Dublin Theatre Festival was comprised of two elements: the main Festival, with leading Irish and international presentations, and a smaller 'fringe' composed of independent theatre companies, mainly Irish but with a number of alternative/cabaret features from overseas.

Although the lion's share of direct production expenditure went on the 'main' Festival, a proportion of Festival funding was allocated to 'fringe' productions considered to be doing original or particularly imaginative work. This was a difficult and unwelcome area of decision-making for a Festival with limited funds, with a number of deserving companies failing to receive what they regarded as their due in terms of Festival support. The advent in the 1990s of a separate fringe organization in receipt of its own allocation of grant aid from the Arts Council was a logical development which, apart from easing the burden on Dublin Theatre Festival management, has undoubtedly increased public awareness of both mainstream and fringe Festival presentations and helped to expand the overall audience for theatre in Dublin.

## Finding the Shows

As I mentioned previously, my own formal involvement with the Dublin Theatre Festival began with my engagement in early 1984 on a consultancy basis to examine the feasibility of the Festival's continuation following the departure of Programme Director Michael Colgan to the Gate Theatre (for which, in my previous role as consultant to the Gate, I have to admit some degree of responsibility). At this time, also, the Festival Director, Brendan Smith, generously accepted the fact that, after twenty-seven years, the burden of the position was becoming too much for him. In effect, it was 'all change' at the Festival.

I concluded that, although, given the shortage of time and resources in hand, it would be imprudent to attempt to mount an event in 1984, with a new management team and realistic grant aid from the Arts Council and other regular funders, the Festival had indeed a future. The Council of the Festival and the Arts Council both agreed with this conclusion.

In the breathing space thus provided, Brendan Smith and Festival Chairman Tim O'Driscoll sounded me out on the prospect of my succeeding Brendan as Festival Director. I had previously worked with Tim on a number of heritage projects under the auspices of An Taisce, the National Trust for Ireland (of which he had also been Chairman), and had greatly valued the experience. I therefore needed little persuasion to work with him again and, after a short period of consideration, accepted the offer of the position of Festival Director. As I had a number of ongoing commitments, the contract specified my availability to the Festival on the basis of three days a week. It was also agreed that, as with the pairing of Brendan Smith and Michael Colgan, the management team would include a Programme Director whose primary task would be to research and recommend for consideration suitable shows for the upcoming Festivals.

Following a series of interviews, the unanimous choice for the position of Programme Director was Michael Scott, whose creative work at the Project and other venues was well known to all of us on the interview panel. The core Festival team was completed by administrators Jane Daly and Mairéad McKeever and fundraiser Myra Geraghty.

Work on compiling the 1985 programme began without delay. Because of the absence of the Festival in 1984, programming had, in effect, to start from scratch. As I mentioned earlier, a great deal of time and effort was expended on trying to 'land' Peter Brook's *Mahabharata*. Michael Scott and I saw the production at the Avignon Festival and at the home venue of the Brook company, Les Bouffes du Nord in Paris, and were hugely impressed. However, the show was fated not to come to Dublin and our attention subsequently focussed on the compilation of a programme which, we determined, would generate the excitement required of a Festival returning after a crucial absence while achieving the appropriate balance of content between Irish and international productions.

In the event, a programme of forty-one productions, twenty-eight Irish and thirteen international, was drawn together. At more than twenty years' remove, I find it hard to select all of the outstanding productions from such a large field. Some which come immediately to mind are the following: Barry McGovern in the premiere of *I'll Go On*; Druid's *Conversations on a Homecoming*; *Tent Meeting*, direct from the Actors' Theatre of Louisville; Molière's *Les Femmes Savantes*, brilliantly presented in rap style by Pistolteatern from Sweden; the first visit to Dublin of Robert Wilson, creator of *Einstein on the*

*Beach*, in *Readings* (Bob also participated in the Festival's international conference, 'The Creative Impulse in Modern Theatre' at TCD); the unique pairing of Siobhán McKenna and Maureen Potter in *Arsenic and Old Lace*; Rough Magic's *Caucasian Chalk Circle*; Hugh Leonard's *The Mask of Moriarty* (unfortunately, the only Leonard premiere during my period as Festival Director); and, of course, *Blood Brothers*, the Willy Russell musical which ran on (and on) after the Festival.

In the 1985 Festival, three very different Irish plays had a particular resonance with audiences: Stewart Parker's masterly *Northern Star*, presented by the Lyric Theatre, Belfast; Tom Mac Intyre's *Rise Up Lovely Sweeney*, the exciting successor piece to his mould-breaking *Great Hunger*; and Hugh Carr's bittersweet *Yesterday's Lovers* which, initially unheralded, proved to be a huge popular success.

The favourable audience and media reception of the 1985 Festival was both a relief and an encouragement to the Festival team. The mood in the Nassau Street office was buoyant and our preparations for the 1986 event were well advanced when the Arts Council 'no funding' bombshell hit us. With the eventual securing of adequate funds for the event, programming recommenced and a final line-up of thirty-two productions, twenty-two Irish and ten international, was achieved. Once again, the public reaction to the Festival was extremely good. While some of this may have been a 'sympathy vote' resulting from public dismay at our Arts Council cutback, I am, of course, disposed to think that the intrinsic merits of the programme accounted for the favourable reception.

By any standards, the programme included several productions which would have graced any international Festival. Among the international productions which gave me particular satisfaction were the *Monkey King* double bill presented by the Peking opera; Grips Theatre Berlin's original musical *Line One*, translated into English especially for our Festival, and the two classics, *Twelfth Night* and *The Cid*, presented by Cheek by Jowl on their first visit to Dublin. The Royal Court's production of Anne Devlin's *Ourselves Alone* brought to the Festival a chilling reminder of the Northern Troubles which so blighted 1980s Ireland. A warmer picture of Ulster life was presented in

Charabanc's presentation of Marie Jones's *The Girls in the Big Picture*. Patrick Mason's production of Frank McGuinness's *Innocence* (portraying a day in the extraordinary life of the painter Caravaggio) and Garry Hynes's new staging of Tom Murphy's powerful *A Whistle in the Dark* (which I had last seen on its London premiere in the early 1960s) were outstanding showcases for the work of two major Irish playwrights. The Festival also marked the emergence of a promising young writer by producing Jim Nolan's *The Boathouse*.

Two Irish productions of Neil Simon pieces in the 1986 Festival enjoyed contrasting fortunes: *They're Playing Our Song* (with music by Marvin Hamlisch of *A Chorus Line* fame) failed to draw audiences to the Olympia; on the other hand, Joe Dowling's vivid presentation of *Brighton Beach Memoirs* at the Gaiety was highly successful. Another hit at the Festival was Rough Magic's sparkling version of the greatest of all Restoration comedies, *The Country Wife*.

The 1987 Dublin Theatre Festival was the smallest in scale of my five events. It consisted of thirty-one shows (one less than the 1986 event), eight of them international, twenty-three Irish. In contrast to the acclaim with which the previous two Festivals had been received, critical rapture in certain quarters was restrained on this occasion (although *The Irish Times*'s final verdict was 'despite the Jonahs, a good Festival'). In large measure, this appeared to be due to a perceived shortage of major new Irish works in the programme. In addition, the Gaiety Theatre, a pivotal venue for the Festival, was unavailable to us in 1987. In part but, of course, not entirely, this was compensated for by the opening of a new venue, the Tivoli.

After an enormous expenditure of Festival resources and energy, notably those of Programme Director Michael Scott, the Tivoli opened its doors with the spectacular Swedish-language production of *Pygmalion* presented by Orion Teatern of Stockholm. The opening, with its teeming downpour of rain, remains one of the most remarkable scenes I have ever witnessed on a Dublin stage.

The second overseas production to catch the public imagination in a significant way during the 1987 Festival was the strongly feminist *Donna Giovanni*, adapted by the Mexican director Jesusa Rodriguez from Mozart and Da Ponte and described by the performers, the all-female Compagnie de Divas, as 'somewhere between commedia dell'arte and cabaret'.

Other notable international presentations lined up for 1987 were the Mickery Theatre (Netherlands) with *Vespers*, Bread and Puppet (USA) with *Life and Death of a Fireman*, the Chorus Theatre of Manipur (India) in *Chakravyuha* and the hugely enjoyable *A Concert for the Theatre*, starring the Broadway diva, Barbara Cook. Barbara's reference to the less-than-glamorous venue in which, owing to the non-availability of the Gaiety, we were forced to house her performance as 'this garage' still brings a twinge of mortification!

Of the home-produced shows in 1987, particular mention has to be made of *Les Liaisons Dangereuses* at the Gate, the revival of Hugh Leonard's early play, *Madigan's Lock* at the Abbey, the visit of Cork Theatre Company with Brian Friel's *Volunteers* and Field Day's gripping production of Stewart Parker's *Pentecost*. On their first visit to a Dublin Theatre Festival, Siamsa Tíre, the national folk theatre of Ireland, achieved full houses at the Olympia, in spite of sniffy remarks about 'peasant culture' which I received from one or two urban sophisticates of my acquaintance.

Two independent companies which remain vibrantly active today, Rough Magic (*The Silver Tassie*) and Storytellers (*The Story of the Widow's Son*), contributed significant work to the 1987 Festival: Declan Hughes directed Sean O'Casey's 'immense black mass of a play' for Rough Magic while Mary Elizabeth Burke-Kennedy brought Mary Lavin's short story, with its wicked choice of endings, vividly to life for Storytellers.

It having been decided by the city fathers and mothers that 1988 constituted the thousandth anniversary of Dublin's foundation by the Vikings, the Dublin Theatre Festival was naturally identified as one of the cultural mainstays of this special year. Under intense pressure, the Council of the Festival agreed to recognize the significance of the occasion by extending the Millennium event to three weeks. The result was a greatly increased workload for the Festival staff which, mercifully assisted by additional grant aid from the Millennium committee and the National Lottery, was able to bring forth the largest programme of events ever mounted by the Festival: forty-five shows, thirteen international, thirty-two Irish.

This Festival was the last of four for which Michael Scott, our 'artistic bloodhound' as I called him (a term of high praise), was Programme Director. In his valedictory remarks about Michael, our Chairman, Dr Tim O'Driscoll, reflecting the feelings of all his colleagues, said: 'His contribution has indeed been a major one, particularly in establishing contact with young audiences.'

To crown his career with the Festival, Michael was asked to develop and direct for 1988 a very special production, an adaptation by himself and Christopher Nolan of Christopher's writings to that date. Christopher himself chose the title *Torchlight and Laser Beams* to illustrate the transformation in his powers of communication brought about by his command of the written word. In his own words, the play 'juxtaposes an able-bodied person's values against a secretly-able-minded cripple's joy of living, despite gross handicap'.

The play, with its magnificent central performance by Conor Mullan, greatly moved audiences at the Gaiety and entranced critics (*The Guardian* described it as 'a dazzling Christopher Nolan adaptation') and its scheduled run was, unsurprisingly, extended to meet the very high level of public demand. Of all the shows produced by the Dublin Theatre Festival during the 1984–1989 period, I would have to say that *Torchlight and Laser Beams* is the one I am most proud to have been involved with.

Perhaps it was the scale of the event or the millennial sensibility infusing the year that made the 1988 Festival something special. Whatever it was, critical and audience reactions were overwhelmingly positive. Michael Coveney in the *Financial Times* described the Festival as 'certainly one to remember'; the *Evening Herald* declared that 'the 29th Dublin Theatre Festival exceeded all expectations'; 'one of the best' was the phrase used by *Irish Stage and Screen*, and the French magazine *Les Temps Modernes* devoted a twenty-page article to the Festival and its importance in terms of world theatre.

Among the many Irish productions which attracted wide acclaim in the 1988 Festival were the two Frank McGuinness offerings: the world premiere of his *Carthaginians* ('electrifying and elegiac' according to the *Financial Times*) and his new version of Ibsen's *Peer Gynt* ('a coruscatingly eloquent and brilliantly staged production' also according to the *Financial Times*); Donal O'Kelly's *Bat the Father, Rabbit the Son* ('dramatic tour de force' in the view of the *Irish Independent*); Brendan Kennelly's adaptation of Euripides's *Medea* ('powerfully written, beautifully staged and acted' said the *Sunday Independent*), and *Women in Arms* from Storytellers and Mary Elizabeth Burke-Kennedy ('a wonderfully fluid production; a deeply satisfying evening' was the verdict of the *Sunday Tribune*).

The international representation at the Dublin Millennium Theatre Festival was varied and, I think it is fair to say, never dull. For the first time, the Festival hosted the Royal Shakespeare Company: their *Hamlet* was memorable for Mark Rylance's intense 'prince on the verge of a nervous breakdown' performance, reflected in the threateningly angled stage setting. *The Irish Times* reviewer saw it as 'the best, most subtle, most deeply affecting characterization of 'Hamlet' it has been my privilege to see'.

In complete contrast to the Shakespearian angst on offer at the Olympia, the brilliant antics of Circus Oz lit up the Gaiety during the first week of the Festival. A fusion of circus, live rock music, comedy and sensational acrobatics (including a scarcely believable 'human fly' routine), the show proved to be 'a copper-bottomed hit' (to quote *The Irish Times* yet again).

In 1988 apartheid was still a cruel reality in South Africa. Out of that grim background, the joyful Amampondo, a group of drummers, musicians, dancers and acrobats from Langa township outside Capetown, brought to Dublin audiences an awareness of the inspiration that cultural expression can bring to an oppressed people. We were honoured to have them in our programme.

Contemporary trends in European dance were showcased for a week at the Olympia Theatre. Two groups, one French, one German, participated in this 'dancefest'. *Docteur Labus*, from the Groupe Émile Dubois featured the brilliant choreography of Jean-Claude Gallotta in a performance interweaving four love stories. Tanz-Forum of Cologne, choreographed by Jochen

Ulrich, fused classical and modern dance with everyday movement to create an incisive self-portrait of a group of dancers drawn from no less than nine countries. It was, perhaps, the only disappointment of the Dublin Millennium Festival that, in contrast to the sell-out audiences at the same theatre for the RSC and Amampondo, and in spite of good reviews, attendances at the international dance presentations were relatively modest.

The sheer diversity of the 1988 Festival raised, not for the first time, the question of whether the programming of the event, or at least the Irish component of it, should follow a thematic line or whether it should simply provide 'something for everyone'. The Dublin Theatre Festival had itself previously triggered a major examination of what constituted the fundamental nature of theatre today: the excitement generated by Kazimierz Braun's Contemporary Theatre of Wroclaw ('theatre as an encounter') at the Festival in the early 1980s (with *Birthrate* and *Anna Livia*) had initiated a discussion on the direction which Irish theatre might take during the remainder of the decade. Our 1985 conference 'The Creative Impulse in Modern Theatre' had been an attempt on the part of the Festival to advance the discussion.

In the event, in spite of the physical innovations of Tom Mac Intyre's theatre pieces and the original work of Maciek Reszczynski (an alumnus of the Wroclaw group) with Theatre Unlimited, which presented *The Murder of Gonzago* (1986) and *Penelope* (1988) at the Festival, Irish theatre remained largely committed, often superbly, as with Friel and Murphy, to the primacy of The Word. This being so, after the Millennium Festival, Dr Helena Sheehan, in a thoughtful article entitled 'Plays Political', raised the question as to whether a theatre festival should be 'an eclectic potpourri' or whether it 'should stand out in terms of thematic quality, with the emphasis on commissioning new work on the cutting edge of coming to terms with contemporary experience'.

In the case of the Dublin Theatre Festival, the financial constraints to which the event was subject, at any rate during the mid to late 1980s, effectively dictated that the eclectic 'something for everyone' route was the one realistically to be taken. Occasionally, however, we did take the risk, as in 1988, of commissioning original works for direct production by the Festival, addressing an issue of relevance to contemporary Ireland. The genesis of *Torchlight and Laser Beams* has been referred to earlier. A second Festival commission in Millennium year, Antoine Ó Flatharta's *City Mission*, dealt with the collision between rural ideals and urban realities. Dr Sheehan found it 'a flawed but reflective and provocative work ... using the conventions of the traditional Abbey play to undermine the ideological foundations of its existence'.

David Grant became the Programme Director shortly after the 1988 event concluded. A Dubliner who worked for five years with the Belfast Festival and who subsequently became editor of *Theatre Ireland* magazine, David had a particular commitment to reflecting in the Festival programme the high level of theatrical activity which had exploded all over Ireland, even in the difficult days of the 1980s.

The programme for the thirtieth Dublin Theatre Festival in 1989 clearly reflected this commitment: the unprecedentedly large line-up of fifty shows included no less than thirty-nine Irish productions. As the programme grew and grew, the arguments for creating a separate fringe event to encompass the burgeoning energies of the independent theatre sector became increasingly compelling. It also became clear that, to accommodate the demand from theatre companies for participation in the event, the 1989 Festival would, like the Dublin Millennium Festival, have to run for three weeks. This time, however, the task had to be undertaken without the benefit of the special grant aid made available in 1988.

The undoubted headline show of the 1989 event was the Moscow Art Theatre's presentation of Chekhov's *The Seagull* at the Abbey. Featuring Innokenti Smoktunovsky, the legendary Russian film Hamlet, the play was performed in Russian with simultaneous translation magnificently delivered by Clive Geraghty. In connection with preparations for bringing the production to Dublin, John Costigan, then of the Abbey Theatre (now Chief Executive of the Gaiety), and I visited Moscow in early 1989, the historic year when the Soviet empire started to crumble. The resonance of current politics in Russia (this was the era of perestroika and glasnost) was inescapable, both in the production itself and in the demeanour of the company members. It was a unique opportunity for John and myself, and subsequently for Dublin audiences, to experience a Chekhov masterpiece performed by Stanislavsky's own company at such an exciting and, in fact, revolutionary moment in Russian history.

As was appropriate in the bicentennial year of another revolution – this time the French Revolution – a strong French element was prominent in the 1989 Festival. An early coup by David Grant was the sourcing of *Freaks*, an extraordinary play adapted by Genevieve de Kermabon from the cult 1932 Tod Browning film. This was a joint production of the Avignon Festival and Peter Brook's Centre Internationale de Créations Théatrales, with a cast almost entirely composed of performers whose unusual physical characteristics gave the piece its cruel name. As presented in the Tivoli, an ideal space for such a free-ranging piece, *Freaks* produced in the capacity audiences a range of complex emotions, building into admiration for a brave and talented group of performers who gave of themselves to draw us into their little-understood world.

Continuing the French theme, Théâtre Nécrobie de Marseille dramatized the vast story of the French Revolution in a two-part presentation entitled *Vivre Libre ou Mourir*, written by (and featuring) Eric Eychenne; and the Arts Theatre, Belfast, presented Derek Mahon's new version of *L'École des Femmes*. To add a Britannic flavour to the Gallic content of the Festival, John Sessions (of *Spitting Image* fame), en route from the West End to New York, presented the seriously irreverent *Napoleon, the Untold American Story*. In a unique Franco-Irish col-laboration, the new Dance Theatre of Ireland, which remains one of the most exciting and innovative dance companies in this country, made its Dublin Theatre Festival debut in 1989 with a celebration of French choreography in *La Beauté des Fleurs*.

The French-sounding name of the Rambert Dance Company, who presented two separate programmes at the Olympia, might have suggested that this was a further contribution to the Bicentenary celebrations. In fact, the company (formerly the even more French-sounding Ballet Rambert), under the artistic direction of Richard Alston and 'at one of the highest points in its history' according to the *Financial Times*, were the acknowledged leading English exponents of contemporary dance. Unfortunately, their visit to Dublin was blighted by a number of injuries sustained in rehearsal, so we did not get to see this superb company at their fabled best.

In 1989, for the first (and, to my knowledge, possibly the last) time, the Dublin Theatre Festival hosted an Irish film premiere. Kenneth Branagh's version of Shakespeare's *Henry V* was screened at the Savoy Cinema and Branagh himself was guest of honour at the event. He also participated in an entertaining post-screening interview with Michael Dwyer, Artistic Director of our sister event, the Dublin Film Festival.

The Irish contribution to the thirtieth Festival was so huge that, in this brief retrospective glance, I can select for mention only a relative handful of shows. Between original plays and adaptations, I can identify twenty new works by Irish writers in the programme for that year. Among new plays, the Abbey Theatre brought the complex Tom Murphy work *Too Late for Logic*; Wet Paint's debut at the Festival gave us Dermot Bolger's *The Lament for Arthur Cleary*; and Druid came with Ken Bourke's *Wild Harvest*. Adaptations by Irish writers included Aidan Mathews's version of Lorca's *The House of Bernarda Alba* at the Gate, Thomas Kilroy's adaptation of Ibsen's *Ghosts* at the Peacock, Storytellers' *The Trial of Esther Waters*, based on the George Moore novel, and *The Wake*, challengingly reduced by Donal O'Kelly and Paul O'Hanrahan from Joyce's *Finnegans Wake*.

In addition to its large programme of performances, the thirtieth Festival had an exceptional number of seminars and workshops. Themes explored included theatre in education, masks and masking, acting styles, open air performance, and the life and work of Stewart Parker. Under the collective heading of *Festivities*, a series of three encounters with leading practitioners dealt with play production, the future of dance in Ireland and contemporary adaptations of the classics (a feature of 1989).

Overall, the event had a programme on a scale which was, by any standards, enormous and which, one can now recognize with the full benefit of hindsight, was guaranteed to strain all of the Festival's resources, human and financial, to the limit or, indeed, beyond it. Nonetheless, the 1989 event, by giving a welcome and a platform to so many independent theatre companies, was, in my view, a significant contributory factor to the vibrant state of Irish theatre throughout the 1990s and into the Celtic Tiger era.

## Finding a Successor

During the period leading up to the 1989 event, I had no idea that this was to be my last Dublin Theatre Festival. In another capacity, as Chairperson of the National Concert Hall, I had been aware that the European Union had designated Dublin as European City of Culture for 1991 and, with the Concert Hall board and staff, I was already, in late 1989, engaged in the preparation of a programme of special musical events to mark this unique occasion. I was also vaguely aware that, a bare fifteen months before the start of Dublin's incumbency, the organizing committee had not yet appointed a director for the event.

Having recently agreed a three-year extension to my original five-year contract with the Dublin Theatre Festival, I was completely unprepared for an approach by the City of Culture organization seeking my acceptance of the position of director of Dublin 1991. This approach came in the very direct form of a personal visit to my office by a member of the City of Culture committee who, by doing so, succeeded in arousing my serious interest in taking on this new challenge.

I reported on this encounter to my Chairman, Tim O'Driscoll, and indicated to him that I was disposed to accept the offer from Dublin 1991, should the Festival be willing to release me from my contract. Although reluctant to accept that our five-year working relationship would be coming to an end, Tim agreed to approach the Theatre Festival Council with a proposal that my contract be waived. Tim stressed that any agreement to this proposal would be subject to the proviso that, until my successor had been appointed and insofar as my duties with Dublin 1991 permitted, I would maintain a 'watching brief' in relation to the Festival. It was understood that I would be closely involved in the identification and selection of my successor.

The Festival Council agreed to this process and I joined the Dublin 1991 organization as director on 1 November 1989. By a sad coincidence, the Festival lost two directors in one week: just a few days before I made the move to the City of Culture office, Brendan Smith, founding Director and, for so long, guiding star of the Festival, died. I would like to think that his final years were made a little more comfortable by the decision of the Festival Council to provide Brendan, on his stepping down as Festival Director in 1984, with a modest pension in recognition of his unique contribution to the creation and growth of the Festival.

I had not stepped down as Festival director without having some inkling of who my successor might be. The pressures of time and finance faced by the Festival in late 1989 and early 1990, coupled with the danger of a loss of momentum, militated against the potentially tortuous process of public advertisement for the position. In any case, an excellent candidate was in the offing.

To my mind, the most suitable person in Ireland to run the event was Tony Ó Dálaigh, formerly of the Irish Theatre Company and Irish National Opera. I was aware through family connections (he and I are married to two sisters) that Tony was, at that juncture, entering the last months of his term as director of the Royal Hospital, Kilmainham (RHK), in which role, which included management of an extensive arts programme, he had been conspicuously successful. I advised Tim O'Driscoll accordingly and, at a meeting attended by Tim, Tony, and myself, it was agreed that, subject to the approval of the Festival Council, Tony would take over as Festival director in March, when his RHK contract expired.

Having started my work with the Dublin 1991 organization, I was dismayed to learn that, because of a shortfall in the funds actually raised from the business sector for the 1989 Festival as compared to the sponsorship income originally reported, Tony was about to inherit a sizeable deficit. I count it a matter of great good fortune that, at just this time, I was able to deliver, under the auspices of Dublin 1991, a generous leading donor to the Festival. The Irish Life Assurance Company stayed the course with the Dublin Theatre Festival for many years and shared in the success of the event in the 1990s.

In 1991, I had one final programming association with the Festival. The calendar for Dublin's year as European City of Culture required a significant theatre element. The main Dublin Theatre Festival that year was appropriately enhanced and expanded to mark the occasion. However, as a counterpoise to the major autumn programme of theatre, a spring event was considered necessary. The result was 'Mayday to Bloomsday' (the title was Tony Ó Dálaigh's), described by *The Irish Times* as 'a lively seven weeks for playgoers from April 20 to June 15.

The 'Mayday to Bloomsday' event was administered by the Dublin Theatre Festival on behalf of Dublin 1991 and, as was appropriate to a cultural celebration with a European connection, it incorporated Russian, Romanian, German, French, British, and Irish themes. The Royal National Theatre's presentation of Molière's *Tartuffe*, performed by an all-Asian cast was particularly international in scope.

It is hard for me to believe that the Dublin Theatre Festival has now reached its fiftieth year. Having had the privilege of knowing personally many of the outstanding figures, now gone from us, who founded and developed the Festival, notably Brendan Smith, Tim O'Driscoll, and Lord Killanin, and having attended my first Festival play all of forty-five years ago, I am strongly aware of how long ago it is since I contributed a link or two to the slender but precious chain which joins the first Festival to the historically significant event of 2007.

# Production History Part Two: 1971–1984

## Dublin Theatre Festival 1971

8–20 March

*Ah Well, It Won't Be Long Now!* by Mary Manning. Olympia Theatre. Directed by Roland Jaquarello.

The Alfred Jarry Pantomime Ensemble. Eblana Theatre.

*Caligula* by Albert Camus. Le Tréteau de Paris at the Peacock Theatre. Directed by Georges Vitaly.

*Celibates* adapted by Allan McCleland from George Moore. Irish Life Theatre. Directed by Allan McCleland.

*Children of the Wolf* by John Peacock. Player Wills Theatre. Directed by Vincent Dowling.

*An Chúis in Aghaidh Íosa* by Diego Fabbri translated by Liam Ó Briain. An Damer. Directed by Frank Dermody.

*The Dáil Debate* by G. P. Gallivan. Peacock Theatre. Directed by Seán Ó Briain.

*The Devil at Work* by Constantine Fitzgibbon. Abbey Theatre. Directed by Alan Simpson.

*Doesn't Anyone Remember Murphy?* by John Quinn. Eblana Theatre. Directed by Eamonn Draper.

*Heartbreak House* by G.B. Shaw. Gate Theatre. Directed by Hilton Edwards.

*It's Later Than You Think* by Jean Anouilh, translated by Lucienne Hill. Edwards-Mac Liammóir Productions at the Gate Theatre. Directed by Hilton Edwards.

*A Loud Bang on June the First* by Wesley Burrowes. Abbey Theatre. Directed by Vincent Dowling.

*Mr. Joyce Is Leaving Paris* by Tom Gallacher. Eblana Theatre. Directed by Robert Gillespie.

*The Morning After Optimism* by Tom Murphy. Abbey Theatre. Directed by Hugh Hunt.

*Murderous Angels* by Conor Cruise O'Brien. Gaiety Theatre. Directed by Laurence Bourne.

*One is One*, written and performed by Julian Chagrin. Peacock Theatre.

*The Patrick Pearse Motel* by Hugh Leonard. Gemini Productions at the Olympia Theatre. Directed by James Grout.

*Partly Furnished* by Barry L. Hillman. Eblana Theatre. Directed by Colm Ó Briain.

*Poc Leim* by Liam Mac Uistin. Peacock Theatre. Directed by Seán Ó Briain.

*Prelude and Fugue* by Clifford Bax. Eblana Theatre. Directed by Eamonn Draper.

*Soft Morning City* compiled from various authors. Tideway Productions at the Player Wills Theatre. Directed by Louis Lentin.


## Dublin Theatre Festival 1972

13–29 March

*Beginning to End: A Selection from the Works of Samuel Beckett* by Samuel Beckett and Jack McGowran. Gaiety Theatre. Directed by Jack McGowran.

*Le Bourgeois Gentilhomme* by J-B.P. Molière. Le Tréteau de Paris at the Player Wills Theatre. Directed by Maurice Jacquemont.

*Brendan* written and performed by Ulick O'Connor. Peacock Theatre. Directed by Tomás Mac Anna.

*Cruiskeen Lawn* adapted by Fergus Linehan, adapted from Myles na Gopaleen (Flann O'Brien). Eblana Theatre. Directed by Barry Cassin.

*The Fourth Kingdom* compiled by Tomás Mac Anna and Adrian Vale. Royal Hibernian Hotel. Directed by Bill Golding.

*Hamlet* by William Shakespeare. Gaiety Theatre. Directed by Ray McAnally.

*Helfrid Foron* at the Peacock Theatre (a mime performance).

*The House of Blue Leaves* by John Guare. Olympia Theatre. Directed by Michael MacAloney and Chris O'Neill.

*Jeannette* by Maurice Kurtz. Gaiety Theatre. Directed by Laurence Bourne.

*The Night Thoreau Spent in Jail* by Jerome Lawrence and Robert E. Lee. American Playhouse Theatre at the Olympia Theatre. Directed by Jerome Lawrence.

*Prisoner of the Crown* by Richard F. Stockton, based on a story idea by Richard T. Herd. Abbey Theatre. Directed by Tomás Mac Anna.

*The Restless Years* by Peter O'Shaughnessy. Dun-Ocean Enterprises at the Tech-Inst Theatre. Directed by Peter O'Shaughnessy.

*Revival* by Tom Gallacher. Eblana Theatre. Directed by Robert Gillespie.

*Richard's Cork Leg* by Brendan Behan, adapted by Alan Simpson. Peacock Theatre. Directed by Alan Simpson.

*Stag Party* by Leonard Webb. Olympia Theatre. Directed by Michael Rudman.

*The Tantalus* by Wesley Burrowes. Player Wills Theatre. Directed by Godfrey Quigley.

*The True Story of the Horrid Popish Plot* by Desmond Forristal. Edwards-Mac Liammóir Productions at the Gate Theatre. Directed by Hilton Edwards.

*The White House* by Tom Murphy. Abbey Theatre. Directed by Vincent Dowling.

## Dublin Theatre Festival 1973

1–13 October

*Bloom of the Diamond Stone* by Wilson John Haire. Abbey Theatre in association with the Royal Court Theatre. Directed by Vincent Dowling.

*Da* by Hugh Leonard. Olympia Theatre. Directed by James D. Waring.

*Escurial* by Michel De Ghelderode. Peacock Theatre. Directed by Roland Jaquarello.

*Gertrude Stein's Gertrude Stein* by Nancy Cole. Player Wills Theatre.

*The Herne's Egg* by W. B. Yeats. Peacock Theatre. Directed by Jim Fitzgerald.

*The Importance of Being Earnest* by Oscar Wilde. Abbey Theatre. Directed by Alan Barlow.

*Irish Music and Poetry.* Dublin Theatre Festival in association with Nora Lever Productions at Christ Church Cathedral. Directed by Nora Lever.

*The Joslyn Circle* by Harding Lemay. Eblana Theatre. Directed by Liam O'Callaghan.

Juliette Greco at the Royal Dublin Society Concert Hall.

*The Last of the Bucks* by Ulick O'Connor. Castletown House. Directed by Tomás Mac Anna and Jim Fitzgerald

*Lord Arthur Saville's Crime* adapted by Constance Cox from Oscar Wilde. World Theatre Productions at the Gresham Hotel.

*Marcella* adapted by Godfrey Quigley from a novel by Brinsley MacNamara. World Theatre Productions at the Olympia Theatre. Directed by Martin Dempsey.

*Noone* by Joe O'Donnell. Edwards-Mac Liammóir Productions in association with Gemini Productions at the Gate Theatre. Directed by Hilton Edwards.

*The Only Street* by Tom Gallacher. Eblana Theatre. Directed by Robert Gillespie.

*Prelude in Kazbek Street* by Micheál Mac Liammóir. Edwards-Mac Liammóir Productions at the Gate Theatre. Directed by Hilton Edwards.

*Prisoner of Second Avenue* by Neil Simon. Eamonn Andrews Studios at the Gaiety Theatre. Directed by Fred O'Donovan.

*Purgatory* by W. B. Yeats. Peacock Theatre. Directed by Jim Fitzgerald.

*Sunshine Boys* by Neil Simon. Gaiety Theatre.

*Tartuffe* by J-B.P. Molière, translated by Donal M. Frame. Special Molière Tri-Centenary Productions at the Royal Dublin Society Concert Hall. Directed by Maurice Jacquemont.

*Under Milk Wood* by Dylan Thomas. London Theatre Company at the Peacock Theatre.

## Dublin Theatre Festival 1974

30 September–12 October

*Black Man's Country* by Desmond Forristal. Edwards-Mac Liammóir Productions at the Gate Theatre. Directed by Hilton Edwards.

*Crock* adapted by Turlough McConnell and David Meade from James Stephens's novel, *The Crock of Gold*. Gaiety Theatre. Directed by Alan Simpson.

*Everything in the Garden* adapted by Edward Albee from the play by Giles Cooper. World Theatre Productions at the Gresham Hotel. Directed by Ann O'Driscoll.

*Feminine Plural* by Leila Blake. Player Wills Theatre.

*The Game's a Bogey* by John McGrath. 7:84 Theatre Company at Dublin City Theatre. Directed by John McGrath.

*The Gathering* by Edna O'Brien. Abbey Theatre. Directed by Barry Davis.

*The Happy Go Likeable Man* adapted by Jim Sheridan from J-B.P. Molière. Peacock Theatre. Directed by Joe Dowling.

*Jacques Brel is Alive and Well and Living in Paris* adapted by Eric Blau and Mort Shuman from Jacques Brel. Eblana Theatre. Directed by Bill Keating.

*Just Libby* by Libby Morris. Player Wills Theatre.

*The Letter* by Noel O'Brien. Four-in-One Players. Project Arts Centre. Directed by Chris O'Neill.

*The Morgan Yard* by Kevin O'Morrison. Olympia Theatre. Directed by Paul Shyre.

*Motherlove* by August Strindberg, translated by Arvid Paulson. Peacock Theatre. Directed by Pat Laffan.

*On the Outside* by Tom Murphy and Noel O'Donoghue. Four-in-One at Project Arts Centre. Directed by Chris O'Neill.

*L'Orfeo* by Monteverdi. Christ Church Cathedral.

*Pride and Prejudice* adapted by Helen Jerome from Jane Austen. Castletown House. Directed by Nora Lever.

*Strongbow* by Maurice Davin Power. Nora Lever Productions at Christ Church Cathedral. Directed by Nora Lever.

*Summer* by Hugh Leonard. Olympia Theatre. Directed by Brian Murray

Théâtre de La Huchette at the Player Wills Theatre, performing the work of Guy de Maupassant and Jacques Prévert. Directed by Nicolas Bataille.

*The Third Policeman* adapted by Eamon Morrissey from the novel by Flann O'Brien. Dublin Comedy Theatre at the Gate Theatre. Directed by Eamon Morrissey.

*Ulysses In Nighttown* adapted by Marjorie Berkentin from James Joyce's *Ulysses*. Abbey Theatre. Directed by Tomás Mac Anna.

## Dublin Theatre Festival 1975

29 September–11 October

*Arms and the Woman* by Sean O'Driscoll. John Player Theatre. Directed by Peter O'Shaughnessy.

*A Borderline Case* by Harry Barton. Gemini Productions at the Eblana Theatre. Directed by Barry Cassin.

*Dreaming (Or Am I?)* by Luigi Pirandello and *The Old Tune* by Robert Pinget, adapted and translated by Samuel Beckett. Peacock Theatre. Directed by Pat Laffan.

*Innish* adapted by Fergus Linehan and Jim Doherty from Lennox Robinson's *Drama at Inish*. Abbey Theatre. Directed by Alan Simpson.

*The Inspector* adapted by Eamon Morrissey, adapted from Nikolai Gogol. Dublin Comedy Theatre at the Gate Theatre. Directed by Desmond Perry.

*Irishmen* by Hugh Leonard. Irish Theatre Company at the Gaiety Theatre. Directed by James D. Waring.

*Love?* and *Plays Without Words* (including mimes by Samuel Beckett). Theatre on the Balustrade at the Gaiety Theatre. Directed by Ladislav Fialka.

*Lulu* by Frank Wedekind. Project Arts Centre. Directed by Agnes Bernelle.

*The Real Charlotte* adapted by Adrian Vale and Terence de Vere White from Somerville and Ross's novel. Edwards-Mac Liammóir Productions at the Gate Theatre. Directed by Hilton Edwards.

*Rhyming Couplets* by Kevin Grattan. Peacock Theatre. Directed by Joe Dowling.

*The Sanctuary Lamp* by Tom Murphy. Abbey Theatre. Directed by Jonathan Hales.

*The Sea Horse* by Edward Moore. Gemini Productions at the Eblana Theatre. Directed by Robert Gillespie.

*So Great a Sweetness*, compiled by Anne Tate from Yeats, Maud Gonne, Katherine Tynan, Lady Gregory, and Edward Martyn. Nora Lever Productions at Castletown House. Directed by Nora Lever.

*Spokesong* by Stewart Parker. World Theatre Productions at the John Player Theatre. Directed by Michael Heffernan.

*Venus and Adonis* by John Blow and *Il Combattimento di Tancredi e Clorinde* by Monteverdi. Christ Church Cathedral. Produced by Anne Makower.

*What a Bloody Circus* by Eugène Ionesco translated by Donal Watson. Peacock Theatre. Directed by Petrika Ionesco.

## Dublin Theatre Festival 1976

27 September–9 October

*Adam and Eve* by Alan Dee. State Cinema, Phibsboro. Choreographed by Mavis Ascott.

*Article Five* by Brian Phelan. Project Arts Centre. Directed by Michael Sheridan.

*The Canning Town Cowboy* by Shane Connaughton. Wilmot Theatrical Services at Coláiste Mhuire. Directed by Pam Brighton.

*The City Whose Lord is a Child* by Henry de Montherlant, translated by Christophe Campos. Eblana Theatre. Directed by Jim Waring.

*Cries from Casement as his Bones are Brought to Dublin* adapted by Paddy Scully from David Rudkin's original radio play. Project Arts Centre. Directed by Paddy Scully.

*Dead Eyed Dicks* by Peter Kind. Eamon Andrews Studio and HM Tennent Ltd. at the Gaiety Theatre. Directed by Lionel Harris. Special preview in aid of Amnesty International.

*The Devil's Own People* by Patrick Galvin. Gemini Productions at the Gaiety Theatre. Directed by James D. Waring.

*Friends* by Kevin O'Connor. Peacock Theatre. Directed by Kevin McHugh.

*The Giant Lobelia* by Harry Barton. Gemini Productions at the Eblana Theatre. Directed by Barry Cassin.

*The Hard Life* adapted by Pat Layde from Flann O'Brien. Peacock Theatre. Directed by Alan Simpson.

*Jack Be Nimble* by Tom Mac Intyre. Peacock Theatre. Directed by Patrick Mason.

*Lysistrata* adapted by Anna Manahan and Agnes Bernelle from Alan A. Summerstein's translation of *Aristophanes*. Amber Productions at the John Player Theatre. Directed by Agnes Bernelle.

*Mobile Homes* by Jim Sheridan. Project Arts Centre. Directed by Peter Sheridan.

*Moby Dick* adapted by Jack Aranson, from Hermann Melville's novel. St. Catherine's. Directed and performed by Jack Aranson.

*More Stately Mansions* by Eugene O'Neill. Nora Lever Productions at the John Player Theatre. Directed by Nora Lever.

*Operation Shield Rock* by Jonas Arnason, translated by Alan Boucher. Icelandic Theatre Company at the Peacock Theatre.

*The Plough and The Stars* by Sean O'Casey. Abbey Theatre. Golden Jubilee Performance. Directed by Tomás Mac Anna.

*The Rivals* by Richard Brinsley Sheridan. Abbey Theatre. Directed by William Chappell.

*The Seventh Sin* by Desmond Forristal. Edwards-Mac Liammóir Productions at the Gate Theatre. Directed by Hilton Edwards.

*A Song of Scandal* adapted by Maureen Charlton and Annette Perry from Richard Brinsley Sheridan. Pavilion Theatre. Directed by Alice Dalgarno.

*The Speakers.* Dublin Theatre Festival in association with the Abbey Theatre present Joint Stock Company at the Abbey Theatre. Directed by Max Stafford-Clark.

*Tales of the Emigrants.* Children's T Company in various locations.

*Tea and Sex and Shakespeare* by Thomas Kilroy. Abbey Theatre. Directed by Max Stafford-Clark.

## Dublin Theatre Festival 1977

3–15 October

*Aisling Mhic Artain* by Eoghan Ó Tuairisc. Peacock Theatre. Directed by Eddie Golden.

*As You Like It* by William Shakespeare. Irish Theatre Company at the Gaiety Theatre. Directed by Joe Dowling.

*Catchpenny Twist* by Stewart Parker. Peacock Theatre. Directed by Pat Laffan.

*Cock-a-doodle-dandy* by Sean O'Casey. Abbey Theatre. Directed by Tomás Mac Anna.

*Conversation About An Absent Lover* by Peter Hacks. Project Arts Centre. Directed by Sean Tracey.

*The Liberty Suit* by Peter Sheridan and Gerard Mannix Flynn. Project Arts Centre at the Olympia Theatre. Directed by Jim Sheridan.

*Living Quarters* by Brian Friel. Abbey Theatre. Directed by Joe Dowling.

*The Mother* adapted by Bertolt Brecht from Maxim Gorky. Project Arts Centre. Directed by Donald Taylor-Black.

*Old World* by Aleksei Arbuzov, translated by Ariadne Nicolaeff. Eblana Theatre. Directed by Chloe Gibson.

*On Baile's Strand* by W. B. Yeats. Project Arts Centre.

*The Proposal* by Anton Chekhov. Irish Theatre Company at Players Theatre. Directed by Andy Hinds.

*Purgatory* by W. B. Yeats. Project Arts Centre. Directed by Jim Sheridan.

*Rings For a Spanish Lady* by Antonio Gala, translated, directed, and adapted by Peter Luke . Gaiety Theatre.

*The Runner Stumbles* by Milan Stitt. Gemini Productions at the Gate Theatre. Directed by Barry Cassin.

*La Serrure* by Jean Tardieu and *La Voix Humaine* by Jean Cocteau. Théâtre Present at the John Player Theatre. With Arlette Thomas and Pierre Peyrou.

*Talbot's Box* by Thomas Kilroy. Peacock Theatre. Directed by Patrick Mason.

*The Twinkling Twins* by Renee de O'Baldai. Irish Theatre Company at Players Theatre. Directed by Andy Hinds.

*Travesties* by Tom Stoppard. Abbey Theatre. Directed by Tomás Mac Anna.

*Trembling Giant* by John McGrath. 7.84 Theatre Company at the John Player Theatre. Directed by John McGrath.

## Dublin Theatre Festival 1978

2–21 October

*L'Aurore Boreale* by Pierre Bourgeade. Monique Couterier at Edmund Burke Hall. Directed by Herve Alexandre.

*Bonfire* by Joe O'Donnell. Gemini Productions at the Eblana Theatre. Directed by Robert Gillespie.

*Catappletits* by Pascal Pettit. Peacock Theatre. Directed by Patrick Laffan.

*Chapter Two* by Neil Simon. Woodside Productions at the Olympia Theatre. Directed by Louis Beachner.

*Dance of Death* by August Strindberg, adapted by Peter O'Shaughnessy. Focus Theatre. Directed by Mary Elizabeth Burke-Kennedy.

*Dance, Dance, Dance.* Mavis Ascott Dance Company at the John Player Theatre. Choreographed by Mavis Ascott.

*Deirdre* by Ulick O'Connor. Edmund Burke Hall. Directed by James Flannery.

*Diarmuid agus Grainne* by Micheál Mac Liammóir. Peacock Theatre. Directed by Joe Dowling.

*Elephant Man* by Bernard Pomerance. Project Arts Centre. Directed by Patrick Mason.

*Emigrants* by Peter Sheridan. Pirate Jenny Company at Project Arts Centre. Directed by Jim Sheridan.

*Encounter in the Wilderness* by Hugh Carr. Edwards-Mac Liammóir Productions at the Gate Theatre. Directed by Agnes Bernelle.

*Fando and Lis* by Fernando Arrabal. Players Theatre. Directed by Martin Drury.

*The Grand Inquisitor* by Ulick O'Connor. Edmund Burke Hall. Directed by James Flannery.

*Heartbreak House* by G.B. Shaw. Irish Theatre Company at the Oscar Theatre. Directed by Edward Golden.

*I'm Not Talking About Soup* by Harry White. University College Dublin at Players Theatre. Directed by Ben Barnes.

*In Sand* by Jack B. Yeats. World Theatre Productions at the Oscar Theatre. Directed by Beryl Fagan.

*Kabale Und Liebe* by Friedrich Schiller. Test Theatre Company, Munich at Edmund Burke Hall.

*Miss Margrida's Way* by Roberto Athayde. Estelle Parsons at Edmund Burke Hall. Directed by Roberto Athayde.

*Mummenschanz*. Swiss Mime Group at the Gaiety Theatre.

*The Playboy of the Western World*, a ballet based on the play by J. M. Synge. Irish Ballet Company at the Olympia Theatre. Choreographed by Joan Denise Moriarty.

*A Prayer for My Daughter* by Thomas Babe. Royal Court Theatre at Project Arts Centre. Directed by Max Stafford-Clark.

*Prometheus Changed*. Living Theatre at the Olympia Theatre. Directed by Julian Beck.

*Proxopera* adapted by Peter Luke from Benedict Kiely. Edwards-Mac Liammóir Productions at the Gate Theatre. Directed by Hilton Edwards.

*Sauce for the Goose* by Georges Feydeau, translated by Peter Meyer. RTÉ Players at the Gaiety Theatre. Directed by Jean Claude Amyl.

*Streamers* by David Rabe. Stage One Players at the Eblana Theatre. Directed by Sean Treacy.

*Submarine* by Ulick O'Connor. Edmund Burke Hall. Directed by
James Flannery.

*The Two Executioners* by Fernando Arrabal. Players Theatre. Directed
by Martin Drury.

*Uncle Vanya* by Anton Chekhov. Abbey Theatre. Directed by Vladimir
Monakhov.

*Victoriana* – works by G.B. Shaw, Guy de Maupassant, and William
McGonagle. Threadbare Theatre Company at Players Theatre.
Directed by John Olohan and Ronan Paterson.

*When Am I Gettin' Me Clothes*? by Pat Ingoldsby. Peacock Theatre.
Directed by Donald Taylor Black.

*Where All Your Dreams Come True* by Jim Sheridan from an original
idea by Annie Kilmartin. Irish Theatre Company at Abbey
Methodist Hall, Dublin. Directed by Paul Brennan.


## Dublin Theatre Festival 1979

1–13 October

*American Buffalo* by David Mamet. Dublin Stage One at the Eblana
Theatre. Directed by Fred Haines.

*Antigone* by Jean Anouilh. University College Cork Drama society at
Players Theatre.

*Birds, Beasts, and Flowers* by John Carroll. Edmund Burke Hall.
Directed by John Carroll.

*Captive Audience* by Desmond Forristal. Edwards-Mac Liammóir
Productions at the Gate Theatre. Directed by Hilton Edwards.

*A Child Growing Up* by David Kemp. John Player Theatre.

*Close of Play* by Simon Gray. National Theatre of Great Britain at the
Olympia Theatre. Directed by Harold Pinter.

*Crooked in the Car Seat* by Brian Lynch. Gemini Productions at the
Eblana Theatre. Directed by Donald Taylor Black.

*Deoraíocht* adapted by Macdara Ó Fatharta from Pádraic Ó Conaire.
Peacock Theatre. Directed by Tomás Mac Anna.

*Doobally Black Way* by Tom Mac Intyre. Calck Hook Dance Theatre
at Edmund Burke Hall. Directed and choreographed by Wendy
Shankin and Doris Seiden.

*Empress Eugénie* by Jason Lindsey. Dublin Theatre Festival in
association with Marianne MacNaghten at Edmund Burke Hall.
Directed by Marianne MacNaghten.

*The Erpingham Camp and Funeral Games* by Joe Orton. Irish Theatre Company at the Gaiety Theatre. Directed by Patrick Mason.

An Evening with Dave Allen. Gaiety Theatre.

*Every Good Boy Deserves Favour* by Tom Stoppard. Olympia Theatre. Directed by Edgar Selge.

*An Giall* by Brendan Behan. An Damer. Directed by Art Ó Briain.

*The Gingerbread Man* by David Wood. John Player Theatre. Directed by Jonathon Lynn.

*The Half Promised Land* by Maeve Binchy. Peacock Theatre. Directed by Pat Laffan.

*Ha'penny Place* by Jim Sheridan. Project Arts Centre. Directed by Peter Sheridan.

*Legs 11* by Bernard Farrell. Moving Theatre Company. Holy Rosary Parish Hall and on tour. Directed by Annie Kilmartin

*A Life* by Hugh Leonard. Abbey Theatre. Directed by Joe Dowling.

*The Nightingale and Not the Lark* by Jennifer Johnston. Peacock Theatre. Directed by Paul Brennan.

*The Passion of Christ.* Greek Theatre Guild Company at Project Arts Centre. Directed by Yannis Houvardas.

Penta Theatre Company of Holland at the Olympia Theatre.

*The Rise and Fall of the City of Mahogany* by Bertolt Brecht. Dublin University Players at Players Theatre.

Royal Ballet of Flanders at the Olympia Theatre.

*Tohu-Bohu* by Pierre Byland and Philippe Gautier. Compagnie Pierre Byland at the Gate Theatre.

## Dublin Theatre Festival 1980

29 September–15 October

*Affluence* by Wesley Burrowes. Irish Theatre Company at the Oscar Theatre. Directed by Christopher Fitz-Simon.

*And Then Came Jonathan* by Michael Judge. John Player Theatre. Directed by Barry Cassin.

*Arachne* by Terez Nelson and *Giselle* by Anton Dolin and John Gilpin. Dublin City Ballet at the Olympia Theatre.

*Blood Weekend* by John Wood, Barbara Vaughen, and Ric Jerrom. Natural Company Theatre of Bath at the Mansion House. Directed by Caroline Maynard.

*Canaries* by Bernard Farrell. Abbey Theatre. Directed by Patrick Mason.

*Le Cirque Imaginaire* by Victoria Chaplin and Jean Baptiste Thiérrée. Gate Theatre.

*Curigh the Shape Shifter* by Mary Elizabeth Burke-Kennedy. Focus Theatre. Directed by Mary Elizabeth Burke-Kennedy.

*Dorothy* by Graham Reid. Oscar Theatre. Directed by Kevin McHugh.

*Forever Young* by Shane Connaughton. Project Arts Centre. Directed by Fred Haines.

*Getting Out* by Marsha Norman. Actors Theatre of Louisville at the Olympia Theatre.

*Hancock's Last Half Hour* by Heathcote Williams. Red Rex Theatre at Project Arts Centre. Directed by Garrett Keogh.

*Hess* by Michael Burrell. Edmund Burke Hall. Directed by Philip Grout.

*I'm Going To Have My Memories Taken Out* by David Stevens. Eblana Theatre. Directed by Bill Keating.

*Lig Sinni gCathú* by Breandán Ó hEithir, adapted by Macdara Ó Fatharta. Peacock Theatre. Directed by Donal Farmer.

*Nightshade* by Stewart Parker. Peacock Theatre. Directed by Chris Parr.

*No Room For Dreamers* by George Hutchinson. Pavilion Theatre.

*Nora Barnacle* by Maureen Charlton. Dublin Theatre Festival at the Eblana Theatre. Directed by Bill Keating.

*Nutcracker Sweet* by David Wood. Whirligig Productions at the John Player Theatre. Directed by David Wood.

*The Rare Oul Times-The Quare New Times* by Pat Abernathy and Dave Marsden. Isosceles Travelling Show at the Mansion House.

*Speak of the Devil* by Fergus Linehan. DK Productions in association with the Olympia Theatre. Directed by William Chappell.

*Sssss – Grrrr Gotcha!* by Brendan and Mary Conroy. Pintsize Puppet Theatre.

*Tales of Five Cities* by Basil Payne. The Mansion House. Directed by Basil Payne.

*Through the Magic Storybook* by Eugene Lambert. Lambert Puppet Theatre at the Mansion House. Directed by Eugene Lambert.

*Translations* by Brian Friel. Field Day Theatre Company at the Gate Theatre. Directed by Art Ó Briain.

*Writer's Cramp* by John Byrne. Project Arts Centre. Directed by Robin Lefèvre.

*Zoz* by Joe O'Donnell. Gemini Productions at the Olympia Theatre. Directed by Tomás Mac Anna.

## Dublin Theatre Festival 1981

### 28 September–10 October

*Alice in Wonderland* adapted and directed by Eugene and Miriam Lambert. Lambert Puppet Theatre at Pintsize Puppet Theatre.

*The Ballad of George Mallory* by Michael Ford. Trinity College Dublin University Drama Society at Players Theatre.

*Birthrate* by Tadeuz Rosewicz. Wroclaw Contemporary Theatre at the Gate Theatre. Directed by Kazimierz Braun.

*Butley* by Simon Gray. Trinity College Dublin University Drama Society at Players Theatre.

*Cabaret*. The People Show at Project Arts Centre.

*Commedia degli Zanni*. Commedia dell'Arte a l'Avogaria at the Gate Theatre. Directed by Carlo Picozzi.

*Creatures from the Swamp*. Moving Picture Mime Show at Edmund Burke Hall. Divisions by Shane Connaughton. The Oscar Theatre. Directed by Pam Brighton.

*The Fabulous Journey of Mac Con Glin* by Peter O'Shaughnessy and Anthony Blinco. John Player Theatre. Directed by Art Ó Briain.

*Forever Yours Marie-Lou* by Michel Tremblay. Cork Theatre Company at the Focus Theatre.

*Gaeilgeoirí* by Antoine Ó Flatharta. Peacock Theatre. Directed by Sean McCarthy.

*Handle with Care*. Moving Picture Mime Show at Edmund Burke Hall.

*Happy End* by Dorothy Lane, Bertolt Brecht, and Kurt Weill. Trinity College Dublin University Drama Society at Players Theatre.

*The Informer* adapted by Tom Murphy from the novel by Liam O'Flaherty. Olympia Theatre. Directed by Tom Murphy.

*The Island* by Athol Fugard. The Repertory Theatre of St. Louis at Edmund Burke Hall. Directed by Jim O'Connor.

*Jennifer's Vacation* by Robin Glendinning. Edwards-Mac Liammóir Productions at the Gate Theatre. Directed by Patrick Laffan.

*A Keane Sense of Humour* adapted by Joe O'Donnell from the works of John B. Keane. Gemini Productions at the Eblana Theatre. Directed by Barry Cassin.

*Ladies' Night.* Actors Theatre of Louisville at the Eblana Theatre. Directed by Jon Jory.

Lar Lubovitch Dance Company at the Olympia Theatre. Choreographed by Lar Lubovitch.

*Macbeth* by William Shakespeare. Natural Theatre Company of Bath at the John Player Theatre.

*The Maids* by Jean Genet. Shared Experience at Project Arts Centre. Directed by Clare Davidson.

*Night and Day* by Tom Stoppard. Abbey Theatre. Directed by Joe Dowling.

*Nocturne for Sybil Vane* by Andrew Finan. Trinity College Dublin University Drama Society at Players Theatre.

*Not Just Yet* by Art Ó Briain. TEAM. Directed by Martin Drury.

*One-Man* by Steven Berkoff at Project Arts Centre.

*Orpheus.* Ballet Theatre Joseph Russillo at the Gaiety Theatre.

*The Queering of the Clone* by Hugh Burns. Legit Theatre Company at An Damer.

*Rite of Spring* and *This is My Company.* Ballet Theatre Joseph Russillo at the Gaiety Theatre.

*The River Bank* by Rabindranath Tagore. Trinity College Dublin University Drama Society at Players Theatre.

*Round and Round the Garden* by Jim Nolan. TEAM. Directed by Martin Drury.

*The Seagull* by Anton Chekhov in a version by Thomas Kilroy. Irish Theatre Company at the Olympia Theatre. Directed by Patrick Mason.

*The Silver Dollar Boys* by Neil Donnelly. Peacock Theatre. Directed by Ben Barnes.

*The Silver Show/ The Silver Princess.* Optical Figurenbuhne at the Eblana Theatre.

*Somewhere Between Frogs and Princes* by Barbara McNamara. Moving Theatre at the Community Theatre. Directed by Annie Kilmartin.

*St. Mark's Gospel* adapted by Alec McCowen. Edmund Burke Hall.

*Su l'Agiare del Flon.* Commedia dell'Arte a l'Avogaria at the Gate Theatre. Directed by Carlo Picozzi.

*The Táin*. Dublin Theatre Festival Presents The Irish Ballet Company at the Olympia Theatre. Choreographed By Joan Denise Moriarty.

*There is no Night* by Sean Moffatt. Trinity College Dublin University Drama Society at Players Theatre.

*Three Sisters* by Anton Chekhov in a version by Brian Friel. Field Day Theatre Company at the Gaiety Theatre. Directed by Stephen Rea.

*Tragedy of Errors* by Gerry Stembridge. Trinity College Dublin University Drama Society at Players Theatre.

*Volpone* by Ben Jonson. A.D.L. at Mansion House.

*What Now, What Next* by Rose Tobin. Trinity College Dublin University Drama Society at Players Theatre.

*The Wind That Shook The Barley* by Declan Burke-Kennedy. Focus Theatre Company at the Oscar Theatre. Directed by Mary Elizabeth Burke-Kennedy.

## Dublin Theatre Festival 1982

27 September–10 October

*The Actor's Nightmare* by Christopher Durang. Cork Theatre Company at the Eblana Theatre. Directed by Fred Haines.

*Anna Livia* by Maciej Slomczynski. Wroclaw Contemporary Theatre at the Gaiety Theatre. Directed by Kazimierz Braun.

*Beds* by Anne Hartigan. Moveable Feast at An Damer. Directed by Robert Gordon.

*Charles Dickens* adapted by Emlyn Williams. Edmund Burke Hall.

*Dylan Thomas Growing Up* adapted by Emlyn Williams. Edmund Burke Hall.

*Games* by James Saunders. St. Patrick's College of Education at University Theatre. Directed by Dermot Higgins.

*Gilly and The Bogeys* by Joe O'Donnell. John Player Theatre. Directed by Michael Scott.

*Home* by Samm-Art Williams. Negro Ensemble Company at the Gate Theatre. Directed by Douglas Turner Ward.

*The Immigrant* by Jim Sheridan. In association with Theatre Passe Muraille at Project Arts Centre. Directed by Jim Sheridan.

*Kill* by Hugh Leonard. Olympia Theatre. Directed by Patrick Mason.

*Kolbe* by Desmond Forristal. Abbey Theatre. Directed by Ray McAnally.

*Laundry and Bourbon* by James McLure. Peacock Theatre. Directed by Ben Barnes.

*Letters Home* by Rose Leiman Goldemberg. Actors Repertory Theatre at Players Theatre.

*Lon Rinn An Chairn* by Seán Ó Broin. Peacock Theatre. Directed by Tomás Mac Anna.

*Louvain 1915* by Barbar Field. Focus Theatre. Directed by Mary Elizabeth Burke-Kennedy.

*Macunaima* by Mario de Andrade. Grupo de Theatro Macunaima at the Gaiety Theatre. Directed by Antunes Filho.

*The Marowitz Hamlet* by Charles Marowitz. UCD Dramsoc at University Theatre. Directed by Gerard Stembridge.

*Mary Makebelieve* by Fergus and Rosaleen Linehan. Peacock Theatre. Directed by Domy Reiter-Sofer.

*Metamorphosis* adapted by Steven Berkoff from Franz Kafka. Oscar Theatre. Directed by Raymond Yeates.

*Pas de Deux* by Hugo Claus. Belgian and Dutch Theatre Company at the Eblana Theatre. Directed by Robert David McDonald.

*The Phoenix* by Michael O'Shea. UCD Dramsoc at University Theatre. Directed by Michael O'Shea.

*The Playboy of the Western World* by J.M. Synge. Druid Theatre Company at the Olympia Theatre. Directed by Garry Hynes.

*The Rock and Roll Show* by Peter Sheridan. Project Arts Centre. Directed by Michael Sheridan.

*Semi-Private* by Mary Halpin. Edwards-Mac Liammóir Productions at the Gate Theatre. Directed by Pat Laffan.

*The Shadow of the Glen* by J. M. Synge. Druid Theatre Company at Players Theatre. Directed by Garry Hynes.

*Sr. Mary Ignatius Explains it All For You* by Christopher Durang. Cork Theatre Company at the Eblana Theatre. Directed by Fred Haines.

*The Stag King* by Carlo Gozzi. A Marionette Production at Douglas Hyde Gallery. Directed by John McCormick.

*Voids* by Liam Lynch. Platform Theatre Group at Lourdes Hall. Directed by Jacqui Dickson.

*We Can't Pay, We Won't Pay* by Dario Fo. Moving Theatre at Community Theatre. Directed by Annie Kilmartin.

*Wedding*. Dance Theatre Bremen at the Gaiety Theatre.

# Dublin Theatre Festival 1983

## 26 September–9 October

*The Blue Macushla* by Tom Murphy. Red Rex Theatre Company at the Mansion House. Directed by Art Ó Briain.

*Castles in the Air* by Martin Lynch. Lyric Theatre, Belfast at the John Player Theatre. Directed by Leon Rubin.

*Charan the Thief* by Habib Tanvir. The Naya Theatre at the SFX Centre. Directed by Habib Tanvir.

*Comedy Store* by Billy Magra. Red Rex Theatre Company at the Mansion House.

*Crimes of the Heart* by Beth Henley. Edwards-Mac Liammóir Productions at the Gate Theatre.

*Fancy Footwork* by Miriam Gallagher. Exit Theatre Group at the Focus Theatre.

*Fascinating Aida* at Project Arts Centre.

The Flying Pickets at Edmund Burke Hall.

*The Former One-On-One Basketball Champion* by Israel Horowitz. Cork Theatre Company at the Mansion House.

*A Galway Girl* by Geraldine Aron. Druid Theatre Company at Edmund Burke Hall. Directed by Maeliosa Stafford.

*The Garden*. Muteki Sha Dance Group at An Damer. Choreographed by Natsu Nakajima.

*The Gigli Concert* by Tom Murphy. Abbey Theatre. Directed by Patrick Mason.

*Hamlet* by William Shakespeare. Collettivo di Parma at the Gate Theatre. Directed by the company.

Henan Acrobatic Troupe at the Gaiety Theatre.

*Horseman Pass By* by Daniel Magee. Platform Theatre Group at Whitefriars Hall. Directed by Jacqui Dickson.

*Imeachtaí Na Saoirse* by Antoine Ó Flatharta. Peacock Theatre. Directed by Raymond Yeates.

*The Kids, The Digs, The Village* by Mick Egan and Peter Sheridan. City Workshop at An Damer.

*Lay Up Your Ends* by Martin Lynch and Charabanc. Charabanc Theatre Company at the John Player Theatre. Directed by Pam Brighton.

London Contemporary Dance Theatre. The Gaiety Theatre. Choreographed by Robert Cohan and Tom Jobe.

*The Man Who Stole from Adolf Hitler* by Tony Browne. Cork Theatre Company at the Mansion House. Directed by Emelie FitzGibbon.

*The Old Woman Broods* by Tadeusz Rozewicz. Project Arts Centre. Directed by Kazimierz Braun.

*Our Jane* by Michael Skelly. Western Union at the Eblana Theatre. Directed by Seán McCarthy.

*The Parrot* by Mary Elizabeth Burke-Kennedy. Tadhg O'Kane Players at the Mansion House. Directed by Mary Elizabeth Burke-Kennedy.

*La Piège de Méduse* by Erik Satie. Compagnie de l'élan at the John Player Theatre. Directed by Erik Laborey.

*Pledges and Promises* by Peter Sheridan. City Workshop at An Damer.

*A Pocket Romeo and Juliet* by Derek Chapman and Deirdra Morris. Focus Theatre. Directed by Derek Chapman.

*Pol* by Alain Didier-Weill. Oscar Mime Company at the Mansion House.

*Pratt's Fall* by Stewart Parker. Western Union at the Eblana Theatre. Directed by Patrick Mason.

*Quilters* by Molly Newman and Barbara Damashek. Denver Centre Theatre Company. Directed by Molly Newman and Barbara Damashek.

*Randy* by Chris Meehan. Oscar Theatre. Directed by Mavis Ascott.

*Scorpions* by Hugh Leonard. Olympia Theatre. Directed by Roy Heayberd.

*The Unexpected Death of Jimmy Blizzard* by Robert Ellison. Peacock Theatre. Directed by Ben Barnes.

*The Unseen Hand* by Sam Shepard. Cork Theatre Company at the Mansion House.

*Women in Power* adapted by John McGrath. 7:84 Theatre Company at SFX Centre. Directed by John McGrath.

*The Wood of the Whispering* by M.J. Molloy. Druid Theatre Company at Edmund Burke Hall. Directed by Garry Hynes.

*Yakety Yak!* The Darts at the Olympia Theatre.


**1984: The Dublin Theatre Festival did not take place.**

# 3 | 'Present Tense' *or* 'It shouldn't happen to a festival programmer!'

David Grant

The highs and the lows: hearing the audience response to seeing Geneviève de Kermabon's adaptation of Tod Browning's cult film *Freaks* on the Tivoli Theatre stage; solving the logistical challenges of getting Footsbarn's *A Midsummer Night's Dream* into the Iveagh Gardens; persuading the Theatre Union of the Russian Federation to bring the independent production, *Tverboul*, to Dublin; the collapse of a major co-production after months of negotiation just weeks before the deadline for the Festival brochure resulting in a last minute scramble for alternatives and many sleepless nights; hearing that the huge and unique *Archaos* circus tent had shredded in a sudden gust of wind.

Looking back on the three frenetic years (1989 -1991) in which my life was dominated by the Dublin Theatre Festival, certain quintessential moments loom largest in memory. Even now, faced with any crisis, I measure it against the enormity of nearly losing Archaos' epic production, *Metal Clown*, which had accounted for a quarter of the then record (1991 European City of Culture) Festival budget of one million pounds. The trace memory of that particular trauma soon causes any current anxiety to evaporate. And I am thankful that Tony Ó Dálaigh and Michael Colgan came forward to do battle with the Archaos management, who despite the Festival rapidly securing a replacement tent, proved tenacious in negotiation. Desperate for survival, they went to the extreme of threatening to pull a special matinee performance for the families of hundreds of employees of the Festival's overall sponsor, Irish Life. In the event, their bluff was called and I still recall the quiet dignity of all those parents and children getting up from the benches and returning to their cars without a murmur while the bewildered circus performers with their chainsaws looked on. But this climactic catastrophe cannot eclipse my overall sense of privilege and satisfaction at having been a small part of the story of the Dublin Theatre Festival.

When it was suggested that I contribute to this collection, my first instinct was to refer to notebooks, programmes, and such other ephemera that were gathering dust in boxes in the attic. But the visceral clarity of certain 'flashbulb' moments in my experience of my Festival years has prompted me to approach this task from the perspective of what Stanislavsky would term 'affective memory'. As a theatre practitioner, now working in the academy, I am interested in how this exercise may illuminate the perspective of the artist-scholar which is the subject of so much continuing debate and discussion within the university context. The idea of 'embodied knowledge' has become a helpful means of explaining the practitioner's perspective. In Donald Rumsfeld's now notorious epistemological taxonomy ('known knowns', 'known unknowns' and 'unknown unknowns'[1]) he neglects the category that can best explain this phenomenon – namely, 'unknown knowns'. Since Donald Schön coined the term 'reflective practitioner' there has been a growing acknowledgement that conventional ways of understanding knowledge need to expand to include a practice-oriented dimension.[2] In the same way that Stanislavsky's 'System' encourages the actor seeking to evoke the reality of an imaginary situation by drawing on contextualized past memories, so I intend to re-imagine significant moments from my actual experience of the Dublin Theatre Festival in order to evoke not just the facts but the flavour of the events.

I have previously experimented with this approach in an attempt to recapture the immediacy of a rehearsal process, but its extension to the more wide-ranging practice of a programmer intrigues me. I have found that the use of the historic present facilitates recall and have been impressed by the use of a similar technique by Dr Bill McDonnell of the University of Sheffield in conveying his experience of previously undocumented community drama performances in West Belfast in the early 1990s.[3] The result is a vibrant account that locates the reader inside the described world and that comes closer to orality than literacy. Walter J Ong demonstrated in his seminal book *Orality and Literacy: The Technologizing of the Word* how writing had over centuries restructured consciousness. The use of present tense narrative offers one way of reversing this effect. Steven Pinker has written extensively on the relationship between language structures and hidden thought processes.[4] It is my contention that revisiting past events in the present tense operates as a mechanism for revealing the 'unknown knowns' of embodied knowledge and it is this approach that I intend to apply to my trace memories of the Dublin Theatre Festival.

Each of the accounts that follow flow from a process of trying to re-immerse myself in the various experiences in order to recapture their immediacy. In the subsequent commentary, I seek to step back from the moment of recalled experience for more objective reflection. Just as the first stage can be compared to the approach of a Stanislavskian actor, so the second reflects Meyerhold's famous formula $N=A1+A2$, where $N$ = the performance, $A1$ the actor as the material he organizes, and $A2$ the actor as the organizer of the material. As a reflective practitioner, I am aware of the same kind of duality, drawing on my own experience while also seeking to understand it.

## Freaks

January 1989, the two hundredth anniversary of the French Revolution. It will be important for the Festival to represent France and AFAA, the French cultural agency have money to spend. With the Moscow Arts Theatre already represented in the programme (a return visit for the Abbey taking *The Field* and *The Great Hunger* to Moscow the previous year), there is pressure to follow the pattern of cultural diplomacy and invite something from the *Comédie Française*. I pack my little suitcase and take off for Paris.

*Fin de Partie* in the company's original production – I thought it would never end. Museum theatre at its most deadly and I have tickets for another performance at the *Comédie Française* tonight. *En route* from my hotel by metro, I have to change trains at the Bouffes du Nord. Brook's theatre seems to beckon to me from across the twilit tracks. Impetuously, I abandon my journey and make my way down to the theatre door. The production is from the Avignon Festival, an adaptation of Tod Browning's controversial 1930s movie, *Freaks*. It is a love story set in a circus freak show where a midget falls for a beautiful trapeze artist who then betrays him for the circus strongman. The members of the freak show wreak a horrible revenge by turning her into a human chicken. I am intrigued to know how this can be rendered live on stage. I'm in luck. There is a ticket left.

I experience the earthy intimacy of the Bouffes du Nord for the first time, its brickwork stripped bare of plaster, the seating embracing the stage. A magical spectacle peopled by a collection of strange and fantastical but deeply human figures (the fat lady, the legless man who walked on his hands, and the 'human sausage' – seemingly just a head carried round on a platter) bewitches me. The story unfolds, culminating in a breath-taking finale in which the trapeze artist is surrounded by the angry 'freaks' who scramble towards her across a huge net high above our heads and covering most of the area of the theatre. As the lights snap to black, I know I must invite this remarkable production to Dublin.

Back at my desk the next day, I laboriously settle to opening the usual mound of mail. First out of its envelope is a proposal for a tour of *Freaks*. A quick conference with Lewis Clohessy, the Festival Director, a phone call to the agent and to AFAA and the deal is soon sealed. I have never felt so certain about a decision.

A visit by Didier, the production's technical director, to the Tivoli (the only viable venue available to us) produces some nail-biting moments, with much sucking of teeth and intakes of breath, but eventually technical solutions are agreed. All we need to do is to locate a snake. *Pace* Saint Patrick, I do not think that this will be a major problem for the Irish theatre.

When the company arrive in Dublin, curiosity gets the better of most of the Festival staff and there are many extra bodies in the aisles as the first performance begins. Those who slip away, having seen just the first appearance of these unusual human forms, later report that the image troubles them. But those who stay the course find the experience of the performance cathartic and rejoice in their shared humanity with the performers.

Later that week, I have a long chat with Geneviève de Kermabon, the show's director, and enjoy the chance to express my huge admiration of her work. She is quietly and modestly appreciative. Around us, in the opulent surroundings of the French Embassy in Adelaide Road, stand the actors in their ordinary clothes. The legless acrobat sips champagne while balancing a well-laden plate on his muscular arms and Jean Claude ('the human sausage') works the room deftly in his motorized wheelchair. I am struck by the power of theatre to dissolve difference.

Looking back on my early experiences of the Festival, it strikes me how much the idea of a theatre that blurred the distinction between conventional drama and more robust forms like circus had come by the late 1980s to be what was expected of foreign visitors to the Dublin Theatre Festival. Soon after taking up the post of Programme Director, I was dispatched to Madrid to see *Els Comediants*, the Barcelona company who had taken the Galway Arts Festival by storm. It was an indication of how far Festival thinking was influenced by Galway, as was later clear in the enthusiasm for *Archaos*. In the event, *Els Comediants* turned out to be unavailable in the period of the Festival, but I believe that *Freaks* was far more than just an equivalent circus-based show, as the response of the audience described above shows.

## The Bulandra's *Hamlet*

It is January 1990. I am in my office in the Festival's Nassau Street offices. The telephone rings. It is John Fairleigh from Queen's University in Belfast. I have previously worked with him on events for the Stewart Parker Trust. He wants to know if I would be interested in a production of *Hamlet* from Romania. The lead actor, Ion Caramitru, whom he met at a conference twenty years before, has taken advantage of the fall of Ceauşescu, in which he has played a part, to re-establish contact. He has become Minister of Culture in the provisional government and there is an invitation for the company to come to London. Am I interested in the show for Dublin? There is a *Tarom* flight returning empty from Belfast to Bucharest in two weeks time having delivered home the last of the winter skiers. John knows the Belfast agent and can get me a seat.

When I get on the plane, clutching my small suitcase, I find every seat is filled with supplies. Apart from me, the passengers include representatives of a local charity and a UTV film crew. I squeeze myself into place between several boxes of disposable nappies. The propellers splutter into life and we take off for Bucharest. It is the most bizarre flight I have ever taken. The charity workers and I exchange stories. There is a palpable sense of adventure. They are worried about getting their supplies, destined for Romanian orphanages, safely through the airport at the end of the flight. I mention that I am being met by the Minister of Culture. Great excitement ensues.

The plane lands and we set off across the runway towards the terminal building. There is an inescapable air of anarchy. As we come indoors I am met by Caramitru and his entourage. I explain the anxieties of my fellow passengers. There is a hurried conversation and someone is deputed to assist them while I am whisked away in a large car. That evening I am collected and taken to Caramitru's apartment where I am greeted by his patrician mother and treated to a fine dinner while Caramitru and his colleagues discuss with me the logistics of their visit to Dublin. I admire the fine furnishings and Caramitru's collection of exquisite orthodox icons, salvaged from churches around Romania which were abandoned under Communism.

Next day I visit the Bulandra Theatre and see the set of *Hamlet*. Its nineteenth-century location could not disguise the clear implication that Claudius and Gertrude were the Ceauşescus – a celebration of the subversive power of classical theatre. Hard for the authorities to censor Shakespeare! The theatre critic Marian Popescu, whom I had previously met at a conference in Moscow, becomes my guide. He shows me the grotesque extravagance of Ceauşescu's palace, the improvised candle-lit shrines and bullet-holes where protesters had died during the revolution and the historic church lifted in its entirety and reset a hundred metres further from the main road so that it did not intrude on the dictator's view. I am about to direct a production of Nicolai Erdman's *The Suicide* for the Dublin Youth Theatre, so he takes me to meet a promising young director who is rehearsing the same play. As is common in the Eastern European tradition, this is the start of a sporadic and lengthy rehearsal process which is expected to last many months. But there is already a sense that the revolution has robbed these theatre artists of their motivation.

I leave the foggy air and grimy streets of Bucharest and fly to Budapest with its smart boulevards and superb restaurants. I am here to visit the Katona Jószef Theatre, whose *Government Inspector* I have recently seen at the Old Vic and am hosted by the state agency responsible for foreign theatre tours. But there is already a sense that Hungary is hungry to embrace the West. Next day, a long train journey to Zagreb in Yugoslavia for IETM (the Informal European Theatre Meeting) where Dragan Klaic's keynote speech ironically refutes the claim that we are witnessing 'the end of history'. Then, onto a performance in which the audience is herded onto one of two cattle trucks, where angry actors play out a war of words – a different language in each truck. The point is lost on us amid the civilized hospitality of Yugoslavian Croatia.

October 1990 – the Bulandra arrive in Dublin after a triumphant reception at London's National Theatre. Prince Michael, claimant to the Romanian throne, has been in the audience. An angry Caramitru emerges with his entourage up the blue carpet of the rickety Nassau Street stairs. How dare we put his company in such accommodation? Yes, he had said student-style accommodation would suffice, but this?! I agree to go back with him to the hostel and discover a huge roomful of metal bunkbeds with a few grubby showers. Shades of a POW camp, or worse ... Despite my embarrassment, there is a limit to what the cash-strapped Festival can do, but a cheap hotel in Gardiner Street is found for the company's leading members. Despite the perceived slight, the wide-eyed response of the company to Dublin is clearly evident and the confusion of one older actor, brought along despite his incipient dementia is deeply touching. They will not deny him this chance to travel after so long a wait.

At the Gaiety Theatre, the distinctive black reflecting floor is in place but an argument is developing over the slides for the *surtitres*. Caramitru says they are too noisy and after further experiment I agree. *Hamlet* is a well known story and we will provide a full synopsis for each member of the audience. The production begins at the end of the play with a stylish fencing match, before flashing back to the beginning. I am gripped by the passion and clear political resonances of the performances. I am transported and oblivious to the strangeness of the language. I am swept along in a surge of history being played out before my eyes.

Next morning on the radio, Gay Byrne could not be further from my point of view.

Although the smallest of the three Festivals I programmed in Dublin, the 1990 event remains my favourite. A reduced budget and the limited availability of venues enforced a necessary discrimination. Whereas the lack of a Festival Fringe had prompted me towards inclusivity in 1989, the need to be more selective undoubtedly produced a Festival of more consistent quality. And the lack of access to venues like the Olympia and Tivoli propelled us towards more imaginative solutions.

## Footsbarn's *A Midsummer Night's Dream*

February 1990: my temporary office on the first floor of 47 Nassau Street. I am struck by the inertness of this dingy room, so full of activity for a few weeks each year that my own files and personal effects have to be consigned to a corner of the administrative office upstairs to make way for the box office team. I open envelopes and start to sort them into piles – invitations to events, unsolicited scripts, and proposal after proposal from managements, agents, and individuals. One stands out – *Mir Caravane,* a pan-European touring festival of circus theatre with companies from Russia, Czechoslovakia, East and West Germany, Spain, and 'England' (in the guise of the French-based Footsbarn Theatre Company whose work I have so enjoyed at the Galway Arts Festival). I make a few phone calls to check it out. It sounds amazing. The *zeitgeist* incarnate. The tour began in Moscow, a trail-blazer for private sponsorship in the new post-*perestroika* era surging through Europe (Prague, Budapest, Berlin) on the tide of political change. I check the schedule against my diary. The last date is in Basel. If I fly there straight from IETM in Zagreb I can catch the final few days.

As I climb out of my airport taxi into a suburban Basel square, I am struck by the incongruity of all these caravans and the circus tent. The bohemian atmosphere of the encampment is at odds with the upright architecture that surrounds it. I seek out John Kilby from Footsbarn and he shows me round. I settle down in the main tent among some Russian clowns. They are ecstatic about the whole experience of the tour. It has defied all the boundaries that have contained the people of Europe for decades. Borders are unnatural. The itinerant circus way is natural.

There is a commotion outside. A police car has pulled up. The policemen get out and walk towards the tent. They are clearly visible as its sides are down. Word filters back that they are acting on complaints from local residents. The nightly birthday parties, the Russians joke! Well, in a company of over a hundred, it's usually someone's birthday most nights. Then suddenly the West German Production Manager who has been talking with them doubles up and I notice an aerosol spray in one of the policemen's hands. Teargas! Before anyone can react, he is bundled into the car which speeds away. Uproar! Eventually the atmosphere settles and darkens. I stay to see some shows, but am in a sombre mood as I return to my hotel.

Next day, when I arrive on site, John asks if I will sit in on a meeting with the local police. Their Production Manager was held overnight but the police chief is now here to make amends. I am one of the few independent witnesses. But as we sit down together, the policeman launches into an immediate apology. He regrets what has happened. But we have to understand, the sedentary Swiss feel threatened by this sudden invasion of nomads. The Iron Curtain may have collapsed, but the Alps stand firm! Afterwards I sit down to negotiate Footsbarn's visit to Dublin. They are keen, but want to perform in their own tent.

I think of the site by the Dublin airport road where I have seen
circus tents before, and my heart sinks. But I determine to find
a way of making this happen. It couldn't be any harder than
negotiating for the Olympia or the Gaiety!

Back in Dublin, we have drawn a blank on where to put the
tent. Then a phone call from Noel Pearson, acting Artistic
Director of the Abbey. Their Festival show for the main stage
has fallen through. Have we anything that would suit. I mention
Footsbarn. Pearson is keen, but I fear for what will be lost in a
conventional venue. But it still looks like the best option so I
agree.

Two weeks later, another call from the Abbey. They are
moving their Peacock show (Michael Harding's *The Misogynist*)
to the main stage. Back to the drawing board about the tent.
Then inspiration strikes Tony Ó Dálaigh – the Iveagh Gardens!
A city centre tent. It seems a godsend. We know we can't have
the Olympia this year, so an extra venue is an added bonus.

When Festival comes, there is a special magic in winding our
way through the Garden's shabby grandeur which seems to fit
perfectly with Footsbarn's makeshift version of *A Midsummer
Night's Dream*. At first, some Festival-goers seem ill at ease,
perching on the wooden benches; but then the play begins to
weave its spell. A Polish Puck who speaks no English dances to
the rhythm of his lines, evoking something primitive and
seminal: the spirit of Eastern Europe free of its chains.

In contrast to the frugal 1990 Festival, Dublin's year as
European City of Culture in 1991 promised exceptional
opportunities and I was keen that we capitalize on this by
proposing an additional Spring programme to be managed by
the Theatre Festival team. In retrospect, this season, which ran
for seven weeks 'From Mayday to Bloomsday', was the most
satisfying experience I had as Programme Director. The format
avoided many of the frustrations of the usual two-week autumn
event. To begin with, the scale was smaller and therefore better
suited to the progressive, experimental work it seemed to me a
festival should be about. Indeed, the total subsidy from the City
of Culture was only £100,000. The use of just two venues (the
Project Arts Centre and the Andrews Lane Theatre)
circumvented the fractious process of negotiating short lets with

the larger theatres. Nor were we at the mercy of the sometimes unpredictable and often autocratic whim of the major production houses. But above all, the momentum of the event was paced more evenly, avoiding audience burnout and allowing more programme flexibility. The programme achieved a perfect balance between new Irish work (Wet Paint, Co-Motion, and Charabanc), classics (Rough Magic with Farquhar, and the Royal National theatre with an Asian version of *Tartuffe*) and overseas work (the Market Theatre, Johannesburg and what turned out to be the post-'Soviet Week').

## The Soviet Week

This is the second time I have flown from Shannon to Moscow with Aeroflot. Last time it was for a meeting of the International Theatre Institute's Critics' Forum, but at least I have some idea what to expect. Alone in the departure lounge (this is really just a refuelling stop for the through-flight from Havana), I remember how grateful I was for the constant companionship of Elizabeth, my interpreter, who quickly taught me the Cyrillic alphabet so I could identify the different Metro stations. As we grew to trust one another, she confided how Russian life contrived to make her live her whole life with a feeling of pervasive guilt at being Jewish. Then a few weeks ago, I received a postcard from her from Tel Aviv. It occurs to me what a crucial role interpreters fulfil in cultural exchanges. On my last trip, I met Sergei Nerubenko, who had been interpreter for the Dublin Youth Theatre when they had visited Moscow. Now it is at his invitation as an official of the Russian Theatre Union that I return. When I began these discussions it was for a 'Soviet Week' as the centrepiece of the one-off 'Mayday to Bloomsday' event the Theatre Festival is producing for Dublin's 1991 City of Culture programme. But discussions with the Soviet Theatre Union, who had been central to the Moscow Arts Theatre visit less than two years before, quickly fizzled out as it became clear with the dismemberment of the USSR that they were penniless. So we had to restart our negotiations with the Theatre Union of the Russian Federation. Just then, my flight is called and I make my solitary way onboard, finding a single empty seat among my exotic fellow passengers.

We land in Moscow and everyone else applauds. I remember that this seems to be an *Aeroflot* custom. Whether from gratitude or surprise I'm not sure, but I join in. With trepidation, I negotiate immigration control, but the uniformed official merely grunts. I see Sergei across the barrier. He greets me warmly and takes me to find my luggage. After more than an hour of looking at an empty carousel we report the bag missing and go with the Theatre Union's driver to Central Moscow and my hotel, swerving regularly to avoid the potholes. Last time I stayed in a vast hotel, one of Stalin's skyscrapers, and shared a corridor with someone whose room had a twenty-four hour guard. I later discovered he was a famous faith-healer, the height of celebrity in the new Russia. This time the hotel is a more modest affair. I check in, and Sergei takes me for lunch. The first two restaurants are state-owned. At the door of each a surly waiter rebuffs us. The first has no water; the second no food. Sergei is exasperated but unbowed. We round the corner to find one of Moscow's new independent businesses – a pizzeria. There is a *Pizza Hut* menu taped above the counter and I wonder is this some sort of franchise. When the lumpish, doughy food arrives it becomes clear that this is aspirational, but definitely a sign of things to come. I mention to Sergei that I am hoping to see members of the independent theatre group whose show, *Tverboul*, I shared a venue with when I took *The Wake* to the Edinburgh Fringe the previous summer. It is a lively and powerful evocation of modern Moscow life: a bare stage, a double bass, an enchanting score – a kind of urban folk music – and suddenly the stage explodes with life, a kaleidoscopic encapsulation of so much changing and so much staying the same. I have their phone number in Moscow, but calls from Ireland have proved impossible. He is non-committal and I realize that independent initiatives are fine for restaurants but theatre companies are another matter. To pursue this one, it looks like I will have to use my limited knowledge of the Cyrillic alphabet to negotiate the metro on my own.

Back in my hotel, I gingerly try the number I have for the director of the *Tverboul* company. Sergei has explained that there are no switchboards in Russia. Every extension has its own unique number. So I am relieved when I am answered by an English speaker. It is the director's mother whom I met at the Traverse and she is excited to hear from me. A rendezvous is quickly arranged for the next day. Sergei soon arrives to take me to a play – *The Medium-Sized Cat* – a satire about the hierarchical nature of the Writers' Union. Despite Sergei's simultaneous translation, I am mystified until I realize the word in the title isn't 'Cat' but 'Hat', the idea being that writers are awarded the right to wear a hat in proportion to their status.

Next day, I am escorted to the office of the Director of the Russian Theatre Union. A drinks trolley is trundled out and I remark on the coincidence that it is exactly the same as the one that had appeared on the stage the previous night. Sergei and his boss rock with laughter. This is no coincidence. This is the only kind of drinks trolley available in the Russian Federation. They have a treat for me. They have arranged a special performance just for me of a production by a theatre company from Perm, a city in Siberia. After almost an hour, our car arrives at a block of flats in a residential area on the outskirts of Moscow. To my surprise, there is a studio theatre in the basement. To my shock, the performance is the same clownish production of Albee's *Zoo Story* I have seen on my last visit to Moscow. This time, on my own, it seems even longer. Back at the hotel my luggage has arrived at last – from New York having been left onboard the Aer Lingus flight I took from Dublin to Shannon. My suitcase is now better travelled than I am.

In the next three days, I see a further five shows. Only one seems right for Dublin – an atmospheric production by a company from Voronezh of a short autobiographical play by Anton Chekhov called *Hospital Ward No. 6*. The others are principally notable for their obsession with 1940s America, exemplified by the frequent use of Glen Miller music. Moscow is clearly obsessed with a forty year-old notion of Western culture. But I do manage to slip away to meet my *Tverboul* contact. They are eager to come to Dublin, but without the support of the Theatre Union with their airfares, how is this to be done?

Sergei arrives at my hotel in some excitement. The Theatre Union has arranged for me to visit Theatre Ilkhom at their home in Tashkent in the Republic of Uzbekistan. We are leaving at once. We make our way to one of Moscow's internal airports. The atmosphere is very different to that in the International Airport – more like a bus station. We join the bustling queue at the foot of a rusty set of steps. Several passengers have chickens in cages. On board, I am offered water from a bakelite beaker and am forbidden by my Theatre Union minders to drink it.

Tashkent is far from being the city of a thousand mosques I had envisioned. Its Spice Route days are far behind it and most of its buildings postdate a devastating earthquake in the 1960s. My palatial but comfortable hotel has clearly been built for party officials and I am put in a suite that I am assured was once occupied by Brezhnev. Out of curiosity I click on the television and am confronted with the image of Mary Robinson!

We are soon off to meet Mark Weil, the Artistic Director of Theatre Ilkhom. As soon as we enter the theatre, housed like the one in Moscow in the basement of a multi-storey building, I feel totally at home. Weil has created a strong sense of community here, working in Russian, but with a company and audiences that include many Uzbeks. It is immediately evident that this is a very special theatrical phenomenon. I am greeted warmly and invited to sign their 'Visitors' Wall'. I happily put my name in the space indicated, just above Peter Brook's. I see two productions, but the obvious choice for Dublin is their mime and clown tribute to Mozart, *Clomadeus*. The theme of the little man confronting reality resonates all too strongly with the mood around us. When after many vodkas at dinner in Weil's house that night I find myself comparing the status of ethnic Russians in Uzbekistan with that of Protestants in Northern Ireland, my anxieties are laughed off with an almost reckless bravado.

Back in Moscow the deal is done. Unenthusiastic as they are about *Tverboul*, if I take *Hospital Ward No. 6* and *Clomadeus* (I can only assume they have done a good deal as agents for this Russian company that is outside their jurisdiction), then I can have *Tverboul*. A quick stop in Arbat Street for some Russian Dolls in the form of the Communist Tsars (Lenin to Gorbachev) and I am safely ensconced in the home-from-home ambience of the Moscow Airport duty-free, courtesy of Aer Rianta.

A news report in the *Observer* in September 2007 provides a tragic postscript. It is reported that Mark Weil has been attacked and killed outside his theatre in Tashkent on the eve of the opening of the new theatre season. Although his assailants remain unknown, it seems likely that they were reacting to his fearless pursuit of work that challenged social attitudes in an increasingly conservative community. His last words were: 'I open a new season tomorrow and everything must happen.'

## The Schiller Theater's *Macbeth*

A meeting with Ingo Roth, an enthusiastic Bavarian, in the Goethe Institute's office near Merrion Square. For the City of Culture Festival he recommends a production of *Macbeth* from the Schiller Theater in Berlin. Ingo is passionate about theatre (I remember him leaving at the interval of an interminable student show because he thought it was over and on discovering the next day that it had only been the interval, returning the next night to see the equally lengthy second half) and has exquisite taste. So I agree at once to go and see the play.

To be in Berlin, scarcely a year after the fall of the Wall, is a surreal experience. The whole city still seems in a state of delayed shock. A Western taxi driver takes me to see a production of Behan's *Hostage* in the Dresdener Theater on the Eastern side, for all the world like Captain Kirk going boldly where no man has been before. The production itself is equally discomforting – lots of abseilers in chintzy frocks. If it didn't have the title on the programme in front of me I would have no idea what I was seeing. Returning to my hotel in the West, I am struck by the way the buildings peter out on either side of the gash left by the now demolished Wall.

*Macbeth* itself is a revelation. A studio production, it evinces a strong sense of compressed scale. A small box set opens periodically to reveal receding corridors of surprising depth. It strikes me as an inversion of Purcarete's *Ubu Roi with Scenes from Macbeth* in that we start with recognisably human figures that mutate through the course of the action into grotesque manikins in exaggerated padded costumes. It is a must-have show. But where to put it?

Back in Dublin I check the tech specs against all available venues. Only the Tivoli has the depth of stage to accommodate the hidden corridors and its owner has not committed to the Festival yet. I ring him up. He remembers that I have delivered the press announcement for the Mayday to Bloomsday Festival in verse. Would I be prepared to write him a verse tribute to recite at his daughter's wedding? It seems a small price to pay.

The first night of *Macbeth* in Dublin is a triumph; a welcome shelter from the Archaos-chaos.

***

Taken together these 'present-tense' accounts illustrate my overall experience as Programme Director for the Dublin Theatre Festival, but they also demonstrate some key characteristics of the Festival at the time. They deal exclusively with the selection of productions from outside Ireland. This reflects the relative powerlessness of the Theatre Festival within the wider Irish theatre infrastructure. When I began working with the Festival, it was in a precarious state, with debts from the previous year exceeding its annual grant from the Arts Council. This meant that the scope for getting involved in originating productions was very limited. For understandable reasons, the main Dublin production houses (the Abbey and the Gate) were fiercely independent and the receiving houses (the Gaiety, the Olympia, and the Tivoli) displayed an ambivalence to the Festival, which though it drew great media attention, was often difficult to accommodate into their year-round programmes. Foreign work, on the other hand, attracted significant financial support from national cultural agencies such as the Goethe Institute and the British Council (though in 1991 in particular, we found ourselves in competition with major international promotions such as the Gate's Beckett Festival ).

At its best however, the Festival was able to connect with the prevailing *zeitgeist*, both within and beyond Ireland. It is no coincidence that so many of the above accounts relate to the collapse of socialism and the changing face of Europe and I feel privileged to have glimpsed this at first hand. But changes within Ireland were also reflected in these Festival programmes.

Lewis Clohessy notes in his memoir my enthusiasm for supporting the expanding production base for theatre throughout Ireland and Druid (Galway), Field Day (Derry), Meridian (Cork), the Arts Theatre and Tinderbox Theatre Company (Belfast), Yew Theatre (Ballina), Theatre Omnibus (Limerick), Galloglass (Clonmel) all found their way into one programme or another. This too reflected the reality of a changing world.

What I hope becomes clear is the variety of ways in which programming comes about and the constraints within which a programmer works. Occasionally, as with *Freaks,* you just strike lucky. More often, you depend on a network of contacts, formal and informal, which builds up over time. When I left in November 1991, Tony Ó Dálaigh invited me to write some recommendations for the future development of the Theatre Festival. I suggested six options: an emphasis on international work, an emphasis on medium to small scale work, a biennial festival, alternating year by year between foreign and Irish work, a longer less intensive Festival, or a Festival built around one major event. As history has shown the emergence, with the main Festival's support, of a vibrant Fringe, pre-empted much of this, but I did have the chance to apply some of these principles when I programmed the theatre content of Derry's year-long IMPACT Festival in 1992. The extraordinary brief was to find one event per month over the year. These included the Abbey with *Dancing at Lughnasa,* the Royal National Theatre with *Fuente Ovejuna,* the Royal Shakespeare Company with Fiona Shaw in *Electra,* the Maly Theatre of Saint Petersburg, Druid with Frank McGuinness's own production of *Carthaginians,* Rough Magic and Charabanc. In my mind's eye, it was the best Dublin Theatre Festival that never was.

---

[1] Department of Defense news briefing, 12 February 2002.

[2] See Donald Schon, *The Reflective Practitioner* (Basic Books, 1983).

[3] Bill McDonnell, 'A Good Night Out on the Falls Road: Liberation Theatre and the Nationalist Struggle in Belfast 1984–1990' in *Radical Initiatives in Interventionist and Community Drama and Politics,* edited by Peter Billingham (Bristol: Intellect, 2004).

[4] Steven Pinker, *The Stuff of Thought* (London: Allen Lane, 2007).

# Production History Part Three: 1985–1994

## Dublin Theatre Festival 1985

23 September–6 October

*Arsenic and Old Lace* by Joseph Kesselring. Gemini Productions at the Gaiety Theatre. Directed by William Chappell.

*Baglady* by Frank McGuinness. Abbey Theatre at An Damer. Directed by Patrick Mason.

*Blood Brothers* by Willy Russell. Olympia Theatre. Directed by Danny Hiller.

*Bouncers* by John Godber. Hull Truck at Edmund Burke Hall. Directed by John Godber.

*Callers* by Graham Reid. Peacock Theatre. Directed by Ben Barnes.

*The Caucasian Chalk Circle* by Bertolt Brecht. Rough Magic Theatre Company at Project Arts Centre. Directed by Declan Hughes.

*Charades* by Lee Dunne. Dublin Youth Theatre. Directed by Joe Dowling

*The Children of Lir* by Patricia Lynch and *The Devil's Bridge* . Lambert Puppet Theatre.

*Conversations on a Homecoming* by Tom Murphy. Druid Theatre Company at the Gate Theatre. Directed by Garry Hynes.

*Dirty Works/Gangsters* by Maishe Mapony. Bahamutsi and Market at Edmund Burke Hall. Directed by Maishe Maponya.

*The Dosshouse Waltz* by Aodhan Madden. Gemini Productions at the Eblana Theatre. Directed by Gerard Stembridge.

*Dreamscapes* by Steve Reich and Philip Glass and *Pie Jesu* by Gabriel Fauré. The Irish National Ballet at the SFX Centre. Choreographed by Charles Czarney and Garry Trinder.

*Early Warnings*. Ludus Dance in Education. Choreographed by David Glass.

*Ex Voto*. Bread and Puppet Theatre at the Lombard Street Studio. Directed by Peter Schumann.

*Father's Lying Dead On The Ironing Board* by Agnes Bernelle. Agnes Bernelle and her Band at Project Arts Centre.

*Les Femmes Savantes* by J-B.P. Molière. Pistolteatern at the Mansion House.

*Forty Coats and The Monster Mystery* by Joe O'Donnell. Dublin Theatre Festival and RTE at Father Matthew Hall. Directed by Avril McCrory.

*Fragments of Isabella* adapted by Michael Scott and Gabrielle Reidy
from the book by Isabella Leitner. City Theatre at An Damer.
Directed by Michael Scott.

*Frocks* adapted by Smock Alley Theatre Company from Aristophanes.
Smock Alley Theatre Company at Project Arts Centre. Directed by
the company

*Gatherers* by Frank McGuinness. Team Theatre Company at Lombard
Street Studio. Directed by Joe Dowling.

*I'll Go On* adapted by Barry McGovern and Gerry Dukes from novels
by Samuel Beckett. The Gate Theatre. Directed by Colm Ó Briain.

*In the Mood.* The Irish National Ballet at the SFX Centre.
Choreographed by Domy Reiter Soffer.

*Insignificance* by Terry Johnson. Vanishing Point Productions at the
Academy. Directed by John M. Farrell and Bill Wertz.

*Ladybag* by Frank McGuinness. Dublin Theatre Festival in association
with Abbey Theatre at An Damer. Directed by Patrick Mason.

Molly Parkin at Project Arts Centre.

*My Lady Luck* by James A. Brown, based on the works of Robert
Service. Eblana Theatre. Performed by Vincent Dowling.

*Northern Star* by Stewart Parker. Lyric Players Theatre, Belfast at the
Olympia Theatre. Directed by Peter Farago.

*Now You're Talkin'* by Marie Jones. Charabanc Theatre Company at
the John Player Theatre. Directed by Pam Brighton.

*The Open Couple* by Dario Fo and Franca Rame. Coláiste Mhuire.
Directed by Brian deSalvo.

*Peg Woffington* by Maureen Charlton. National Concert Hall.

*Readings* by Robert Wilson. Coláiste Mhuire.

*Rise Up Lovely Sweeney* by Tom Mac Intyre. Peacock Theatre.
Directed by Patrick Mason.

*Souper Sullivan* by Eoghan Harris. Abbey Theatre. Directed by Tomás
Mac Anna.

*La Strada*, adapted from Federico Fellini by Seija Hyvonen-Mammen.
Pantomimteatern at the John Player Theatre.

*Tent Meeting* by Levi Lee, Larry Lawson, and Rebecca Alworth
Wackler. The Actors Theatre of Louisville at Gleeson Hall. Directed
by Norman Rene.

*Tub, Lovers and Speed.* Jennifer Muller/The Works at the Gaiety
Theatre. Choreographed by Jennifer Muller.

*Twilight Companies* by Brian McGrath. Drolleries Theatre Company at the Academy Theatre. Directed by Paul Moore.

*Two or Three Trapezes*. Théâtre à Bâtir at Mansion House.

*Up N' Under 11* by John Godber. Hull Truck at Edmund Burke Hall. Directed by John Godber.

*Yesterday's Lovers* by Hugh Carr. Kite Productions at the Eblana Theatre. Directed by Barry Cassin.


## Dublin Theatre Festival 1986

29 September–12 October

The Beijing Opera at the Gaiety Theatre. Directed by Wang Peilin.

Ben Elton. Edmund Burke Hall.

*Brighton Beach Memoirs* by Neil Simon. Gaiety Theatre. Directed by Joe Dowling.

*The Cid* by Corneille. Cheek by Jowl at the Mansion House. Directed by Declan Donnellan.

*The Country Wife* by William Wycherley. Rough Magic Theatre Company at Project Arts Centre. Directed by Lynne Parker.

*The Girls in the Big Picture* by Marie Jones. Charabanc Theatre Company at the SFX Centre. Directed by Andy Hinds.

*Have a Nice Day* by Tom O'Neill. The Actors Company at the Focus Theatre. Directed by Tony Coleman.

*The House of Bernarda Alba* by Federico Garcia Lorca. Irish National Ballet at the Abbey Theatre. Directed by Annelli Vuorenjuuri-Robinson.

*Innocence: the Life of Caravaggio* by Frank McGuinness. Gate Theatre. Directed by Patrick Mason.

The King with the Donkey's Ears. Lambert Puppet Theatre.

*Line One* by Voker Ludwig. Grips Theatre Berlin at the Olympia.

*Macbeth* by William Shakespeare. Smock Alley at Project Arts Centre. Directed by The Company.

*The Murder of Gonzago* by Maciek Reszczynski. Theatre Unlimited at An Damer. Directed by Maciek Reszczynski.

*Nor I... but...* by Vidar Eggertsson. The Egg Theatre at An Damer. Directed by Vidar Eggetsson.

*Ourselves Alone* by Anne Devlin. Royal Court Theatre at the John Player Theatre. Directed by Simon Curtis.

*The Physicists* by Frederick Durrenmatt. Players Theatre.

*The Puppeteer From Lodz* by Gilles Segal. Siren Productions at
Coláiste Mhuire. Directed by John P. Kelly.

*Private Death of a Queen* by Aodhan Madden. Gemini Productions at
the Eblana Theatre. Directed by Gerry Stembridge.

*Saol i mBás Pháidí Joe* by Micheál Mac Cárthaigh. Peacock Theatre.
Directed by Brendan Ellis.

*Shades of the Jolly Women* by Peter Sheridan and Jean Doyle. Project
Arts Centre.

*Single Line Traffic.* Dublin Contemporary Dance Theatre at Lombard
Street Theatre. Choreographed by Yoshiko Chuma.

*They're Playing Our Song* by Neil Simon, with music by Marvin
Hamlisch. Olympia Theatre.

*Twelfth Night* by William Shakespeare. Cheek By Jowl at the Mansion
House. Directed by Declan Donnellan.

*A Whistle in the Dark* by Tom Murphy. Abbey Theatre. Directed by
Garry Hynes.

*A Woman of No Importance* by Oscar Wilde. Stragedays Theatre
Company at Players Theatre.

*You Can't Deep Freeze a Red Hot Mamma.* Smock Alley at Project
Arts Centre. Directed by Derek Chapman.

## Dublin Theatre Festival 1987

28 September–11 October

*Another Day* by Tom O'Neill. Focus Theatre. Directed by David
McKenna

*Berlin Berlin* by Rudolph Bernauer. Project Arts Centre. Directed by
Peter O'Brien.

Chakravyuha Chorus Theatre (India) at the Mansion House. Directed
by Ratan Thiyam.

*A Concert for the Theatre.* Barbara Cook at the Edmund Burke Hall.
Directed by Wally Harper.

*Diary of a Madman* adapted by Tim McDonnell from Nikolai Gogol.
Focus Theatre/John Everett Productions at Project Arts Centre.
Directed by Deirdre O'Connell.

*Disasters of War*, Parts One and Two. Brith Gof Company (Wales).
Performed by Mike Pearson and Nicholas Ros.

*Domestic Bliss* by Sue Broadway and Dave Spathaky. The Ra Ra Zoo at Coláiste Mhuire. Directed by Emil Wok.

*Donna Giovanni* devised by the company. Companias Divas, DTF, and LIFT at the Olympia Theatre. Directed by Jesusa Rodriguez.

*Each His Own Wilderness* by Doris Lessing. Focus Theatre. Directed by Siobhan Murphy.

*Heartstone* by Jim Nolan. TEAM at Lombard St. Studios. Directed by Annie Kilmartin.

*The Invisible Man* by Jennifer Johnston. Peacock Theatre. Directed by Caroline FitzGerald.

*The Last Hero* by Donald Freed. Lone Eagle and Dublin Theatre Festival at the Peacock Theatre. Directed by Ken Albers.

*Les Liaisons Dangereuses* by Christopher Hampton (after Choderlos de Laclos). The Gate Theatre. Directed by Ben Barnes.

*Life and Death of A Fireman*. Bread and Puppet Theatre at the Mansion House. Directed by Peter Shumann.

*Liverpool Fantasy* by Larry Kirwan. Eblana Theatre. Directed by Geoffrey Sherman.

*Madigan's Lock* by Hugh Leonard. Peacock Theatre. Directed by Vincent Dowling.

*Mother of all the Behans* adapted by Peter Sheridan from the book by Brian Behan. Peacock Theatre. Directed by Peter Sheridan.

Pas de Deux Dance Company. National Gallery. Choreographed by Roy Galvin.

*Pentecost* by Stewart Parker. Field Day at the John Player. Directed by Patrick Mason.

*A Phoenix Too Frequent* by Christopher Fry. An Damer. Directed by Gerry Walsh.

*The Pub Bombers* by James O'Brien. Giro Theatre at the Olympia Theatre. Directed by James O'Brien.

*Pygmalion* by G.B. Shaw. Orion Theatre (Sweden) at the Tivoli Theatre. Directed by Lars Rudolfsson.

*Remember Mauritania* by Aodhan Madden. Peacock Theatre. Directed by Claire Wilson.

*Shock Treatment* by Pat Courtenay. Beg, Borrow and Steal Company at the Cathedral Club.

Siamsa Tire at the Olympia Theatre. Directed by Fr. Pat Ahern and Oliver Hurley.

*The Silver Tassie* by Sean O'Casey. Rough Magic Theatre Company at Project Arts Centre. Directed by Declan Hughes.

*The Story of the Widow's Son* by Mary Lavin. Storytellers Theatre Company at Project Arts Centre. Directed by Mary Elizabeth Burke-Kennedy.

*Ulysses* adapted by Anthony Cronin and others. Abbey Theatre. Directed by Ann Myler.

*Vespers* by Ritsaert ten Cate. Mickery Theatre at Coláiste Mhuire.

*Volunteers* by Brian Friel. John Player Theatre. Directed by Gerry Barnes.

## Dublin Millennium Theatre Festival 1988

26 September–15 October

*Autumn Dances*. Irish Theatre Ballet at the Mansion House. Choreographed by Babil Gandara.

*Bat The Father, Rabbit The Son* by Donal O'Kelly. Rough Magic Theatre Company at the Mansion House. Directed by Declan Hughes.

*Bloomsday*. Dublin Contemporary Dance Theatre at Lombard Street Studio. Choreographed by Jerry Pearson.

*Carthaginians* by Frank McGuinness. Peacock Theatre. Directed by Sarah Pia Anderson.

*Circus Oz*. Gaiety Theatre. Directed by Robin Laurie and Emil Wolk.

*City Mission* by Antoine Ó Flatharta. John Player Theatre. Directed by Michael McCaffrey.

*Colours: Jane Barry Esquire* by Jean Binnie. Abbey Theatre. Directed by Jude Kelly.

*Departed* by Joe O'Byrne. Co-Motion Theatre Company at the Lombard Street Studio. Directed by Joe O'Byrne.

*Did you see that?* written, directed and performed by Mark Britton and Krissie Illing. Project Arts Centre.

*Docteur Labus*. Groupe Emile Dubois at the Olympia Theatre. Directed by Jean-Claude Galotta.

*Hamlet* by William Shakespeare. Royal Shakespeare Company at the Olympia Theatre. Directed by Ron Daniels.

*I Can Give You A Good Time* by Gilly Frazer. Kite Productions at Project Arts Centre. Directed by Barry Cassin.

*The Joan Collins Fan Club* by Julian Clary. Edmund Burke Hall.

*Josephine in the Night* by Aodhan Madden. Peacock Theatre. Directed by Caroline FitzGerald.

*Laurel and Hardy* by Tom McGrath. Smock Alley at An Damer. Directed by Malcolm Douglas.

*Medea* by Euripides, in a new version by Brendan Kennelly. Medea Productions at the RDS. Directed by Raymond Yeates.

*Peer Gynt* by Henrik Ibsen in a new version by Frank McGuinness. Gate Theatre. Directed by Patrick Mason.

*Penelope* by Maciek Reszczynski. Theatre Unlimited at Project Arts Centre. Directed by Maciek Reszczynski.

*Recollections of a Furtive Nudist* by Ken Campbell. Project Arts Centre. Directed by Gillian Brown.

*Serious Money* by Caryl Churchill. Rough Magic Theatre Company at Project Arts Centre. Directed by Lynne Parker.

*She's Your Mother Too You Know* by Ena May. Focus Theatre. Directed by Ena May.

Simon Fanshawe and Jenny Lecoat. Project Arts Centre.

*A Sober Black Shawl* by Tomás Mac Anna. Gemini Productions at An Damer. Directed by Tomás Mac Anna.

*State of Emergency*. Amampondo at the Olympia Theatre.

*A Thin Red Line* by Seamus Moran. Íomhá Ildánach at Edmund Burke Hall. Directed by Matthew Skinner.

*Torchlight and Laser Beams* by Christopher Nolan. Gaiety Theatre. Directed by Michael Scott.

*Übungen für Tanzer*. Tanz-Forum Cologne at the Olympia Theatre. Choreographed by Jochen Ulrich.

The Vicious Boys in Cabaret. Edmund Burke Hall.

*Women in Arms* by Mary Elizabeth Burke-Kennedy. Storytellers Theatre Company at the John Player Theatre. Directed by Mary Elizabeth Burke-Kennedy.

Interactions

# Dublin Theatre Festival 1989

19 September–8 October

*Bare Essentials* by Tom O'Neill. Brass Tacks Theatre Company at the Damer. Directed by Rebecca Roper.

*Cinema* by Rambert Dance Company, Olympia Theatre.

*Contrariwise or Lewis Carroll – A Conundrum.* Key Theatre Company at Andrews Lane Theatre. Directed by Eamonn Hunt

*The Country of the Young* by Susie Burke. Cauldron Productions at Andrews Lane Theatre. Directed by Brenda Dillon.

*Courage, The Adventuress.* The Medieval Players at Andrews Lane Theatre. Directed by Carl Heap.

*Crossing Water* by Jane Mooney and Sue Mayo. Still Standing Dance Theatre at Lombard St. Studio.

*Dark Elegies* by Rambert Dance Company. Olympia Theatre.

*Dionysia* by Hugh Carr. R.I.A.M. Directed by Hugh Carr

*Dream Walker* by Antoine Ó Flatharta. TEAM at Lombard St. Studio. Directed by Patrick Sutton

*Edmond* by David Mamet. Seven Woods Theatre Company at Andrews Lane Theatre. Directed by Frank Conway

*Enter An Angel* by Mark Patrick. Kite Productions at Andrews Lane Theatre. Directed by Barry Cassin.

*Excuse My Dust* by Paul Ryan. Round Table at the Mansion House. Directed by Patricia Martin.

*Facets of Eve* by Dario Fo and Franca Rame. Project Arts Centre.

*Flying Fish and The Cook's Hat* by Annie Olds. Still Standing Dance Theatre at Lombard St. Studio.

*Freaks*, adapted by Geneviève de Kermabon from Tod Browning's film. Avignon Festival at Tivoli Theatre. Directed by Geneviève de Kermabon.

*The Ghost of Saint Joan* by Joe O'Byrne. Co-Motion Theatre Company at Black Church. Directed by Joe O'Byrne

*Ghosts* by Henrik Ibsen in a version by Thomas Kilroy. Gemini Productions at the Peacock Theatre. Directed by Michael Scott.

*The House of Bernarda Alba* by Federico Garcia Lorca, in a version by Aidan Mathews. Gate Theatre. Directed by Ben Barnes.

*A Hundred Years of Cabaret* by Agnes Bernelle. Project Arts Centre.

*The Johnny Patterson Travelling Circus*. Theatre Omnibus at the Royal Hospital.

*Joyicity* by Ulick O'Connor. Peacock Theatre. Directed by Caroline FitzGerald

*Judith* with Roberta Carreri. Odinteatret. Project Arts Centre.

*La Beauté des Fleurs*. Dance Theatre of Ireland at Lombard St. Studio. Choreographed by Isabelle Dubouloz and Pierre Doussaint.

*La Corbière* by Anne Hartigan. Moveable Feast Theatre Company at Project Arts Centre. Directed by Cathy Leeney

*The Lament For Arthur Cleary* by Dermot Bolger. Wet Paint Arts at Project Arts Centre. Directed by David Byrne.

*The Life of Napoleon* by John Sessions. Renaissance Theatre Company at the Olympia Theatre. Directed by Kenneth Branagh.

*Lives Worth Living* by Lawrence Evans and Jane Nash. Graffiti at Lombard St. Studio. Directed by Emelie FitzGibbon.

*Molly's Rock* by Ken Robbins. Andrews Lane Theatre. Directed by Claire Wilson.

*My Name, Shall I Tell You My Name?* by Christina Reid. Yew Theatre Company at Andrews Lane Theatre. Directed by Pieree Campos.

*Our Country's Good* by Timberlake Wertenbaker. Rough Magic Theatre Company at Tivoli Theatre. Directed by Declan Hughes.

*Pulau Dewata*. Rambert Dance Company, Olympia Theatre.

*Savages* by Christopher Hampton. Pigsback Theatre Company at Lombard St. Studio. Directed by Martin Munroe.

*The School For Wives* by J-B.P. Molière in a new version by Derek Mahon. Arts Theatre Belfast at the John Player Theatre. Directed by Nick Philippou.

*The Seagull* by Anton Chekhov, translated by Elisaveta Fen. Moscow Art Theatre at the Abbey Theatre. Directed by Oleg Yefremov.

*The Second Grand Confabulation Of Drum Ceat* by Sydney Bernard Smith. Andrews Lane Theatre. Directed by Sydney Bernard Smith.

*Septet* by Rambert Dance Company. Olympia Theatre.

*Skeffington* by Rosalind Scanlon. An Damer. Directed by Rosalind Scanlon

*Soldat* by Rambert Dance Company. Olympia Theatre.

*A Soldier's Tale* by Igor Stravinsky. Opera Theatre Company. Project Arts Centre. Directed by Derek Chapman.

*Sounding*. Rambert Dance Company, Olympia Theatre.

*Strong Language*. Rambert Dance Company. Olympia Theatre.

*Tine Chnámh* by Liam Ó Muirthile. On The Bank at Project Arts Centre. Directed by Fiach Mac Conghail.

*Too Late For Logic* by Tom Murphy.     Abbey Theatre. Directed by Patrick Mason.

*Traffic On Dame Street* by Mr. Trellis and Dermot Carmody. Andrews Lane Theatre.

*The Trial of Esther Waters* by George Moore. Storytellers Theatre Company at John Player. Adapted and directed by Mary Elizabeth Burke-Kennedy.

*Vivre Libre ou Mourir* by Eric Eychenne. Théâtre Necrobie de Marseille at Andrews Lane Theatre. Directed by Eric Eychenne.

*The Wake*, adapted by Donal O'Kelly and Paul O'Hanrahan from James Joyce. Project Arts Centre. Directed by David Grant.

*Wild Harvest* by Ken Bourke.     Druid Theatre Company at Lombard St. Studio. Directed by Andy Hinds.

*A Woman Alone* by Dario Fo and Franca Rame. Fand Productions at Lombard Street Studio. Directed by Ronan Smith.

## Dublin Theatre Festival 1990

1–14 October

*Adult Child/Dead Child* by Claire Dowie. Andrews Lane Theatre. Directed by John Kearns.

*All Being Well* by Damian Gorman. Replay at the Gaiety Theatre. Directed by Ian McElhinney.

*Apollo: To the Moon* by Mary Hall Surface. Tivoli Theatre. Directed by Mary Hall Surface.

*The Audition* by Rudolph Sirera. Moving Parts Theatre Company at Andrews Lane Theatre. Directed by Guy Charlton.

*The Big Sea* by Colin Teevan. Galloglass at Andrews Lane Theatre. Directed by Simon Bayly.

*The Bread Man* by Frank McGuinness. Gate Theatre. Directed by Andy Hinds.

*The Complete Works of William Shakespeare* by Jess Borgeson, Adam Long, Reed Martein, Daniel Singer. The Reduced Shakespeare Company at Andrews Lane Theatre.

*Danton's Death* by Georg Buchner. Communicado at the John Player Theatre. Directed by Gerry Mulgrew.

*Dead Dad Dog* by John McKay. Graffiti at City Arts Centre. Directed by Emelie FitzGibbon.

*The Edge.* Trestle at the John Player Theatre. Directed by John Wright.

*Endangered Species.* The Kosh at Lombard Street Studio. Directed by Johnny Hutch and Michael Murwitzer.

The Fabulous Singlettes at the Gaiety Theatre.

*The Fetch* by John Maher. Andrews Lane Theatre. Directed by Owen Roe.

*Fluidofiume* by Enrico Frattaroli. Stravagario Maschere Theatre at Project Arts Centre. Directed by Enrico Frattaroli.

*Goodnight Siobhan* by Jeannane Crowley. Royal Court Theatre at the Gate Theatre. Directed by John Dove.

*Hamlet* by William Shakespeare. Bulandra Theatre at the Gaiety Theatre. Directed by Alexandru Tocilescu.

*The Heart Laid Bare* by Hugh Carr. Dry Bread Theatre Company at Andrews Lane Theatre. Directed by Barry Cassin.

*I Can't Get Started* by Declan Hughes. Rough Magic Theatre Company at Project Arts Centre. Directed by Lynne Parker.

*In High Germany* by Dermot Bolger. Gate Theatre. Directed by David Byrne.

*Jacob's Ladder* by Sure Aldred. Andrews Lane Theatre. Directed by Jackie Fletcher.

*Just the One* by Eamon Morrissey. Dublin Comedy Theatre at the Tivoli Theatre.

*Kitty O'Shea* by Tom Mac Intyre. Peacock Theatre. Directed by Ben Barnes.

*Live and Cracking.* Crack '90 at Mother Redcaps Tavern.

*Mac* by Henry Hudson. Scenario Productions at Lombard Street Studio. Directed by Claire Wilson.

*Mamie Sighs* by Donal O'Kelly. Peacock Theatre. Directed by John Olohan.

*Man to Man* by Manfred Karge. Lombard Street Studio. Directed by Brian Brady.

*A Midsummer Night's Dream* by William Shakespeare. Footsbarn Travelling Theatre at Iveagh Gardens.

*Misogynist* by Michael Harding. Abbey Theatre. Directed by Judy Friel.

*Mulletman and Gulliver* by Donal O'Kelly and Charlie O'Neill. City Arts Centre. Directed by Patrick Sutton.

*Poor Beast in the Rain* by Billy Roche. The Angels Club at Andrews Lane Theatre. Directed by Brian deSalvo.

*Return to Go.* Other People Theatre Company at Andrews Lane Theatre. Directed by Eilish Kelly.

*Shadowtackle* by Anne Barrett. TEAM Theatre Company at City Arts Centre. Directed by Patrick Sutton.

*The Sinking of Titanic and Other Matters* by Joe O'Byrne. Co-Motion Theatre Company at SFX Centre. Directed by Joe O'Byrne.

*Tarry Flynn* by Patrick Kavanagh. Playwrights and Actors Company at the Tivoli Theatre. Directed by Kevin McHugh.

*Tressell* by the company. Popular Productions at Larkin Hall.

*Volpone* adapted by Johnny Hanrahan from Ben Jonson. Meridian Theatre Company at the John Player Theatre. Directed by Johnny Hanrahan and John Browne.

*Waiting for Godot* by Samuel Beckett. Sanwoollim Theatre at Project Arts Centre. Directed by Yuong Woong Lim.

*The Waking of Brian Boru* by Michael Harding. Theatre Omnibus City Arts Centre.

*Wandrin' Star* by Julian Clary. Gaiety Theatre.

*A Weill Entertainment.* Opera Theatre Company at Mother Redcaps Tavern.

*Zero Crossing.* I-Contact at the Douglas Hyde Gallery. Choreographed by Snaggy O'Sullivan.

## Irish Life Dublin Theatre Festival 1991

1–20 October

*As You Like It* by William Shakespeare. Cheek By Jowl at the Riverbank Theatre. Directed by Declan Donnellan.

*Baal* by Bertolt Brecht. Íomhá Ildánach at the Eblana Theatre. Directed by Maire O'Higgins.

*Blues In The Night* by Sheldon Epps. Centre Stage Productions and Excalibur Productions Ltd at the Tivoli Theatre. Directed by Carole Todd.

*Breath, That Time, A Piece of Monologue* by Samuel Beckett. Gate Theatre. Directed by Judy Friel.

*The Brittonioni Brothers*. Forkbeard Fantasy at Andrews Lane Theatre.

*The Broken Kiss* by Martin Dolan. 3 New Plays, 3 New Directors at Open House. Directed by Marton Dolan.

*Candlemas Night* by Aodhan Madden. 3 New Plays, 3 New Directors at Open House. Directed by Conall Morrison.

*Come and Go, Act Without Words II*, and *Play* by Samuel Beckett. Gate Theatre. Directed by Lucy Bailey.

*Cook Dems.* Bobby Baker at Andrews Lane Theatre.

*Derives* by Phillipe Genty. The Phillipe Genty Company at the Gaiety Theatre. Directed by Phillipe Genty.

*Digging For Fire* by Declan Hughes. Rough Magic Theatre Company at Project Arts Centre. Directed by Lynne Parker.

*Dinner Dance* by David Pownall. The Kosh at Newman House. Directed by Michael Merwitzer.

*Donny Boy* by Robin Glendinning. Tinderbox Theatre Company at Lombard Street Studio. Directed by David Grant.

*The Dracula Meditations* by Paul O'Hanrahan. Balloonatics Theatre Company at Project Arts Centre. Directed by Mary Cloake.

*Drawing on a Mother's Experience.* Bobby Baker at Andrews Lane Theatre.

*Endgame* by Samuel Beckett. Gate Theatre. Directed by Antoni Libera.

*Footfalls, Rough for Theatre 1* and *Rockaby* by Samuel Beckett. Gate Theatre. Directed by Derek Chapman.

*From Fogarty's Cave* by Ric Knowles. Mulgrave Road Co-Op at Andrews Lane Theatre. Directed by Terry Tweed.

*Glad* by Jeremy Weller. Grassmarket Project at City Arts Centre. Directed by Jeremy Weller.

*Hamlet* by William Shakespeare. The Tokyo Globe Company at the Tivoli Theatre. Directed by Kohji Orita.

*Hang All The Harpers* by Shane Connaughton and Marie Jones. DubbelJoint Theatre Company at the Olympia Theatre. Directed by Pam Brighton.

*Happy Days* by Samuel Beckett. Gate Theatre. Directed by Caroline FitzGerald.

*Howling Moons, Silent Sons* by Deirdre Hines. Pigsback Theatre Company at Project Arts Centre. Directed by Jim Culleton.

*Infidel* by Roger Gregg. Graffiti Theatre Company at City Arts Centre. Directed by Emelie FitzGibbon.

*Krapp's Last Tape* by Samuel Beckett. Gate Theatre. Directed by Pat Laffan.

*Macbeth* by William Shakespeare. The Schiller Theater at the Tivoli Theatre. Directed by Katharina Thalbach.

*Machnamh* and *Through An Eye Of Stone*. Composed by Mícheál Ó Súilleabháin. Daghda Dance Company at Newman House. Performed and choreographed by Olive Beecher, Paul Johnson, and Mary Nunan.

*The Madame MacAdam Travelling Theatre* by Thomas Kilroy. Field Day Theatre Company at the Gaiety Theatre. Directed by Jim Nolan.

*Medea: Sex War* by Tony Harrison. Volcano Theatre Company at City Arts Centre. Directed by Janek Alexander.

*Metal Clown*. Archaos Circus in Tallaght.

*Monrovia Monrovia* by Karl McDermott. Andrews Lane Theatre.

*Not I, What Where, Act Without Words I* by Samuel Beckett. Gate Theatre. Directed by Colm Ó Briain.

*Ohio Impromptu, Rough For Theatre II, Catastrophe* by Samuel Beckett. Gate Theatre. Directed by Pierre Chabert.

*One Last White Horse* by Dermot Bolger. Peacock Theatre. Directed by David Byrne.

*Potestad* by Eduardo Pavolvsky. Lyric Theatre Belfast at Andrews Lane Theatre. Directed by Joe Devlin.

*The Power of Darkness* by John McGahern after Leo Tolstoy. Abbey Theatre. Directed by Garry Hynes.

*The Ring* by Richard Wagner. Pocket Opera Company at the Gaiety Theatre. Directed by Peter Beat Wyrsch.

*The Shadow of a Gunman* by Sean O'Casey. The O'Casey Theatre Company at the Olympia Theatre. Directed by Shivaun O'Casey.

*Sixteen to Ninety One* by Colm Quilligan and Veronica Coburn. Writers Ireland and the OPW at Kilmainham Gaol. Directed by Colm Quilligan and Veronica Coburn.

*Tears From A Long Time Ago* by Martina Lynch. Graffiti Theatre Company at City Arts Centre. Directed by Emelie FitzGibbon.

*The Táin Bó Cuailgne* adapted by Joe O'Byrne. Co-Motion Theatre Company at the SFX Centre. Directed by Joe O'Byrne.

*That Mad One With The Hair* by Pom Boyd. Let Loose Productions at Project Arts Centre. Directed by Julina Plunkett-Dillon.

*A View From the Bridge* by Arthur Miller. Focus Theatre. Directed by Brian deSalvo.

*Waiting for Godot* by Samuel Beckett. Gate Theatre. Directed by Walter Asmus.

*Weave the Red Thread* by Bill Hammond. 3 New Plays, 3 New Directors at Open House. Directed by John Breen.

*Winds of Change.* Ludus Dance Company at Newman House. Directed by Jane Mooney.

*Words of Pride and Passion.* Terry Neason at Andrews Lane Theatre.

## Irish Life Dublin Theatre Festival 1992

5–17 October

*The Ash Fire* by Gavin Kostick. Pigsback Theatre Company at Project Arts Centre. Directed by Jim Culleton.

*An Baile Seo Againne Inniu* by the company. Aisteiori Bhreanainn at Coláiste Mhuire.

*The Ballad Of the Limehouse Art* by Tim Newton. Louder than Words at Andrews Lane Theatre. Directed by Ruth Ben-Tovim.

*Billy Club Puppets* adapted by Padraic Cullen and Peter Sheridan from Federico Garcia Lorca. Second Level Theatre Project at Project Arts Centre. Directed by Padraic Cullen and Peter Sheridan.

*Billy Liar* by Keith Waterhouse and Wilis Hall. Royal National Theatre at the Riverbank Theatre. Directed by Tim Supple.

*Blood and Ice* by Liz Lochhead. Smashing Times Theatre at the Dublin Writers Museum. Directed by Kevin Lavin.

*The Bosco Road Show.* Puppet Magic at City Arts Centre.

*The Colour of Your Money*, with a score by Fergus Johnston. Rubato Ballet at RHA Gallery.

*Desirs Parade* by Phillipe Genty. The Phillipe Genty Theatre Company at the Gaiety Theatre. Directed by Phillipe Genty.

*Dixie* by Sean McArthy. Storytellers Theatre Company at the Riverbank Theatre. Directed by Mary Elizabeth Burke-Kennedy.

*The Dogs* by Donal O'Kelly. Rough Magic Theatre Company at Project Arts Centre. Directed by Lynne Parker.

*Dolores* by Darina Mac Anna. Circe Productions at Players Theatre. Directed by Mairead McGrath.

*Each Woman in Her Own Time.* Nite Songs and DGOS Opera Ireland at Andrews Lane Theatre. Directed by Michael McCafferty.

*The Emergency Session* by Arthur Riordan. Rough Magic Theatre Company at Project Arts Centre. Directed by Declan Hughes.

*Festoons.* Illustrated Touring Theatre Company at Dublin City College.

*Fine Day for a Hunt* by Tom Mac Intyre. Punchbag Theatre Company at Andrews Lane Theatre. Directed by Sean Killian.

*Frank Pig Says Hello* by Pat McCabe. Co-Motion Theatre Company at Lombard Street Studio. Directed by Joe O'Byrne.

*Frog and Toad*, adapted by the company. Graffiti Theatre at City Arts Centre. Directed by Emilie FitzGibbon.

*Get Hur* by Ray Dobbins. Bloolips at Project Arts Centre. Directed by Bette Bourne.

*Grease* by Jim Jacobs and Warren Casey. Edward Farrell at the Olympia Theatre. Directed by Carole Todd.

*Hat Talk* written, performed, and directed by Bette Bourne. Project Arts Centre.

*Here Come Cowboys* by Colin Teevan. TEAM at City Arts Centre. Directed by Patrick Sutton.

*The Iceman Cometh* by Eugene O'Neill. Abbey Theatre. Directed by Robert Falls.

*In the Corset Department of Clery's.* The Crack 90s at Project Arts Centre.

*Les Justes - Na Firéin*, by Albert Camus, in a new version by the company. Aisteiori Bhreanainn at Coláiste Mhuire.

*Justice* by Hugh Murphy. Point Fields Theatre at Andrews Lane Theatre. Directed by Joe Devlin.

*Lake Horses* devised by the company and scripted by Paul Conway, Gerard Lee, Judy Lunny, Michelle Manahan, and Peter Sheridan. Second Level Theatre Project at Project Arts Centre. Directed by Peter Sheridan.

*The Little Mermaid* by Hans Christian Anderson. Jytte Agbildstroms Teatre of Denmark at City Arts Centre.

*Love of a Pig* by Leslie Caveny. Theatre West and The Usual Suspects at Andrews Lane Theatre. Directed by Bob McCracken.

*The Midnight Court* by Brian Merriman, translated by Frank O'Connor. Lisgold Productions at Andrews Lane Theatre. Directed by Barry Cassin.

*Momix Classics.* Momix at the Gaiety Theatre. Choreographed by Moses Pendleton.

*Moths* by Martin Lynch. Citywide Community Theatre Project at Andrews Lane Theatre. Directed by Lenny Mullan.

*Never Had It So Good* by Caroline Seymour, Finola Geraghty, Maeve Murphy. Trouble and Strife at Andrews Lane Theatre. Directed by Jessica Dromgoole.

*Nothing Adds Up in this Crazy World* by Tom O'Brien. Comic Souffle at Dublin City College.

*One for the Road* by Willy Russell. Theatre O at the Eblana Theatre. Directed by Terry O'Dea.

*Revelations, Indictments, and Confessions* by Michael McCarthy and Greg Holman. Second City at Andrews Lane Theatre. Directed by Michael Napier and Nate Herman.

*Ripley Bogle* adapted by Sean O'Tarpaigh from Robert McLiam Wilson. Bualadh Bos at Andrews Lane Theatre. Directed by Paul Mills.

*Shaker* by Nicholas McInerny. Touchdown Theatre Company at Andrews Lane Theatre. Directed by Annie Griffin.

*Sick Dying Dead and Black* by Bernie Downes. Second Level Theatre Project at Project Arts Centre. Directed by Carol Scanlan and Peter Sheridan.

*Silverlands* by Antoine Ó Flatharta. Peacock Theatre. Directed by Andy Hinds.

*Sinne Clann Tom* by Padraig Ó Gillogain. Aisteiori Bulfin at Coláiste Mhuire. Directed by Tony De Barra.

*The Splitting of Latham* by Michael Duke. Benchtours at Players Theatre. Directed by Magdalena Schamberger.

*The Streets of Dublin* by Dion Boucicault in a new version by Fergus Linehan. Acewise Productions at the Tivoli Theatre. Directed by Brian deSalvo.

*Summer* by Edward Bond. Focus Theatre. Directed by Peter O'Shaughnessy.

*Tartuffe* by J-B.P. Molière in a new version by Michael West. Gate Theatre. Directed by Alan Stanford.

*The Three Little Pigs*. Lambert Puppet Theatre at City Arts Centre.

## Irish Life Dublin Theatre Festival 1993

4–16 October

*Al Andalus*. Antonio Vargas Flamenco Dance Theatre at the Olympia Theatre. Choreographed by Antonio Vargas.

Avner the Eccentric. Samuel Beckett Theatre.

*Brothers of the Brush* by Jimmy Murphy. Peacock Theatre. Directed by David Byrne.

*Buffalo Bill Has Gone To Alaska* by Colin Teevan. Pigsback Theatre Company at Andrews Lane Theatre. Directed by Jim Culleton.

*The Challenge* by Gilbert Dupuis. Dynamo Theatre Company at the Riverbank Theatre. Directed by Alain Fourier.

*Dance for Another Place* written and choreographed by John Scott. Irish Modern Dance Theatre at Project Arts Centre.

*A Doll's House* by Henrik Ibsen, translated by John Tinsdale. Gate Theatre. Directed by Karel Reisz.

Ennio Marchetto at the Olympia Theatre.

*Eye of the Storm* by Charles Way. Tehatr Gwent at City Arts Centre. Directed by Gary Meredith.

*F!* devised by the company from a scenario by David Grant. Wet Paint Arts at the Riverbank Theatre. Directed by David Grant.

*Famine* by Tom Murphy. Abbey Theatre. Directed by Garry Hynes.

*Fishy Tales* by Enda Walsh. Graffiti Theatre Company at City Arts Centre. Directed by Emelie FitzGibbon.

*Foggy Hairs and Green Eyes* by Tom Mac Intyre. Punchbag Theatre at Project Arts Centre. Directed by David Quinn.

*For Company/Territorial Claims*. Daghdha Dance Company at Project Arts Centre. Choreography by Mary Nunan.

*Hatchet Plan* by the company. Parti-Pris Theatre Company at Andrews Lane Theatre. Directed by Nick Herrett and Toby Jones.

*The Illusion* adapted by Peter Sheridan from Corneille. Charabanc Theatre Company at the Samuel Beckett Theatre. Directed by Peter Sheridan.

*Jenufa* by Leoš Janaček. Opera Theatre Company at the Samuel Beckett Theatre. Directed by Lindsey Posner.

*Kabarett Valentin* by David Lavender and Colin Granger. Umbrella Theatre at Bank of Ireland Arts Centre. Directed by David Lavender.

*Katie Has Been Drowned* by Alex van Warmerdam. The Mexican Hound at the Tivoli Theatre. Directed by Alex van Warmerdam.

*Keely and Du* by Jane Martin. Olympia Theatre. Directed by Caroline FitzGerald.

*The Nest* by Frank Xavier Kroetz. Andrews Lane Theatre. Directed by Ray Yeates.

*Night After Night* by Neil Bartlett and Nicholas Bloomfield. Gloria at the Samuel Beckett Theatre. Directed by Neill Bartlett.

*A Nightmare for C. Darwin*, composed, choreographed and directed by Shanghai Taro. The Shanghai Taro Butou Koushi at the Samuel Beckett Theatre.

Odissi Classical Dance from India. Edmund Burke Hall.

*One Man* written, performed, and directed by Steven Berkoff. The Gaiety Theatre.

*Opera* by Enrico Frattaroli. Stravagario Maschere at Project Arts Centre. Directed by Enrico Frattaroli.

*The Other Side of Paradise* by John Kane. Andrews Lane Theatre. Directed by Susie Fuller.

*Othello* by William Shakespeare. Second Age at the Tivoli Theatre. Directed by Alan Stanford.

*Para* by Joe O'Byrne. Co-Motion Theatre Company at the Riverbank Theatre. Directed by Joe O'Byrne.

Paul Merton at the Olympia Theatre.

*Plastered*. Trestle Theatre Company at Andrews Lane Theatre.

*Sandra/Manon* by Michel Tremblay. Andrews Lane Theatre. Directed by Vanessa Fielding.

*Slice of Life* by Tara Farrell and Niamh Dowd. Very Special Arts Ireland at City Arts Centre. Directed by Emelie FitzGibbon.

*Talking to the Wall* by Gerard Mannix Flynn. Far Cry at Project Arts Centre. Directed by Conall Morrison.

*The Taffetas* by Rick Lewis. American Theater Works at the Gaiety Theatre. Directed by Arthur Whitelaw.

*The Tempest* by William Shakespeare. Island Theatre Company at Kilmainham Gaol. Directed by Terry Devlin.

*The Way of the World* by William Congreve. Rough Magic Theatre Company at Project Arts Centre. Directed by Lynne Parker.

*The Well* by Ken Bourke. TEAM at City Arts Centre. Directed by Susie Kennedy.

*The Winter's Tale* by William Shakespeare. Royal Shakespeare Company at the Gaiety Theatre. Directed by Adrian Noble.

## Irish Life Dublin Theatre Festival 1994

3–16 October

*The American Century* by Murphy Guyer. The Usual Suspects at Andrews Lane Theatre. Directed by Bob McCracken.

*Anorak of Fire* by Stephen Dinsdale. Project Arts Centre. Directed by Sarah Frankcom.

*Buile Shuibhne/Sweeny* adapted by Páraic Breathnach and devised by the company. Macnas at Coláiste Mhuire. Directed by Rod Goodall.

*Chamber Music* by Hugh Leonard. Abbey Theatre. Directed by Patrick Mason.

Chinese State Circus at the RDS.

*Christy Don't Leave So Soon* and other pieces. CandoCo Dance Company at the Samuel Beckett Theatre. Choreographed by Adam Benjamin and Celeste Dandeker with Lea Parkinson.

*Cinderella*. Tandarica Theatre at Father Matthew Hall. Directed by Silviu Purcarete.

*The Comeback* adapted by Isse Ogata. London Stage Company at Andrews Lane Theatre. Directed by David Duly.

*Come Down From the Mountain John Clown*, devised and directed by the company. Barabbas... The Company at the Samuel Beckett Theatre.

*Decameron 646* Adapted by Silviu Purcarete from Giovanni Boccaccio. Teatrul Anton Pann at the Tivoli Theatre. Directed by Silviu Purcarete.

Fascinating Aida at the Olympia Theatre. Directed by Nica Burns.

*From The Diary of Virginia Woolf* by Dominick Argento and *Twelve Poems of Emily Dickinson* by Aaron Copland. Opera Theatre Company at the National Concert Hall.

*The Good Thief* by Conor McPherson. Loopline Theatre Company at the Furnace. Directed by Conor McPherson.

*Hanging Around*, by the company. Trestle Theatre Company at Andrews Lane Theatre.

*The Happy Prince* by Oscar Wilde. Graffiti Theatre Company at Father Matthew Hall. Directed by Emelie FitzGibbon.

*Her Body Doesn't Fit Her Soul.* Wim Vandekeybus/Ultima Vez at the Olympia Theatre. Choreographed and directed by Wim Vandekeybus.

*Hidden Charges* by Arthur Riordan. Rough Magic Theatre Company at Project Arts Centre. Directed by Lynne Parker.

*Hope.* Composed By Kaffe Matthews. Desperate Optimists at Project Arts Centre.

*The Kiss* by Michael Harding. Project Arts Centre. Directed by Michael Harding.

*Loco County Lonesome* by Pat McCabe. Co-Motion Theatre Company at the Olympia Theatre. Directed by Joe O'Byrne.

*Macbeth* by William Shakespeare. Second Age Theatre Company at the Riverbank Theatre. Directed by Alan Stanford.

*The Mai* by Marina Carr. Peacock Theatre. Directed by Brian Brady.

*Mary and Lizzie* by Frank McGuinness. Smashing Times at the Crypt. Directed by Jo Mangan.

*Molly Sweeney* by Brian Friel. Gate Theatre. Directed by Brian Friel.

Nuova Compagnia Di Canto at Castle Hall.

*Observe the Sons of Ulster Marching Towards the Somme* by Frank McGuinness. Abbey Theatre. Directed by Patrick Mason.

*Oscar* by David Norris. Playwrights and Actors Company at Andrews Lane Theatre. Directed by Caroline FitzGerald.

*Out of Line* by Maeve Ingoldsby. TEAM at Father Matthew Hall. Directed by Susie Kennedy.

*Peacemaker* by David Holman. Visible Fictions at Father Matthew Hall. Directed by Mark Leese.

*The Rider.* Derevo at the Samuel Beckett Theatre. Directed and choreographed Anton Adasinsky.

*Riders on the Storm* by Emily Casey and William Kennedy. Very Special Arts Company at City Arts Centre. Directed by Gerry Morgan.

*The Risen People* by James Plunkett. Gaiety Theatre. Directed by Peter and Jim Sheridan.

*Ruby Red,* with music by Michael Scott. Irish Modern Dance Theatre at the Tivoli Theatre. Choreographed by John Scott.

*Snow White and The Yellow Packs* by Karen Egan. Zenda Productions at City Arts Centre. Directed by Karen Egan.

*The Street of Crocodiles* adapted by Simon McBurney from Bruno Schultz. Théâtre de Complicité at the Olympia Theatre. Directed by Simon McBurney.

*Trickledown Town* by Donal O'Kelly. Calypso Theatre Company at City Arts Centre. Directed by Kenneth Glenaan.

*True Lines* devised by the company. Bickerstaffe Theatre Company at the City Arts Centre. Directed by John Crowley.

*Virginia Minx at Play.* Emilyn Claid at Project Arts Centre. Choreographed by Emilyn Claid.

*Voices of the Disappeared.* Gaiety Theatre. Readings in aid of Amnesty International.

*Whatever the Weather.* Brouhaha at Players Theatre. Directed by Alain Gautre.

*Zboide, des pissenlites aux etoiles,* by the company with music by Christopher Roche. Turak Theatre D'Objets at Father Matthew Hall. Directed by Michael Laubu.

# 4 | Dublin Theatre Festival in the 1990s

Tony Ó Dálaigh

I was always interested in theatre and, from my arrival in Dublin at the age of seventeen, I attended more plays than films, including once at the old Abbey, in what turned out to be the third last performance of *The Plough and the Stars* before the 1951 fire, with Marie Kean playing Bessie Burgess. Her usual role was Mrs Gogan but the regular Bessie of the time, Eileen Crowe, was making a film. The final lines 'Keep the home fires burning' were sung by Ray McAnally.

When the Abbey transferred to the Queen's, I saw almost everything there including the first night of *The Country Boy*, which became a staple for the next decade, and *House Under Green Shadows* by a colleague in the Department of Defence, Maurice Meldon, who was tragically killed soon afterwards by a fall from a bicycle as he left work. I was cycling just 100 yards behind.

At the Gate, where it cost a mere shilling in the last four rows, Edwards/Mac Liammóir and Lord Longford alternated, presenting a contrasting fare to the Abbey. I particularly remember seeing Micheál as the twin brothers in *Ring Round the Moon* and *The School for Scandal* with Aidan Grennell in a wig that seemed at least two feet high.

In the mid-1950s, I did some acting with a group, The Revellers, in the Department of Defence, and in Irish at An Damer and from 1962 with the newly founded Strand Players. I once read an obituary of a theatre manager which quoted him as saying 'I could not act so it had to be administration'. I was a very average actor, could only 'play myself' and somehow administration crept in. The late Riobárd Mac Gabhráin in Gael Linn which funded An Damer asked me to become part-time manager. As it added £3 a week to my wages of £9, I accepted without hesitation. Around the same time, I agreed to help found – with Gerald Duffy, Edwin FitzGibbon, Martin Dempsey, and Colman Pearce – and manage a small-scale opera company, Irish National Opera, which gave over 500 performances in thirty counties from 1965 until 1985 when Arts Council grants were withdrawn.

This touring experience led to my being appointed in 1974 as full time General Manager of Irish Theatre Company, the first State-funded professional touring company. I got leave of absence for a maximum of four years from my Department – then Education – and spent a stimulating time with Artistic Directors Phyllis Ryan, the late Godfrey Quigley and, for the final two years, Joe Dowling. Highlights were a revival of Fergus Linehan's *Black Rosie* with Anita Reeves showing the comic facility that later made her one of our finest actresses, *Irishmen*, a triple-bill by Hugh Leonard with Donal McCann in two highly contrasting roles and Joe Dowling's first ITC production, *Thieves Carnival*, with a terrific young cast. Joe's later successes with the company included his first *Juno and the Paycock*, *As You Like It*, and the Beatles musical *John, Paul, George, Ringo and Bert*.

As a regular playgoer, the Dublin Theatre Festival loomed large each year in my calendar. In its first year, 1957, I saw *The Rose Tattoo* toward the end of its run after the furore and the arrest of its Director Alan Simpson. Little did I imagine that, thirty-three years later, I would be appointed Director of the Festival.

After my stint with ITC, I went back to the Department of Education for eight years, but I had got the management bug so was delighted when I was asked by Roinn an Taoisigh to become Director of the Royal Hospital Kilmainham for four years. When the decision was made to locate IMMA there, I applied for early retirement as I knew little or nothing about modern art. Just then, Lewis Clohessy was moving from the festival to run Dublin's year as European City of Culture and I was thrilled when the DTF Board asked me to succeed him.

My first weeks were traumatic. The Festival had always been under-funded. Its Arts Council grant was £100,000 and most years the organization carried a substantial deficit. I am no great shakes at finance, as my wife Mags will testify – she took over our household accounts quite early in our marriage – but it became clear in the first month or so, from the deluge of invoices flooding the letter box, that we were in serious trouble. A major part of the problem was that forecasts of sponsorship in 1989 were, to put it mildly, over-optimistic. For example, a new sponsor was entered as being likely to contribute £5000. In reality, they came up with £500.

The net result was an accumulated deficit of £145,000 and looming disaster. One of my memories of those fraught days is of the Chairman, Dr Tim O'Driscoll, furiously smoking a huge cigar in my office while, next door, I was trying to placate an angry car-hire executive holding a fistful of invoices by promising him payment 'as soon as our grant arrives' and countering his demand for an immediate cheque by assuring him it was certain to bounce as we literally had no credit left.

Informal talks between myself and Phelim Donlon, Drama Officer of the Arts Council, led to a tacit understanding that a special ex-gratia grant of £40,000 would be forthcoming if the hierarchy of the DTF board would step down and allow younger members to be promoted. This tactic for partially solving the problem was simultaneously jeopardized by a meeting of the Chair and another senior Board Member with Taoiseach Charles Haughey, who promised them £50,000 from his Department. Tim O'Driscoll rang with the 'good news' from Dublin Airport – he was en route to London. I tried to disguise the shock in my voice as I remembered what had happened to Irish Theatre Company and Irish National Ballet who each got larger once-off figures directly from the Government and never received a subsequent penny either from them or the Arts Council. All I could muster to Tim was a croaked 'well done'.

I sat in my office for all of five minutes before confidentially informing Phelim Donlon who was equally appalled. He brought his Director, Adrian Munnelly, and his Chairman into the loop, which resulted in a call from 70 Merrion Square to Government buildings saying in essence 'Hands off, we are dealing with the problem'. I then got a call from Richard Stokes, Assistant Secretary, Roinn an Taoisigh, to say that the Taoiseach was withdrawing his offer. I then had the problem of phoning Tim in his London hotel with the bad news. Of course, he was furious. 'How could the Arts Council have known?' The best I could muster was 'Roinn an Taoisigh leaks like a sieve'.

In the event, Tim and three other older members resigned and Gabriel Moloney was elected Chair with Eithne Healy taking a more prominent role than heretofore. Gay proved to be a great networker and persuaded many leading businessmen to come to our rescue by making a one-off donation. He raised, in all, some £55,000 thus bringing our deficit down to a manageable £50,000.

I was lucky in my first year that David Grant, who had worked with Lewis Clohessy in 1989, was still Programme Director. He managed, with slim resources, to put together a lively programme. One of the surprise successes was The Reduced Shakespeare Company doing bits from all of the Bard's thirty-seven plays in ninety minutes. Joe Dowling, while directing in Canada some months earlier, tipped me off about the show. During a tour of Ireland the following year, one of the group met the then Manager of Hawk's Well Theatre, Sligo, and married her. She soon became the administrative brain behind the company. They went on to world-wide success with cloned companies and played in the West End for many years.

The biggest show of 1990 was a Romanian *Hamlet* which, before the fall of the Ceauşescus, was seen in Romania as a parable of a corrupt head of state and his wife. The lead was played by Ion Caramitru who returned many years later to star as Janáček at the Gate in Brian Friel's play *Performances*, and who is now head of the National Theatre in Bucharest. The British Council set up a Dublin office in 1990 and its Director, the late Ken Churchill, helped us to present two exciting shows, the unique Footsbarn in *A Midsummer Night's Dream* and the Scottish company Communicado in *Danton's Death*. 1991 was certainly the most dramatic of my ten years with the blowing away of the Archaos tent and the cancellation of two performances before a substitute tent of sufficient size could be imported. The Festival's fortunes were much improved through the generous sponsorship of Irish Life who became title sponsors in recognition of Dublin's year as European City of Culture. Irish Life later agreed to remain as our main sponsor for a further four years.

Fergus Linehan, who joined the Festival as Programme Director two years later, felt that there were four stunning imports in 1991: *As You Like It*, an all-male production from Cheek By Jowl; *Macbeth* from the Schiller Theater, Berlin; *Hamlet* (with the same actor playing Hamlet AND Ophelia); and Phillipe Genty Company in *Derives*. The most successful new play of the year was Rough Magic's *Digging for Fire* by Declan Hughes. The big event of 1991, however, was the staging of all nineteen plays by Samuel Beckett, which later went to New York and the Barbican. And, of course, the original 1991 Beckett Festival production of *Waiting for Godot* has been all over the world since then and toured to all thirty-two Irish counties in Autumn 2008. But we had many downsides. Apart from the Archaos crisis, three productions from Northern Ireland – *The Madam MacAdam Travelling Theatre, Hang All the Harpers*, and *The Shadow of a Gunman* – were critically mauled and attracted very small audiences.

1992 was a 'holding' year. Money was tight and we were limited in the number of affordable visiting shows. Phillipe Genty returned with *Desirs Parade* and the Royal National Theatre brought a disappointing *Billy Liar*. The Abbey and Peacock had two excellent productions, *The Iceman Cometh* with Brian Dennehy and Garry Hynes' production of *Silverlands* by Antoine Ó Flatharta. There were also two quirky successes – *Frank Pig Says Hello* from Co-Motion, and Arthur Riordan's *The Emergency Session* with the immortal lines from de Valera 'I'm an ancient Irish monument, I'm CELTIC and I'm CROSS'.

Thanks to the British Council, we were able in 1993 to host the RSC in Adrian Noble's stunning production of *The Winter's Tale*. The Abbey provided a timely revival of Tom Murphy's *Famine* and Rough Magic staged a stylish *The Way of the World* in the round at the Project. The year was not without drama with two productions in the published programme being cancelled because the leading actor in both cases went AWOL.

I have many favourite shows from my ten years but the one I treasure most is *The Street of Crocodiles* from Théâtre de Complicité in 1994, which got thumbs down from Gerry Colgan in *The Irish Times* but, happily, raves elsewhere. The Gate presented Brian Friel's *Molly Sweeney* while, at the Peacock, Marina Carr had her first big success with *The Mai*. The UK company of disabled actors CandoCo amazed audiences at the Samuel Beckett Centre. The biggest disappointment was *Decameron 646* at the Tivoli. I had seen this production by Silviu Purcarete in Bucharest in a small space and found it exciting. It simply withered in a bigger venue. After the opening night, a friend asked me 'Were you drunk when you saw this in Romania?' 1994 also marked the first professional production of a play by Conor McPherson, *The Good Thief*, performed by Garrett Keogh.

After Cheek by Jowl's wonderful Shakespeare in 1991, their production of *The Duchess of Malfi* in 1995 proved a huge disappointment – undercast and largely inaudible in the Gaiety. It was the only occasion we had to make refunds – the morning after the opening our phones were jammed with complaining customers. Footsbarn, however, came with an imaginative version of *The Odyssey*, Fiona Shaw performed *The Waste Land* in the derelict Magazine Fort in Phoenix Park, and Opera Circus were hilarious in *Kill Me, I Love You...Too*. The future Tony Award winner Briain F. O'Byrne was a charismatic Michael Collins in *Good Evening, Mr Collins* at the Peacock and my all time favourite one man show *The Tale of Teeka* (*l'Histoire du Loi*) came from Quebec, which seems to have an endless supply of cutting-edge theatre companies.

1996 brought our biggest ever show – Purcarete's *Les Danaides* with a Romanian cast of six principals, a chorus of fifty men and fifty women and a crew of twenty-five, making 131 in all. The unflappable Felicity O'Brien looked after their needs – hotel, transport, meals etc. The RSC performed *The Comedy of Errors* at DCU – in pre-Helix days – while Bernard Farrell's *Stella by Starlight* was a popular success at the Gate with a very funny denouement featuring vasectomy. Slava's *Snowshow* blew audiences – including Taoiseach John Bruton – away at the Gaiety, while Marie Jones's *Stones in his Pockets* made its first Dublin appearance. This initial production was but a shadow of Ian McElhinney's later one which began at the Lyric Belfast and went on to conquer Dublin, the West End, and Broadway with Conleth Hill and Sean Campion.

The opening show of 1997 was Cirque Plume, a French circus with stunning musical acts. Other successful visiting companies were Robert Lepage's Ex Machina in *Elsinore*, a one-man *Hamlet*, two Purcarete productions (*Phaedra* and *Titus Andronicus*) from Craiova, Romania, and *Dead Souls* from the Canadian company Carbone 15. The big Irish successes were *The Leenane Trilogy* from Druid, which packed the Olympia for two weeks, and Thomas Kilroy's *The Secret Fall of Constance Wilde* directed by Patrick Mason at the Abbey.

In 1998, a Spanish company complete with white horse, filled the Shelbourne Hall at the RDS venue with their *Carmen*, the Maly St Petersburg brought *Stars in the Morning Sky* and the Italian Romeo Castellucci gave us a highly controversial *Giulio Cesare* at the Beckett Centre. My favourite show of that year was *Tinka's New Dress*, a one-man show by Ronnie Burkett, who manipulated sixty-plus puppets on a 'magic roundabout'. He was peeved at being moved to Coláiste Mhuire (to make room for *Giulio Cesare*) and peppered his show with witty anti-Festival barbs, including complaining that I had told him that Coláiste Mhuire was Irish for 'beautiful theatre'.

My final year did not quite match 1998 but we did have one of our finest visiting shows – the marathon *Cloudstreet* from Australia at the SFX, where we supplied every member of the audience with an interval bag containing a sandwich, fruit, and a drink. While there were no outstanding new Irish plays – *Boomtown* was a rare failure from Rough Magic – there were three other highly original imports – Gesher (an all-Russian Israeli company) in *The Village*, Mabou Mines in *Peter and Wendy*, and Shared Experience with *Jane Eyre*.

Up to 1994, it was usual to have over forty productions in the Festival. In early 1995, the Festival Council held an all-day policy meeting at Royal Hospital Kilmainham. It was chaired by Séamus Páircéir and two fundamental decisions were made: to gradually reduce the number of productions to around 20 and to encourage the emergence of a fringe. As a result a vibrant fringe did emerge under Jimmy Fay and the number of productions dropped from forty in 1994 to thirty-three, then twenty-five, twenty-four and finally to twenty in 1999.

My ten years in 47 Nassau Street were the most fulfilling of my life and I would like to acknowledge the tremendous support I received from Fergus Linehan, Ciarán Walsh, Tammy Dillon, David Grant, Mairéad McKeever, many part-time workers, the Council and my two Chairs, Gay Moloney and Eithne Healy.

# Production History Part Four: 1995–2008

# Irish Life Dublin Theatre Festival 1995

## 2–14 October

*Ages of Man* by Richard Hayter. Selections from Shakespeare, performed in the Footsbarn tent at the Iveagh Gardens.

Bob Downe at the Olympia Theatre.

*Buddleia* by Paul Mercier. The Passion Machine at Project Arts Centre. Directed by Paul Mercier.

*City Life* by Issei Ogata. London Stage Company at the Samuel Beckett Theatre. Directed by Yuzo Morita.

*Dances with Intent*. CoisCéim Dance Theatre at the Samuel Beckett Theatre. Choreographed by David Bolger with Diana Richardson.

*Double Helix* devised and written by the company. Bickerstaffe at Andrews Lane Theatre. Directed by John Crowley.

*The Duchess of Malfi* by John Webster. Cheek By Jowl at the Gaiety Theatre. Directed by Declan Donnellan.

*Earwigs* by Maeve Ingoldsby. Barnstorm Theatre at the Ark. Directed by Patrick Sutton.

Eddie Izzard at the Gaiety Theatre.

*An Evening With Queen Victoria* by Katrina Hendrey. Clarion/Seven Muses at the Gaiety Theatre. Directed by Katrinia Hendrey.

*Fixing Bill Haley* by Ken Bourke. TEAM at City Arts Centre. Directed by Patrick Sutton.

*Good Evening Mr. Collins* by Tom Mac Intyre. Peacock Theatre. Directed by Kathy McArdle.

*Kill Me, I Love You...Too* devised by the company. Opera Circus at Andrews Lane Theatre. With directorial contributions from David Glass, Peta Lily, Kathryn Hunter and Marcello Magni.

*Kirkle* by Paula Meehan. TEAM at The Ark. Directed by Susie Kennedy.

*A Lie of Beauty* by Samuel Barber. Muziektheater Transparant at Andrews Lane Theatre. Directed by Guy Coolen.

*The Lithium Waltz* by Barry McKinley. Black Box Theatre at Andrews Lane Theatre. Directed by Paul Brennan.

*The Medium* adapted by Anne Bogart from writings by Marshall McLuhan. Saratoga International Theater Institute (SITI) at the Samuel Beckett Theatre. Directed by Anne Bogart.

*The Modern Husband* by Paul Godfrey. Actors Touring Company at Andrews Lane Theatre. Directed by Nick Philippou.

*My Boyfriend's Back* by Julian Clary. Olympia Theatre.

*A Night at the Cotton Club.* Jiving Lindy Hoppers/Harry Strutters/Hot rhythm Orchestra at the Gaiety Theatre.

*No Need to Argue*, written by students from Pobalscoil Neasáin, Baldoyle. Very Special Arts at City Arts Centre. Directed by Gerry Morgan.

*The Odyssey* adapted from Homer by the company. Footsbarn Travelling Theatre at Iveagh Gardens.

*The Only True History of Lizzie Finn* by Sebastian Barry. Abbey Theatre. Directed by Patrick Mason.

*A Peaceful Man*, written by Torun Lian from texts by Henry Michaux and Fernando Pessoa. Teater Figur at the Samuel Beckett Theatre. Directed by Anne-Mali Soether.

*Pentecost* by Stewart Parker. Rough Magic Theatre Company at Project Arts Centre. Directed by Lynne Parker.

*The Picture of Dorian Grey* adapted by Gavin Kostick from Oscar Wilde. Gate Theatre. Directed by Alan Stanford.

*Public Enemy* by Kenneth Branagh. Irish Arts Centre at Andrews Lane Theatre. Directed by Kenneth Branagh.

*Pyjamas* by Nino D'Introna, Graziano Melano, Giacomo Ravicchio. Teatro dell'Angolo at The Ark. Directed by Nino D'Introna and Giacomo Ravicchio.

*Sardines* by Michael West. Pigsback Theatre Company at the Samuel Beckett Theatre. Directed by Michael West.

*Seasaw* by Dennis Foon. Green Thumb Theatre Company at the Ark.

*Staying Married* written, performed and directed by Moira Keefe and Charlie Oates. Domestic Rep at Andrews Lane Theatre.

*The Tale of Teeka* by Michel Marc Bouchard. Les Deux Mondes at the Samuel Beckett Theatre. Directed by Daniel Meilleur.

*The Waste Land* by T. S. Eliot. Fitzroy Productions at the Magazine Fort, Phoenix Park. Directed by Deborah Warner.

# Dublin Theatre Festival 1996

7–19 October

*Aladdin* adapted for the stage by Gianni Franceschini. Aida at The Ark.

*And, Suddenly...* Susanne Linke/Urs Dietrich at the Peacock Theatre. Choreographed by Susanne Linke and Urs Dietrich.

*Balor* adapted by Páraic Breathnach. Macnas at the Olympia Theatre. Directed by Rod Goodall.

Cirque Eloize at the Gaiety Theatre.

*The Comedy of Errors* by William Shakespeare. Royal Shakespeare Company at Dublin City University. Directed by Tim Supple.

*Dealer's Choice* by Patrick Marber. Royal National Theatre at the Gaiety Theatre. Directed by Patrick Marber.

*Dog Man* by Claudette Sutherland. Usual Suspects at Andrews Lane Theatre. Directed by Bob McCracken.

*The Flesh Addict* by Gavin Kostick. Pigsback Theatre Company at the Temple Bar Music Centre. Directed by Jim Culleton.

*Hard To Believe* by Conall Morrison. Bickerstaffe Theatre Company at Andrews Lane Theatre. Directed by Conall Morrison.

*Indulgence.* Desperate Optimists at Arthouse.

*Island*, devised by the company. Tam Tam (Holland) at the Ark.

*Kitchensink* by Paul Mercier. Passion Machine at Andrews Lane Theatre. Directed by Paul Mercier.

*Last Night's Fun* by Dermot Healy. Theatre Omnibus at Project Arts Centre. Directed by Dermot Healy.

*Les Danaides*, after Aeschylus. Offshore International Cultural Project at the National Basketball Arena. Directed by Silviu Purcarete.

*Northern Star* by Stewart Parker. Rough Magic Theatre Company at the Samuel Beckett Theatre. Directed by Lynne Parker.

*Obstacles*, devised by the company. Tam Tam (Holland) at the Ark.

*Over the Stone* by Mari Rhian Owen. Arad Goch at The Ark.

*Road Movie* by Godfrey Hamilton. Starving Artists at the Peacock Theatre. Directed by Lorenzo Mele.

*SAPA* created by Malcolm McClay and Jeff Becker. Crisus (USA) at Project Arts Centre.

*She Stoops to Folly* adapted by Tom Murphy from Oliver Goldsmith. Abbey Theatre. Directed by Patrick Mason.

*Snowshow* created by Slava Polunin. Gaiety Theatre.

*Stella by Starlight* by Bernard Farrell. Gate Theatre. Directed by Ben Barnes.

*Stones in His Pockets* by Marie Jones. DubbelJoint Productions at the Tivoli Theatre. Directed by Pam Brighton.

*Strokehauling* devised by the company. Barabbas... The Company at Project Arts Centre. Directed by Raymond Keane.

*Tailesin* written and directed by Jeremy Turner. Arad Goch at the Ark.

*Tailor's Requiem* by Gavin Quinn. Pan Pan Theatre Company at Project Arts Centre. Directed by Gavin Quinn.

*Trainspotting* adapted by Harry Gibson from Irvine Welsh. GandJ Productions at the Olympia Theatre. Directed by Harry Gibson.

*The Two Souls of Guarrancine*. Movimento Danza at the Peacock Theatre. Choreographed by Gabriella Stazio.

*Urban Minefields* by Oscar McLennan and Anne Seagrave. Oscar McLennan at Project Arts Centre.

*You Must Tell the Bees* devised by Tom Mac Intyre. Irish Modern Dance Theatre at the Peacock Theatre. Choreographed by John Scott.

## Dublin Theatre Festival 1997

6–18 October

*A Border Worrier* by John Byrne. Project @ The Mint.

The Amazing Adventures of Mr. De Wit. Theatre Kameleon at The Ark.

*A Touch of Light* by Patricia O'Donovan. The Train Theatre at The Ark. Directed by Patricia O'Donovan.

Cirque Plume at the RDS.

*Dead Souls*. Carbone 15 at the Samuel Beckett Theatre. Directed by Gilles Maheu.

*Elsinore* by Robert Lepage. Ex Machina at the Gaiety Theatre. Directed by Robert Lepage.

Fascinating Aida at the Gaiety Theatre. Directed by Nica Burns.

*Henry and the Seahorses*. Teatergruppen Mariehonen at The Ark.

*Here Lies Henry* created by Daniel MacIvor and Daniel Brooks. Da Da Kamera at Project @ The Mint. Directed by Daniel Brooks.

*It's a Slippery Slope* written and performed by Spalding Gray. Tivoli Theatre.

*The Leenane Trilogy: The Beauty Queen of Leenane, A Skull in Connemara* and *The Lonesome West* by Martin McDonagh. Druid Theatre Company and the Royal Court Theatre at the Olympia Theatre. Directed by Garry Hynes.

*Massive Damages* by Declan Lynch. Passion Machine at the Tivoli Theatre. Directed by Gerard Stembridge.

*Measure for Measure* by William Shakespeare. Edinburgh International Festival, Nottingham Playhouse, and the Barbican at the Gaiety Theatre. Directed by Stéphane Braunschweig.

*Melonfarmer* by Alex Johnson. Peacock Theatre. Directed by Jimmy Fay.

*Milseog an tSamhraidh* by Éilis Ní Dhuibhne. Amharchlann de hÍde at the Samuel Beckett Theatre. Directed by Kathy McArdle.

*New Kid* written and directed by Dennis Foon. Green Thumb Theatre at The Ark.

*Parallel Lines*, excerpts from *Ulysses* by James Joyce, with music by David Paul Jones. Theatre Cryptic at Project @ The Mint. Directed by Cathie Boyd.

*Phaedra* after Seneca and Euripides. National Theatre of Craiova at the SFX Centre. Directed by Silviu Purcarete.

*Scraping the Surface* by Vic Albert. Theatre Terrific at The Ark.

*The Secret Fall of Constance Wilde* by Thomas Kilroy. Abbey Theatre. Directed by Patrick Mason.

*Titus Andronicus* by William Shakespeare. National Theatre of Craiova at the SFX City Theatre. Directed by Silviu Purcarete.

*Viper's Opium* by Godfrey Hamilton. Starving Artists at Andrew's Lane Theatre. Directed by Lorenzo Mele.

*The Weeping of Angels* by Joseph O'Connor. Gate Theatre. Directed by Alan Stanford.

## Dublin Theatre Festival 1998

5–17 October

*Amazing Grace* by Michael Harding. Peacock Theatre. Directed by Brian Brady.

*By the Bog of Cats* by Marina Carr. Abbey Theatre. Directed by Patrick Mason.

*Carmen* by Salvadora Távora. La Cuadra de Sevilla at the RDS. Directed by Salvadora Távora.

Circus Ethiopia at the Gaiety Theatre.

*The Cry of the Chameleon*. Anomalie/Josef Nadj at the National Basketball Arena. Directed and choreographed by Josef Nadj.

*Diamonds in the Soil* devised by Patrick O'Reilly. Macnas at the Olympia Theatre. Directed by Mikel Murfi.

*Giulio Cesare* after William Shakespeare. Societas Raffaello Sanzio at the Samuel Beckett Theatre. Directed by Romeo Castellucci.

*Hellcab* by Will Kern. Tamarind Theatre Company at the Tivoli Theatre. Directed by Jennifer Markowitz.

*L is for Elephant* by Jean-Frédéric Messier, translated by Richard Simas. Théâtre des Confettis at The Ark. Directed by Jean-Frédéric Messier.

*Miss Tong Tong*. Theater Waidspeicher/Puppentheater Erfurt at The Ark.

*Native City* by Paul Mercier. Passion Machine at the Tivoli Theatre. Directed by Paul Mercier.

*The Salvage Shop* by Jim Nolan. Red Kettle at the Gaiety Theatre. Directed by Ben Barnes.

*Shakespeare's Villains – A Masterclass in Evil* by Steven Berkoff. East Productions at the Olympia Theatre. Directed by Steven Berkoff.

*Stars in the Morning Sky* by Alexander Galin. Maly Drama Theatre of St. Petersburg at the Gaiety Theatre. Directed by Lev Dodin.

*Tinka's New Dress* created by Ronnie Burkett. Ronnie Burkett's Theatre of Marionettes at Coláiste Mhuire.

Certified Lunatic and Master of the Impossible. Tomas Kubinek at The Ark.

*Uncle Vanya* by Anton Chekhov in a new version by Brian Friel. Gate Theatre. Directed by Ben Barnes.

# Dublin Theatre Festival 1999

4–16 October

*Arabian Nights* adapted by Dominic Cooke. Young Vic Theatre Company at the Olympia Theatre. Directed by Dominic Cooke.

*Boomtown* by Pom Boyd, Declan Hughes, and Arthur Riordan. Rough Magic Theatre Company at Meeting House Square. Directed by Lynne Parker.

*Cloudstreet* , adapted by Nick Enright and Justin Monjo from the novel by Tim Winton. Company B Belvoir/Black Swan Theatre at the SFX Centre. Directed by Neil Armfield.

*Comedians* by Trevor Griffiths. Bickerstaffe Theatre Company at Andrew's Lane Theatre. Directed by Jimmy Fay.

*The Diary of One Who Vanished*, a song cycle by Leoš Janaček with lyrics in a new version of Ozek Kalda's poems by Seamus Heaney. English National Opera at the Gaiety Theatre. Directed by Deborah Warner.

*Dolly West's Kitchen* by Frank McGuinness. Abbey Theatre. Directed by Patrick Mason.

*The Half-Chick and Two Tales*. Storybox Theatre at The Ark.

*House Clown* conceived by Damien Bouvet. Compagnie Voix-Off at The Ark.

*Into the West* adapted from Jim Sheridan's screenplay by Greg Banks. Travelling Light Theatre Company at The Ark. Directed by Greg Banks.

*Jane Eyre* adapted by Polly Teale from the novel by Charlotte Brontë. Shared Experience at the Gaiety Theatre. Directed by Polly Teale.

*The Map Maker's Sorrow* by Chris Lee. Peacock Theatre. Directed by Brian Brady.

*Peter and Wendy* adapted from the novel by J.M. Barrie by Liza Lorwin. Mabou Mines at the Tivoli Theatre. Directed by Lee Breuer.

*The Plains of Enna* by Pat Kinevane. Fishamble at the Tivoli Theatre. Directed by Jim Culleton.

*Scenes From an Execution* by Howard Barker. The Wrestling School at the Civic Theatre. Directed by Howard Barker.

*The Spirit of Annie Ross* by Bernard Farrell. Gate Theatre. Directed by Ben Barnes.

*The Village* by Joshua Sobol. Gesher Theatre at the Olympia Theatre. Directed by Yevgeny Arye.

*The Wall of Cloud* by Raymond Deane. Opera Theatre Company at the Samuel Beckett Theatre. Directed by Jason Byrne.

You Say What I Mean But What You Mean Is Not What I Said. Hot Mouth at the Civic Theatre.

*Zany Waves*. Compagnie Coatimundi at The Ark.

## eircom Dublin Theatre Festival 2000

### 30 September–12 October

*Aquarium* by Lucio Diana, Roberto Tarasco, Adriana Zamboni. Teatro Settimo at The Ark.

*Barbaric Comedies* by Ramón María del Vallé-Inclán in a new version by Frank McGuinness. Edinburgh International Festival, Abbey Theatre, and DTF at the Abbey Theatre. Directed by Calixto Bieito.

*bedbound* by Enda Walsh. New Theatre. Directed by Enda Walsh.

*Down the Line* by Paul Mercier. Peacock Theatre. Directed by Lynne Parker.

*Dracula, The Music and Film* by Philip Glass. National Concert Hall.

*Dublin Carol* by Conor McPherson. Gate Theatre. Directed by Robin Lefèvre.

*Genesi* by Romeo Castellucci and the company. Societas Raffaello Sanzio at the O'Reilly Theatre. Directed by Romeo Castellucci.

*God's Gift* adapted by John Banville from Heinrich von Kleist's *Amphytron*. Barabbas... The Company at the O'Reilly Theatre. Directed by Veronica Coburn.

*Hamlet* by William Shakespeare. Royal National Theatre at the Gaiety Theatre. Directed by John Caird.

*The Inspector* adapted from Nikolai Gogol's *The Government Inspector*. Footsbarn Travelling Theatre at Iveagh Gardens. Directed by Paddy Hayter.

*The Librarian's Fantasy* written and directed by Ezéchiel Garcia-Romeu and François Tomsu. Théâtre Granit Scène Nationale de Belfort at the Bank of Ireland Arts Centre.

*Light* adapted by Simon McBurney and Matthew Broughton from the book by Togny Lindgren, and devised by the company. Théâtre de Complicité at the Gaiety Theatre. Directed by Simon McBurney.

*The Lost Days of Ollie Deasy* created by Macnas and Mikel Murfi. Macnas at the Mansion House. Directed by Mikel Murfi.

Masked Marvels and Wondertales by Michael Cooper. The Ark.

*Mur-Mur* by Yvan Côté, Jacqueline Gosselin, Robert Dion, Daniel B. Hétu, Pierre Leclerc, and Guylaine Paul. Dynamo Théâtre at The Ark. Directed by Robert Dion.

*The Small Poppies* by David Holman. Company B at the Tivoli Theatre. Directed by Neil Armfield.

*The Well* devised by Tony Mac Mahon and John Comiskey. Abhann Productions at Vicar Street. Directed by John Comiskey.

## eircom Dublin Theatre Festival 2001

1–14 October

*Bailegangaire* by Tom Murphy. Peacock Theatre. Directed by Tom Murphy.

*Famine* (a reading) by Tom Murphy. Abbey Theatre. Directed by Patrick Mason.

*The Gigli Concert* by Tom Murphy. Abbey Theatre. Directed by Ben Barnes.

*Guess Who's Coming for the Dinner* by Roddy Doyle. Calypso Productions at Andrew's Lane Theatre. Directed by Bairbre Ní Chaoimh.

The Harlem Gospel Choir at the Olympia Theatre.

*Ich Liebe Dich* adapted by Gavin Friday and Martin Seezer from the music of Kurt Weil. Tivoli Theatre. Directed by John Comiskey.

*Labyrinth – Mystery of the Monster in the Maze* by Andy Cannon and David Troughton. Wee Stories for Children Theatre Company at The Ark.

*Le Costume* by Can Themba, adapted by Mothobi Mutoatse and Barney Simon, in a French adaptation by Marie-Helene Estienne. Théâtre des Bouffes du Nord at the Tivoli Theatre. Directed by Peter Brook.

*Macbeth* after William Shakespeare. Blue Raincoat Theatre Company at the Tivoli Theatre. Directed by Niall Henry.

*Mambrú*. La Compaòia Markeliòe at The Ark.

*Minuit* by James Carlès . Compagnie James Carlès at The Ark.

*The Morning After Optimism* by Tom Murphy. Peacock Theatre. Directed by Gerard Stembridge.

*The Mystery of Charles Dickens* by Peter Ackroyd. Ambassador Theatre Group/Act Productions at the Gaiety Theatre. Directed by Patrick Garland.

*Oyster* by Inbal Pinto. Inbal Pinto Dance Company at the Olympia Theatre. Directed by Avshallom Pollack.

*Rose Rage* adapted from Shakespeare's *Henry VI* plays by Edward Hall and Roger Warren. The Watermill Theatre at the O'Reilly Theatre. Directed by Edward Hall.

*The Sanctuary Lamp* by Tom Murphy. Peacock Theatre. Directed by Lynne Parker.

*Scaramouche Jones* by Justin Butcher. Rebbeck Penny at the Samuel Beckett Theatre. Directed by Rupert Goold.

*Three Short Plays. Come on Over* by Conor McPherson, directed by Conor McPherson; *White Horses* by Neil Jordan, directed by Neil Jordan; *The Yalta Game* by Brian Friel after Anton Chekhov, directed by Karel Reisz. Gate Theatre.

Tindersticks. Humanitat at the Olympia Theatre.

*Washday* by Joanna Williams. Little Bigtop Theatre for Children at The Ark. Directed by John Lee.

*Woyzeck* after Georg Büchner with music and lyrics by Tom Waits and Kathleen Brennan. Betty Nansen Theatre at the Gaiety Theatre. Directed by Robert Wilson.

*A Whistle in the Dark* by Tom Murphy. Abbey Theatre. Directed by Conall Morrison.


## Dublin Theatre Festival 2002

### 30 September–12 October

*Ariel* by Marina Carr. Abbey Theatre. Directed by Conall Morrison.

*Blowfish* by Veronica Coburn. Barabbas... The Company at The Ark. Directed by Veronica Coburn.

*Closing Time* by Owen McCafferty. Royal National Theatre at the Tivoli Theatre. Directed by James Kerr.

*Conversations on a Homecoming* by Tom Murphy. Lyric Theatre, Belfast at the Gaiety Theatre. Directed by Conall Morrison.

*Done Up Like a Kipper* by Ken Harmon. Peacock Theatre. Directed by Pat Kiernan.

*Glengarry Glen Ross* by David Mamet. Steppenwolf Theatre Company at the Olympia Theatre. Directed by Amy Morton.

*The Hand* by Donal O'Kelly. Liberty Hall Theatre. Directed by Donal O'Kelly.

*Jimmy* by Marie Brassard. Infrarouge Théâtre, Quebec, at the Samuel Beckett Theatre. Directed by Marie Brassard.

Marianne Faithful at the Olympia Theatre.

*The Mysteries* conceived and created by Mark Dornford-May and Charles Hazlewood. Broomhill Opera at the Gaiety Theatre. Directed by Mark Dornford-May.

*The Notebook* and *The Proof* adapted for the stage by Carly Wijs, Robby Cleiren, Rysard Turbiasz, and Gunther Lesage from the works of Agota Kristof. De Onderneming at the Samuel Beckett Theatre.

*One Helluva Life* by William Luce. Tivoli Theatre. Directed by Bryan Forbes.

*See You Next Tuesday* adapted by Ronald Harwood from Francis Veber's *Le Dîner de Cons*. Gate Theatre. Directed by Robin Lefèvre.

*Sive* by John B. Keane. Druid Theatre Company at the Olympia Theatre. Directed by Garry Hynes.

*Tokyo Notes*. Seinendan Theatre Company at the Samuel Beckett Theatre. Directed by Oriza Hirata.

*What Ever: An American Odyssey in Eight Acts* by Heather Woodbury. Liberty Hall Theatre. Directed by Dudley Saunders.

## Dublin Theatre Festival 2003

29 September–11 October

*Bear, The Story of a Hero* written by Marije van der Sande with lyrics by Wim Meuwissen. Tam Tam objektentheatre at The Ark. Directed by Wim Hofman.

*Boy Called Rubbish* devised and created by Ellis Pearson and Bheki Mkhwane. Ellis and Bheki at The Ark.

*Casio Tone* devised by Sergio Pelagio and Silvia Real. Producões Real Pelagio at The Ark.

*Duck* by Stella Feehily. Abbey Theatre presents Out of Joint and Royal Court Theatre at the Peacock Theatre. Directed by Max Stafford-Clark.

*the far side of the moon* by Robert Lepage. Ex Machina at the O'Reilly Theatre. Directed by Robert Lepage.

*Fascinating Aida: One Last Flutter*. Liberty Hall Theatre. Directed by Christopher Luscombe.

*Flamenco Republic*. Compañía María Pagés at the Olympia Theatre. Artistic direction by María Pagés.

*Giselle* by Michael Keegan-Dolan. Fabulous Beast at the Samuel Beckett Theatre. Directed by Michael Keegan-Dolan.

*Hamlet* by William Shakespeare. Birmingham Repertory Theatre and Edinburgh International Festival at the Olympia Theatre. Directed by Calixto Bieito.

*Hurl* by Charlie O'Neill. Barabbas... The Company at the Tivoli Theatre. Directed by Raymond Keane.

*The Lieutenant of Inishmore* by Martin McDonagh. Royal Shakespeare Company at the Olympia Theatre. Directed by Wilson Milam.

*Mythos* adapted by Rina Yerushalmi from Aeschylus's *Oresteia*, translated by Aharon Shabtai and Shimon Buzaglo. ITIM Theatre Ensemble and the Cameri Theatre of Tel Aviv at the Tivoli Theatre. Directed by Rina Yerushalmi.

*Performances* by Brian Friel. Gate Theatre. Directed by Patrick Mason.

*The Shape of Metal* by Thomas Kilroy. Abbey Theatre. Directed by Lynne Parker.

*Sharon's Grave* by John B. Keane. Druid Theatre Company at the Gaiety Theatre. Directed by Garry Hynes.

The Tiger Lillies at Liberty Hall Theatre.

*Tommy Tiernan's Original Stories for Children* by Tommy Tiernan and Yvonne McMAhon. Tommy Tiernan at The Ark.

*The Woman Who Walked into Doors* based on the novel by Roddy Doyle with music by Kris Defoort and libretto by Guy Cassiers and Kris Defoort. Dublin Theatre Festival and Opera Ireland present Het muziek Lod and Ro Theatre at the Gaiety Theatre. Directed by Guy Cassiers.

# Dublin Theatre Festival 2004

23 September–9 October

*Buffo* conceived and performed by Howard Buten. The Ark.

*The Dandy Dolls* by George Fitzmaurice, *Purgatory* by W. B. Yeats, and *Riders to the Sea* by J. M. Synge. Peacock Theatre. Directed by Conall Morrison.

*Death of a Salesman* by Arthur Miller. Guthrie Theatre at the Gaiety Theatre. Directed by Joe Dowling.

*Envelopes and Packages* by Charlot Lemoine. Vélo Théâtre at The Ark.

*Frankie and Johnny in the Clair de Lune* by Terrence McNally. Steppenwolf Theatre Company at the Olympia Theatre. Directed by Austin Pendleton.

*The Gigli Concert* by Tom Murphy. Abbey Theatre. Directed by Ben Barnes.

*I Do Not Like Thee, Dr. Fell* by Bernard Farrell. Abbey Theatre. Directed by Martin Drury.

*Improbable Frequency* by Arthur Riordan and Bell Helicopter. Rough Magic Theatre Company at the O'Reilly Theatre. Directed by Lynne Parker.

*James X* by Gerard Mannix Flynn. Far Cry Productions at the Liberty Hall Theatre. Directed by Pam Brighton.

*No Comment* by Jesse De Pauw, Charles L. Mee, and Jan Lauwers. Jan Lauwers and Needcompany at the Samuel Beckett Theatre. Choreographed by Tijen Lawton and Jan Lauwers.

*Observe the Sons of Ulster Marching Towards the Somme* by Frank McGuinness. Abbey Theatre. Directed by Robin Lefèvre.

*Othello* by William Shakespeare. Cheek By Jowl at the Tivoli Theatre. Directed by Declan Donnellan.

*Portia Coughlin* by Marina Carr. Peacock Theatre. Directed by Brian Brady.

*Portofino Ballade* by Peter Rinderknecht. Theatre en Gros et en Detail at The Ark. Directed by Andreas 'Paulchen' Günther with Peter Rinderknecht.

*Shining City* by Conor McPherson. Gate Theatre and the Royal Court Theatre at the Gate Theatre. Directed by Conor McPherson.

*Tom Thumb* adapted and directed by Marcello Chiarenza, translated by Patrick Lynch. Lyngo Theatre Company at The Ark.

*Trad* by Mark Doherty. Galway Arts Festival at Andrew's Lane Theatre. Directed by Mikel Murfi.

*Tragedia Endogonidia* by Romeo Castellucci. Societas Raffaello Sanzio at the Samuel Beckett Theatre. Directed by Romeo Castellucci.

*Twelfth Night* by William Shakespeare. Chekhov International Theatre Festival at the Olympia Theatre. Directed by Declan Donnellan.

*The Well of the Saints* and *The Tinker's Wedding*. Druid Theatre Company at the Tivoli Theatre. Directed by Garry Hynes.

## Dublin Theatre Festival International 2005

30 September–15 October

*Battle of Stalingrad: A Requiem* by Rezo Gabriadze. Rezo Gabriadze Theatre-Studio at the Samuel Beckett Theatre. Directed by Rezo Gabriadze.

*Betrayal* by Harold Pinter. Gate Theatre. Directed by Robin Lefèvre.

*Bloody Sunday: Scenes from the Saville Inquiry* edited by Richard Norton-Taylor. Tricycle Theatre at the Abbey Theatre. Directed by Nicolas Kent with Charlotte Westenra.

*Brontë* by Polly Teale. Shared Experience in association with Guildford's Yvonne Arnaud Theatre and the Lyric Hammersmith at Project Arts Centre. Directed by Polly Teale.

*The Bull* by Michael Keegan-Dolan. Fabulous Beast Dance Theatre at the O'Reilly Theatre. Directed by Michael Keegan-Dolan.

*Hamlet* by William Shakespeare. The Abbey Theatre and The Lyric Theatre Belfast at the Peacock Theatre. Directed by Conall Morrison.

*I Am My Own Wife* by Doug Wright. Delphi Productions at the Gaiety Theatre. Directed by Moisés Kaufman.

*Laurel and Hardy* by Tom McGrath. Royal Lyceum Theatre Company, Edinburgh at the Olympia Theatre. Directed by Tony Cownie.

*Lords of the Railway* created by the company from an idea by Peter Mueller. Theater Handgemenge at The Ark. Directed by Markus Joss.

*Old Times* by Harold Pinter. Gate Theatre. Directed by Michael Caven.

*Queen of Colours* by Eva Noell and Paul Olbrich. Erfreuliches Theater Erfurt at The Ark. Directed by Eva Noell and Paul Olbrich.

*Romeo and Juliet* by William Shakespeare. OKT/Vilnius City Theatre at the Gaiety Theatre. Directed by Oskaras Korsunovas.

*Short Stories* created and performed by Hugo Suarez and Inés Pasic. Teatro Hugo and Ines at The Ark.

*Some Girls Are Bigger Than Others* conceived by Andrew Wale and Perrin Manzer Allen with the songs of Morrissey and Marr (*The Smiths*). Glynis Henderson Productions and the Lyric Hammersmith at the Olympia Theatre. Directed by Andrew Wale.

*Tshepang* by Lara Foot Newton. Mopo Productions at the Samuel Beckett Theatre. Directed by Lara Foot Newton.

*White Cabin* by Maxim Isaev and Pavel Semchenko. AKHE at Project Arts Centre.

*White Star* after an idea by Vanessa Van Durme. Victoria at the Samuel Beckett Theatre. Directed by Lies Pauwels.

*The Winter's Tale* by William Shakespeare. A Watermill Theatre production by Propeller at the Abbey Theatre. Directed by Edward Hall.

*The Worlds of Fingerman* by Inés Pasic. Gaia Teatro at The Ark. Directed by Inés Pasic.

## Dublin Theatre Festival International 2006

28 September–14 October

*Aalst: A True Story* conceived by Pol Heyvaert. Victoria at Project Arts Centre. Directed by Pol Heyvaert.

*Alice Trilogy* by Tom Murphy. Peacock Theatre. Directed by Tom Murphy.

*The Bonefire* by Rosemary Jenkinson. Rough Magic Theatre Company at Project Arts Centre. Directed by Lynne Parker.

Cabaret Décadanse at the Laughter Lounge.

*Came So Far For Beauty – An Evening of Leonard Cohen Songs* conceived and conducted by Hal Willner. The Point Theatre.

*Emilia Galotti* by Gotthold Ephraim Lessing. Deutsches Theater Berlin at the Gaiety Theatre. Directed by Michael Thalheimer.

*Empress of India* by Stuart Carolan. Druid Theatre Company at the Abbey Theatre. Directed by Garry Hynes.

*Everyday* by Michael West and the company. The Corn Exchange at the Samuel Beckett Theatre. Directed by Annie Ryan.

*The Exonerated* by Jessica Blank and Eric Jensen. Liberty Hall Theatre. Directed by Bob Balaban.

*Festen* adapted by David Eldridge from the film by Thomas Vinterberg, Mogens Rukov, and Bo hr. Hansen. Gate Theatre. Directed by Selina Cartmell.

*Hedda Gabler* by Henrik Ibsen. Schaubühne am Lehniner Platz at the Abbey Theatre. Directed by Thomas Ostermeier.

*La Tempête* by William Shakespeare, translated by Normand Chaurette. 4D Art at the O'Reilly Theatre. Directed by Michel Lemieux, Victor Pilon, and Denise Guilbault.

*Letting Go of that Which You Most Ardently Desire* by Gerrard Mannix Flynn. Far Cry Productions. Various locations in Dublin.

*Lifeboat* by Nicola McCartney. Catherine Wheels Theatre Company at The Ark. Directed by Gill Robertson.

*Orestes* by Helen Edmundson based on Euripides. Shared Experience in association with Guilford's Yvonne Arnaud Theatre at the Olympia Theatre. Directed by Nancy Meckler.

*Product* by Mark Ravenhill. Paines Plough at Project Arts Centre. Directed by Lucy Morrison.

*Rattledanddisappeared* by András Vinnai and Viktor Bodó. Katona József Theatre at the O'Reilly Theatre. Directed by Viktor Bodó.

*The Syringa Tree* by Pamela Gien. The Olympia Theatre. Directed by Larry Moss.

*There's a Rabbit in the Moon.* Vélo Théâtre at The Ark. Directed by Francesca Bettini.

*The Vacationers* by Maxim Gorky. Omsk State Drama Theatre at the Gaiety Theatre. Directed by Evgeny Marchelli.

Ute Lemper at the Olympia Theatre.

## Ulster Bank Dublin Theatre Festival 2007

26 September–14 October

*Bistouri* by Alain Moreau. Tof Théâtre at The Ark. Directed by Alain Moreau.

*BLACKland* devised by the company. Krétakör at the O'Reilly Theatre. Directed by Arpad Schilling.

*bobrauschenbergamerica* by Charles L. Mee. SITI Company at Project Arts Centre. Directed by Anne Bogart.

*C41 and datamatics [ver.1.0]* by Ryoji Ikeda. Irish Museum of Modern Art.

*Fragments* by Samuel Beckett. Théâtre des Bouffes du Nord and the Young Vic Theatre at the Tivoli Theatre. Directed by Peter Brook.

*The Giraffe's Journey* by Robert Abbiati. The Ark.

*Gorgeous Morons* by Bradford Scobie and Julie Atlas Muz. New Theatre.

*The Grand Inquisitor* adapted by Marie Helene Estienne from Dostoevsky's *Brothers Karamazov*. Théâtre des Bouffes du Nord at the Tivoli Theatre. Directed by Peter Brook.

*Hibiki*. Sankai Juku at the Gaiety Theatre. Directed and choreographed by Ushio Amagatsu.

*The History Boys* by Alan Bennett. National Theatre of Great Britain at the Olympia Theatre. Directed by Nicholas Hytner.

*Homeland* created and performed by Laurie Anderson. Olympia Theatre.

*House/Boy* by Nicky Paraiso. New Theatre. Directed by Ralph B. Pena.

*The Idiots* by Lars von Trier. Pan Pan at Project Arts Centre. Directed by Gavin Quinn.

*Is This About Sex?* By Christian O'Reilly. Rough Magic Theatre Company at the Pavilion Theatre, Dun Laoghaire. Directed by Lynne Parker.

*Ivanov* by Anton Chekhov. Katona József Theatre at the O'Reilly Theatre. Directed by Tamas Ascher.

*James Son of James* by the company. Fabulous Beast Dance Theatre at the Samuel Beckett Theatre. Directed by Michael Keegan-Dolan.

*Kebab* by Gianina Carbunariu, translated by Philip Osment. Royal Court Theatre, Pentabus Theatre Company and Ulster Bank Dublin Theatre Festival at Project Arts Centre. Directed by Orla O'Loughlin.

*La Marea* by Mariano Pensotti, translated by Conor Hanratty. Quartière Bloom. Directed by Mariano Pensotti.

*Long Day's Journey into Night* by Eugene O'Neill. Druid Theatre Company at the Gaiety Theatre. Directed by Garry Hynes.

*Minor Matters* by Gitte Kath und Jakob Mendel. Junges Ensemble Stuttgart at The Ark. Directed by Brigitte Dethier.

*On the Case* conceived by Debra Batton. Legs on the Wall at George's Dock. Directed by Debra Batton and Mark Murphy.

*The Playboy of the Western World* by Bisi Adigun and Roddy Doyle from the play by J.M. Synge. Abbey Theatre. Directed by Jimmy Fay.

*The Pride of Parnell Street* by Sebastian Barry. Fishamble at the Tivoli Theatre. Directed by Jim Culleton.

*Private Peaceful* by Michael Morpugo, adapted by Simon Reade. Scam Theatre and Bristol Old Vic at The Ark. Directed by Simon Reade.

*Radio Macbeth* adapted by the company from the play by William Shakespeare. SITI Company at Project Arts Centre. Directed by Anne Bogart and Darron L. West.

*Reggie Watts*. Created and performed by Reggie Watts at the New Theatre.

*Road to Nowhere* staged by No Theater. Young@Heart at the O'Reilly Theatre. Directed by Bob Climan and Roy Faudree.

*The Seagull* by Anton Chekhov. Krétakör at Project Arts Centre. Directed by Arpad Schilling.

*small metal objects* devised by Simon Laherty, Sonia Teuben, Bruce Gladwin, Genevieve Morris, and Jim Russell. Back to Back Theatre at Mayor Square. Directed by Bruce Gladwin.

*Sonos 'E Memoria* by Gianfranco Cabbidu and Paulo Fresu. Improvised Music Company at Vicar Street.

*Traces*, conceived and directed by the company. The 7 Fingers/Les 7 doigts de la main at the Olympia Theatre.

*Uncle Vanya* by Anton Chekhov in a version by Brian Friel. Gate Theatre. Directed by Robin Lefèvre.

*Woman and Scarecrow* by Marina Carr. Peacock Theatre. Directed Selina Cartmell.

## Ulster Bank Dublin Theatre Festival 2008

22 September–12 October

*The Attic Under the Sky* from an idea by Sara Topsøe-Jensen. Carte Blanche at The Ark. Directed by Malco Oliveros.

*Between the Devil and the Deep Blue Sea* by Suzanne Andrade. 1927 at Project Arts Centre. Directed by Suzanne Andrade.

*Black Watch* by Gregory Burke. National Theatre of Scotland at the RDS. Directed by John Tiffany.

*Caligula* by Albert Camus in a new version by David Greig. CHRG at Project Arts Centre. Directed by Conor Hanratty.

*Cat on a Hot Tin Roof* by Tennessee Williams. The Corn Exchange at Project Arts Centre. Directed by Annie Ryan.

*Circus*, devised and directed by Raymond Keane. Barabbas... The Company at the Samuel Beckett Theatre.

*The Cripple of Inishmaan* by Martin McDonagh. Druid Theatre Company and Atlantic Theater at the Olympia Theatre. Directed by Garry Hynes.

*Delirium*, adapted by Enda Walsh from Dostoevsky's *The Brothers Karamazov*. Created by Theatre O. The Peacock Theatre. Directed by Joseph Alford.

*Dodgems* by Charlie O'Neill. CoisCéim Dance Theatre at the O'Reilly Theatre. Directed and choreographed by David Bolger.

*The End of Everything Ever*, devised and directed by the company. NIE (New International Encounter) at The Ark.

*ENGLAND* by Tim Crouch. News from Nowhere at Dublin City Gallery: The Hugh Lane. Directed by Karl James and a smith.

*First Love* by Samuel Beckett. Gare St. Lazare Players at Project Arts Centre. Directed by Judy Hegarty Lovett.

*Gatz*, A verbatim presentation of F. Scott Fitzgerald's *The Great Gatsby*. Elevator Repair Service at Project Arts Centre. Directed by John Collins.

*Happy Days* by Samuel Beckett. National Theatre of Great Britain at the Abbey Theatre. Directed by Deborah Warner.

*Heart of Darkness* by Joseph Conrad. Lily Productions at Number 10. Performed by Gavin Kostick.

*Hedda Gabler* by Henrik Ibsen in a version by Brian Friel. Gate Theatre. Directed by Anna Mackmin.

*It's Only the End of the World* by Jean-Luc Lagarce. A.L.O.D.H.E. at the Pavilion Theatre, Dun Laoghaire. Directed by Manuel Orjuela Cortes.

*La Omision de la Familia Coleman* by Claudio Tolcachir. Timbre 4 at the Pavilion Theatre, Dun Laoghaire. Directed by Claudio Tolcachir.

*The Magic* Flute, adapted from Mozart's opera by Mark Dornford-May, with words and music by Mandisi Dyantyis, Mbali Kgodintsi, Pauline Malefane, and Nolufefe Mtshabe. An Eric Abraham - Isango/Portobello Production at The Gaiety Theatre. Directed By Mark Dornford-May.

*Metamorphosis* by Franz Kafka, adapted and directed by David Farr and Gisli Orn Gardarsson. Vestuport Theatre and Lyric, Hammersmith at the Olympia Theatre.

*Rank* by Robert Massey. Fishamble at the Helix. Directed by Jim Culleton.

*That Night Follows Day* by Victoria and Tim Etchells. Victoria at Project Arts Centre. Directed by Tim Etchells.

*Waves* devised by Katie Mitchell and the company. National Theatre of Great Britain at the Samuel Beckett Theatre. Directed by Katie Mitchell.

*While We Were Holding It Together*, concept by Ivana Müller. Project Arts Centre. .

*The Wolf and the Goat*, translated by Richard R. Nybakken. Compagnia Rodisio at The Ark.

*The Year of Magical Thinking* by Joan Didion. National Theatre of Great Britain at the Gaiety Theatre. Directed by David Hare.

*You Are Here* by Ioanna Anderson. Living Space Theatre Company in association with Bedrock Productions at Quartière Bloom. Directed by Tara Derrington.

# 5 | Dublin Theatre Festival in the Twenty-First Century

Fergus Linehan

I have to begin with the admission that I've resisted writing this article. Peter Brook once said that the most important quality a theatre should have is combustibility – it should be burnt to the ground regularly. If that is true of theatre buildings, it is even more pertinent for festivals, the most ephemeral of all arts institutions. Most of my professional life has been wrapped up in this seasonal activity and yet at the end of each event I still fantasize of wandering around the Festival HQ on the last day, dousing the office with petrol and flicking a match over my shoulder as I walk out. I tend to resist reminiscences.

My first meaningful encounter with the Dublin Theatre Festival was as a teenager. My father [also Fergus Linehan] was Arts Editor of *The Irish Times* and I would immerse myself in shows for two weeks in a way that I found exhilarating and liberating. Even into the late-1980s an exposed nipple had the capacity to cause a sensation in the media and, thanks to the draconian licensing laws, the prospect of a late night bar that sold something other than foul German wines was a cause for celebration. Looking back at some of the programmes from these years it's hard not to see them as somewhat limited but, in the context of the bleakness of the 1980s, they represented a rare spark of ambition and optimism. With virtually no resources at their disposal, the arts organizations of the time were left to scramble around playing politics with miniscule budgets. Those lucky few charged with leading our major institutions were paid what a junior office worker would get today and put together full programs with budgets and funding that would barely get a single production onstage in 2008. As is often the case in the arts, the absence of resources led to a vacuum which was filled with politics, intrigue, and treachery. Large boards overseen by even larger councils spent torturous hours in wild and woolly power struggles which were enthusiastically reported by the media. The Dublin Theatre Festival was one such organization, defined as much by crises, skulduggery, and intrigue as anything that ever made it to the stage.

Like many institutions and organizations throughout Ireland, the Festival underwent major changes that mirrored the seismic change the country underwent at the end of the twentieth century. Gay Moloney, Chairman of the Festival in the early 1990s, often recounted how, when he first joined the board, the average age was teetering somewhere around the seventy-five mark.

My first professional encounter with the Festival was in 1992 when I performed (very badly) in a production of Christopher Hampton's play *Savages*. The evening was saved by a magnificent performance by Tom Murphy, a truly great actor who died tragically in 2007. As well as acting, I was one of the producers of the show and several months after we had finished we were still trying to extract our box-office receipts from the Festival office. Eventually we climbed the creaking stairs of 47 Nassau Street to demand our money. The offices could only be described as bizarre. I was reminded of the stories you read about the Gardaí breaking into a home and finding the body of an old person who hasn't left their cottage for twenty years. Buried in the detritus was a plastic shopping bag full of ticket stubs – this was poured out onto the table – yikes!

Four years later I climbed these stairs again, this time as the new General Manager. The same grungy anarchy seemed to permeate every inch of the place and it was only the extraordinary patience of the administrator Mairead McKeever that seemed to stop the whole place from sinking into the ground. That and the completely unfounded optimism of our Director Tony Ó Dálaigh , who was blissfully unbothered by the apocalyptic scenario facing the organization. Cometh the hour cometh the man – in all honesty I think that anyone other than Tony would have taken one look at the state of the Dublin Theatre Festival and run a mile. It was only someone with his combination of charisma, political nous, and financial naivety that could have carried the Festival over what surely should have been its downfall – that and the steely determination of Gay Moloney who would drag us all into his office for regular eight a.m. meetings. At one of these he savaged me for not knowing the exact balance of our bank account. With virtually no assets, a very modest turnover and a frighteningly large deficit carried forward, the solvency of the company was pretty much non-existent. Trading continued due to kind words from our sponsor Irish Life, clever cash-flow from the Arts Council, and critically a general sense that a man with Gay Moloney's reputation would find a way to knock us back into shape. And knock he did! It wasn't until 1996 that the Festival could really start to think beyond the spreadsheet. Reading over Tony's contribution to this book and how he negotiated a financial bail out, it brings home how little money was about. The fact that £50,000 was such a big deal that it involved the Taoiseach, senior civil servants, and the Head of the Arts Council seems laughable now but, at the time, it was regarded as a very serious investment.

This isn't to say that good work wasn't staged during these years, but the focus was always on the finances. Festivals are extremely delicate flowers and a moment of loose governance or bad planning can sentence them to years of rebuilding or extinction. Careering from crises to crises is sometimes mistaken for artistic ambition and too often, leaders who wreak financial havoc are subsequently painted as victims of small minded boards and petty media. The truth, in my opinion, is that growing a festival or deepening its relationship with its community is the end result of hundreds of small things done well rather than flashes of bravado.

Despite the fact that I am not the tidiest of people, circumstances required that I become Felix to Tony's Oscar and we found a way of working together that was effective and great fun. As well as having to be the organized one, I also had to take on the role of bad cop. Tony Ó Dálaigh is a very nice man. The financial and operational climb was extremely tough, especially for someone in their mid twenties, who didn't know very much about anything. In 1993, the first year of our 'computerized' booking system, we double booked the entire dress circle for the opening night of the RSC's production of *The Winter's Tale*. I sat on the stairs of the Gaiety Theatre with the company cheque book passing out refunds to an angry mob. In 1995 when Deborah Warner's production of *The Waste Land* at the fort in the Phoenix Park wasn't ready on time, we kept the audience circling the city in a bus with our box-office manager reading them T.S. Eliot's text over the tannoy. As late as 1999 I found myself nailing toilet seats to bowls as the public waited outside at the opening of *Cloudstreet* in the SFX. Indeed on the morning of their arrival, the *Cloudstreet* company, recently arrived from Australia, found that we hadn't had enough money to book an early check in. We arrived in our offices to find many of the leading figures of Australian theatre asleep under our desks.

Some of the theatres were (and in some cases still are) terrible dives. On one occasion, the special branch sniffer dog, checking for explosives emerged from the stalls of one such venue with a large rat in its mouth. But no matter how embarrassing, unforgivable or unhygienic the circumstances, Tony would turn up beaming and exclaim 'Isn't this great!' And to a large degree it was. To be employed doing something you loved, to be allowed to create something that, given your budget and experience, you have no right to create, and to be part of the evolution of Irish theatre was a rare and exhilarating privilege.

Once we got our head above water we had the room to improve the consistency of our programming. Ever the generous one, Tony encouraged me to get more involved in the creative side of things and in 1997 named me Deputy Director. That year we produced a programme that, given the resources available to us, astonishes me to this day: Martin McDonagh's

*Leenane Trilogy*, Robert Lepage's *Elsinore*, Cirque Plume, Carbone 14's *Dead Souls*, Spalding Gray's final fully produced work, and a double bill by Romanian director Silviu Purcarete.

The 1997 Festival changed the international profile of the event. There was a sense that we had gained promotion, however tentative, back to the premier league. Beyond Tony a number of people really stand out from this period – Ciaran Walsh and Felicity O'Brien and later Maura O'Keeffe. At the time I didn't realize how rare it was to be surrounded by people who had a deep commitment to and profound knowledge of theatre, dance and music. The level of debate and discussion was, in retrospect, remarkably rigorous and I'm sure I didn't realize or properly acknowledge it at the time. I know that each of them has rare qualities of leadership and creativity. With a tightly knit young team with an international outlook, the scandals of Archbishop McQuaid seemed very distant. Despite some good work, the 1998 and 1999 Festivals did not quite reach the heights of 1997. In particular 1999 proved especially difficult. *The Diary of One Who Vanished*, on paper a dream team of tenor Ian Bostridge, director Deborah Warner, and translator Seamus Heaney, turned out to be a twenty-seven minute recital on a bare stage. Given that it was Tony's last year I was very disappointed we didn't send him off with more of a bang.

The second half of the 1990s was also characterized by the Chairmanship of Eithne Healy. It was often rather patronizingly said that Eithne brought a degree of style to the Festival, but God knows we needed it. With Tony in his 1970s civil servant suits, me in my poor man's Gordan Geko get up, and Ciaran in his Godspell sweatshirt we did not cut much of a dash. Beyond our sartorial limitations we did need to improve both our brand and our way of dealing with the world. Eithne led us sensitively through this process and built a wide constituency of support that still functions today. People join not-for-profit boards for different reasons. In truth it is often to push their own social, political, or cultural agenda. People like Eithne Healy do it from a deep felt belief in art, its broader conversation with the nation, and a sense of service. These seem like old-fashioned qualities but they are shared by the most valuable members of every board I have served or served on.

In 1995 I met with a young director called Jimmy Fay, who was running an excellent new theatre company, Bedrock. What began as a discussion about six or seven small productions testing the limits of what theatre could be, ended up as the first Dublin Fringe Festival. Produced for a total budget of approximately £10,000 it proved a huge success. I remember standing with Jimmy on the opening night and, as there was no advance booking system, neither of us had any idea whether anyone was going to show up. Like all good fringes, however, it was answering a need. A loose alliance of theatre, dance, and cabaret artists was galvanized by the Fringe and in its early years it grew exponentially, hosting works by Conor McPherson, Mark O'Rowe, and Enda Walsh. Although I understand the argument, personally I think it is a great pity that the Fringe decided to move its dates away from those of the Dublin Theatre Festival. What was gained in logistical ease never compensated for the loss of intensity and profile. It is one thing to step into a well established festival, it's quite another to start one from scratch. Three people stand out in this regard: firstly Jimmy Fay, whose sheer charisma and brazen chutzpah kick-started the whole thing, secondly, Irene Kernan, who managed the unmanageable, and, thirdly, Jack Gilligan from Dublin City Council, who was the first to put his hand up with financial support. Later, Australian Vallejo Gantner became Director of the Fringe and subsequently a good friend. For a short time we even shared a house together before I left for Sydney to run the Festival here and he to New York to Performance Space PS122.

In 1999 the board appointed me Festival Director, due to start with the 2000 Festival. Of the five Festivals I presided over I feel one was institutionally important but artistically flawed (2000), two were strong (2001 and 2003) and two had great moments but were inconsistent (2002 and 2004). Overall I feel the Festival held its own during these years. In footballing parlance we were a mid-table contender – consistently presenting major international work and producing interesting projects – but I don't think we were giving Edinburgh or Avignon any sleepless nights about their pre-eminence. I realize the footballing analogy is very glib, but the truth is festivals do ebb and flow like clubs. Some like the Chicago Festival or Glasgow's Mayfest simply disappear, other such as Brighton or Belfast Festivals rise up full of gusto but then fall back again. The big ones always seem to be there or thereabouts.

In artistic terms, 2001 was the most coherent programme I presided over. The dense survey of the work of Tom Murphy at the Abbey was countered by the intuitive simplicity of Peter Brook's *Le Costume* and the visual pyrotechnics of Robert Wilson's *Woyzeck*. 2001 taught me an important message about our expectations of the media. Staging a work by Robert Wilson is regarded as a watershed for a growing festival. It requires a high degree of financial backing, technical ability, and a good international reputation. The work was, without question the centrepiece of the Festival, but when I opened the Sunday papers most had not even reviewed it. The truth is that for a generation of Irish journalists theatre remains an artform of knotty literary works and the central purpose of the Festival is to find the great Irish play. In this world, a new piece of writing in a studio theatre will always trump a visiting work, regardless of scale or form. This tension around the Festival's purpose has always been one of the programming challenges and is not unique to the Dublin Theatre Festival.

One of the issues that plagued the Festival in both 2000 and 2001 was the indecision of the Arts Council. The organization was enjoying the booming economy and ticket sales, sponsorship and the overall profile of the Festival was on the up. With a very active Chair in Moya Doherty, a new Director and an ambitious title sponsor there was a genuine sense of momentum. This created something of a crisis for the Arts Council of the time – a crisis that reflected a broader question. The conditions were now in place whereby the Festival could achieve the sort of ticket sales and sponsorship required to deliver an event of major international significance. The question was – were the Arts Council willing to take that leap and live with the institutional responsibilities that would create down the line? In the end the Arts Council didn't really know what to do with us. They were supportive and increased funding in the period but the idea of establishing the Festival on the model of the Avignon or Vienna Festivals seemed too much for them. In the end they decided to use the additional funding to create a huge range of micro festivals. This inability to deal on a large scale was characteristic of so much that seemed to be going on in public life. We could finance and construct ten small theatres around Dublin but we couldn't seem to build a new National Theatre. We could fix up every little football club in the country but we couldn't build a National Stadium. Those small theatres and festivals have enriched communities all over Ireland but there are certain things that small organizations cannot do and our continuing reluctance to think and act big can have the effect of keeping the arts ghettoized and powerless. This would only be a moan from the grave were it not for the fact that it's clear that an even more potent opportunity has opened up again for the Dublin Theatre Festival over the past twelve months – a new young Director, enthusiastic media, and an engaged public, and strong corporate support have aligned to create the perfect conditions for the Festival to take a huge leap forward.

The rarefied atmosphere of a festival certainly encourages theatre companies to stretch their wings but sometimes festivals feel the need to step outside of the existing structures and to take on the role of producer. Over the five years that I was Director we dipped our toe in the water as producers with differing results. Our intention was to produce work that we felt was of international standard but did not fit into the usual Irish theatre calendar. We got off to a blistering start with Enda Walsh's *bedbound* in 2000, a claustrophobic diamond of a play, which went on to win many awards and tour all over the world. The following year we tried to harness the anarchic imagination of Gavin Friday with an evening of Kurt Weill music called *Ich Liebe Dich*. To this day I'm uncertain whether it was a work of genius or truly awful. 2002 brought mixed results with Donal O'Kelly's *The Hand*. To my great frustration, as a producer, I never felt I could give Donal the support he needed, and there is still something extraordinary within his work that remains unrealized. At full tilt he is the natural inheritor of the Irish storytelling tradition, but he has a shyness and modesty within him that seems to resist that mantle. 2003 saw a co-production with a young choreographer called Michael Keegan-Dolan. This was the perfect example of how and why a festival should take a producing role. Michael was an outsider who had got ahead of the institutions of Irish theatre and dance. While others were agonizing about single lines of dialogue or minor phrases of movement, he was filling vast open spaces with characters who screamed out the hilarity and barbarity of twenty-first century rural Ireland. *Giselle* became the talking point of the 2003 Festival. 2004 saw Mannix Flynn's *James X* with an accompanying exhibition. This was a deeply moving project and one that I was very proud to have been part of. The producing of these projects was handled by Felicity O'Brien, who became increasingly central to the shaping of the Festival over the course of these years. Some day someone very smart will talk Felicity into leading a major festival.

One of the strongest supporters of the Festival's producing arm was our Chairman Peter Crowley. Peter had come to our Board when his wife Clodagh, then working for The Ark, told me he was looking to get involved. Most Chairmen spend their time tempering the erratic ambitions of their Artistic Directors but, with Peter, the opposite was more often the case. He was drawn towards the more radical and innovative parts of the programme and promoted them with evangelical zeal to his often bewildered colleagues in the corporate world. Peter is one of those people who make Dublin a better place in which to live. He consistently gathers together unlikely groups of people and shakes them out of their complacency.

2003 brought an agonizingly close coup. We produced a series called 'Playing Politics' and to our enormous surprise Arthur Miller agreed to visit the Festival and do a public interview with Director Joe Dowling. Miller has been a major figure in my life, through his work for the theatre but also as an essayist. Our wild excitement was crushed two weeks out when we got an email to say that Mr. Miller had fallen ill and his doctors were refusing to let him travel. Little did we know that this was the beginning of a period that would eventually lead to his passing in February 2005.

In early 2004 on a month-long trip around Australia, I did an interview for the post of Director of the Sydney Festival. I

returned home in early March to find that I had been offered
the job for the 2006–2008 Festivals. Even though discussions
had been amicable this was something of a shock. Of particular
difficulty was the issue that I would have to start at the end of
2004, which would mean handing over the Dublin Theatre
Festival Directorship a year earlier than planned. Over the
course of a hectic weekend I went back and forth on the phone
with Australia and met with my chair, Peter Crowley. I am
extremely flattered that Peter didn't give up without a fight, but
in the end the board approved my leaving at the end of the 2004
Festival. My friend Sean Doran, who had done a spell as
Director of the Perth Festival wrote that I would 'return to us in
several years time as either an archbishop or a politician'.

The final programme which I presided over was grounded in
a visit by the Guthrie Theater of Minneapolis with Joe Dowling's
beautiful production of *Death of a Salesman*. Joe's 1996
production of the same play had been one of the reasons I had
gone into the theatre and to finish off my time at the Festival
with this work was a great honour. The hardest part of 2004
came with our production of Romeo Castellucci's production
*Tragedia Endogonidia*. Romeo had astonished Festival
audiences twice before with *Guilio Cesare* in 1998 and *Genesi* in
2000. *Tragedia Endogonidia* called for a scene where a small
infant was left in the middle of a large stage alone. Although
nothing happened during this scene, both before and after there
were particularly brutal images onstage. It should be noted that
the child was not in the same building when this happened.
While onstage the child could see its mother but the audience
was unaware of this and the effect was chilling. On opening
night the baby fell over and was extremely upset. The curtain
took an eternity to close and the image was unbearable. After
the show I was deeply conflicted as to whether we should go
ahead with the rest of the week's performances. The logic was
straightforward – what had happened was that a baby was
sitting up, tumbled over, wailed for a minute, and his mother
then picked him up, an occurrence that happens every day of
the week. As an act of theatre, however, it felt like we had
overstepped the mark. Romeo was equally upset and we
discussed the matter carefully. In one sense the work had been

too powerful – the imagery of innocence was simply too potent when juxtaposed with images of cruelty and terror. The following day talk radio lit up and I took quite a few blows on air. I said to our team that I wanted to deal with every complaint, and I spent the day talking the matter over with members of the public who were genuinely furious at what they had seen. The rest of the performances did go ahead and interestingly, with some small changes, the image seemed less controversial but equally powerful. Indeed one night we had an incredibly jolly and inquisitive baby who galloped around the stage and had the audience in fits of laughter – not quite what we were after.

The other strong memory that came from 2004 was Declan Donnellan's superb all male Russian production of *Twelfth Night*. There are times when our job is as simple as getting out of the artist's way and this was one of them. Substantial, hilarious and utterly accessible, it was a reminder of how a great Festival show can refresh the palate and replenish the appetite. One of the first things I did when I was confirmed as Director of Sydney Festival was to make sure it would be in our 2006 programme

There are many moments that I haven't gone into which remain sources of great pride and there are people who may not have popped up in these anecdotes but who were critical to any success we enjoyed. The enduring brilliance and guile of Michael Colgan on our Board saw us sidestep many problems and take opportunities when they presented themselves; the precision and patience of Ross Keane in our office ensured that in the midst of all the talk we actually got things done; and the eternal good humour of Gerry Lundberg reminded us that it was no crime to have a bit of fun.

It's hard not to get sentimental about my time at the Dublin Theatre Festival but it's a dangerous way to go. For every fond memory there's a few that have been repressed; for every big catch there were many that got away and for all the moments of principle there are compromises which undoubtedly blot my copybook. However, overall I think that we got some very good work over the line and strengthened the organization. My mother once said to me to be wary of shows that were 'more fun to be in that to be at'. Similarly, those of us charged with leading festivals have to guard against leaving our best work in the locker room, by devoting our energies to extraordinary inter-continental adventures. Keeping the event relevant to many remains one of the most challenging and critical parts of the job.

The Festival has always reflected the broader changes that take place in Irish society. Over the period of my involvement we increasingly saw work which charted the emergence of enormous individual freedoms and prosperity which in turn released forms of social and moral anarchy. The truth, a commodity so elusive in the works of Brian Friel, seemed now to rise to the surface wildly and unpredictably. We became far more outraged about a child onstage than a flash of nudity and our attention span certainly shortened but perhaps intensified. As I prepare for my last festival here in Sydney, I am fascinated to see how the 2008 Dublin Theatre Festival will reflect the world in which it finds itself. The 2007 program was probably the best Dublin Theatre Festival to date and while the maxim that 'every time a friend of mine succeeds a little part of me dies' may have a glimmer of truth, I dearly hope all concerned build on last year's success and take the Festival to new heights.

# Bibliography

Abalkin, N., *Sistema stanislavskogo i sovetskii teatr* (Moscow: Iskusstvo, 1950).

Adams, Michael, *Censorship: The Irish Experience* (Dublin: Sceptre, 1968).

Armfield, Neil, 'Director's Note', *Eircom Dublin Theatre Festival Booklet*, p. 3.

Awde, Nick, 'Review of *Cloudstreet*', *The Stage* 23 September 1999, p. 4.

Bachelard, Gaston, *The Poetics of Space*, trans. Maria Jolas (Boston, Mass.: Beacon Press, 1994).

Bakhtin, Mikhail, *Rabelais and His World*, trans. Hélène Iswolsky (Bloomington, IN: Indiana University Press, 1984).

Barthes, Roland, *The Roland Barthes Reader*, ed. and trans. Susan Sontag (London: Vintage, 1993).

Benedict, David, 'Trains and Boats and Planes', *The Independent* 8 September 1999, p. 21.

Benjamin, Walter, 'The Work of Art in the Age of Mechanical Reproduction', *Illuminations* (New York: Schocken Books, 1969).

Ben-Messahel, Salhia, *Mind the Country: Tim Winton's Fiction* (Perth: University of Western Australia Press, 2006).

Beuys, Joseph, *What is Art?* (London: Clairview, 2004).

Blake, James J., 'Irish-Language Theater in the 1990s: Slógadh to Teilifís na Gaeilge', *New Hibernian Review* (Summer 1999), pp. 147-52.

Blythe, Ernest, 'Ireland's Contribution to World Theatre', *The Irish Times* 27 May 1957, p. 16.

Bodolazov, L., 'Veter stranstvii', *Sovetskaia kul'tura* 22 January 1982, p. 3.

Boland, John, 'Prose & Cons', *Hibernia* 27 September 1979.

Boland, Rosita, 'Front Row', *The Irish Times* 21 October 1999, p. 18.

Boland, Rosita, 'Theatre Festival Ups and Downs', *The Irish Times* 21 October 1999, p. 18.

Bourne, Randoph, 'Trans-National America', *Atlantic Monthly*, July 1916 (January 31, 2008): http://www.swarthmore.edu/SocSci/rbannis1/AIH19th/Bourne.html

Braun, Edward, ed. and trans., *Meyerhold on Theatre* (London: Eyre Methuen, 1969).

Braun, Edward, 'Meyerhold: the Final Act', *New Theatre Quarterly* 33 (February 1993), pp. 3-15.

Brodskaia, G, 'Chekhov v khudozhestvennom teatre 1970-kh godov', *Chekhov i teatral'noe iskusstvo*, eds A. Al'tshuller, J.M. Synge. (Leningrad: LGITMiK, 1985), pp. 190-91.

Brook, Peter, *There Are No Secrets: Thoughts on Acting and Theatre* (London: Methuen, 1993).

Brown, Ismene, 'Absolute Clowns', *The Daily Telegraph* 16 January 2001, p. 23.

Brown, Terence, *Ireland, A Social and Cultural History, 1922-2002* (London: Harper Perennial (1981) 2004).

Buscovic, Alix, *Cloudstreet*: Riverside Studios, *What's On* 22 September 1999.

Carr, Marina, *Ariel* (Oldcastle: Gallery Press, 2002).

Carr, Marina, *Plays 1* (London: Faber and Faber, 1999).

Carr, Mary, 'It's Not Up My Street', *The Evening Herald* 11 October 1999, p. 22.

Casanova, Pascale, *The World Republic of Letters* (Cambridge: Harvard UP, 2004).

Chaillet, Ned, 'Hugh Leonard', *Contemporary Dramatists*, ed. D.L. Kirkpatrick, 4th edn (Chicago; London: St. James, 1988), 322.

Chambers, Lilian, et al., eds, *Theatre Talk: Voices of Irish Theatre Practitioners* (Dublin: Carysfort Press, 2001).

Clarke, Jocelyn, 'Calling the Shots', *Sunday Tribune* 3 October 1999, p. 12.

Clarke, Jocelyn, 'Review of 'Chamber Music'', *Sunday Tribune* 28 August 1994, p. B7.

Cleary, Joe, *Outrageous Fortune: Capital and Culture in Modern Ireland* (Dublin: Field Day Publications, 2007).

Colgan, Gerry, 'Oh, What a Lovely War', *The Irish Times* 14 October 1993, p. 12.

Colgan, Gerry, 'Review of *The Dogs*', *The Irish Times* 15 October 1992, p. 8.

Colgan, Gerry, 'Reviews the eircom Dublin Theatre Festival 2000', *The Irish Times* 6 October 2000, p. 13.

Conley, Susan, 'The Fabulous Beast Within: Michael Keegan-Dolan in conversation with Susan Conley'. Programme, *The Story of the Bull* (Dublin Theatre Festival 2005).

Connell R.W. and James R. Messerschmidt, 'Hegemonic Masculinity. Rethinking the Concept', *Gender and Society* 19.6 (2005), pp. 829-59.

Connell, R.W., 'A Very Straight Gay: Masculinity, Homosexual Experience, and the Dynamics of Gender', *Americomman Sociological Review* 57.6 (1992), pp. 735-51.

Conquest, R, *The Politics of Ideas in the USSR* (London: The Bodley Head, 1967).

Conrad, Kathryn, 'Queer Treasons: Homosexuality and Irish National Identity', *Cultural Studies* 15.1 (2001), pp. 124-37.

Crawley, Peter, 'Review of *The Bonefire*', *The Irish Times*, 2 October 2006, p. 12.

Crawley, Peter, 'The Rough Guide to Growing New Talent', *The Irish Times* 11 February 2004, p. 6.

Csikszentmihalyi, Mihaly, *Beyond Boredom and Anxiety* (Michigan: Jossey-Bass Publishers, 1975).

Deane, Seamus, ed., *The Field Day Anthology of Irish Writing* (Derry: Field Day; Cork: Cork University Press, 1991).

Dening, Penelope, 'Stormy Weather', *The Irish Times eircom Dublin Theatre Festival Supplement* 25 September 1999, p. 1.

Derrida, Jacques, *Writing and Difference* (Chicago: University of Chicago Press, 1978).

Dollimore, Jonathan, *Sexual Dissidence, Augustine to Wilde, Freud to Foucault* (Oxford: Clarendon Press, 1991).

Dowling, Vincent, 'Director's Note on *The Gentle Island*', Olympia Theatre programme for *The Gentle Island*, (commenced Tuesday, 30 November 1971), n.p.

Elam, Keir, *The Semiotics of Theatre* (London : Routledge, (1980) 2002).

Enright, Nick and Justin Monjo, *Cloudstreet: Adapted from the novel by Tim Winton* (Sydney: Currency Press in association with Company B. Belvoir and Black Swan Theatre, 2004).

Evans, David T., *Sexual Citizenship: The Material Construction of Sexualities* (London: Routledge, 1993).

Farrell, Michael, *The Apparatus of Repression*, Field Day Pamphlet, 11 (Derry: Field Day Theatre Company, 1986).

Fleming, N.C. and Alan O'Day, eds, *The Longman Handbook of Modern Irish History Since 1800* (Harlow: Pearson Education Limited, 2005).

Foucault, Michel, *Discipline and Punish: The Birth of the Prison* (New York: Vintage Books, 1979).

Fouéré, Olwen, 'Journeys in Performance: On Playing in *The Mai* and *By the Bog of Cats*', *The Theatre of Marina Carr: 'before rules was made'*, eds Cathy Leeney and Anna McMullan (Dublin: Carysfort Press, 2003), pp. 160-71.

Freud, Sigmund, *Two Short Accounts of Psycho-Analysis* (London: Pelican, 1972).

Fricker, Karen, 'Giselle', *The Guardian* 3 October 2003.

Friel, Brian, *Selected Plays of Brian Friel* (London: Faber and Faber, 1984).

Friel, Brian, *The Gentle Island* (The Gallery Press: Dublin, 1973).

Frye, Northrop *Anatomy of Criticism* (Princeton and Oxford: Princeton University Press, 1957; 2000).

Geertz, Clifford, *The Interpretation of Cultures* (Ann Arbor: University of Michigan Press, 1973)

Gorman, Sophie, 'Family epic with magical touch', *Irish Independent* 11 October 1999, p. 16.

Gregory, Augusta, *Our Irish Theatre: A Chapter of Autobiography* (Gerrards Cross, Bucks: Colin Smythe, 1972).

Grene, Nicholas, ed., *Talking About Tom Murphy* (Dublin: Carysfort Press, 2002).

Grene, Nicholas *The Politics of Irish Drama* (Cambridge: Cambridge University Press, 1999).

Harraway, Donna, Simians, Cyborgs and Women: the Reinvention of Nature (London: Free Association, 1991).

Harris, Claudia, 'The Beckett Festival,' *Theatre Journal* 44.3 (1992), p. 407.

Harris, Susan Cannon, *Gender and Modern Irish Drama* (Bloomington and Indianapolis: Indiana University Press, 2002).

Healy, Rachel, 'Sydney Festival '98', Summer Arts, *Sydney Morning Herald*, 4 January 1998, p. 29.

Hickey, Des and Gus Smith, 'Leonard: Difficult to Say "No"', *A Paler Shade of Green* (London: Leslie Frewin Publishers, 1972) 191-201.

Houlihan, Con, 'Plumbing the Depths of Success', *Evening Press* 5 October 1979.

Hutcheon, Linda, *A Poetics of Postmodernism* (New York and London, p, Routledge, 1988)`.

Jackson, Joe, 'The healing touch', interview with Frank McGuinness by Joe Jackson, *Irish Independent* 21 April 2002, p.2.

James, William, *The Varieties of Religious Experience, A Study in Human Nature* (1902) (New York: Penguin Books, 1982).

Keating, Sara, 'Frank views from a very 'short fuse'', *The Irish Times* 24 November 2007, *Weekend Review*, p. 5.

Kelly, Henry, 'Henry Kelly Talks to Madame Maria Knebel', *The Irish Times* 3 October 1968, p. 6.

Kelly, Seamus, 'Chekhov's classic as in Russia', *The Irish Times* 9 October 1968, p. 10.

Kelly, Seamus, 'Cold light of truth on the frustrations of aging bachelors', *The Irish Times* 8 October, 1968.

Kelly, Seamus, 'Theatre Festival First Nights', *The Irish Times* 8 October 1975, p. 10.

Kilroy, Thomas. *Talbot's Box* (Oldcastle: Gallery Books, 1979).

Kilroy, Thomas, 'Groundwork for an Irish Theatre', *Studies* 48 (1959) , pp. 192-8.

Kilroy, Thomas, 'The Irish Writer: Self and Society, 1950-80', *Literature and the Changing Ireland*, ed. Peter Connolly (Gerrards Cross: Colin Smythe, 1982), pp. 175-87.

Kilroy, Thomas, *The Death and Resurrection of Mr Roche* (London: Faber and Faber:, 1969).

Knebel', Mariia, "Vishnevyi sad' v Irlandii', *Teatr* (May 1969), pp. 158-66.

Knebel', Mariia. 'Dublin: Ebbi-teatr', *Sovetskaia kul'tura* 7 January 1969, p. 3.

Knebel', Mariia, *Vsia zhizn*, 2nd ed. (Moscow: Iskusstvo, 1993).

Knowles, Richard, 'From Dream to Machine: Peter Brook, Robert Lepage, and the Contemporary Shakespearean Director as (Post)Modernist' in *Theatre Journal* (50, 2), May 1998, pp. 189-206.

Knowles, Richard, 'Reading *Elsinore*: The Ghost and the Machine', *Canadian Theatre Review* 111 (Summer 2002), pp. 82-7.

Knowlson, James, *Damned to Fame: The Life of Samuel Beckett* (New York: Simon and Schuster, 1996).

Korotkov, M, 'Irlandiia znaet Chekhova', *Sovetskaia kul'tura* 5 December 1978, p. 3.

Kristeva, Julia, *Revolution in Poetic Language* (New York: Columbia University Press, 1984).

Lacy, Stephen, *British Realist Theatre: The New Wave in its Context 1956-1965* (London and New York: Routledge, 1995).

Lavender, Andy, *Hamlet in Pieces* (London: Nick Hern, 2001)

Leeney, Cathy and Anna McMullan, eds, *The Theatre of Marina Carr: 'before rules was made'* (Dublin: Carysfort Press, 2003).

Leland, Mary, 'Review of *Is This About Sex?*', *The Irish Times* 12 September 2007, p. 2.

Leonard, Hugh, 'Chamber Music', *Sunday Independent* August 14 1994, 6L.

Leonard, Hugh, 'Production Note', *Stephen D: A Play in Two Acts* (London and New York: Evans Plays, 1964).

Leonard, Hugh, 'The Unimportance of Being Irish', *Irishness in a Changing Society*, The Princess Grace Irish Library (Gerrards Cross: Colin Smythe, 1988), pp. 18-29.

Leonard, Hugh, 'Unprofessional Conduct', *Evening Press* 28 September 1979, p. 10.

Leonard, Hugh, *Home Before Night* (London: Penguin, 1981).

Leonard, Hugh, *Moving* (London: Samuel French, 1995).

Leonard, Hugh, *Selected Plays of Hugh Leonard*, ed. S.F. Gallagher (Gerrards Cross: Colin Smythe, 1992).

Leonard, Hugh, *The Mask of Moriarty* (Dublin: Brophy Books, 1987).

Linehan, Fergus, 'Take heart, theatre lovers, the circus is in town', *The Irish Times* 16 September 1989: Weekend, p. 3.

Linehan, Fergus, 'The Future of Irish Drama: A discussion between Fergus Linehan, Hugh Leonard, John B. Keane and Brian Friel', *The Irish Times* 12 February 1970.

Long, Angela, 'Aussie marathon dazzles the Irish', *The Irish Times* 11 October 1999, p. 13.

Lyotard, Jean-Francois, *The Lyotard Reader* (Oxford: Basil Blackwell, 1989)

Mackrell, Judith 'Fabulous Beast', *The Guardian* 7 February 2008.

Marcuse, Herbert, *Eros and Civilisation* (London: Allen Lane, 1970).

Mays, J.C.C. 'Irish Beckett, A Borderline Instance', *Beckett in Dublin*, ed. S.E. Wilmer (Dublin: Lilliput Press, 1992), pp. 133-46.

McCallum, John, 'Epic experience overflows with human spirit', *The Australian*, 6 January 1998, p. 9.

McDonnell, Bill, 'A Good Night Out on the Falls Road: Liberation Theatre and the Nationalist Struggle in Belfast 1984–1990', *Radical Initiatives in Interventionist and Community Drama and Politics*, ed. Peter Billingham (Bristol: Intellect, 2004), pp. 25-54.

McGuinness, Frank, 'Surviving the 1960s: three plays by Brian Friel, 1968-71', *The Cambridge Companion to Brian Friel*, ed. Anthony Roche (Cambridge: Cambridge University Press, 2006), pp. 18-29.

McGuinness, Frank, *Plays 2* (London: Faber, 2002).

McKeon, Belinda, 'Taking Up Where Synge Left Off', *The Irish Times* 29 September 2004, p. 14.

McLeod, Chris, 'Saints be Praised', *Arts Today, The West Australian* 2 March 1995, p. 8.

Meany, Helen, 'James Son of James' *The Guardian* 5 October 2007.

Meierkhol'd, V.E., *Stat'i, pis'ma, rechi, besedy: 1891-1917* (Moscow: Iskusstvo, 1968).

Menand, Louis, 'Now What I Wonder Do I Mean by That?' *Slate Magazine* 20 August 1996 (2 August 2007): http://samuel-beckett.net/theater.html.

Merriman, Victor, 'Decolonisation Postponed: The Theatre of Tiger Trash' *Irish University Review* 29.2, Autumn/Winter, 1999, pp. 305-17.

Millis, David E, and John Meredith, eds, *The Reedy River Songbook* (Sydney: New Theatre, 1954).

Moffat, Sean, 'The Gentle Island', *Theatre Ireland* 18 (1989), p. 48.

Morash, Christopher. *A History of Irish Theatre, 1601-2000* (Cambridge: Cambridge University Press, 2002).

Morgan, Joyce, 'Cloud's Silver Lining', *Sydney Morning Herald* 6 January 1998, p. 29.

Murphy, Paul, 'The Myth of Benightedness After the Irish Renaissance: the drama of George Shiels', *Moving Worlds* 3.1 (Winter 2003), pp. 45-58.

Murphy, Thomas, *A Whistle in the Dark* (Dublin: The Gallery Press, 1984).

Murray, Christopher, Review of *The Mask of Moriarty*, *Irish University Review* (Autumn/Winter 1988), p. 137.

Nandy, Ashis, The Intimate Enemy: Loss and Recovery of Self Under Colonialism (Delhi: Oxford University Press, 1983).

Newman, Jeremiah, 'Ireland in the Eighties: Our Responsibility', *Christus Rex*, 25.3 (1971), p. 181.

Norris, David, 'Homosexual People and the Christian Churches in Ireland', *The Crane Bag*, 5.2 (1981) .

Nowlan, David, "Uncle Vanya' at the Abbey', *The Irish Times* 26 September 1978, Arts, p. 8.

Nowlan, David, 'Moscow Art theatre in "The Seagull" at the Abbey', *The Irish Times* 21 September 1989, p. 12.

Nowlan, David, "The Caucasian Chalk Circle' at the Project', *The Irish Times* 3 October 1985, p. 12.

Nowlan, David, '*Cloudstreet* SFX Theatre', *The Irish Times* 11 October 1999, p. 13.

Nowlan, David, 'Playwrights' Failure Casts Gloom on Festival', *The Irish Times* 18 October 1990, p. 8.

Nowlan, David, 'The Leningrad choices', *The Irish Times* 18 February 1988, p. 14.

Nowlan, David, 'Uncle Vanya Opens at the Abbey', *The Irish Times* 5 October 1978, p. 10.

Nowlan, David, 'Why International Plays Help Irish Writing', *The Irish Times* 2 May 1985, p. 10.

Nugent, Ann, 'Joys and Sorrows Made Real', *The Canberra Times* 12 January 1988, p. 11

O Gairbhi, Tadhg, 'Thirsty for good stout and bad company', *The Irish Times* 27 September 2004, p. 13.

O'Carroll, Íde and Eoin Collins, eds, Lesbian and Gay Visions of Ireland: Towards the Twenty-First Century (London: Cassell, 1995).

O'Cleary, Conor, 'Choice of Abbey play defended', *The Irish Times* 17 February 1988, p. 13.

O'Cleary, Conor, 'Choice of play splits Abbey company', *The Irish Times* 12 February 1988, p. 11.

O'Cleary, Conor, 'Democracy brings crisis to Russian theatre', *The Irish Times* 8 February 1988, p. 12.

O'Connor, Kevin, 'Kevin O'Connor at Dublin Theatre Festival', *The Stage and Television Today* 23 October 1975, p. 19.

O'Toole, Fintan, 'A brilliantly disturbing theatrical coup', *The Irish Times* 23 September 1989.

O'Toole, Fintan, 'Second Opinion', *The Irish Times* 13 September 1994, p. 8.

O'Toole, Fintan, 'When Survival Depends on the Luck of the Draw', *The Irish Times* 5 November 1988, p. 25.

O'Toole, Fintan, *Critical Moments: Fintan O'Toole on Modern Irish Theatre*, eds Julia Furay and Redmond O'Hanlon (Dublin: Carysfort Press, 2003).

O'Toole, Fintan, *The Ex-Isle of Ireland* (Dublin: New Island Books, 1997).

Parry, Jan 'There's only one way to see *Giselle*', *Sunday Observer* 27 February 2005.

Pearson, Noel, 'Theatre Festival was worthwhile', *Evening Press* 18 October 1975.

Pettitt, Lance, 'Gay Fiction – 2', *Graph* 7 (1989-90), p. 13.

Phelan, Mark, 'Modernity, Geography and Historiography: (Re)-Mapping Irish Theatre History in the Nineteenth Century', *The Performing Century: Nineteenth-Century Theatre's History*, eds Tracy C. Davis and Peter Holland (London: Palgrave Macmillan, 2007), 135-58.

Phelan, Peggy, *Unmarked: The Politics of Performance* (London: Routledge, 1993).

Pilkington, Lionel, Theatre and the State in 20th Century Ireland: Cultivating the People (London and New York: Routledge, 2001).

Pilkington, Lionel, 'Irish Theater Historiography and Political Resistance', *Staging Resistance: Essays on Political Theater*, eds Jeanne Colleran and Jenny S. Spencer (Ann Arbor: University of Michigan Press, 1988), pp. 13-30.

Pugwail, Nick, 'Cloudstreet', *L.A.M.* 28 September 1999, p. 27.

Rebellato, Dan, 1956 and All That: The Making of Modern British Drama (London: Routledge, 2002).

Riding, Alan, 'Finding New Audiences for Alienation', *New York Times* 11 June 2000, p. 24.

Rockwell, John, 'Festivals: Lincoln Center Festival Program Book, July 1996', *Outsider: John Rockwell on the Arts 1967-2006* (New York: Limelight Books, 2006), p. 351.

Rose, Kieran, *Diverse Communities: The Evolution of Gay and Lesbian* Politics (Cork: Cork University Press, 1994).

Rudnitskii, Konstantin, 'Vremia i mesto', *Klassika i sovremennost'* (Moscow: Nauka, 1987).

Rudnitsky, Konstantin, *Meyerhold the Director* (Moscow: Nauka, 1969).

Schechner, Richard, 'Restoration of Behavior', *Studies in Visual Communication* 7 (1981), pp. 2-45.

Schon, Donald, *The Reflective Practitioner* (New York: Basic Books, 1983).

Segal, Lynne, Slow Motion: Changing Men, Changing Masculinities (London: Virago, 1990).

Senelick, Laurence, *The Chekhov Theatre* (Cambridge: Cambridge University Press, 1997).

Shakh-Azizova, T.K. Dolgaia zhizn' traditsii', *Chekhovskie chteniia v Ialte*, eds Kuleshov, et. al. (Moscow: Kniga, 1976).

Shevtsova, Maria, 'Lev Dodin' *Fifty Key Directors*, eds Shomit Mitter and Maria Shevtsova (Abingdon: Routledge, 2005), p. 203.

Shevtsova, Maria, *Dodin and the Maly Drama Theatre* (London: Routledge, 2004).

Shvidkoi, Mikhail, 'The Effect of *Glasnost*: Soviet Theater from 1985 to 1989', *Theater* 3 (Fall 1989), pp. 7-20.

Simpson, Alan, *Beckett and Behan and a Theatre in Dublin* (London: Routledge and Kegan Paul, 1962).

Singleton, Brian, 'Festival Fallout', *Irish Theatre Magazine* 1.4 (autumn/winter 1999), p. 13.

Smeliansky, Anatoly, 'Chekhov at the Moscow Art Theatre', *The Cambridge Companion to Chekhov*, eds Vera Gottlieb and Paul Allain (Cambridge: Cambridge University Press, 2000).

Smeliansky, Anatoly, *The Russian theatre after Stalin*, trans. Patrick Miles (Cambridge: Cambridge University Press, 1999), pp. 16-30.

States, Bert O, *Great Reckonings in Little Rooms: On the Phenomenology of Theatre* (Berkeley and London: University of California Press, 1985).

*Sunday Press*, 'President's praise for Tom's play', *The Sunday Press* 12 October 1975, p. 11.

Swift, Carolyn, *Stage by Stage* (Dublin: Poolbeg, 1985).

Titley, Alan, 'Neither the Boghole nor Berlin: Drama in the Irish Language from Then Until Now', *Players and Painted Stage*, ed. Christopher Fitz-Simon (Dublin: New Island Books, 2004).

Waldrop, M. Mitchell, 'Do-It-Yourself Universes', *Science* (1987)

Washburn, Martin, 'Alive and Well', *Village Voice* 20 August 1996, p. 78.

Waterman, Stanley, 'Carnivals for Elites? The Cultural Politics of Arts Festivals', *Progress in Human Geography* 22.1 (1998), pp. 54-74.

Whelan, Gerard with Carolyn Swift, *Spiked: Church-State Intrigue and the Rose Tattoo* (Dublin: New Island, 2002).

White, Victoria.' Women Writers Finally Take Centre Stage', *The Irish Times* 15 October 1998.

White, Victoria, 'Shop Window or Closed Shop', *The Irish Times* 1 October 1993, p. 14.

Williams, Tennessee, *The Rose Tattoo and Other Plays* (London: Penguin, 1978).

Wills, Clair, *That Neutral Island, A Cultural History of Ireland During the Second World War* (London: Faber and Faber, 2007).

Winship, Lyndsey 'Belly Laughs and Grisly Murder' *The Telegraph* 23 September 2007.

Woodworth, Paddy, 'A Light Shining Through the Chaos', *The Irish Times* 26 October 1991, p. 32.

Woodworth, Paddy, 'Chekhov and the Moscow Art today', *The Irish Times* 16 September 1989: Weekend, p. 5.

Yefremov, Oleg, 'A Path to Chekhov', *Chekhov on the British Stage*, ed. and trans. Patrick Miles (Cambridge: Cambridge University Press, 1993), pp. 126-35.

# Notes on Contributors

**Lilian Chambers** has had a life-long passion for theatre. She was awarded an M.A. in Theatre Studies from NUI Dublin and is a founding director of Carysfort Press. She co-edited *Theatre Talk – Voices of Irish Theatre Practitioners* and *The Theatre of Martin McDonagh – A World of Savage Stories*. She has been a member of the Friends Council of the Dublin Theatre Festival since its inception

**Lewis Clohessy** has been a freelance arts and environment consultant since 1982. In 1984, he was appointed Director of the Dublin Theatre Festival, a post he held until 1989, when he left to direct Dublin's year as European City of Culture, 1991. He has been Chair of many cultural organizations, including the National Concert Hall, Music Network, Dublin Organ Festival, and Dublin Film Festival.

**Tanya Dean** is a freelance theatre critic, and former General Manager of *Irish Theatre Magazine*. She is currently studying for a Masters of Fine Arts in Dramaturgy and Dramatic Criticism in Yale.

**Ros Dixon** is Lecturer in Drama and Theatre Studies in the English Department at NUI, Galway. She is a specialist in Soviet theatre history and has written several articles on the work of Anatolii Efros, and on modern productions of the works of Chekhov, Gogol, and Turgenev. She is currently engaged in research on productions of Russian plays in Ireland and Irish plays in Russia, a study that concerns issues of translation, adaptation, and cross-cultural exchange, and which is supported by a grant from the Irish Research Council for the Humanities and Social Sciences.

**Christopher Fitz-Simon** was born in Belfast and brought up in the Eleven Houses of the title of his recent memoir of World War II in Northern Ireland and the Emergency in the Free State. In TCD he was Chairman of D.U. Players and Editor of *Icarus*. One of the earliest drama directors in RTE TV, he was later Artistic Director of the Lyric Theatre, Belfast, and Literary Manager and Artistic Director of the National Theatre Society. Among his books are *The Boys* and *The Abbey Theatre: the first 100 Years*.

**Lisa Fitzpatrick** holds a Ph.D. from the University of Toronto, where she wrote her thesis on postnationalism and Irish theatre. She lectures in Drama at the University of Ulster, and her current research interests are contemporary performance in Ireland, women's writing, and the performance of violence.

**David Grant** studied law at Cambridge, but became bewitched by the Edinburgh Fringe and spent the next two decades working in the arts including two years as Managing Editor of *Theatre Ireland* magazine, three years as Programme Director of the Dublin Theatre Festival and six years as Associate Director of Belfast's Lyric Theatre. Since 2000 he has been a Lecturer at Queen's University, where he is Head of Drama Studies.

**Nicholas Grene** is Professor of English Literature at Trinity College, Dublin, a Fellow of the College, and a Member of the Royal Irish Academy. He has published widely on Shakespeare and on modern Irish drama, including *The Politics of Irish Drama* (Cambridge UP, 1999) and *Shakespeare's Serial History Plays* (Cambridge UP 2002). He is the chair of the Irish Theatrical Diaspora and with Chris Morash, co-edited *Irish Theatre on Tour* (Carysfort Press, 2005). His most recent books are *Yeats's Poetic Codes* (Oxford University Press, 2008) and (also co-edited with Chris Morash), John Devitt, *Shifting Scenes: Irish Theatre-Going, 1955-85* (Carysfort Press, 2008).

**John P. Harrington** is Dean of the School of Humanities, Arts, and Social Sciences at Rensselaer Polytechnic in Troy, New York. He is the author of *The Life of the Neighborhood Playhouse on Grand Street*, *The Irish Play on the New York Stage*, and *The Irish Beckett*, as well as editor of a new Irish Theatrical Diaspora volume, *Irish Theater In America*, and W. W. Norton's newly enlarged anthology *Modern and Contemporary Irish Drama*.

**Sara Keating** is a freelance theatre critic and arts writer. In 2006 she received a PhD from the Samuel Beckett Centre, Trinity College for her research on twentieth-century Irish drama. She currently teaches contemporary Irish drama at NYU Tisch School of the Arts, Dublin.

**Thomas Kilroy** has written sixteen plays for the stage. He was a board member of Field Day. In the 2004 *Irish Times* Theatre Awards he was given a Special Tribute Award for his contribution to theatre and in 2008 he received the Pen Ireland Cross Award for Literature.

**Peter Kuch** is the inaugural Eamon Cleary Professor of Irish Studies at the University of Otago, New Zealand. His published work includes books and articles on Yeats, Joyce, Eliot, Irish theatre, literary theory, and several Australian writers. He is currently writing a cultural history of the performance of Irish theatre in Australia and New Zealand. He directs the Irish Film Festival in Dunedin and Auckland.

**Cathy Leeney** lectures in Drama Studies at the Drama Studies Centre, School of English, Drama and Film at UCD. She led the establishment of the MA in Directing for Theatre at UCD in 2005, and her research interests and publication topics include twentieth century Irish theatre, contemporary Irish theatre and performance, women in performance, scenography, and directing.

**Fergus Linehan** was a founding Director of Pigsback Theatre Company (now Fishamble Theatre Company), General Manager, Deputy Director, and Director of the Dublin Theatre Festival and has produced numerous independent productions.

He lives in Sydney, Australia, where he is currently Festival Director and Chief Executive of the 2006 – 2009 Sydney Festivals, Australia's largest annual cultural event.

**Patrick Lonergan** lectures in drama at NUI Galway. He is a theatre critic for *The Irish Times* and *Irish Theatre Magazine*, and his books include *Globalization and Theatre: Irish Drama in the Celtic Tiger Era* (2008). He is Academic Director of the Synge Summer School.

**Tony Ó Dálaigh** was a Civil Servant, mainly in Department of Education, where he was Private Secretary to four Ministers. He escaped for four years (1974-8) as Chief Executive of Irish Theatre Company, the first State-aided touring company. He was Director of Royal Hospital Kilmainham (now IMMA) 1986-90 after which he was appointed Director of Dublin Theatre Festival. Earlier he was co-founder of Strand Players, part-time Manager of An Damer (Irish Language Professional Theatre Company), and co-founder and Manager of Irish National Opera. He is now a semi-retired Arts Consultant.

**Fintan O'Toole** is assistant editor of *The Irish Times*. His books include *Tom Murphy – the Politics of Magic*; *A Traitor's Kiss: The Life of Richard Brinsley Sheridan*; *Shakespeare is Hard But So Is Life*; and *White Savage: William Johnson and the Invention of America*.

**Lionel Pilkington** teaches drama and theatre studies, Irish theatre history, colonialism and cultural theory, and cultural politics at NUI, Galway. His publications include *Theatre and the State in 20th Century Ireland: Cultivating the People* (Routledge, 2001).

**Emilie Pine** lectures in modern drama in the School of English, Drama and Film at University College Dublin. She is currently writing a book on memory and contemporary Irish culture. Emilie is on the Board of the Durrell School of Corfu and is Associate Editor of the *Irish University Review*.

**Alexandra Poulain** is Professor of Irish studies at Université Charles de Gaulle-Lille III (France). She writes on Irish theatre from Boucicault to the present day. Her book *Homo Famelicus:*

*Le théâtre de Tom Murphy* was published in 2008 by Caen University Press. She also translates Irish plays for the French stage.

**Shaun Richards** is Professor of Irish Studies at Staffordshire University. He is the co-author (with David Cairns) of *Writing Ireland: Colonialism, Nationalism and Culture* (1988) and the editor of *The Cambridge Companion to Twentieth-Century Irish Drama* (2004), and has published widely on Irish drama in major journals and edited collections.

**Carmen Szabó** is a lecturer in Drama and Theatre Studies at University College Dublin. She has published articles and a book on Irish and Northern Irish theatre. Her current research focuses on performance studies, science, technology, and applied mathematics in the theatre. She is part of the committee for History and Philosophy of Science at University College Dublin.

# Index

**CARYSFORT
PRESS**

The Press aims to produce high quality publications which, though written and/or edited by academics, will be made accessible to a general readership. The organisation would also like to provide a forum for critical thinking in the Arts in Ireland, again keeping the needs and interests of the general public in view.

The company publishes contemporary Irish writing for and about the theatre.

**Carysfort Press** was formed in the summer of 1998. It receives annual funding from the Arts Council.

The directors believe that drama is playing an ever-increasing role in today's society and that enjoyment of the theatre, both professional and amateur, currently plays a central part in Irish culture.

*Editorial and publishing inquiries to:*

**CARYSFORT PRESS Ltd**

58 Woodfield, Scholarstown Road,
Rathfarnham, Dublin 16,
Republic of Ireland

T (353 1) 493 7383  F (353 1) 406 9815
e: info@carysfortpress.com
**www.carysfortpress.com**

## ECHOES DOWN THE CORRIDOR:
## IRISH THEATRE – PAST, PRESENT, AND FUTURE

EDITED BY PATRICK LONERGAN
AND RIANA O'DWYER

This collection of fourteen new essays explores Irish theatre from exciting new perspectives. How has Irish theatre been received internationally - and, as the country becomes more multicultural, how will international theatre influence the development of drama in Ireland? These and many other important questions.

ISBN      978-1-904505-25-9
€20

## GOETHE AND ANNA AMALIA:
## A FORBIDDEN LOVE?

BY ETTORE GHIBELLINO, TRANS. DAN FARRELLY

In this study Ghibellino sets out to show that the platonic relationship between Goethe and Charlotte von Stein – lady-in-waiting to Anna Amalia, the Dowager Duchess of Weimar – was used as part of a cover-up for Goethe's intense and prolonged love relationship with the Duchess Anna Amalia herself. The book attempts to uncover a hitherto closely-kept state secret. Readers convinced by the evidence supporting Ghibellino's hypothesis will see in it one of the very great love stories in European history – to rank with that of Dante and Beatrice, and Petrarch and Laura.

ISBN      978-1-904505-24-2
EAN       9781904505242
€25

## MODERN DEATH: THE END OF HUMANITY
TRANS: DAN FARRELLY

Modern Death is written in the form of a symposium, in which a government agency brings together a group of experts to discuss a strategy for dealing with an ageing population. The speakers take up the thread of the ongoing debates about care for the aged and about euthanasia. In dark satirical mode the author shows what grim developments are possible.

ISBN 978-1-904505-28-0
€8

## SHIFTING SCENES:
## IRISH THEATRE-GOING 1955-1985
NICHOLAS GRENE AND CHRIS MORASH

Transcript of conversations with John Devitt, academic and reviewer, about his lifelong passion for the theatre. A fascinating and entertaining insight into Dublin theatre over the course of thirty years provided by Devitt's vivid reminiscences and astute observations.

ISBN 978-1-904505-33-4
€10

## IRISH THEATRE IN ENGLAND,
## IRISH THEATRICAL DIASPORA SERIES: 2
EDITED BY RICHARD CAVE AND BEN LEVITAS

Irish theatre in England has frequently illustrated the complex relations between two distinct cultures. How English reviewers and audiences interpret Irish plays is often decidedly different from how the plays were read in performance in Ireland. How certain Irish performers have chosen to be understood in Dublin is not necessarily how audiences in London have perceived their constructed stage personae. Though a collection by diverse authors, the twelve essays in this volume investigate these issues from a variety of perspectives that together chart the trajectory of Irish performance in England from the mid-nineteenth century till today.

ISBN 978-1-904505-26-6
€20

## SILENCED VOICES
## HUNGARIAN PLAYS FROM TRANSYLVANIA
SELECTED AND TRANSLATED BY
CSILLA BERTHA AND DONALD E. MORSE

The five plays are wonderfully theatrical, moving fluidly from absurdism to tragedy, and from satire to the darkly comic. Donald Morse and Csilla Bertha's translations capture these qualities perfectly, giving voice to the 'forgotten playwrights of Central Europe'. They also deeply enrich our understanding of the relationship between art, ethics, and politics in Europe.

ISBN 978-1-904505-34-1
€25

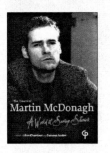

## EDNA O'BRIEN
## 'NEW CRITICAL PERSPECTIVES'
EDITED BY KATHRYN LAING
SINÉAD MOONEY AND MAUREEN O'CONNOR

The essays collected here illustrate some of the range, complexity, and interest of Edna O'Brien as a fiction writer and dramatist…They will contribute to a broader appreciation of her work and to an evolution of new critical approaches, as well as igniting more interest     in the many unexplored areas of her considerable oeuvre.

ISBN 1-904505-20-1
€20

## THE THEATRE OF MARTIN MCDONAGH
## 'A WORLD OF SAVAGE STORIES'
EDITED BY LILIAN CHAMBERS AND
EAMONN JORDAN

The book is a vital response to the many challenges set by McDonagh for those involved in the production and reception of his work. Critics and commentators from around the world offer a diverse range of often provocative approaches. What is not surprising is the focus and commitment of the engagement, given the controversial and stimulating nature of the work.

ISBN 1-904505-19-8
€35

## IRELAND ON STAGE:
## BECKETT AND AFTER
EDITORS: HIROKO MIKAMI, MINAKO
OKAMURO, NAOKO YAGI

A collection of ten essays on contemporary Irish theatre. The focus is primarily on Irish playwrights and their works, both in text and on the stage, in the latter half of the twentieth century. The essays range from Samuel Beckett to Brian Friel, Frank McGuinness, Marina Carr, and Conor McPherson. There is frequent reference back to Wilde, Yeats, Synge, Shaw, O'Casey, and Joyce.

ISBN     978-1-904505-23-5
€20

## BRIAN FRIEL'S DRAMATIC ARTISTRY
## 'THE WORK HAS VALUE'
EDITED BY DONALD E. MORSE, CSILLA
BERTHA, AND MÁRIA KURDI

*Brian Friel's Dramatic Artistry* presents a refreshingly broad range of voices: new work from some of the leading English-speaking authorities on Friel, and fascinating essays from scholars in Germany, Italy, Portugal, and Hungary. This book will deepen our knowledge and enjoyment of Friel's work.

ISBN 1-904505-17-1
€25

## OUT OF HISTORY
## 'ESSAYS ON THE WRITINGS OF
## SEBASTIAN BARRY'

EDITED WITH AN INTRODUCTION BY CHRISTINA
HUNT MAHONY

The essays address Barry's engagement with the
contemporary cultural debate in Ireland and also
with issues that inform postcolonial criticial theory.
The range and selection of contributors has
ensured a high level of critical expression and an
insightful assessment of Barry and his works.

ISBN 1-904505-18-X
€20

## IRISH THEATRE ON TOUR
## IRISH THEATRICAL DIASPORA SERIES: 1

EDITED BY NICHOLAS GRENE AND
CHRIS MORASH

'Touring has been at the strategic heart of
Druid's artistic policy since the early eighties.
Everyone has the right to see professional
theatre in their own communities. Irish theatre
on tour is a crucial part of Irish theatre as a
whole'. *Garry Hynes*

ISBN 1-904505-13-9
€20

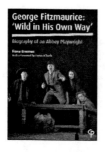

## GEORGE FITZMAURICE:
## 'WILD IN HIS OWN WAY'

BIOGRAPHY OF AN ABBEY PLAYWRIGHT
BY FIONA BRENNAN
WITH A FOREWORD BY FINTAN O'TOOLE

Fiona Brennan's...introduction to his
considerable output allows us a much greater
appreciation and understanding of Fitzmaurice,
the one remaining under-celebrated genius of
twentieth-century Irish drama.
*Conall Morrison*

ISBN 1-904505-16-3
€20

## IRISH LITERATURE FEMINIST PERSPECTIVES
## IASIL STUDIES IN IRISH WRITING

EDITED BY PATRICIA COUGHLAN AND
TINA O'TOOLE

The collection discusses texts from the early 18th
century to the present. A central theme of the book
is the need to renegotiate the relations of feminism
with nationalism and to transact the potential
contest of these two important narratives, each
possessing powerful emancipatory force. *Irish
Literature: Feminist Perspectives* contributes incisively
to contemporary debates about Irish culture, gender
and ideology.

ISBN 978-1-904505-35-8
€20

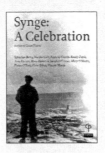

## EAST OF EDEN
### NEW ROMANIAN PLAYS
### EDITED BY ANDREI MARINESCU

Four of the most promising Romanian playwrights, young and very young, are in this collection, each one with a specific way of seeing the Romanian reality, each one with a style of communicating an articulated artistic vision of the society we are living in.
*Ion Caramitru, General Director Romanian National Theatre Bucharest*

ISBN 1-904505-15-5
€10

## SYNGE: A CELEBRATION
### EDITED BY COLM TÓIBÍN

A collection of essays by some of Ireland's most creative writers on the work of John Millington Synge, featuring Sebastian Barry , Marina Carr, Anthony Cronin, Roddy Doyle, Anne Enright, Hugo Hamilton, Joseph O'Connor, Mary O'Malley, Fintan O'Toole,  Colm Toibin, Vincent Woods.

ISBN 1-904505-14-7
€15 Paperback

## POEMS 2000–2005
### BY HUGH MAXTON

Poems 2000-2005 is a transitional collection written while the author – also known to be W. J. Mc Cormack, literary historian – was in the process of moving back from London to settle in rural Ireland.

ISBN 1-904505-12-0
€10

## HAMLET
### THE SHAKESPEAREAN DIRECTOR
### BY MIKE WILCOCK

"This study of the Shakespearean director as viewed through various interpretations of HAMLET is a welcome addition to our understanding of how essential it is for a director to have a clear vision of a great play. It is an important study from which all of us who love Shakespeare and who understand the importance of continuing contemporary exploration may gain new insights."

*From the Foreword, by Joe Dowling, Artistic Director, The Guthrie Theater, Minneapolis, MN*

ISBN 1-904505-00-7
€20

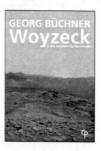

## GEORG BÜCHNER: WOYZECK
### A NEW TRANSLATION BY DAN FARRELLY

The most up-to-date German scholarship of
Thomas Michael Mayer and Burghard
Dedner has finally made it possible to establish
an authentic sequence of scenes. The widespread view that this play is a prime example of
loose, open theatre is no longer sustainable.
Directors and teachers are challenged to "read
it again".

ISBN 1-904505-02-3
€10

## MUSICS OF BELONGING:
## THE POETRY OF MICHEAL O'SIADHAIL
### EDITED BY MARC CABALL AND DAVID F. FORD

An overall account is given of O'Siadhail's life, his
work and the reception of his poetry so far. There
are close readings of some poems, analyses of his
artistry in matching diverse content with both
classical and innovative forms, and studies of
recurrent themes such as love, death, language,
music, and the shifts of modern life.

Paperback €25
ISBN 978-1-904505-22-8

Casebound €50
ISBN: 978-1-904505-21-1

## CRITICAL MOMENTS
### FINTAN O'TOOLE ON MODERN IRISH THEATRE
### EDITED BY JULIA FURAY & REDMOND O'HANLON

This new book on the work of Fintan O'Toole,
the internationally acclaimed theatre critic and
cultural commentator, offers percussive analyses
and assessments of the major plays and
playwrights in the canon of modern Irish
theatre. Fearless and provocative in his
judgements, O'Toole is essential reading for
anyone interested in criticism or in the current
state of Irish theatre.

ISBN 1-904505-03-1
€20

## THE THEATRE OF MARINA CARR
### "BEFORE RULES WAS MADE"- EDITED BY ANNA MCMULLAN & CATHY LEENEY

As the first published collection of articles on
the theatre of Marina Carr, this volume explores
the world of Carr's theatrical imagination, the
place of her plays in contemporary theatre in
Ireland and abroad and the significance of her
highly individual voice.

ISBN 0-9534-2577-0
€20

## THEATRE TALK

VOICES OF IRISH THEATRE PRACTITIONERS
EDITED BY LILIAN CHAMBERS &
GER FITZGIBBON

"This book is the right approach - asking
practitioners what they feel."
*Sebastian Barry, Playwright*

"... an invaluable and informative collection of
interviews with those who make and shape the
landscape of Irish Theatre."
*Ben Barnes, Artistic Director of the Abbey Theatre*

ISBN 0-9534-2576-2
€20

## SACRED PLAY

SOUL JOURNEYS IN CONTEMPORARY
IRISH THEATRE BY ANNE F. O'REILLY

'Theatre as a space or container for sacred play
allows audiences to glimpse mystery and to
experience transformation. This book charts how
Irish playwrights negotiate the labyrinth of the
Irish soul and shows how their plays contribute
to a poetics of Irish culture that enables a new
imagining. Playwrights discussed are:
McGuinness, Murphy, Friel, Le Marquand Hartigan,
Burke Brogan, Harding, Meehan, Carr, Parker,
Devlin, and Barry.'

ISBN 1-904505-07-4
€25

## THEATRE OF SOUND

RADIO AND THE DRAMATIC IMAGINATION
BY DERMOT RATTIGAN

An innovative study of the challenges that radio
drama poses to the creative imagination of the
writer, the production team, and the listener.

"A remarkably fine study of radio drama –
everywhere informed by the writer's
professional experience of such drama in the
making... A new theoretical and analytical
approach – informative, illuminating and at all
times readable." *Richard Allen Cave*

ISBN 0-9534-2575-4
€20

## PLAYBOYS OF THE WESTERN WORLD

PRODUCTION HISTORIES
EDITED BY ADRIAN FRAZIER

'Playboys of the Western World is a model of
contemporary performance studies.'

'The book is remarkably well-focused: half is a series
of production histories of Playboy performances
through the twentieth century in the UK, Northern
Ireland, the USA, and Ireland. The remainder focuses
on one contemporary performance, that of Druid
Theatre, as directed by Garry Hynes. The various
contemporary social issues that are addressed in
relation to Synge's play and this performance of it
give the volume an additional interest: it shows
how the arts matter.' *Kevin Barry*

ISBN 1-904505-06-6
€20

## THE THEATRE OF FRANK MCGUINNESS

STAGES OF MUTABILITY
EDITED BY HELEN LOJEK

The first edited collection of essays about
internationally renowned Irish playwright Frank
McGuinness focuses on both performance and
text. Interpreters come to diverse conclusions,
creating a vigorous dialogue that enriches
understanding and reflects a strong consensus
about the value of McGuinness's complex work.

ISBN 1-904505-01-5
€20

## THE DRUNKARD

TOM MURPHY

'The Drunkard is a wonderfully eloquent play.
Murphy's ear is finely attuned to the glories and
absurdities of melodramatic exclamation, and
even while he is wringing out its ludicrous
overstatement, he is also making it sing.'
The Irish Times

ISBN 1-904505-09-0
€10

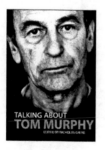

## TALKING ABOUT TOM MURPHY

EDITED BY NICHOLAS GRENE

Talking About Tom Murphy is shaped around the
six plays in the landmark Abbey Theatre Murphy
Season of 2001, assembling some of the best-
known commentators on his work: Fintan
O'Toole, Chris Morash, Lionel Pilkington,
Alexandra Poulain, Shaun Richards, Nicholas
Grene and Declan Kiberd.

ISBN 0-9534-2579-7
€15

## THE POWER OF LAUGHTER

EDITED BY ERIC WEITZ

The collection draws on a wide range of
perspectives and voices including critics,
playwrights, directors and performers. The result is
a series of fascinating and provocative debates
about the myriad functions of comedy in
contemporary Irish theatre. *Anna McMullan*

As Stan Laurel said, it takes only an onion to cry.
Peel it and weep. Comedy is harder. These essays
listen to the power of laughter. They hear the
tough heart of Irish theatre – hard and wicked
and funny. *Frank McGuinness*

ISBN 1-904505-05-8
€20

## THREE CONGREGATIONAL MASSES
### BY SEÓIRSE BODLEY,
### EDITED BY LORRAINE BYRNE

'From the simpler congregational settings in the Mass of Peace and the Mass of Joy to the richer textures of the Mass of Glory, they are immediately attractive and accessible, and with a distinctively Irish melodic quality.' *Barra Boydell*

ISBN 1-904505-11-2
€15

## THE IRISH HARP BOOK
### BY SHEILA LARCHET CUTHBERT

This is a facsimile of the edition originally published by Mercier Press in 1993. There is a new preface by Sheila Larchet Cuthbert, and the biographical material has been updated. It is a collection of studies and exercises for the use of teachers and pupils of the Irish harp.

ISBN 1-904505-08-2
€35

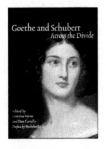

## GOETHE AND SCHUBERT
### ACROSS THE DIVIDE
### EDITED BY LORRAINE BYRNE & DAN FARRELLY

Proceedings of the International Conference, 'Goethe and Schubert in Perspective and Performance', Trinity College Dublin, 2003. This volume includes essays by leading scholars – Barkhoff, Boyle, Byrne, Canisius, Dürr, Fischer, Hill, Kramer, Lamport, Lund, Meikle, Newbould, Norman McKay, White, Whitton, Wright, Youens – on Goethe's musicality and his relationship to Schubert; Schubert's contribution to sacred music and the Lied and his setting of Goethe's Singspiel, Claudine. A companion volume of this Singspiel (with piano reduction and English translation) is also available.

ISBN 1-904505-04-X
Goethe and Schubert: Across the Divide. €25

ISBN 0-9544290-0-1
Goethe and Schubert: 'Claudine von Villa Bella'. €14

## GOETHE: MUSICAL POET, MUSICAL CATALYST
### EDITED BY LORRAINE BYRNE

'Goethe was interested in, and acutely aware of, the place of music in human experience generally - and of its particular role in modern culture. Moreover, his own literary work - especially the poetry and Faust - inspired some of the major composers of the European tradition to produce some of their finest works.' *Martin Swales*

ISBN 1-904505-10-4
€30

## GOETHE AND SCHUBERT 'CLAUDINE VON VILLA BELLA'

### EDITED BY LORRAINE BYRNE & DAN FARRELLY

Goethe's Singspiel in three acts was set to music by Schubert in 1815. Only Act One of Schuberts's Claudine score is extant. The present volume makes Act One available for performance in English and German. It comprises both a piano reduction by Lorraine Byrne of the original Schubert orchestral score and a bilingual text translated for the modern stage by Dan Farrelly. This is a tale, wittily told, of lovers and vagabonds, romance, reconciliation, and resolution of family conflict.

ISBN 0-9544290-0-1
€14

## PROSERPINA: GOETHE'S MELDODRAMA WITH MUSIC BY CARL EBERWEIN, ORCHESTRAL SCORE AND PIANO REDUCTION

### EDITOR: LORRAINE BYRNE BODLEY; PREFACE BY NICHOLAS BOYLE

This score, the first edition of Eberwein's setting of Goethe's melodrama, Proserpina, offers an unprecedented examination of Goethe's text and overturns the accepted image of the artist as unmusical. Carl Eberwein's dramatic setting of Goethe's melodrama, Proserpina, for solo voice (speaking part) and orchestra, with a choral finale, is highly dramatic in impact and beautifully orchestrated.

ISBN HB: 9781904505273;  PB: 9781904505297
€28

## A HAZARDOUS MELODY OF BEING: SEOIRSE BODLEY'S SONG CYCLES ON THE POEMS OF MICHEAL O'SIADHAIL

### EDITED AND WITH AN INTRODUCTION BY LORRAINE BYRNE BODLEY

This apograph is the first publication of Bodley's O'Siadhail song cycles and is the first book to explore the composer's lyrical modernity from a number of perspectives. Lorraine Byrne Bodley's insightful introduction describes in detail the development and essence of Bodley's musical thinking, the European influences he absorbed which linger in these cycles, and the importance of his work as a composer of the Irish art song.

ISBN 978-1-904505-31-0 (paperback)
€25

## THEATRE STUFF (REPRINT)

CRITICAL ESSAYS ON
CONTEMPORARY IRISH THEATRE
EDITED BY EAMONN JORDAN

Best selling essays on the successes and
debates of contemporary Irish theatre at home
and abroad.

Contributors include: Thomas Kilroy, Declan
Hughes, Anna McMullan, Declan Kiberd, Deirdre
Mulrooney, Fintan O'Toole, Christopher Murray,
Caoimhe McAvinchey and Terry Eagleton.

ISBN 0-9534-2571-1
€20

## URFAUST

A NEW VERSION OF GOETHE'S
EARLY "FAUST" IN BRECHTIAN MODE
BY DAN FARRELLY

This version is based on Brecht's irreverent and
daring re-interpretation of the German classic.

"Urfaust is a kind of well-spring for German
theatre… The love-story is the most daring and
the most profound in German dramatic
literature." Brecht

ISBN 0-9534257-0-3
€10

## IN SEARCH OF THE
## SOUTH AFRICAN IPHIGENIE

BY ERIKA VON WIETERSHEIM
AND DAN FARRELLY

Discussions of Goethe's "Iphigenie auf Tauris"
(Under the Curse) as relevant to women's issues
in modern South Africa: women in family and
public life; the force of women's spirituality;
experience of personal relationships; attitudes to
parents and ancestors; involvement with religion.

ISBN 0-9534-2578-9
€10

## THE STARVING
## AND OCTOBER SONG

TWO CONTEMPORARY IRISH PLAYS
BY ANDREW HINDS

The Starving, set during and after the siege of
Derry in 1689, is a moving and engrossing
drama of the emotional journey of two men.

October Song, a superbly written family drama
set in real time in pre-ceasefire Derry.

ISBN 0-9534-2574-6
€10

## SEEN AND HEARD (REPRINT)

SIX NEW PLAYS BY IRISH WOMEN
EDITED WITH AN INTRODUCTION
BY CATHY LEENEY

A rich and funny, moving and theatrically
exciting collection of plays by Mary Elizabeth
Burke-Kennedy, Síofra Campbell, Emma
Donoghue, Anne Le Marquand Hartigan,
Michelle Read and Dolores Walshe.

ISBN 0-9534-2573-8
€20

## UNDER THE CURSE

GOETHE'S "IPHIGENIE AUF TAURIS",
IN A NEW VERSION BY DAN FARRELLY

The Greek myth of Iphigenie grappling with the
curse on the house of Atreus is brought vividly
to life. This version is currently being used in
Johannesburg to explore problems of ancestry,
religion, and Black African women's spirituality.

ISBN 0-9534-2572-X
€10

## HOW TO ORDER
*TRADE ORDERS DIRECTLY TO*

CMD
Columba Mercier Distribution,
55A Spruce Avenue,
Stillorgan Industrial Park,
Blackrock,
Co. Dublin

T: (353 1) 294 2560
F: (353 1) 294 2564
E: cmd@columba.ie

*FOR SALES IN NORTH AMERICA
AND CANADA*

Dufour Editions Inc.,
124 Byers Road,
PO Box 7,
Chester Springs, PA 19425,
USA

T: 1-610-458-5005
F: 1-610-458-7103